INSIGHT GUIDE

ITALY

Discovery
CHANNEL

APA PUBLICATIONS

Part of the Langenscheidt Publishing Group

L

ABOUT THIS BOOK

Editorial

Managing Editor
Emily Hatchwell
Editorial Director
Brian Bell

Distribution

UK & Ireland
GeoCenter International Ltd
The Viables Centre , Harrow Way
Basingstoke, Hants RG22 4BJ
Fax: (44) 1256-817988

United States
Langenscheidt Publishers, Inc.
46–35 54th Road, Maspeth, NY 11378
Fax: (718) 784-0640

Canada
Prologue Inc.
1650 Lionel Bertrand Blvd., Boisbriand
Québec, Canada J7H 1N7
Tel: (450) 434-0306. Fax: (450) 434-2627

Worldwide
**Apa Publications GmbH & Co.
Verlag KG (Singapore branch)**
38 Joo Koon Road, Singapore 628990
Tel: (65) 865-1600. Fax: (65) 861-6438

Printing

Insight Print Services (Pte) Ltd
38 Joo Koon Road, Singapore 628990
Tel: (65) 865-1600. Fax: (65) 861-6438

©2000 Apa Publications GmbH & Co.
Verlag KG (Singapore branch)
All Rights Reserved

First Edition 1985
Fourth Edition (Updated) 1999
Reprinted 2000

CONTACTING THE EDITORS
Although every effort is made to
provide accurate information, we
live in a fast-changing world and
would appreciate it if readers
would call our attention to any
errors or outdated information
that may occur by writing to us:
**Insight Guides, P.O. Box 7910,
London SE1 1WE, England.
Fax: (44 20) 7403-0290.
insight@apaguide.demon.co.uk**

This guidebook combines the
interests and enthusiasms of
two of the world's best known
information providers: Insight Guides,
whose titles have set the standard
for visual travel guides since 1970,
and Discovery Channel, the world's
premier source of nonfiction television
programming.

The editors of Insight Guides provide practical advice and general
understanding about a
destination's history,
culture, environment,
people, and institutions.
Discovery Channel and
www.discovery.com, its
Website, help millions
of viewers explore

their world from the comfort of their
own home and also encourage them
to explore it first hand.

How to use this book

Insight Guides has a proven
formula of informative and well-
written text paired with a fresh
photojournalistic approach. The
books are carefully structured,
both to convey a better understanding of each place and its
culture, and to guide readers
through its myriad
attractions:

◆ The first section, with a
yellow colour bar, covers
Italy's classical **history**
and rich, lively modern

EXPLORE YOUR WORLD

Above: Venice's Piazza San Marco

culture in authoritative **features** written by experts.

◆ The main **Places** section, with a blue bar, provides a run-down of all the places worth seeing. Places of major interest are cross-referenced by numbers or letters to specially drawn maps.

◆ The **Travel Tips** listing section at the back of the book provides recommendations on travel, hotels and restaurants, as well as an Italian phrasebook, with a menu reader.

The contributors

This is the Fourth Edition of the *Insight Guide: Italy*. To help make a good book even better, managing editor **Emily Hatchwell** enlisted the expertise of Italy specialists, including two Insight regulars: **Lisa Gerard Sharp** and **Christopher Catling**. **Fred Mawer** wrote a new chapter on Sardinia.

Nicky Swallow helped update the Places chapters and Travel Tips. Editors **Harriet Salisbury, Jeff Evans, Liz Clasen** and **Jane Ladle** brought the new elements together into a coherent whole.

The authors included wine writers **James Ainsworth** and **Margaret Rand**, and **Bruce Johnston**, a journalist for the *Daily Telegraph*. **Ginger Künzel** wrote about the Italian Alps and the Trentino-Alto Adige region, and **Susie Boulton** contributed to the sections on Venice.

Much of this new edition builds on the work of **Katherine Barrett**. She wrote the chapters on Rome and Famous Travellers. **Clare McHugh** wrote many of the chapters on Italian history and the chapters on the northern provinces.

It is to **Alberto Rossatti** that the book owes much of its native expertise. Other contributors to the original guide included **Benjamin Swett, Jacob Young, Claudia Angeletti, Kathleen Beckett, Melanie Menagh, Peter Spiro** and **George Prochnik**.

Like all Insight Guides, this book owes a lot to its photographs, many of which are by **John Heseltine, Albano Guatti**, and **Bill Wassman**.

Map Legend

▬ ▪▪	International Boundary
▬ ▬ ▬	Region Boundary
⊖	Border Crossing
▬ ▪ ▬	National Park/Reserve
▬ ▬ ▬	Ferry Route
Ⓜ	Metro
✈	Airport
🚌	Bus Station
🅿	Parking
❶	Tourist Information
✉	Post Office
✝ ♁ ♂	Church/Ruins
☽ ♀	Mosque
✡ ✡	Synagogue
♂ ♂	Castle/Ruins
∴	Archaeological Site
∩	Cave
🗿	Statue/Monument
★	Place of Interest

Places of interest in the **Places** section are cross-referenced to maps by number (e.g. ❶). A symbol at the top of each right-hand page tells you where to find the relevant map.

Contents

Portofino in
Liguria,
once a
humble
fishing
village and
now an
exclusive
resort

Travel Tips

Insight on ...

Information panels

Places

THE ETERNAL SEDUCTRESS

Italy, with her unrivalled beauty and baffling contradictions,

continues to seduce and enchant those who are drawn to her

Italy, like the sorceress Circe, tantalisingly beautiful and at the same time treacherous, has attracted kings, scholars, saints, poets and curious travellers for centuries. The spell of the "Eternal Seductress", as men have dubbed her, which once drew people across stormy mountains and seas, now leads them into hardly less turbulent airports and train stations.

Italy has always seemed somewhat removed from the rest of Europe: physically by mountains and sea, spiritually by virtue of the Pope. In the eyes of outsiders, the Italians themselves are characterised by extremes: at one end of the spectrum, the gentle unworldliness of St Francis, and, at the other, the amoral brilliance of Machiavelli; on the one hand, the curiosity of Galileo or the genius of Michelangelo, on the other, the repressive dogmatism of Counter Reformation Jesuits. There have been those who thought the Italians were unworthy of Italy, and others, such as the English novelist E.M. Forster, who considered them "more marvellous than the land".

This book believes that Italy and the Italians are equally worthy of attention. It explores the land and its people, from Calabrian villagers to Milanese sophisticates and delves into their justly famous treasures, from Etruscan statues to Botticelli's radiant *Birth of Venus*. Special features celebrate Italian passions – films, fashion, opera and food – while the history section threads its way through a tumultuous past, from the legendary founding of Rome by Romulus and Remus to the Renaissance, reunification, Mussolini and the Mafia.

In Italy the past is always present: a housing development rises above a crumbling Roman wall; ultra-modern museums display pre-Roman artifacts; old people in tiny mountain villages preserve customs which are centuries old while their grandchildren roar into the future on shiny new Vespas.

This is the country which inspires imagination in the dull, passion in the cold-hearted, rebellion in the conventional. Whether you spend your sojourn in Italy under a brightly coloured beach umbrella on the Riviera, shopping in Milan or diligently examining churches and museums, you cannot be unchanged by Italy. At the very least, you will receive a highly pleasurable lesson in living. Whether you are struck by the beauty of a church facade rising from a perfectly proportioned piazza, the aroma of freshly carved *prosciutto*, or the sight of a stylish passer-by spied over the foam of your *cappuccino*, there is the same superb sensation: nowhere else on earth does just living seem so extraordinary.

PRECEDING PAGES: St Peter, Rome; welcome to Venice; artistic endeavours at Piazzale Michelangelo, Florence; a quiet afternoon in Scanno in Abruzzo.
LEFT: young visitor to St Mark's Basilica in Venice.

FAMOUS TRAVELLERS

Italy has long been a "paradise of exiles", a haven for visitors in search of classical heritage and humanity, sunlight and passion

As Dr Johnson declared, "A man who has not been to Italy is always conscious of an inferiority," a sentiment still shared by many travellers more than 200 years later. Ever since the Romantic era, Italy has resonated with travellers in search of solace and enlightenment, cultural riches and religious renewal. A reverence for the Classical legacy or the Renaissance has been mingled with affection for the musical culture and an infatuation with art, landscape, Catholicism and cuisine. A clerical creation of E.M. Forster's claims: "I do believe that Italy really purifies and ennobles all who visit her. She is the school as well as the playground of the world."

Above all, Italy has been seen as sublimely civilised, a soothing enchantress who would erase all cares. For past travellers, attitude determined experience: Italy became a picturesque canvas, a place of beauty, longing, moral decay and sexual liberation. In particular, the country represented a holiday haven for repressed northerners drawn to the lotus-eating life of the South. The allure of Italy still draws on this landscape of the senses, a subconscious invitation for projections of aversions and fears as well as desires. Yet whatever their motives, travellers concur on the seductive spell of Italy. On his way to Rome in 1852, the artist Frederick Leighton spoke for many visitors to come: "A faithful lover I return, after six years of longing absence, to the home of my inward heart."

The Grand Tour

The Grand Tourists had great cultural pretensions and treated Italy as a finishing school for the soul. The Victorian itinerary was virtually unchanged since the Romantic era: a brief visit to Venice was followed by autumn in Florence, Rome for Christmas and New Year, then to Naples or Taormina in Sicily until Easter spelt a return to Rome. Gilded youth roamed the summits of Etna and Vesuvius, poked about in

Roman palaces and postured in romantic ruins. Privileged visitors declaimed in Venetian galleries, posed at the Milan opera and gathered in fashionable cafés such as Doney's in Florence and Caffè Greco in Rome. Shelley (1792–1822), the Romantic poet par excellence, had a novelettish affair with an Italian countess and

boasted that he had "Florenced and Romed and Galleried and Conversationed".

As for wintering resorts, the Adriatic was ignored in favour of the French or Italian Riviera. Yet while the Côte d'Azur was treated as a sanatorium for the middle and upper classes, Italian cities and resorts were seen as artistic universities and pleasure domes. Historian John Pemble portrays Victorian and Edwardian Italy as appealing to "oversize personalities whose voices, gestures, and passions required high ceilings, strong light, and stupendous views". San Remo was a case apart: by the 1880s it was favoured by spinsters, censorious clerics and those who found Monte Carlo too brash.

LEFT: the heroine of Hawthorne's *The Marble Faun* has an assignation in Perugia. **RIGHT:** Percy Bysshe Shelley.

Aesthetes came in search of the picturesque, escaping the frigid capitals of northern Europe and North America. Italy inspired travel memoirs by Goethe and Stendhal, Dickens and Henry James, writers who focused on curious byways rather than the well-trodden highways. In turn, painters such as Poussin and Turner painted the sublime light while the Romantic poets reflected the sunlight of the South in their writings. Virtually no Victorian writer, painter or sculptor of note failed to visit Italy. As for musicians, Liszt,

> **AN AMERICAN IN ROME**
>
> In time, American writer Henry James even became fond of "the barbarisms, miseries and uncleannesses of Rome".

and Henry James considered the city "the aesthetic antidote to the ugliness of the rest of the world, that is, of Anglo-Saxondom in particular". Yet James, like Marcel Proust, also had an affinity for Venice: "It is a fact that almost everyone interesting, appealing, melancholy, memorable, odd seems to have gravitated to Venice ... the deposed, the defeated, the wounded or even only the bored have seemed to find there something that no other place could give".

Until the 1870s, the British moved as a herd

Chopin, Tchaikovsky and Wagner were all deeply affected by Italy. Venice inspired Wagner to write *Tristan and Isolde*.

"Infatuated aliens"

This was how Henry James (1843–1916) described his fellow-travellers, devoted to Italian art and culture. In literature, Rome, Florence and Venice receive most paeans of praise. This is reflected in Henry James's view of Milan as "perhaps the last of the prose capitals rather than the first of the poetic". By the 1880s, Florence had become the most favoured residential city for foreigners. But each major city had its admirers. John Gibson, the 19th-century sculptor, called Rome "the very university of art",

in Italy, from Venice to Florence and Rome. The American George Hillard wrote in the 1840s: "No one could visit these cities without being constantly aware of the fastidiousness of English hygiene, the chill of English manners, and the sibilance of English speech." American novelist W.D. Howells declared Venice in October to be "the month of sunsets and the English". As for Rome, stylish Via Condotti was known as "*il ghetto inglese*" while "*inglese*" ("English") became a generic term for all foreigners.

E.M. Forster (1879–1970) saw Italy as liberating "the undeveloped heart" of the English. In *A Room with a View* (1908), his repressed heroine is rescued by voluptuous, pagan Italy. The Welsh poet Dylan Thomas (1914–53) needed no such introduction to Tuscan life. He spent an agreeable time quaffing Chianti and praising the endless pine trees, "the cypresses at the hilltop which tell one all about the length of death, [and] the woods deep as love and full of goats".

In time, what Henry James called "the bark of Chicago" came to be as common as British English in Italy. The Americans tended to be more critical, daring to expose Italy to a burst of realism or mockery. To Mark Twain (1835–1910), "The Arno would be a very plausible river if they would pump some water into it." His compatriot Henry James was equally scathing about the riverside houses: "Anything more battered and befouled, more cracked and disjointed, dirtier, drearier and poorer, it would be impossible to conceive." Yet James, the epitome of the civilised traveller, was the one who best appreciated daily life: "Our picture of Italy is … of happy processes, accidents, adventures, a generous acceptance of goodly appearances."

A romantic vision

In general, French writers convey a more romantic vision of Italy. In Rome, Emile Zola (1840–1902) succumbed to the melancholy beauty of the Colosseum: "a world where one loses oneself amidst death-like silence and solitude". In Florence, Santa Croce sent Stendhal's head reeling: "I went in constant fear of falling to the ground". This aesthetic sickness, now known as "Stendhal's Syndrome", also affected Maupassant, Proust and Monet. Proust (1871–1922) set part of *A la Recherche du Temps Perdu* in Venice, while George Sand (1804–76) described the city in very sensuous terms: "The bases of the *palazzi*, where oysters used to cling to stagnant moss, are covered in mosses of tender green, and the gondolas glide between two carpets of velvety, beautiful verdure".

The Germans were equally entranced by Italy. In 1788, Goethe (1749–1832) experienced the pleasurable terror of the Roman Catacombs. Venice, too, appealed to his poetic nature: "This strange island-city, this heaven-like republic". Thomas Mann (1875–1955) chose ambivalence over waxing lyrical. The protagonist in *Death in Venice* falls under the Venetian spell, but there is an inherent criticism in his praise: "This was

Venice, the fair frailty that fawned and that betrayed, half fairy tale, half snare".

Frederick Faber, a visitor to Pisa in 1843, praised "the voluptuous silent poetry which Italy engenders". To many, the scenery was as aesthetically pleasing as the art. Faced with such a paradise, "nine out of ten English tourists either gush or cant," declared one Victorian visitor. Virginia Woolf (1882–1941) did neither, invoking: "the Arno flowing past with its usual coffee-coloured foam". The Tuscan landscape has inspired some of the loveliest modern poetry. Elizabeth Jennings praises the perfection of the Florentine setting: "Take one bowl,

one valley … And then set cypresses up/So dark that they seem to contain their repeated shadows/In a straight and upward leap". Charles Tomlinson writes of cypresses "Folded in like a dark thought/For which the language is lost".

Italy was unique in offering an equally rich Classical and Christian inheritance. Romantic taste favoured Classical ruins and Renaissance architecture. Then came a Victorian taste for Gothic buildings and medieval madonnas, which prevailed until World War I. Ruskin's writings on Venice and Florence helped to turn the art treasures of Italy into a supremely Christian preserve. By implication, Classical art was seen as spiritually impoverished. Henry James was almost a lone voice in rebelling against the

LEFT: Piranesi's fanciful drawing of Hadrian's Villa.
RIGHT: Mme de Stael, author of *Corinne*, a romance between an Italian poetess and a Scottish laird.

prevailing aesthetic: "art is made for us, not we for art". Despite the superiority of Tuscan art, the critic Bernard Berenson (1865–1959) preferred vibrant Venetian art: "The Florentines were too attached to classical ideals of form and composition … too academic, to give embodiment to the throbbing feeling for life and pleasure".

For travellers steeped in Classical lore, the romance of Roman ruins was heightened by nostalgia for lost glory. "Who can visit such a place of beauty and decay," intoned Gladstone, "without feeling that it opens his mind to what he never knew before and cannot hope to recall elsewhere?". The Romantic poet Edgar Allan

Apart from nostalgia, travellers sought escape from the oppressiveness and cold of northern climes. The pessimism of the Protestant mind longed for the perceived sunniness and passion of the Latin disposition. Italy was seen as an incantation, a feminine, luxuriant, sensual country. In a climate of sexual tolerance, the casualties of modern life could seek comfort and acceptance. Italy became a place for elopement, with Robert and Elizabeth Browning fleeing to Pisa in 1846. For moral exiles, this realm of enchantment represented a Faustian pact of temptation and fall. The South, particularly Capri, was known for tolerance towards homo-

Poe marvelled at "the grandeur, gloom and glory" of the Colosseum, then in a parlous state. Sicily and Pompeii provoked a similarly lyrical response: an exquisite sadness and ruminations on the pathos, transience and futility of life.

Sensitive visitors felt a longing for an irrecoverable past, the cultivated melancholy of time travellers who had come too late to a world too old. D.H. Lawrence (1885–1930) lamented the passing of a pagan civilisation: "The Etruscans had a passion for music and an inner carelessness the modern Italians have lost".

LATIN PASSION

Lord Byron (1788–1824) famously declared of Italy: "a woman is virtuous who limits herself to her husband and one lover".

sexuality. In Sorrento, writer Norman Douglas celebrated "elemental and permanent things, casting off outworn weeds of thought" with an illiterate peasant boy.

The perceived moral licence of Italy was an invitation to explore and dare to meet one's destiny. A beguiling story was spun around the poetic yet tragic deaths of Shelley and Keats in Italy. Retreating to sunnier climes was seen as both a promise and a lure, not without torment for the soul. In *Middlemarch*, George Eliot's heroine, Dorothea, has her smothered sensibilities stirred in Rome: on honeymoon there, she compares the sensuous and expansive city with her arid husband. Yet most northern spirits flourished in the noon-day heat. The appeal of expatriate spinsterhood was manifold, with a dizzy round of musical evenings and lively gatherings in Florence and Rome. However, there was little inter-marriage between Italians and foreigners, save for the exchange of a high-sounding southern title for a northern dowry.

Native prejudice

In cultivating the romance of Italy, travellers have had their prejudices. "The country, especially Naples, swarms with pick-pockets", declared one 18th-century guidebook. Yet past travellers generally only knew the natives as servants and rarely commented on the relative poverty of most Italians. Despite his entrée into Italian life, Shelley still ridiculed "countesses [who] smell so of garlic that an ordinary Englishman cannot approach them".

Travellers have always wanted to preserve the mystique, potency and passion of Italy. However, to an Anglo-Tuscan such as Iris Origo (1902–1980), "The real gulf lay between the mere tourist and the established Anglo-Florentine". In World War II, she knew old ladies "who preferred the risk of a concentration camp to a return to England". Yet even paradise can become ennervating to exiles such as Alan Moorehead (1910–83): "Presently I began to suffer from that dreadful ennui that must overtake all self-appointed exiles who live in beautiful places in the sun. One lovely day succeeds another … But as things were, it mattered not in the least to me who won the local elections or whether the hail destroyed the grapes or whether Florence defeated Turin at football."

The decline of paradise has long been a common refrain, with travellers railing against the vulgarity of tourism. "His gondolier, being in league with various lace-makers and glass-blowers, did his best to persuade his fare to pause" – even in Thomas Mann's Venice, the fleecing of tourists was part of the Italian experience. Mary McCarthy, the American critic, wrote: "Contrary to popular belief, there are no

back canals where a tourist will not meet himself, with a camera, in the person of the other tourist crossing the little bridge. And no word that can be spoken in this city that is not an echo of something said before." Not that foreign travellers have the last word. Pietro Aretino, the 16th-century writer, indulged in a little *schadenfreude* at the expense of the cultural invaders of his country: "And who would not laugh till he cried at the sight of a boatload of Germans who had just reeled out of a tavern being capsized into the chilly waters of the Canal".

Italy continues to befuddle visitors' senses. When asked what made life worth living,

Harold Acton, the grand old man of letters, replied: "Writing a book, dinner for six, travelling in Italy with someone you love … I believe Florence has given me all this." Henry James's words will also strike a chord: "One grows irresistibly and tenderly fond of the unanalysable loveableness of Italy … the whole place keeps playing such everlasting tunes on one's imagination." Nor can the pleasures of serendipity be underestimated as part of the allure. As E.M. Forster realised: "And the traveller who has gone to Italy to study the tactile values of Giotto, or the corruption of the Papacy may return remembering nothing but the blue sky and the men and women who live under it." ❑

LEFT: Goethe poses in front of an idealised Italian landscape. **RIGHT:** Elizabeth Barrett Browning, who together with her husband, Robert, formed the nucleus of an artistic community in Florence.

CARTA GEOGRAFICA GENERALE DELL' ITALIA

I SVIZZERI
Walese

I GRIGIONI

Valtellina

VESCOVATO DI TRENTO

Vicentino

Trento
Riva
Feltre
Ceneda
Treviso

Chambery
Aosta
Vagona
Bergamasco
Lago d'Iseo
Ladrone
Vicenza

DUCATO DI SAVOJA

S. Gio. di Morienne

DUCATO DI MILANO

Bergamo
Brescia
CASTIGLIONE
Bresciano

REPUBBLICA DI VENEZIA

Padova
Padovano
Este

PIEMONTE

Vercelli
Novara
Milano
Lodi
Cremona
MANTOVA
DUCATO DI
Verona
Veronese
Legnago
Rovigo

Susa
Torino
Casale
Pavia
Pizzighitone
SABIONETA
GUASTALLA
Ferrara
Zelo
Ferrarese
Comacchio

Brianzon
Embrun
MONFERRATO
Asti
Tortona
Alessandria
Piacenza
Busseto
Parma
Reggio
MIRANDOLA
Pieve
Modena
Romagna

CONTADO DI NIZZA

Salazzo
Mondovi
Aqui
Alba
DUCATO DI PARMA

Fiorenzuola
Rossena
Edifici
DUCATO DI MODENA
Bologna
Bolognese
Faenza
Forli

FRONTIERA DI FRANCIA

Torriglia

REPUBBLICA DI GENOVA

Brugneto
Frignano
Vergato

Tenda
Albenga
Gillete
Ventimiglia
Noli
Final
Genova
Neri
Sestri di Levante
Sardana
Pistoja

MONACO

MARE DI GENOVA

MASSA

REPUBBLICA DI LUCCA

Lucca
Pisa
Pisano
Fiorenza
Firenze
GRAN DUCATO DI

I. di S. Margarita

Arno F.
Livorno
Volterra
Siena
Arezzo
S. Gimino

I. de Gorgona

Vada
Colle
Montieri
Casole

I. de Capri

Monzano
TOSCANA
Chiusi
Orvi

Piombino
Porto Terraio

Grossetto

I. d'Elba
Bastia

Orbitello
Porto Longone
Ercole

Pianosa I.
MARE DI TOSCANA

S. Fiorenzo

Nebbio
Mariana

Calvi

Mare Tirreno

C. Rosso

Aleria
Corsica
ISOLA DI CORSICA
Aleria distrutta

Golfo di Ajano

Ajazzo
Corbini
Porto Vecchio
I. delle Corsi
Bonifacio

Scala di

Isole della Maddalena

I. Asinara
C. Aragonese
Lico
Sardi
Terranoua
Haudaro

Terra Nova

C. Comin

Saisaro
Oscare
Orase

C. della Cacca
Algeri

ISOLA
Tortoli

C. de Bosa
Bosa

E REGNO DI

Dosolo

C. S. Marco

Oristagni
Orirstagno
SARDEGNA

Palermo
S. Vito
Valle di Mazara
Iato
Trapano
Tori
Mazara

Toralba
Cagliari
Villa di Chiesa
S. Michele
M. Santo

I. di S. Pietro

I. S. Antioco
Capo Tavolaro

MARE MEDITERR

Decisive Dates

FROM ORIGINS TO THE ROMAN EMPIRE

2000–1200 BC Tribes from Central Europe and Asia, the Villanovans, settle in northern Italy.
c. 900 BC Etruscans arrive in Italy.
753 BC Legendary date of Rome's founding.
750 BC Greeks start to colonise southern Italy.
509 BC Rome becomes a republic.
390 BC Gauls sack Rome, but are expelled.
343–264 BC Rome gains ascendancy in Italy.
264–146 BC Punic Wars; Rome extends conquests abroad; destruction of Carthage.

58–51 BC Caesar conquers Gaul.
50–49 BC Caesar crosses Rubicon, occupies Rome and is made dictator.
44 BC Caesar assassinated.
27 BC Octavius proclaimed Princeps, as Augustus Caesar; the start of *Pax Romana*.
AD 96–192 Golden century of peace; empire reaches its greatest extent.
303 Persecution of Christians under Diocletian.
306–337 Constantine makes Christianity the state religion and Constantinople the capital.
393 The empire is divided into eastern and western halves.
5th century Invasions by Visigoths, Huns, Vandals, and Ostrogoths.
410 Sack of Rome by Alaric the Goth.

476 End of Western Roman Empire. Ostrogoth general Odoacer deposes Emperor Romulus Augustus and assumes the title King of Italy.

MEDIEVAL ITALY

535–553 Justinian brings all Italy within rule of Eastern emperor.
568 Lombards (a Germanic tribe) overrun much of Italy; peninsula divided into Lombard state ruled from Pavia and Byzantine province centred at Ravenna.
752 The pope asks the Frankish king, Pepin the Short, to join the fight against the Lombards.
774 Charlemagne, son of Pepin the Short, is made king of the Lombards.
800 Charlemagne is crowned Holy Roman Emperor by Pope Leo III and establishes Carolingian Empire.
827 Saracens capture Sicily.
9th century Carolingian Empire disbands, leaving behind rival Italian states.
951 Saxon king Otto I becomes king of the Lombards; the following year he is crowned Holy Roman Emperor.
11th century Normans colonise Sicily and southern Italy.
1076 Pope Gregory VII and Emperor Henry IV become embroiled in power struggle that will last for nearly 200 years.
1155 Guelphs, who take the side of the pope, clash with the Ghibellines, who follow the new emperor, Frederick Barbarossa.
1167 Lombard League of cities formed, to oppose the emperor.
1176 Pope Alexander III and Frederick Barbarossa are reconciled.
1227–1250 The power struggle resumes, and the papacy is, finally, the victor.

LATE MIDDLE AGES AND RENAISSANCE

1265 Charles of Anjou becomes king of Sicily.
1282 French settlers in Sicily are massacred.
1302 Anjou dynasty established in Naples.
1348 Black Death kills one third of Italians.
1309–77 Papacy established at Avignon.
1377 Papacy moves back to Rome.
1442 Alfonso V, King of Aragon, is crowned king of the "Two Sicilies" (Naples and Sicily).
1447 Francesco Sforza replaces the Visconti in Milan.
1469–92 Lorenzo de' Medici leads Florence; peak of Renaissance.
1494 Wars of Italy begin with invasion of

French King Charles VIII; battle of Fornovo; Medici driven from Florence.

CENTURIES OF FOREIGN DESPOTISM

1503–13 Julius II is pope; Rome is now centre of the Renaissance.
1525 Battle of Pavia; Spaniards capture French king.
1527 Rome sacked by Charles V's imperial troops; Venice now centre of artistic activity.
1534 Founding of the Jesuits.
1540 Inquisition unleashed on Italy.
1559 Treaty of Cateau-Cambrésis confirms Spanish control of Italy.
1700–13 War of the Spanish Succession ends Spanish domination; Austria becomes main foreign power on peninsula.
1796 Napoleon invades Italy; brings ideals of French Revolution; founds several republics.
1808 French capture Rome for second time, and exile the pope.
1814 Overthrow of French rule.

TOWARDS ITALIAN UNITY

1815 Congress of Vienna; Venice given to Austria, who once again dominates Italy.
1820–31 Abortive uprisings against Austria; formation of secret patriotic societies, such as the Carbonari.
1831 Mazzini founds Young Italy movement.
1848 Uprisings across Italy against Austria led by Charles Albert, king of Piedmont; early successes followed by Austrian backlash. Charles Albert grants constitution.
1852 Cavour becomes prime minister of Piedmont.
1854 Piedmont enters the Crimean War.
1859–60 With the help of France, Piedmont annexes most of northern Italy. Garibaldi's "Thousand" conquer Sicily and Naples.
1861 Victor Emmanuel II of Piedmont proclaimed King of Italy.
1866 Venice annexed to Italy.
1870 Italian troops enter Rome; unification completed; Rome becomes capital.

MODERN ITALY

1882 Triple Alliance agreed between Italy, Germany and Austria.
1896 Italians defeated at Adowa, Ethiopia.

PRECEDING PAGES: 18th-century map of Italy, when it was a collection of independent states. **LEFT:** Francesco Petrarch, Renaissance poet. **RIGHT:** Pope John Paul II.

1900 Anarchist assassinates King Umberto I. Victor Emmanuel III is crowned king.
1915 Italy joins Allies in World War I.
1919 Italian claims largely ignored at peace conference; rise of Fascism.
1922 Mussolini's march on Rome.
1935 War against Ethiopia.
1939 Seizure of Albania.
1940 Italy joins Germany in World War II.
1943 Allies land in Sicily. Mussolini deposed, later rescued by Germans to found puppet government in the North. In September, provisional government in the South surrenders.
1944 Liberation of Rome; abdication of King Victor Emmanuel III.

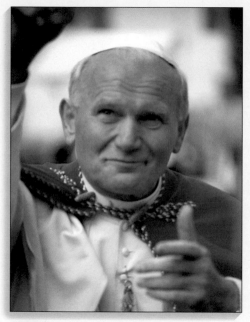

1945 Mussolini killed by partisans.
1946 Italy declared a republic.
1957 Treaty of Rome: Italy joins Common Market as one of six founder members.
1950s–60s Italy's "economic miracle".
1966 Floods in Venice and Florence.
1978 Former premier Aldo Moro kidnapped and killed.
1980 Earthquake strikes Campania.
1990 Emergence and swift rise of the secessionist Northern League.
Early 1990s Corruption scandals rock Italy.
Late 1990s Extensive privatisation as part of the preparation for European Monetary Union.
1999 Work continues in preparation for the celebrations for the Holy Year 2000.

BEGINNINGS

Many primitive tribes settled in Italy, but under the Greeks
and the Etruscans it became the centre of the ancient world

As school children have noticed for years, Italy looks like a boot. The long, narrow peninsula sticking out of Europe's underbelly is perpetually poised to kick Sicily westward. This peculiar shape made Italy a natural site for early civilisation. The Alps, which cut across the only land link with the rest of Europe, protected the peninsula from the barbarians who roamed Northern Europe, while the Mediterranean, which surrounds the three remaining sides, served as a highway, first to bring civilisation to the peninsula and later to export it.

The land itself contains two separate regions: the northern continental, and the southern peninsular. Together the two parts cover an area of about 250,000 sq km (97,000 sq miles). The northern section is a plain, bordered on the north and northwest by the Alps and on the south by the Apennines. Once a vast bay of the Adriatic, this plain was gradually filled with nitrate-rich silt from the Po, the Adige and other rivers, and became the most fertile region in Italy.

Mountainous spine

The Apennine range, the so-called backbone of Italy, dominates the peninsular section of the country. These mountains zig-zag down from the French Alps and the coast of Liguria in the northwest, through northern Tuscany and southeast to the Adriatic coast, and veer west again to the Strait of Messina, between Sicily and the toe of the boot. In the central province of Abruzzi the peaks of the Gran Sasso d'Italia soar as high as 2,912 metres (9,700 ft).

It is no coincidence that the early inhabitants of Italy flourished in the west, on the lowland plains north and south of Rome. Here there are a few natural harbours and long rivers. The Tiber, Arno, Livi and Volturno are easily navigated by small craft, and their valleys provide easy communication between the coast and the interior. What is more, the plains of Tuscany, Latium and Campania comprise fertile farm-

LEFT: an Etruscan statue of Apollo. RIGHT: a Greek temple at Selinunte in Sicily.

land, thanks to a thick layer of ash and weathered lava from the many once-active volcanoes.

Around 200,000 years before the founding of Rome, only cave-dwelling hunter-gatherers lived on the Italian peninsula. However, with the Indo-European migrations (2000–1200 BC), tribes of primitive peoples poured into Italy

from Central Europe and Asia. These tribes lived in round huts clustered in small villages. The Villanovans, as the tribesmen are called, were farmers who could make and use iron tools. They cremated their dead and placed the ashes in tall, clay or bronze urns.

Villanovan culture spread from its original centre around Bologna south to Tuscany and Latium. Nowhere, however, did settlements grow to the size of towns; and Villanovans are not known for any great artistic achievements.

The transformation of Italy from a primitive backwater to the centre of the ancient world was due to the Greeks and the Etruscans. Both sailed across the sea in search of rich new land. They sowed the first seeds of civilisation on the peninsula in the early 8th century BC.

Greek colonists settled in Sicily and on the west coast near modern-day Naples. Most came in search of land to farm, for Greece had insufficient arable land to feed the entire population. Others were political refugees: whenever a Greek king was overthrown, all his followers were required to flee.

On arriving in Italy, Greek settlers formed independent cities, each loosely linked to their city of origin on the Greek mainland. One of the

MASTERS OF THE VINE

The Greeks were the first to bring both the vine and the olive under cultivation.

soldiers. But after years of inconclusive fighting the Greek leaders gave up the struggle.

The colonists still argued among themselves, and therefore failed to become a dominant political power in Italy. They did, however, become the major cultural and artistic force. Italian natives were eager to trade for Greek luxury goods, the like of which they had never seen. Soon Greek bronze and ceramic ware was dispersed throughout Italy and provided natives with new and sophisticated art patterns to imitate; the architecture and sculpture in the Greek

earliest colonies was at Cumae, by the Bay of Naples. Greeks from Euboea, an island northeast of Athens, settled there in about 770 BC. Other Euboeans founded Rhegion (modern Reggio di Calabria), at the tip of the boot, a few years later. The Corinthian city of Syracuse on Sicily ultimately became the most powerful of the Greek colonies. The colonists farmed the land around their cities, and traded with mainland Greece. They soon prospered and made important contributions to Italian agriculture.

During the 5th century, both Syracuse and Athens tried to establish rival empires out of the Greek colonies in Italy. Numerous battles were fought and many Italian natives were drafted as

cities also served as models. The civilising influence of the Greeks went beyond the visual arts. The natives adapted the Greek alphabet for their own Indo-European tongues and each native group soon had its own letters. By example, the Greeks also taught the Italian natives about modern warfare, lessons that they later used against their Greek teachers. The Italians learnt how to fortify towns with high walls of smooth masonry, and the value of shock troop tactics with armoured spearmen.

But exceptional wealth and knowledge did not enable the Greeks to control Italy, and failure to unify the natives under Greek leadership left great political opportunities wide open.

In about 800 BC, Etruscans settled on the west coast where Tuscany (Etruscany) and Lazio are today. The origins of the Etruscans still puzzle scholars. The Greek historian Herodotus claimed that they came from Asia Minor, driven by revolution and famine at home to seek new lands. However, recent archaeological evidence suggests that Etruscan culture derives from a small group of Phoenicians from Palestine who landed in Italy and imparted to the natives the knowledge they had brought from the East.

Wherever they came from, the Etruscans were a highly civilised people who had a hearty appetite for life. Hundreds of Etruscan tombs

dent, but they were grouped in a loose confederation for religious purposes. Representatives of the cities would gather regularly to worship the 12 Etruscan gods, but that was the extent of their political unity. Their fascination with religion far surpassed their desire for political power.

Vital trade routes

Each Etruscan city supported itself by trade. Eager to obtain luxury goods from the Greek colonists, the Etruscans developed overland routes to reach the Greek cities. These cut straight through Latium, the plain south of the Tiber occupied by Italian natives called Latins.

have survived, many with wall paintings depicting dancing, dinner parties and music-making. Other paintings show battle and hunting scenes.

The Etruscans were also extremely skilled craftsmen. Their speciality was metal working. Italy was rich in minerals, and trade in metal goods soon became the basis of an active urban society. Cities sprang up where previously there had been only simple villages. Each of the Etruscan cities (there were 12 in all) was indepen-

LEFT: an ancient Greek dives gracefully into the unknown in a fresco from a tomb at Paestum.
ABOVE: the she-wolf suckling Romulus and Remus, the mythical founders of Rome.

One of their trading posts on the route south was a Latin village called Rome, originally only a cluster of mud huts. Under the influence of the Etruscans, the settlement flourished. They drained the swamp that became the Roman Forum and built grand palaces and roads.

For 300 years from the late 8th century BC, Etruscan kings ruled Rome. But, by the 5th century BC, their power was fading. In the North, Gauls overran Etruscan settlements in the Po Valley. Next, Italic tribesmen from the Abruzzi threatened the main Etruscan cities. Then, in the South, the Etruscans went to war against the Greeks. The Romans chose this moment to rebel against their Etruscan masters. ❏

ROME RULES THE WORLD

Between its legendary founding by Romulus and its sacking by barbarians,
Rome presided over one of our greatest civilisations

The historians of Ancient Rome wrote their own version of events leading to the overthrow of the Etruscan kings. They drew upon legends about Rome's past and claimed that the city had only temporarily fallen under Etruscan rule. According to legend, Rome was founded by the descendants of gods and heroes.

In his epic, the *Aeneid*, Virgil tells how Aeneas, a hero of Homeric Troy, journeyed west after the sack of Troy to live and rule in Latium. In the 8th century one of his descendants, the Latin princess Rhea Silvia, bore twin sons, Romulus and Remus, fathered by the god Mars. Her uncle, King Amulius, angry because the princess had broken her vow of chastity as a Vestal Virgin, locked her up and abandoned the boys on the river bank to die. They were found there by a she-wolf who raised them. As young men, the brothers led a band of rebel Latin youths to find a new home. As they approached the hills of Rome, a flight of eagles passed overhead – a sign from the gods that this was an auspicious site for their new city.

Rape and revolt

Rome was ruled by Etruscan kings until 509 BC when the son of King Tarquinius Superbus raped a Roman noblewoman, Lucretia. She killed herself in shame and Roman noblemen rose in revolt against the Etruscans.

The leader of the Roman revolt, Lucius Junius Brutus, may have been an actual historical figure. In Roman legend he is the founder of a republic, a vigorous leader, and a puritanical ruler. The historian Tacitus wrote that he was so loyal to Rome that he watched without flinching as his two sons were executed for treason.

In the war against the Etruscans, Rome was also aided by Cincinnatus, a simple Roman farmer who left his plough to help his city. He was so able that he rose quickly to the rank of general. But once the fight was won, he surrendered his position of power and returned to his life as an ordinary citizen.

These stories of Rome's early heroes reveal a lot about the Roman character. For the Romans, *pietas* – dutiful respect to one's gods, city, parents and comrades – was all-important.

Because of this, the heroes of legend were very useful propaganda tools within the empire.

Upon the overthrow of the Etruscans, Rome's leaders founded a republic based on the Greek model, and the Senate, a group of Rome's leading citizens who previously had advisory roles in government, took control of the city.

Roman conquests

During the next 200 years Rome conquered most of the Italian peninsula. But Carthage, a city in North Africa founded by the Phoenicians, controlled the western Mediterranean. If Rome was ever to expand its borders across the Mediterranean, Carthage had to be defeated.

LEFT: the *Augustus of Prima Porta* shows a youthful emperor looking to Rome's future of *Imperium sine fine* (rule without end). **RIGHT:** Hannibal's Carthaginian forces cross the Alps during the Second Punic War.

The initial clash between the two cities, the First Punic War (264 BC), began as a struggle for the Greek city of Messina on Sicily. By the time it was over, in 241 BC, the Romans had driven the Carthaginians out of Sicily completely. The island became Rome's first province. Three years later Rome annexed Sardinia and Corsica, and further military triumphs followed. When Rome conquered Cisalpine Gaul (northern Italy) and extended its borders to the Alps, it alleviated the threat of invasion by the Gauls.

War broke out again in 218 BC when the brilliant Carthaginian general Hannibal embarked on an ambitious plan to attack Rome from the

north via Spain, the Pyrenees and the Alps. Rome eventually counterattacked Carthage, and Hannibal was forced to return and defend his homeland. He was defeated in 202 BC at the battle of Zama, southwest of Carthage.

Final defeat of Carthage

The Third Punic War was almost an afterthought. Carthage, stripped of many of its possessions 50 years earlier, had regained much of its commercial power. When the Carthaginians challenged Rome indirectly, the Romans razed the city of Carthage and ploughed salt into the soil. The Carthaginians were sold into slavery.

The blessings of peace were mixed. Rome was now more prosperous than ever before, but only the middle class and the rich benefited. For the common people, many of whom had served their city faithfully during the wars, peace meant greater poverty as the menial jobs on which they had depended were now filled by slaves. Independent farmers, who traditionally formed the backbone of the Roman state, sold their land to the owners of great estates, who used slaves to work it. These displaced farmers joined the Roman mob or wandered Italy seeking work.

The Senate's usual way of dealing with potentially explosive situations was to feed the masses bread and entertain them with circuses. But eventually a patrician, Tiberius Gracchus, challenged the exploitative system. Elected tribune in 133 BC, he campaigned to reintroduce a law limiting the size of the great estates, and proposed redistributing state-owned farming and grazing land among the poor. The Senators, many of them wealthy landowners, blocked Tiberius's plan, and when he persisted and ran for re-election as tribune they engaged assassins to murder him and his supporters.

Gaius the populist

Tiberius's spirit did not die with him. Eleven years later, his brother Gaius was elected tribune. An effective speaker, he was popular with the Roman masses. Once in office, he called for sweeping land reform. Again the Senate struck back viciously. The Roman people were incited to riot, and Gaius was blamed. He was killed or forced to kill himself (the records are not clear), and his followers were imprisoned.

The power of the army commanders now became the determining factor in Roman politics. The general Gaius Marius, son of a farmer, returned to Rome from triumphant campaigns in Africa determined to smash the power of the despised Senate. To the Roman people, Gaius Marius was a god-like figure who had transformed the Roman citizen legions into a professional army. He and his supporters butchered the senatorial leaders and thousands of aristocratic Romans.

This fateful action, taken in the name of liberty, opened the way to dictatorship. The Senate turned to Silla, a rival general and a patrician by birth, who answered Marius's violence with a blood-bath of his own. After Marius's death in 86 BC, Silla posted daily lists of people to be executed by his henchmen. He then conducted equally bloody campaigns abroad.

Silla returned to Rome and ruled as absolute dictator. The Senate could put no check on him for it had opened the door for him to take power. The Republic was dead, the victim of three centuries of empire building.

Enter Pompey the Great

For two years the streets of Rome ran with blood. But in 79 BC Silla grew tired of ruling and retired to his estate near Naples. Civil war broke out again. Silla's successor was another general, Gnaeus Pompeius, called Pompey the Great. He

army across the flooded Rubicon river (the border between Cisalpine Gaul and Italy), against the orders of the Senate. With Caesar heading toward the capital, Pompey quickly left for Greece, taking his own small army and most of the Senate with him. Pompey had planned to strike back at Caesar from Greece having secured an adequate army, but Caesar moved first. He attacked Pompey's allies in Spain, then in Greece, forcing Pompey to flee to Egypt where he was eventually killed in 48 BC.

Caesar returned to Rome in triumph. The masses believed that his victories proved he was divinely appointed to rule Rome. For the first

restored many liberties suspended by Silla, but failed to go far enough for the rioting masses.

Pompey's solution was to join forces with two other military men, Crassus and Julius Caesar, and form the Triumvirate, a ruling body of considerable power and influence. This arrangement was successful at first but when Crassus died in 53 BC, the two remaining leaders quarrelled. For several years Pompey and Caesar eyed each other warily. Then, in 49 BC, Caesar, after his successful campaign in Gaul, led his

LEFT: Julius Caesar raised patrician eyebrows when he put his face on a coin. **ABOVE:** Emperor Augustus built the monumental *Ara Pacis* to celebrate peace.

BEWARE THE IDES OF MARCH

An Etruscan soothsayer had warned Caesar to beware of misfortune that would strike no later than 15 March 44 bc. On that day – the Ides of March – Caesar was scheduled to address the Senate. On his way to the Senate chamber he passed the soothsayer. Caesar remarked that the Ides had come safely. The Etruscan replied that the day was not yet over. In the chamber, Caesar was surrounded by conspirators and stabbed 23 times. When he saw that Marcus Junius Brutus, a patrician he had treated like a son, was among his murderers, he murmured "Et tu, Brute?" ("You too, Brute?") and died.

time in decades there were no riots in the capital. But the upper classes were wary of Caesar's monarchical tendencies. While factions within the Senate heaped honours on the new ruler, hoping for favours in return, many patricians watched suspiciously as Caesar had statues of himself raised in public places and his image put on coins. A conspiracy formed against him.

After Caesar's death, Mark Antony, Caesar's co-consul and Octavian, his grand-nephew, joined forces to pursue and murder the conspirators. Despite their cooperation, but in fact he was the first emperor of Rome. Unlike his grand-uncle before him, he took care not to offend the republican sentiments of the Romans, and therein lay the key to his success. He allowed the Senate the outward trappings of power and influence, but little of the reality. Uninterested in status symbols or ostentation, he lived and dressed simply. The competence and sensitivity with which Augustus reigned made for an unprecedented period of peace and prosperity; and for some 200 years after Augustan reform, the Mediter-

> **CHARACTER BUILDER**
>
> Augustus, first emperor of Rome, outlawed prostitution and drunkenness and strengthened divorce laws.

the two were never good friends. Initially they collaborated with an army leader, Lepidus, to form an uneasy Second Triumvirate, but the arrangement faltered when Antony fell in love with the Egyptian queen Cleopatra and rejected his wife, Octavian's sister, to marry her. In revenge, Octavian turned the Senate against Mark Antony, then declared war on his former partner. When defeat was imminent, Antony and Cleopatra committed suicide.

Augustus and the Pax Romana

Octavian's triumphant return to Rome marked the beginning of a new era. He called himself simply "Augustus", meaning "the revered one", ranean world basked in a *Pax Romana*, a Roman peace.

Before Augustus assumed power, the republican institutions had been unable to administer the vast territories Rome now controlled. Military dictatorship had been the result. To meet this challenge Augustus created a personal bureaucracy within his household. In addition to footmen and maids, he also had tax collectors, governors, census takers, and administrators as his "servants". He allowed this personal civil service to grow to a size sufficient to run the empire, but kept it under tight control. At first, many members of the nobility refused to join: they believed that any office in the household, however influential, was too close to personal service. But poor men of talent joined Augustus readily, and throughout his reign the Empire ran smoothly.

With peace, art and literature flourished. The poet Virgil, who had lived through the civil wars and military dictatorships, paid tribute to Augustus's achievements in the *Aeneid*; the poet Horace likened the emperor to a helmsman who had steered the ship of state into a safe port. Augustus himself took part in the artistic resurgence and set about rebuilding the capital. He claimed that he had found Rome a city of brick and left it a city of marble.

Augustus reigned for 41 years and set the tone of Roman leadership for the next 150. None of his successors had his ability, but his institutional and personal legacy did much to preserve peace in the flourishing Roman world.

The mad and the bad

The Emperor Tiberius had none of his step-father's sense of proportion, nor his steadiness. He began his reign with good intentions, but he mismanaged many early problems. He spent the last 11 years of his reign at his villa on Capri, from where he issued a volley of execution orders. The historian Suetonius wrote (in the translation by Robert Graves), "Not a day, however holy, passed without an execution; he even desecrated New Year's Day. Many of his victims were accused and punished with their children – some actually by their children – and the relatives forbidden to go into mourning."

Rome was relieved when Tiberius died, only to find that there was worse to come. Caligula, his successor, ruled ably for three years, then ran wild. His derangement may have been due to illness, or simply the pressures of high office. He insisted that he was a god, formed his own priesthood and erected a temple to himself. He proposed his horse be made consul. Finally a group of his own officers assassinated Caligula, and Rome was rid of its most hated ruler.

The officers took it upon themselves to name the next emperor. Their choice was Claudius, grandson of Augustus, whom they found hiding behind a curtain in the palace after the assassination. Many thought Claudius a fool, for he stuttered and was slightly crippled, but he

proved a good and steady ruler. He oversaw the reform of the civil service, and the expansion of the Roman Empire to include Britain.

Claudius was poisoned by his ambitious wife Agrippina, who pushed Nero, her son by a previous marriage, on to the throne. Like Tiberius before him, Nero started out with good intentions. He was well-educated, an accomplished musician, and showed respect for the advice of others, especially senators. But the violent side of his nature soon became apparent. He poisoned Brittanicus, Claudius's natural son, and tried to do the same to his mother, but she had taken the precaution of building up an immu-

nity to the poison. In the end Nero accused her of plotting against him, and had her executed.

Nero's excesses caused alarm among Rome's citizens. When a fire destroyed the city in AD 64, he was accused of starting it. In fact he was away from the city at the time and stories of him fiddling while Rome burned are probably untrue.

Nero lost his throne after the Roman commanders in Gaul, Africa and Spain rebelled. When the news reached the capital riots broke out and the Senate condemned him to death as a public enemy. With no hope left, Nero killed himself in AD 68. His suicide threw the empire into greater turmoil. He left no heir and therefore the rebellious commanders fought amongst

LEFT: a reconstruction of the Colosseum.
RIGHT: Emperor Nero with his tigress, Phoebe.

themselves for a year until a legion commander, Vespasian Flavius, emerged as emperor.

Vespasian proved a wise emperor, and his rule ushered in a period of peace. There was a short time of troubles when his son, Domitian, became emperor; but, by the time he died, the Senate was powerful enough to appoint its own emperor, Nerva, a respected lawyer from Rome.

Nerva was the first of the "five good emperors" who reigned from AD 96 to 180. He was followed by Trajan, Hadrian, Antoninus Pius and Marcus Aurelius – all educated men, interested in philosophy and devoted to their duties. They were loved by the people of Rome for

administering their vast Empire well and successfully defending its borders.

Decline and fall

During the period between the death of Marcus Aurelius and the sack of Rome in the 5th century, it became increasingly difficult to defend the Empire from barbarians. Between AD 180 and 285, Rome was threatened in both the east and the west by barbarian tribes. The Empire doubled the size of the army. The drain on manpower and resources caused an economic crisis, and the powerful army could place emperors on the throne and remove them at will. Most of these "barracks emperors" served for less than

three years and never even lived in the capital.

Plague also struck Rome, which weakened the Empire and made it more vulnerable to enemy attack. On all sides wars raged. In the east, the revived Persian Empire threatened Syria, Egypt and all of Asia Minor. In the west, Franks invaded France and Spain.

Major political reform was undertaken by Emperor Diocletian in 286. He believed the Empire could no longer be ruled by one man, so he divided it into eastern and western regions. He chose Nicomedia in Asia Minor as his capital and appointed a soldier named Maximinus to rule the west from Milan.

Unfortunately this arrangement did not end quarrels about the succession. Constantine marched on Rome in 311 to assert his right to the throne. While on the road, however, he claimed that he had a vision. The sign of the cross appeared in the sky with the words: "By this sign win your victory." As a result, when Constantine defeated his rival, Maxentius, and emerged as the sole emperor, he ruled as a Christian and granted religious freedom to existing Christians.

In 324, he took a step further and confirmed Christianity as the state religion. Not all citizens followed the new faith; some notable families remained true to their pagan beliefs. But Constantine's conversion established Christianity, which had been spreading through the Empire since the time of Nero, as the religion of the Roman state and thus of the Western world. Under his auspices, or in the decades which followed his reign, the first Christian churches of Rome were built. These included the earliest constructions of the five patriarchal churches of which the pope himself was the priest: San Pietro (St Peter's), San Giovanni in Laterano, San Paolo fuori le Mura, San Lorenzo fuori le Mura and Santa Maria Maggiore. Together with the catacomb churches of San Sebastiano and Santa Croce in Gerusalemme along the Via Appia, these soon became centres of pilgrimage.

Despite the conversion to Christianity, the Empire continued to decline. In 330, Constantine decided to move the capital east, and make a fresh start in his new city of Constantinople. Back in Italy, the barbarians gradually moved closer. The city of Rome was sacked in 410. ❑

LEFT: one of the "barracks emperors", probably Valerian.

Life in the Empire

In more than 60 treatises on morality, Plutarch (AD 46–126) laid down what was expected of a Roman gentleman. It was a damnable luxury to strain wine or to use snow to cool drinks. It was "democratic and polite" to be punctual for dinner; "oligarchical and offensive" to be late. Conversation over dinner ought to be philosophical, like debating which came first, the chicken or the egg. Salt fish was scooped up with a single finger, but two could be used if the fish was fresh. There was only one permissible way for a Roman gentleman to scratch himself, and so on.

It would be naive to think that all Romans obeyed Plutarch's strictures. Life was as diverse as in any modern capital, with an elegant high society at one end of the scale, vicious louts at the other, and every permutation in between. The one common factor was probably a passion for bathing. With underground furnaces heating the water, the baths got bigger and bigger. The well-preserved Caracalla baths could disgorge 1,600 glowing Romans per day.

In the early days, relations between patricians and plebeians were codified, as were family matters. Patricians were the source of "tranquillity", mainly by lending an ear to plebeians' problems and dispensing advice. In return, plebeians had to stump up money when the patrician was held to ransom or could not settle his debts. Money made available in such circumstances was not a loan but a plebeian's privilege, for which he was supposed to be grateful. On the other hand, plebeians were not enslaved and could switch allegiance from an unsatisfactory patrician to one more suitable.

Divorce was introduced relatively late. At first, marriage was permanent and wives automatically acquired half the conjugal property. However, husbands exercised the ultimate sanction in that they were legally entitled to murder wives for serious offences, such as poisoning the children or making duplicates of their private keys. Fathers were prevented from selling sons into slavery once the boys had married.

Citizens bombarded bureaucrats with complaints about the quality of life in Rome: disgraceful traffic congestion and refuse collection; preposterous fashions like men experimenting with trousers; escalating inflation; homosexuals getting too big for their boots; the filthy habit of smoking dried cow

RIGHT: a fresco in the Casa dei Vettii in Pompeii.

dung, and so forth. The most castigated men in Rome were unscrupulous property developers who set fire to a building they wanted and then, as the flames went up, offered the uninsured owner a pittance. As soon as the deal was struck, the developer summoned a private fire brigade parked around the corner.

In a spiritual context, the lives of the Romans were wrapped up in astrology and mysticism. The spread of Bacchic rites in republican Rome alarmed the government, which called them: "This pestilential evil ... this contagious disease". Senators "were seized by a panic of fear, both for the public safety, lest these secret conspiracies and noctur-

nal gatherings contain some hidden harm or danger, and for themselves individually, lest some relatives be involved in this vice."

The social decadence supposedly behind the downfall of Rome had its own decorum. Petronius Arbiter, author of the *Satyricon*, orchestrated Nero's orgies. He later fell out with Nero and was ordered to take his own life. Petronius invited friends to a farewell banquet where he sat with bandages wrapped around wrists which he discreetly slashed as the evening progressed. The controlled bleeding enabled him to sustain repartee up to the moment his head slumped. It is not known whether he expressed a parting thought on the interesting question of the chicken and the egg.

THE MIDDLE AGES

A period that saw Lombard, Saracen and Norman invasions

and clashes between emperor and pope

For four centuries after the sack of Rome in AD 410, barbarian invaders, including the Goths and the Lombards, battled with local military leaders and the Byzantine emperors for control of Italy. Under these conditions, the culture and prosperity that had characterised ancient times faded. The Roman Empire had unified Italy and made it the centre of the world, but after its demise Italy became a provincial battlefield. Since none of the rival powers could control the whole of Italy, the land was divided, and it remained so until the 19th century.

The Dark Ages began with a series of Visigoth invasions from northern and eastern Europe. The emperors in Constantinople were still in theory the rulers of Italy, but for decades they accepted first the Visigoth and later the Ostrogoth leaders as *de facto* kings. Justinian I, who became emperor in Constantinople in 527, longed to revive the splendour of the Empire and sent the brilliant general Belisarius to regain direct control of Italy. But, although he met with initial success – he captured Ravenna from the Goths in 540 – a new group of barbarians soon appeared on Italy's borders: the Lombards.

Invaders from the north

The Lombards were German tribesmen from the Danube Valley. They swiftly conquered most of what is now Lombardy, Venetia and Tuscany, causing the inhabitants of the northern Italian cities to flee to eastern coastal regions where they were protected by the Byzantines, who still controlled the seas. Many settled around the lagoon of Venice.

Meanwhile the Lombards altered the system of government. They replaced the centralised Roman political system with local administrative units called "duchies", after the Lombard army generals who were known as *duces*. Within each duchy a *duce* ruled as king. The land was distributed to groups of related Lombard families, each headed by a free warrior, who owed limited feudal allegiance to his king but had a free hand on his own land. This, along with the Byzantines' continuing control of many provinces, meant Italy was effectively divided.

The radical changes that the Lombards brought to Italy's administration did not affect

Raiser Justinian. (483—565.) Raiserin Theodora. († 548.)

the Church. Indeed, in Rome the bishopric rose to new prominence because the emperors in Constantinople were too distant to exert any temporal or spiritual authority.

Greatest among the early popes was Gregory I (589–603), a Roman by birth, a scholar by instinct and training, and a great statesman. He persuaded the Lombards to abandon the siege of Rome, and helped achieve peace in Italy. He sent missionaries to Northern Europe to spread the word of God and the influence of Rome, and sent the first missionaries to the British Isles.

Gregory's successors reorganised the municipal government of Rome, and effectively became rulers of the city. It was inevitable that

LEFT: the 6th-century Pope Gregory the Great, one of many early popes who was canonised.

RIGHT: Emperor Justinian with his wife, Theodora.

the popes would eventually clash with the emperor in Constantinople. In 726, Emperor Leo decreed that veneration of images of Christ and the saints was forbidden and that all images were to be destroyed. The pope opposed his decree on the grounds that the Church in Rome should have the final say on all spiritual matters, and organised an Italian revolt against the emperor. The Lombards joined the revolt on the side of the popes and used the opportunity to chase the Byzantines out of Italy.

GREGORY THE GREAT

The pope who made peace with the Lombards to save Rome also gave his name to Gregorian chant, and sent St Augustine to England.

Western Europe. To unify his vast territories under Christian auspices, he had Pope Leo crown him Holy Roman Emperor at St Peter's in Rome on Christmas Day 800.

Charlemagne lived only 14 years after his coronation, and none of his successors matched him in ability; authority fell into the hands of Frankish counts, Charlemagne's vassals who had accompanied him south and been granted land of their own. As representatives of the crown, they were required to raise troops, but they used these

After the imperial capital, Ravenna, fell to the Lombard army in 751, the popes, feeling more directly threatened by the powerful Lombards than by an absent emperor, sought a new ally and turned to the Franks for help.

Pepin, king of the Franks, invaded Italy in 754. He reconquered the imperial lands but ceded control to the pope. Twenty years later, Pepin's son, Charlemagne, finished his father's work by defeating and capturing the Lombard king, confirming his father's grant to the papacy, and assuming the crown of the Lombards.

Charlemagne then returned to the North and campaigned against the Saxons, Bavarians and Avars, making himself ruler of a large part of

forces to fight each other for land and power.

This period of feudal anarchy was also marked by invasions. In the South the Saracens invaded Sicily in 827, and for the next 250 years Sicily was an Arab state. Sicily also became a base for raids on the Italian mainland, and Charlemagne's great-grandson, Louis II, who was emperor for 25 years, failed to raise an organised defence against them. The Lombard dukes in the South, whom Charlemagne had not conquered completely, allied themselves with these invaders against the Carolingian emperor. What success Louis had was overshadowed by Pope Leo IV's defence of Rome and the naval victory against the Saracens at Ostia.

The Normans in the south

In the early 11th century, small groups of Normans arrived in southern Italy. Adventurers and skilled soldiers, they would fight for anyone who would pay: Greek, Lombard and Saracen alike. In return they asked for land.

Soon landless men from Normandy arrived to fight, settle and conquer for themselves. The papacy lost no time in allying itself with this powerful group of Christians. In the 1050s, the Norman chief, Robert Guiscard, conquered Calabria in the toe of Italy. Pope Nicholas II "legitimised" Norman rule of the area by calling it a papal fief then investing Guiscard as its king.

Despite external opposition (from the eastern and western emperors) and occasional domestic rebellions, Roger's son and grandson were able to preserve the regime. Only when William II died in 1189, leaving no heir, did civil war break out and Norman control of southern Italy end.

During the 9th and 10th centuries, the papacy was controlled by Roman nobles. The men they picked for office were often corrupt. After the Emperor Otto I arrived in Rome in 962, he insisted that no pope could be elected until the emperor had named a candidate. But by reforming the papacy, the emperors started a trend that would have far-reaching consequences.

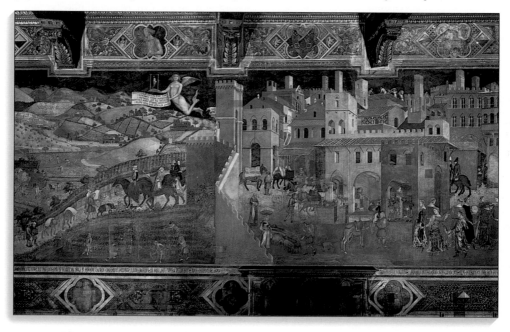

Robert's nephew, Roger, conquered Sicily. He was crowned king in Palermo in 1130 and ruled over the island and his uncle's mainland possessions. He was a tolerant ruler, and his court became a magnet for Jewish, Greek and Arab scholars. Still visible today are the architectural achievements of this sophisticated culture. Brilliant examples of Arab-Norman architecture can be seen in Palermo and at the cathedrals of Monreale and Cefalù.

LEFT: glittering mosaics, such as this one of the Emperor Justinian, are glittering reminders that Ravenna was once the capital of Byzantium.
ABOVE: fresco in Siena's town hall.

In the 11th century, the popes strove to reform the church further by imposing a strict clerical hierarchy. Throughout the Holy Roman Empire, bishops were to be answerable to the pope, and priests to bishops. A single legal and administrative system would bind all members of the clergy together. These reforms immediately angered all lay rulers from the emperor down.

The struggle reached a climax when Emperor Henry IV invested an anti-reform candidate as archbishop of Milan in 1072. As a result, Pope Gregory VII decreed that an investiture by a non-cleric was forbidden and excommunicated Henry. For three days in the cold winter of 1077, the humbled emperor stood in the courtyard of a

Tuscan castle where Gregory was staying, and pleaded for a reconciliation with the pope.

Henry was forgiven. However, he failed to keep his promise to recognise the claims of the papacy, and a new civil war broke out. Gregory's supporters were defeated initially and he was carried off to Salerno and death, but his successors worked to ensure the triumph of Gregory's cause, and the emperors were forced to concede their rights of investiture in 1122.

During the years of the investiture controversy and the ensuing civil wars, the cities of northern and central Italy grew rich and powerful. The emperors were too distracted to admin-

ister them directly. Around the same time, Mediterranean commerce was revived. With new wealth at their disposal, the cities forced the nobles in the countryside to acknowledge their supremacy. The Italian city-states were born. The strong and separate identity of the city-states is one of the leitmotifs of Italian history, influencing the pattern of future political affiliations, fostering separate schools of art, architecture and music, and largely determining regional attitudes today.

The maritime republics of Venice, Genoa and Pisa were foremost among the Italian cities, but inland cities that were situated on rich trade routes also prospered. Milan and Verona lay at

the entrance to the Alpine passes, Bologna was the chief city on the Via Emilia, and Florence had sea access via the river Arno and controlled two roads to Rome.

The growing political power of the city-states was an important factor in renewed conflict between emperor and pope during the 13th century. Emperor Frederick II (1197–1250) tried to build a strong, centralised state in Italy. The cities that supported him kept their rights of self-government, but were forced to join an imperial federation. The cities that opposed him, wanting complete political autonomy, found an ally in Pope Gregory IX who secretly had imperial designs of his own. Northern Italy became a battlefield for civil war between the Guelfs, supporters of the pope, and the Ghibellines, allies of the emperor.

By the time Frederick died in 1250, without instituting his reforms, the Guelf cause was won. The alliance of pope and the city-states had ruined imperial plans for a unified Italy.

The age of Dante

The Guelfs beat the Ghibellines decisively, but a feud broke out between two Guelf factions: the Blacks and the Whites. This split was especially severe in Florence where the Blacks defended the nobles' feudal tradition against the Whites, rich magnates who were willing to give merchants a voice in government.

Pope Boniface VIII sided with the Blacks and worked to have all prominent Whites exiled from Florence in 1302. Among the exiles was Dante Alighieri, who went on to write *La Divina Commedia* (*The Divine Comedy*), a literary masterpiece that promoted Tuscan Italian to the status of a national tongue and also reveals much about the politics of the period.

Dante put his faith in the Holy Roman Empire, convinced that it could and should usher in a new period of cultural and political prominence for Italy. When Henry VII became Holy Roman Emperor in 1308, he wanted to revive imperial power in Italy and set up a government that was neither Guelf nor Ghibelline. But the cities refused to support him. Dante's home town, Florence, was the centre of the resistance to imperial plans. ❏

LEFT: an illuminated manuscript made for the Dukes of Milan in the late 14th century. **RIGHT:** Dante Alighieri, as painted by Andrea del Castagno.

THE RENAISSANCE

Free from foreign interference, the city-states flourished and witnessed an unprecedented cultural awakening

The constant fighting in northern Italy subsided in the early 14th century when both the popes and the emperors withdrew from Italian affairs. After Henry VII's demise, the emperors turned their attention to Germany. Meanwhile, the influence of the papacy declined after a quarrel between Pope Boniface and King Philip of France in 1302. The pope insisted that Philip had no right to tax the French clergy; the king's response was to send his troops to capture the pope. French pressure ensured that the next pope was a Frenchman, Clement V, and he moved the papacy from Rome to Avignon, where it stayed until 1377.

The people of Italy were thus free from outside interference during the 14th century and the Italian cities grew stronger, richer and bigger than any in Europe. Against the political background of the supremacy of the city-state, a new culture bloomed and new ideas flourished. Rulers tried new methods of administration. Scholars were allowed to rediscover the pagan past. Wealthy merchants became lavish patrons of the arts. Through their commissions, artists experimented with a new, more realistic style.

Plague and depression

Not even the Black Death – the terrible outbreak of bubonic plague that ravaged Europe in the 14th century – could smother the new cultural awakening. But the plague did cause great human suffering and a prolonged economic depression. During several months of 1347 the death rate was 60 percent in some Italian cities. The merchants' solution to the declining profits of the period was to change the way they did business. Their innovations included marine insurance, credit transfers, double-entry bookkeeping and holding companies – all of which eventually became standard business practice.

To be a good businessman in the early Renaissance required a basic education: read-

ing, writing and arithmetic. But the more complicated business became, the more knowledge was needed, including an understanding of law and diplomacy, and of the ways of the world. Thus the traditional theological studies of the Middle Ages were replaced by the study of ancient authors and of grammar, rhetoric, history and moral philosophy. This education became known as *studia humanitatis*, or humanities.

Humanism grew partly out of the need for greater legal expertise in the expanding world of Mediterranean commerce. To learn how to administer their new, complex societies, lawyers looked back at the great tenets of Roman law. As they studied the codes of the ancients, they grew to appreciate the cultural riches of that long-buried civilisation. All aspects of Italian life were re-examined in the light of this new humanism. One way of life was thought to be ideal – that of the all-round man based on classical models. The Renaissance

LEFT: Titian's portrait of Pope Julius II, a great patron of the arts. **RIGHT:** relief by Ghiberti from the "Gates of Paradise" of the Baptistry of St John in Florence.

man was a reincarnation of rich, talented Roman philosophers.

Despots and republics

Italians of the 14th century were citizens of particular cities, not members of a national unit. They revered local saints, believed myths that explained the origin and uniqueness of their city, and feuded with other cities. Rulers encouraged artists and writers to glorify their towns.

There were a few experiences and conditions that many cities shared. As the authority of the popes and the emperors declined, life in the cities became increasingly violent. Leading captain would extend his powers until he controlled the entire city. Then he was in a strong enough position to make his office hereditary. This was how the della Scala family in Verona, the Carrara in Padua, the Gonzaga in Mantua and the Visconti in Milan came to power.

Once established, a despot would centralise all agencies of the government under his supervision. His power would be threatened only if he overstepped what his subjects could tolerate.

Some cities, including Venice, Florence, Siena, Lucca and Pisa, did not succumb to despotism until quite late in their history: the merchants were so powerful that rulers such as

families fought each other constantly, and often came into conflict with groups lower on the social ladder which wanted a role in the political life of the city. The remedy to this bloody civil strife was the rule of one strong man. The pattern was repeated over and over again in northern Italy. Traditional republican rule which could not keep order was replaced by a dictatorship. Sometimes a leading faction would bring in an outsider, known as a *podestà*, to end the chaos – for example, the lordship of the Este Family in Ferrara was established in this way. More often, the future despot was originally a *capitano del popolo* – the head of the local police force and citizens' army. Over time, this the Medici only survived by winning their support. In these cities republicanism flourished briefly, but even so the merchants dominated the organs of the republican government.

During the 14th and 15th centuries, northern and central Italy changed from an area speckled with tiny political units to one dominated by a few large states. Both republics and despots were expansionist in outlook. They would conquer their smaller neighbours, and construct out of the lands they gained a new regional state with increased economic resources.

Of the Italian city states, the most successful and the most powerful, was Milan. During the 14th century, the authoritarian Visconti family led the city to innumerable military and political victories until it was the largest state in northern Italy.

The Visconti regime may have been, in its efficiency, unlike anything Europe had seen for centuries, but for the Milanese people it had great drawbacks. The personal brutality of the Visconti controlled Milan. The regime could not rely on the loyalty of the populace for its survival. When the Visconti line died out in 1447, the Milanese declared a republic, but it was not strong enough to rule over all the restive towns Milan now controlled. When, in 1450, Francesco Sforza, a famous general who had served the Visconti, overthrew the republic and became the new duke, ruling with his wife Bianca Visconti, many Milanese were relieved.

The Republic of Florence

The spectacular transformation of Florence from a small town in the 1100s to the commercial and financial centre it had become by the end of the 14th century was based on the profitable wool trade. The wool guild of Florence, the *Arte della Lana,* imported wool from northern Europe and dyes from the Middle East. Using the city's secret weaving and colouring techniques, guild members produced a heavy red cloth that was sold all over the Mediterranean area. Wool trade profits had provided the initial capital for the banking industry of Florence. Since the 13th century, Florentine merchants had lent money to their allies, the pope and powerful Guelf nobles. This early experience led to the founding of formal banking houses, and made Florence the financial capital of Europe.

The leading merchant guilds of Florence spent their wealth on art. The city was a showcase of the best of Renaissance sculpture, painting and architecture. In the second half of the 13th century a building boom began with the construction of the Bargello, the Franciscan church of Santa Croce, and the Dominican church of Santa Maria Novella. Arnolfo di Cambio designed the cathedral and the Palazzo Vecchio. The *Arte della Lana* paid for the con-

---

LEFT: *The Battle of San Romano* by Paolo Uccello, showing the victory of Florence over Siena in 1432.
RIGHT: Cosimo the Elder, the Medici patriarch.

struction and decoration of the cathedral. The city hired Giotto to design the Campanile which is named after him, and in 1434 they had Brunelleschi finish the great dome.

The rich men of Florence controlled the city government through the *Parte Guelfa*. With membership came the right to seek out and persecute anyone with "Ghibellistic tendencies". Other political non-conformities were also not tolerated. Members of lesser guilds who demanded a greater share of power, or joined

THE VISCONTI TOUCH

The eminent Renaissance historian Jacob Burckhardt admired the "strict rationalism" of Visconti's Milan and called its government a work of art.

with the lower classes to fight the *Parte Guelfa*, were annihilated. However, in the early 15th century the violence of class war escalated. The unenfranchised artisans struck back repeatedly. At this point the rich merchants allowed Cosimo de' Medici to rise to the leadership of Florence.

The 15th century was the golden age of the Renaissance. All the economic, political and cultural developments of the previous century had set the stage for a period of unprecedented artistic and intellectual achievement. To live in Italy at this time was to live in a new world of cultural and commercial riches. Italy was truly the centre of the world.

The political history of the century divides

into two parts. Until 1454 the five chief states of Italy were busy expanding their borders, or strengthening their hold on territories,which meant fighting many small wars. The soldiers who fought them were mostly *condottieri* (mercenaries). After 1454 came a period of relative peace, when the states pursued their interests through alliances. These years saw the greatest artistic achievement, when Italian states of all sizes became cultural centres.

Italian wars of the Late Middle Ages and Early Renaissance had traditionally been fought by foreign mercenaries, but by the 15th century the mercenaries were more likely to be Italian. Men of all classes and from all parts of Italy joined the ranks of the purely Italian companies to fight northern wars for rival nobles. The *condottieri* looked upon war as a professional, technical skill. In battle, the object was to lose as few men as possible but still win. Soldiers were too valuable to be sacrificed unnecessarily. The countryside, however, suffered heavily as village after village was plundered. The *condottieri* did not hesitate to take what they could even though they were very well paid. They were bound by no patriotic ties, only by a monetary arrangement, so an important captain could always be bought by the enemy.

One of the greatest *condottieri* was Francesco Sforza. Sforza had inherited the command of an army upon his father's death in 1424. He fought first for Milan and then for Venice in the northern wars until Filippo Visconti sought to attach him permanently to Milan by marrying him to his illegitimate daughter, Bianca.

Visconti died in 1447 leaving no heir, and Milan declared itself a republic. Sforza was expected to captain the new republican forces. Instead he went into exile. But when the republican government proved incompetent he turned his forces on the city and starved Milan into surrender. The chief assembly of the republic invited him to be the new duke of the city.

Peace and the Italian League

Sforza, the great soldier, was instrumental in bringing peace to northern Italy. He signed, and encouraged others to sign, the Treaty of Lodi, which led to the Italian League of 1455. This was a defensive league between Milan, Florence and Venice that the king of Naples and the pope also respected. It was set up to prevent any one of the great states from increasing its powers at the expense of its weaker neighbours, and to present a common national front against attack.

The smaller states of Italy benefited most from the new league. Previously, they had spent vast resources on defence against the larger states. "This most holy League upon which depends the welfare of all Italy," wrote Giovanni Bentivoglio, a citizen of Bologna, in 1460.

During the decades of peace in Italy, Florence experienced its own Golden Age under the rule of the Medici family. The historian Guicciardini described the Florence of Lorenzo de' Medici as follows: "The city was in perfect peace, the leading citizens were united, and their author-

ity was so great that none dared to oppose them. The people were entertained daily with pageants and festivals; the food supply was abundant and all trades flourished. Talented and able men were assisted in their careers by the recognition given to arts and letters. While tranquillity reigned within her walls, externally the city enjoyed high honours and renown."

In part, the success of the Medici was a public relations coup. They allowed the Florentines to believe that the city government was still a great democracy. Only after Lorenzo's death, when Florence was briefly ruled by his arrogant son, did the citizens realise that their state, for all its republican forms, had drifted into the control of one family. They then quickly exiled the Medici and drafted a new constitution. Until then, both Cosimo and Lorenzo de' Medici had dominated Florence while shrewdly never appearing to be more than prominent citizens. They did this partly by manipulating the elections for the *Signoria,* Florence's city council, but the real base of their power lay in their acceptance by the city's leading citizens.

The Medici did more than simply rule and successfully keep the peace. They promoted art

PRINCELY ADVICE

Macchiavelli was inspired by Lorenzo de' Medici when he wrote in *The Prince*: "A ruler must emulate the fox and the lion, for the lion cannot avoid traps and the fox cannot fight wolves."

and culture in Florentine life. When the famous humanist Niccolò Niccoli died, Cosimo acquired his book collection and attached it to the convent of San Marco, creating the first public library in Florence. Cosimo also had Marsilio Ficino trained to become head of the new Platonic Academy and make Florence a centre of Platonic studies. He supplied Donatello with classical works to inspire his sculpture. Lorenzo de' Medici grew up in the atmosphere his grandfather had created and when he became leader

---

LEFT: Francesco Sforza married Bianca (**ABOVE**), natural daughter of the last of the Visconti rulers, to become despot of Milan.

of Florence he also was a great patron of the arts. For his employees he was a peer as well as a patron. His poetry was widely admired.

An end to the peace

When Lorenzo de' Medici died in 1492, the fragile Italian League that had kept Italy at peace and safe from any foreign attacks died with him. Ludovico il Moro, the lord of Milan, immediately quarrelled with the Neapolitan king and proposed to the king of France that he, Charles VIII, conquer Naples and the surrounding states. Ludovico offered finance and safe passage through the North of Italy. Charles readily accepted and so began a truly demoralising chapter of Italian history.

The internal disarray in Italy at the time was so great that the French troops faced no organised resistance. The new leader of Florence, a Dominican friar named Girolamo Savonarola, preached that Charles was sent by God to regenerate the Church and purify spiritual life. Other Italians also welcomed the French. They believed that the invaders would rid Italy of decadence and set up governments with natives in key posts. Only when these ideas proved illusory could Italian patriots recruit an army and challenge the French.

The French and Italians met near the village of Fornovo on 6 July 1495. The Italians, led by General Francesco Gonzaga, looked certain of victory: they outnumbered the French two-to-one, and they could launch a surprise attack against their enemy. But the Italian strategy fell apart. Crucial troops could not cross the river to the French position. General Gonzaga entered the fiercest fighting and did not direct the battle as a whole, and some Italian soldiers left the battle to capture the French king's booty. When the battle ended, four thousand men had died – the majority of them Italian.

"If the Italians had won at Fornovo, they would probably have discovered then the pride of being a united people ... Italy would have emerged as a respectable nation ... a country which adventurous foreigners would think twice before attacking," wrote Luigi Barzini in *The Italians.* Instead, the defeat at Fornovo broke the Italian spirit and led to 30 years of foreign interventions, bloody conflicts, civil wars and revolts. ❑

RENAISSANCE ART

The revolution in art and architecture which began in Florence gave us our greatest treasures. It also set the stage for Mannerism

Italian art shone brightest during the Renaissance when, as in most disciplines, a revolution took place. The Early Renaissance (1400–1500), the *Quattrocento*, introduced new themes that altered the future of art. Ancient Greece and Rome were rediscovered and with them the importance of man in the here and now. The human body surfaced as a new focal point in painting and sculpture. The discovery of perspective changed architecture.

The Early Renaissance centred on Florence. The city wanted to be seen as "the new Rome" and public works flourished. First was Lorenzo Ghiberti's commission for sculpting the gilded bronze north doors (1403–24) of the Baptistry, won in a competition with Filippo Brunelleschi in 1401. Ghiberti's more famous east doors (1424–52) are so dazzling that Michelangelo called them "the Gates of Paradise".

Classical architecture

It was Filippo Brunelleschi (1377–1466) who championed the new classically inspired architecture. After losing the Baptistry door competition, he went to Rome to study the proportions of ancient buildings. His studies led him to design such masterpieces as the dome of Florence cathedral, the arcade fronting the Innocenti orphanage, the church of San Lorenzo (1421–69), the Pazzi Chapel of Santa Croce (begun 1430–33), and Santo Spirito, all in Florence. You need no yardstick to appreciate the use of mathematical proportions. The overriding impression is of harmony, balance and calm.

If Brunelleschi was the most noted architect, Donatello (1386–1466) excelled in sculpture. His work expresses a new attitude to the human body. The figure of St George, made for the church of Orsanmichele and now in the Museo del Bargello, is not only a realistic depiction of the human form, but also a work of psychological insight. His *Gattamelata* (1445–50) in

LEFT: Michelangelo's *David*, in the Accademia in Florence. RIGHT: the anguish of Adam and Eve, from Masaccio's *Expulsion from Paradise*.

Padua was the first equestrian statue cast in bronze since Roman times, and his bronze *David* (1430–32), in the Bargello, was the first free-standing nude statue since antiquity.

The groundwork for the revolution in painting was laid a century earlier by Giotto (1267–1337). His frescoes – in Florence's Santa Croce,

in Padua's Cappella degli Scrovegni, and Assisi's Basilica di San Francesco – depart from the flat Byzantine style and invest the human form with solidity and volume, and the setting with a sense of space and depth. His breakthrough was carried further by the Early Renaissance's most noted painter, Masaccio (1401–28). His Florentine frescoes of *The Holy Trinity with Virgin and St John* in Santa Maria Novella (1425), and *The Life of St Peter* in the Brancacci Chapel of Santa Maria del Carmine (1427), display all the traits characteristic of the Renaissance: the importance of the human form, distinct under its clothing; human emotion; and the use of perspective.

Domenico Veneziano moved to Florence in 1439 and introduced pastel greens and pinks awash in cool light. The palette was picked up by his assistant, Piero della Francesca (1416–92), for his frescoes at San Francesco in Arezzo (1466). These are marvels of pale tone as well as mathematics – heads and limbs are variations of geometric shapes: spheres, cones and cylinders.

The artistic revolution in Florence soon spread to other parts of Italy. Leon Battista Alberti (1404–72), an author of noted treatises on sculpture, painting and architecture, introduced the tracing of classic motifs (columns, arches) on the exteriors of buildings, such as on

Michelangelo, Bramante, Raphael and Titian. Unlike their predecessors, who were thought of as craftsmen, they were considered to be creative geniuses capable of works of superhuman scale, grandeur and effort. Their extravaganzas were made possible by a new source of patronage – the papacy. Having returned to Rome from exile in Avignon, the popes turned the Eternal City into a centre of culture. The art of the High Renaissance is marked by a move beyond rules of mathematical ratios or anatomical geometrics to a new emphasis on emotional impact. The increasing use of oil paints, introduced to the Italians in the late 1400s, began to

the Palazzo Rucellai in Florence (1446–51) and the Malatesta Temple in Rimini (1450).

Giovanni Bellini (1430/1–1516) triumphed in Venice. In his *Madonna and Saints* in San Zaccaria (1505), the grandeur of Masaccio's influence is tempered by Flemish detail.

Detail most delicately expressed is the hallmark of Sandro Botticelli (1444/5–1510). The Uffizi Gallery houses the allegorical *Primavera* (1480) and the lovely *Birth of Venus* (1489).

The High Renaissance

The High Renaissance (1500–1600) was the heyday of some of the most celebrated artists in the entire history of art: Leonardo da Vinci,

replace egg tempera and opened new possibilities for richness of colour and delicacy of light.

Leonardo da Vinci (1452–1519) was born near Florence but left the city to work for the Duke of Milan, primarily as an engineer and only secondarily as a sculptor, architect and painter. In Milan, Leonardo painted the *Last Supper* (1495–98), in Santa Maria delle Grazie. The mural – an unsuccessful experiment in oil tempera, which accounts for its poor condition – is a masterpiece of psychological drama.

Leonardo also exploited new techniques in painting. *Chiaroscuro* (literally, light and dark) – the use of light to bring out and highlight three-dimensional bodies – is vividly seen in the whirl of bodies in the *Adoration of the Magi* (1481–82) in the Uffizi. Another invention was *fumato*, a fine haze that lends a dreamy quality to paintings, enhancing their poetic potential.

In 1503, Pope Julius II, a great patron of the arts, commissioned the most prominent architect of the day, Donato Bramante (1444–1514), to design the new St Peter's. Bramante had earlier made his mark with the classically inspired gem, *The Tempietto* (1502), in the courtyard of Rome's San Pietro in Montorio. The pope's directive for

> **CLASSIC REVIVAL**
>
> Bramante revived concrete, used by the Ancient Romans and abandoned in favour of brick or cut stone during the Middle Ages.

figures with a dignity, volume and beauty inspired by Hellenistic precedents, yet given new emotional impact. It has been said that Michelangelo sought to liberate the form of the human body from a prison of marble: an allegory for the struggle of the soul, imprisoned in an earthly body, and a condition ripe for themes of triumph and tragedy. The tension imbues his best-known works: *David* (1501–04) in Florence's Accademia; *Moses* (1513–15) in Rome's San Pietro in Vincoli, and the beloved *Pietà* in St Peter's.

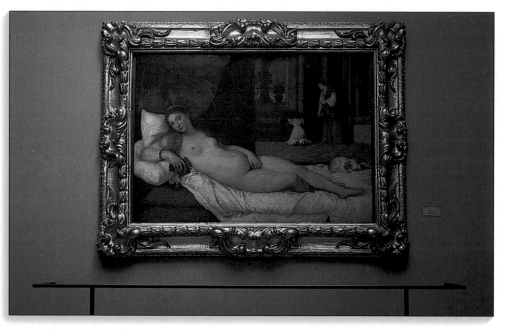

the new project was to create a monument which would surpass any of Ancient Rome. Working with a stock of classic forms (domes, colonnades, pediments) Bramante revolutionised architecture with his revival of another classic technique: concrete, which enables greater flexibility and monumental size.

Bramante died before his design was realised. In 1546, Michelangelo was put in charge of the project, and St Peter's gained its present form.

Michelangelo Buonarroti (1475–1564) first astounded the world with his sculpture: human

Julius II commissioned Michelangelo to paint the Sistine Chapel ceiling. The result, which was completed in only four years (1508–12), is a triumph of human emotions unleashed by the human condition: man's creation, his fall, and his reconciliation with the Lord.

Michelangelo returned to the Sistine Chapel in 1534 to paint the spectacular *Last Judgement*. In the intervening years he went to Florence to complete the Medici Chapel of San Lorenzo (1524–34) and the Laurentian Library (begun 1524) where the drama of the design outweighs many functional considerations. Michelangelo's architectural genius culminates in his redesign of Rome's Campidoglio (1537–39). This open

LEFT: Botticelli's *Primavera* in the Uffizi in Florence.
ABOVE: Titian's *Venus of Urbino*, also in the Uffizi.

piazza, flanked by three facades, became the model for modern civic centres.

While Michelangelo was busy on the Sistine Chapel ceiling, a young artist from Urbino was working nearby, decorating a series of rooms in the Vatican Palace. This artist, soon to be known as the foremost painter of the High Renaissance, was Raffaello Sanzio, or Raphael (1483–1520). His masterpiece in this series is the *School of Athens* (1510–11). The dramatic grouping of philosophers around Plato and Aristotle suggests the influence of Michelangelo; the individualised intention of each recalls Leonardo's *Last Supper*.

In Venice, the paintings of Giorgione da Castelfranco (1476/8–1510) have all the charm and delicacy of Bellini's; they also favour poetic mood over subject matter (*The Tempest* [1505] in Venice's Galleria dell'Accademia is a perfect example), prefiguring the Romantic movement.

Also looking ahead to the freer brushwork and shimmering colours of the Impressionists is the Venetian Titian (1488/90–1576). He mastered the technique of oil painting, and left a legacy of richly coloured, joyously spirited religious pictures as well as masterful portraits. ❑

ABOVE: Parmigianino's *Madonna with the Long Neck* in the Uffizi. **RIGHT:** Caravaggio's *Bacchus*.

THE MANNERISTS

The drama of Leonardo, the theatricality of Michelangelo, the poetic moodiness of Giorgione: all set the stage for the Mannerist phase of High Renaissance art, when the serenity and calm classicism that characterised the works of Raphael were abandoned. In Mannerism the human form is paramount, yet it is usually depicted in strained, disturbing poses and violent colours.

Mannerist artists include Angelo Bronzino, Jacopo Pontorno and Rosso Fiorentino, who revelled in the use of bold colours, dramatic poses and heightened emotions. This unnatural look grew out of the work of artists such as Michelangelo, who had begun to exaggerate human features to create tension and drama – in the over-large head and hands of *David*, for example, or the contorted pose of the Virgin in his *Doni Tondo*, in the Uffizi Gallery.

Expression of an "inner vision" at the expense of reality was vital to Mannerism. In Fiorentino's *The Descent from the Cross* (1521) in Volterra's Pinacoteca, the angularly draped figures bathed in an unreal light stir feelings of anxiety and tension. His friend Pontormo (1494–1557) is also known for works of unexpected colour, unnaturally elongated figures and disquieting mood.

Bronzino (1503–72), Pontormo's pupil and adopted son, epitomises Mannerism's achievements in his psychological portraits of Cosimo I, his wife, Eleanor of Toledo, and her son, Giovanni de' Medici (1550), in the Uffizi Gallery.

Parmigianino (1503–40) used distortion merely for effect. In his *Madonna with the Long Neck* (1535), in the Uffizi, the figures are extremely elongated, the setting is fantastical, and the inspiration for the work – Raphael's fluid grace – is exaggerated beyond recognition.

In Venice, Tintoretto (1518–94) combined the bold style, rich colours and glowing light inspired by Titian with a mystical inclination. His attempt to depict religion's great mystery – the transubstantiation of bread into the body of Christ – results in the haunting *Last Supper* (1592–94) in San Giorgio Maggiore, Venice, with its swirling angels created out of vapours.

In architecture, Andrea Palladio (1518–80), like his predecessor Alberti, wrote theoretical studies of Ancient architecture. His own designs – including the Villa Rotonda, Vicenza (1567–70) and San Giorgio Maggiore, Venice (1565) – are based on classical concepts, and have influenced architects from Inigo Jones to Thomas Jefferson, and even architects today.

BIRTH OF A NATION

After centuries of foreign domination and a prolonged struggle,
Italy emerged in 1870 as a united independent kingdom

The seeds of Italian patriotism, crushed by the battle of Fornovo in 1495, lay virtually dormant for three centuries. After Fornovo, all the armies of Europe came to Italy and fought among themselves for a share of the spoils. Spain, the most powerful nation in Europe at the time, eventually emerged as the clear master of Italy. The pope crowned King Charles V of Spain Holy Roman Emperor in 1530 and Charles and his descendants ruled Italy for more than 150 years. The country was burdened by heavy taxation, and under Spanish influence liberty and native energy and initiative declined. The papacy was no less oppressive; the rules of the Inquisition, the Index and the Jesuit Orders forced many Italians to flee.

Under the Spaniards and later (after the 1713 Treaty of Utrecht) under the equally oppressive Austrians, Italy lost its reputation as a cultural centre. But the 1789 French Revolution inspired many Italians, and the ideals of republicanism spread rapidly. Patriots dreamt of an independent Italian republic modelled on France.

When Napoleon invaded Italy in 1796, the people rose against the Austrians and a series of republics was founded. For three years the whole peninsula was republican and under French rule. But in March 1799, an Austro-Russian army expelled the French from northern Italy and restored many of the local princes. In Naples, the republicans held out for a few months before they, too, had to surrender.

To work against the foreign oppressors and their local sycophants, Italian patriots joined secret societies, such as the Carbonari. In their love of ritual they resembled the Freemasons, but they had a serious goal: to liberate Italy.

The Risorgimento

In 1800 Napoleon won back most of Italy. The kingdom that he founded lasted only briefly but, by proving that the country could be a single

unit, it gave Italian patriots new inspiration. From the Congress of Vienna in 1815, which reinstated Italian political divisions, until Rome was taken in 1870 by the troops of King Victor Emmanuel II of Savoy (who also ruled over Piedmont and Sardinia), the history of Italy was one continuous struggle for reunification.

CAVOUR.
(From a contemporary print in Bianchi's *Cavour*.)

The period is a complex one. Many northern and southern Italians wanted the peninsula to become one nation but there was no agreement as to who would rule or how it should be achieved. Some believed in peaceful evolution. Others, like Giuseppe Mazzini, wanted to revive the Roman republic. Some were for a kingdom of Italy under the House of Savoy.

In 1848, a year of revolt all over Europe, the first Italian war for independence was fought. First, rebellions in Sicily, Tuscany and the Papal States forced local rulers to grant constitutions to their citizens. In Milan, news of Parisian and Viennese uprisings sparked the famous "five days" when the occupying Austrian army was

LEFT: Giuseppe Garibaldi, a prominent leader of the Risorgimento. **RIGHT:** Camillo Benso Count of Cavour, Italy's first great statesman.

driven from the city. A few days later, Charles Albert of Savoy sent his army to pursue the Austrians, and the revolution began in earnest.

Charles Albert was soon supported by troops from other Italian states; however, the tide turned when the pope refused to declare war on Catholic Austria. The newly confident Austrians drove Charles Albert's army back into Piedmont. He abdicated months later, and the House of Savoy signed a peace treaty.

Garibaldi and Cavour

Venice and the Roman Republic continued the fight. In Rome, Mazzini led a triumvirate that

it was now the only Italian state with a free press, an elected parliament, and a liberal constitution. Piedmont-Savoy was also blessed, from 1852, with a brilliant prime minister, Count Camillo Cavour, who was devoted to the cause of Italian unity. Cavour went to England and France to raise support for the Italian cause. He contributed Piedmontese troops to the Crimean War, and thus won a seat at the peace conference, where he brought the Italian question to the attention of Europe's most important statesmen. Although Cavour made no tangible gains at this meeting, he won moral support.

Europe was thus not surprised when France

governed the city with a true democratic spirit despite the siege conditions. The commander of the city's armed forces was Giuseppe Garibaldi, a life-long Italian patriot, who had honed his fighting skills as a mercenary in the revolutions of South America, where he had fled after being convicted of subversion in Piedmont. Now he and his men faced the combined strength of the Neapolitans, the Austrians and the French. It was French forces that entered the city on 3 July 1849, the day after Garibaldi escaped into the mountains. The following month the Venetians succumbed to an Austrian siege.

The treaty the Austrians had signed with the House of Savoy kept them out of that region, so

and Piedmont went to war with Austria three years later. The French king, Napoleon III, and Cavour had agreed that, after the expected victory, an Italian kingdom would be formed for the Piedmontese king, Victor Emmanuel, and Nice and French Savoy would be returned to France. The people of the Italian dukedoms rushed to proclaim their allegiance to Victor Emmanuel.

Unfortunately, the French soon tired of fighting and decided to make a quick peace with Austria. The Austrians agreed to let Lombardy become part of an Italian Federation (with Austrian troops still in its garrisons), but the Veneto region went back to Austria and the dukes of Modena and Tuscany were reinstated.

In Italy, there was general outrage. Cavour resigned in protest, but first he arranged plebiscites in Tuscany and Modena. Citizens refused to have their dukes back and voted to become part of Piedmont.

Garibaldi and 1,000 red-shirted volunteers sailed for Sicily from Genoa on 5 May 1860. His arrival was a signal for the overthrow of Bourbon rule on the island. Garibaldi quickly declared himself dictator in the name of Victor Emmanuel. After fierce fighting, with the aid of Sicilian rebels Garibaldi entered Palermo

PATRIOT AND DEMOCRAT

Giuseppe Mazzini founded the Young Italy movement and agitated frenetically for unification from 1830–70.

divided over whether to take Rome by force or to negotiate a settlement with the Romans.

Finally, in 1870, after the French were weakened by a defeat in the Sudan, Italian troops fought their way into the city through Porta Pia. The pope barricaded himself in the Vatican. For half a century, no pope emerged to participate in the life of the new Italy.

The new government of all Italy was a parliamentary democracy with the king as executive. The most powerful men in the early days of the Italian state were the loyal

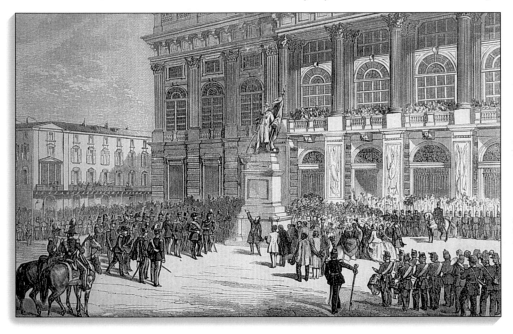

in triumph. Inspired by his success, men from all over Italy now came to help him and, on 7 September, Naples fell to the patriots.

Meanwhile, Victor Emmanuel gathered troops and marched south to link up with Garibaldi and his men. The two groups met at Teano, and the kingdom of Italy was declared. The new kingdom did not include Rome, however: the pope preached against the patriots, and the French had garrisoned troops there to protect the city. The victorious nationalists were

LEFT: Garibaldi and Victor Emmanuel II of Savoy join forces at Teano.
ABOVE: celebration of Italian unity in Turin.

Piedmontese parliamentarians who were largely responsible for its creation and for designing the administration of the whole peninsula.

However, once the government moved down to Rome, this group began to splinter. The left came to power under a new prime minister, Agostino Depretis. In parliament, Depretis had shown great skill as a legislator and manipulator, but as prime minister he could not organise his party or set forth a coherent national policy. His rivals on the right had done no better, but their opposition made it hard for him to accomplish much. This was the start of the breakdown of the party system in Italy, the effects of which are discernible even today. ❑

THE 20TH CENTURY

Wars, Fascism, corruption scandals ... with remarkable resilience,
Italy has survived every challenge the century has presented

As governments so often do during times of rapid change and relative instability at home, Italy began to look abroad for confirmation of its hard-won independence. Relations with France had cooled during the final fight for unification; when France occupied Tunisia, a traditional area of Italian influence, they became positively chilly. Italy's response was to sign the Triple Alliance with Germany and Austro-Hungary, providing for mutual defence in the event of war.

Under the conservative governments of Francesco Crispi (1887–91, 1893–96), Italy also joined the scramble for colonies in North Africa. Crispi successfully colonised Eritrea, but when he tried to subdue Ethiopia (Abyssinia), the Italian army suffered a humiliating defeat at Adwa which led to Crispi's resignation. A later colonising attempt during the Italo-Turkish War (1911–12) ended in victory and the Italian occupation of Libya and the Dodecanese Islands.

North–South divide

At home, the years leading up to World War I were marked by the division that still plagues the country today: relative wealth in the North and extreme poverty in the South. The economy was overwhelmingly agricultural, and the government's protectionist policies left Italy increasingly isolated from other European markets. The industrial boom of the late 1800s, mostly in textiles and refining, was confined to the North. The crushing economic conditions in the South fuelled a wave of emigration. In the last years of the century, nearly half a million people a year set out for the New World.

When World War I began with Austria's attack on Serbia in July 1914, Italy had not been consulted, in breach of the terms of the Triple Alliance. In consequence, on 2 August, Prime Minister Antonio Salandra declared Italy's neutrality. Public opinion began to swing in the direction of the Allies. To help win Italy over,

the Allied governments dangled the possibility of territorial gains: for instance, Rome was offered the chance to gain the "unrecovered" provinces of Trieste and Trentino, long held by the Austro-Hungarian Habsburg Empire. In addition, Italy would receive the upper valley of the River Adige, plus various North African

and Turkish properties. Finally swayed, in April 1915 Italy signed the secret Treaty of London. A month later, the government broke the Triple Alliance and entered the war on the Allied side.

Seldom had a country been so ill-prepared for war. Italy's army was poorly equipped, and Austrian troops had already dug into defensive positions in Alpine strongholds along the 480-km (300-mile) shared border. For Italy the war was a costly stalemate; of the 5.5 million men mobilised, 39 percent were killed or wounded.

At the postwar conference table, although Prime Minister Vittorio Emanuele Orlando sat with the victors, he was hardly regarded as an equal. Despite his protests, the Treaty of Lon-

LEFT: Benito Mussolini in 1928.
RIGHT: statue of Victor Emmanuel II in Venice.

don was ignored. In the end the Treaty of St Germain (10 September 1919) gave Italy Trento and the Alto Adige, as well as Trieste. But Fiume, Dalmatia and the other promised territories were negotiated away by the Allies.

Disappointment in the peace talks, combined with the social and economic toll of the war, produced chaotic domestic conditions. Soon there was talk that Italy had won only a "mutilated victory" despite its wartime sacrifice. Inflation soared. Factory workers took to the streets, and peasants clamoured for land reform.

Into this power vacuum marched Benito Mussolini and his Fascist Party. When he

founded the party in 1919, Mussolini played on the worst fears of all Italians. To those who fretted over the "mutilated victory", he was a chest-thumping nationalist. To placate the rich he denounced Bolshevism, although he himself had once been a socialist. To the middle classes he pledged a return to law and order, and a corporate state in which workers and management would pull together for the good of the country.

By mid-1922, Fascism had become a major political force. When workers called for a general strike, Mussolini made his move. On 28 October, 50,000 members of the Fascist militia converged on Rome. Although Mussolini's supporters held only a small minority in parliament,

the sight of thousands of menacing Fascists flooding the streets of the capital was enough to topple the tottering government of Prime Minister Luigi Facta. Refusing to sanction a state of siege, King Victor Emmanuel III instead handed the reins of government to Mussolini.

Once in control, Mussolini quickly pushed through an act assuring the Fascists a permanent majority in the parliament. After questionable elections in 1924, he dropped all pretence of collaborative government. Italy was now a dictatorship. At Christmas of that year, he declared himself head of the government, responsible only to the king. Fascist fronts took over all the rights once held by unions and management organisations and national corporations were set up to supervise every phase of the economy.

Within two years all parties except the Fascists were banned, and opposition activists were jailed or forced into exile or underground. Anyone Mussolini could not subject by will or law was crushed by force.

Trains that ran on time

Despite its ugly underbelly, on the surface Fascism seemed to work. Weary of inflation, strikes and street disturbances, Italians eagerly embraced their severe new government and its charismatic *Duce*, or leader. This spontaneous response to Fascist rule was reinforced by a strong propaganda campaign. Mussolini promised to restore to Italy the glories of Ancient Rome, and for a time promises were enough.

Soon, however, the government could show results. The economy firmed, trains ran on time, huge public works projects were launched, and Mussolini even made peace with the Vatican, hammering out the Lateran Treaty (1929), which ended the 50-year rift between Rome and the Catholic Church. He also set out on an imperial campaign, restoring control over Libya, which had been ignored during and after World War I. In October 1935, Italian troops crossed the border of Eritrea and headed for the Ethiopian capital of Addis Ababa. The League of Nations protested, but took no action. Six months later, *Il Duce* announced to an hysterical Piazza Venezia crowd that, finally, Rome had begun to reclaim its empire.

The international outcry over the Ethiopian occupation left Rome isolated. The one government willing to overlook Mussolini's expansionism was in Berlin, where Adolf Hitler's

Nazis had held power since January 1933. Both Germany and Italy had supported General Francesco Franco's nationalist troops in the Spanish Civil War (1936–39), and this cooperation led eventually to the signing of the Pact of Steel between Berlin and Rome in May 1939.

Three months later, Hitler invaded Poland. Within days, Britain and France declared war on Germany. At first the Rome government remained neutral, as it had in 1914, arguing that Berlin's surprise attack on Poland

BLACKSHIRTS

This name was originally given to supporters of Mussolini's Fascist party, who wore distinctive black shirts in the 1920s; it was later linked with the Nazi SS and with Oswald Mosley's British Union of Fascists.

Eager to pull off his own battlefield coup, in the autumn of 1940 Mussolini set his sights on taking Greece. But the Greeks fought back fiercely. The Italians suffered many casualties, and only Nazi intervention prevented a likely Italian defeat. The war was also going badly for the Axis Powers in North Africa, and eventually even the Nazi General Erwin Rommel could not prevent the collapse. Heartened by their desert victories, in 1943 American and British troops captured Sicily.

did not require an automatic military response. In any case, most Italians opposed intervention, and the army was ill-prepared for war. But as Hitler claimed victory after victory – in Denmark, Norway and Belgium, and with France near collapse – the lure of sharing the spoils of war proved irresistible. On 10 June 1940, Italy entered the war, just before the fall of France. But from the start it was obvious to Mussolini that he was Hitler's inferior in their alliance.

LEFT: the Palazzo della Civiltà del Lavoro in Rome's EUR district. ABOVE: the 6th-century abbey of Montecassino in Lazio, which was destroyed by Allied bombs in 1944 but subsequently re-built.

The beginning of the end was in sight. From their base in Sicily, the Allied forces began to bomb the Italian mainland, and Italian public morale sank to a new low. On 25 July 1943, the Grand Council of Fascism voted to strip *Il Duce* of his powers. Mussolini refused to step down, but the next day, King Victor Emmanuel ordered his arrest. Mussolini was detained in an inaccessible hotel in the Abruzzi mountains. However, in September German air commandos airlifted him to Munich.

Chaos broke out in the final days of the war. To placate the Germans, who would otherwise have occupied the entire country, Prime Minister Marshal Pietro Badoglio publicly declared that Italy would fight on. In secret, however, he entered negotiations with the Allies, who by then had fought their way as far north as Naples. Above that line was the hastily organised *Repubblica Sociale Italiana,* headed by the liberated *Duce.* But the Italian Social Republic was simply a puppet regime of Berlin, and Mussolini spent most of his time brooding on the judgement history would pass on him.

As the Allies fought northwards, the Italian Resistance, or the Corps of Volunteers for Liberty, felt safe enough to begin widespread activities. Combined, the forces managed to liberate Rome on 4 June 1944; Florence followed on 12

August. The Germans and Mussolini lasted out the winter behind the so-called "Gothic line" in the Apennines, but by spring 1945 that effort too had collapsed. Mussolini tried to escape into Switzerland disguised as a German soldier, but Italian partisans found him, and the next morning he was shot. His body was hauled into Milan and hung by a rope for the public to see.

Recovery and resiliency

In the immediate postwar period, Italy suffered greatly. At the peace conferences there was no representative from Rome. The Italian colonies, won at such cost, were taken away. Reparations

A distinctive feature of Italian politics has been the influence of the Italian Communist Party (PCI). In the postwar years, the party cleaved to the Soviet Union's political line, and Rome's centrist government kept the Communists at arm's length. But under Enrico Berlinguer, PCI secretary 1972–84, the party's orientation changed. It often led the so-called Eurocommunism movement, in favour of more independence from Moscow; it scolded the Soviets for human rights abuses and the Russian invasion of Afghanistan; and on economic issues the PCI grew ever more centrist, prompting some to dub it a "Marxist party

without Marx". By 1981 the PCI could count on about a third of the popular vote and it was second only to the Christian Democrats (DC) in size.

Catholicism and Communism have been the two dominant political cultures of postwar years, with the Communist heartland in central Italy. The collapse of Communism in Eastern Europe led to the PCI splitting into the mainstream Democratic Party of the Left (PDS) and the hardline Communist Refoundation splinter group. After the upheavals of the 1990s, the Christian Democrats were dissolved and the PDS came to power as part of a left-wing coalition.

had to be paid to the Soviet Union and Ethiopia. The political system needed a complete overhaul. In elections in June 1946, voters decided 54–46 in favour of making the country a republic, thus formally ending the days of the monarchy. The economy was in disarray, although the European Recovery Programme (the Marshall Plan) helped to ease the burden from 1948.

After a brief alliance that included the Socialists and Communists, the Christian Democrat leader, Alcide de Gasperi, gained control of government, dropping his leftist partners, and for more than a decade centrist coalitions ran the country. In the early 1960s, the Christian Democrats, Socialists, Social Democrats and Republicans formed a coalition government. They ruled, in various combinations, until 1968.

Fuelled by cheap labour, the economy developed rapidly after World War II. During the 1950s there was a steady migration from rural areas to the cities and from South to North. Heavy industry such as chemicals, iron, steel and autos took off. In 1957, Italy became a founding member of the European Community. By the mid-1960s, manufacturing overtook agriculture as the main source of GNP, and observers hailed Italy's "economic miracle".

Terrorism and scandals

A few years later, however, the boom had gone bust, Italy was dubbed the "sick man of Europe", and social ills set in. By far the worst was terrorism. From the late 1970s, kidnappings, knee cappings and murders were a fact of life. The murder, in 1978, of former Christian Democratic prime minister Aldo Moro by the left-wing *Brigate Rosse* (Red Brigade) spurred new anti-terrorist measures, and eventually 32 Red Brigade members were imprisoned for the deaths of Moro and 16 others. Neo-fascist terrorism also plagued the country, culminating, in 1980, in a bomb blast at Bologna station which killed 84 people. Crime of another sort gripped the nation in May 1981, when Pope John Paul II was shot by Turkish-born Mehmet Ali Agca.

Dogged effort helped to cut inflation, and in 1985 Bettino Craxi's government imposed tighter tax-collection laws. Although inflation remained fairly high, and the lira was unsteady,

the economy grew, and Italy briefly overtook France and Britain in the economic league.

Troubles were in store, however. In the 1990s a wave of corruption scandals rocked the state. In 1992, it was alleged that some £67 million (US$100 million) had been shared out among the leaders of the five parties governing Italy in coalition in 1990. Two former premiers were convicted of being chief recipients. After that, veteran prime minister Giulio Andreotti was charged with having links with the Mafia, and Umberto Bossi, leader of the Lega Nord (Northern League), was convicted of corruption, as were leading figures outside politics, from

industrialists (Ferruzzi and Fiat) to fashion designers. The brief premiership of media magnate Silvio Berlusconi in 1994 also stumbled over accusations of corruption.

These scandals unleashed a volley of reforms spearheaded by the first left-wing government in Italy's postwar history. In order to create stronger, more durable governments, the system of proportional representation was changed to a largely first-past-the-post system. Measures were taken to prune Italy's public sector; and along with attempts to reform the welfare sector and meet the requirements of European Monetary Union, there were also determined efforts to confront organised crime. ❑

LEFT: Silvio Berlusconi, media magnate and former prime minister. **RIGHT:** Umberto Bossi, leader of the Lega Nord (Northern League).

THE MAFIA

With its tradition of private justice and its code of silence, or omertà
the Mafia remains Italy's biggest blight

To many, the notion of the Mafia conjures up images of the *lupara*, or sawn-off shotgun used by the Sicilian underworld; corpses dripping with blood; and onlookers standing by, helpless and resigned. The Mafia may somehow affect the majority of Sicilians, but local attitudes are changing profoundly.

The revulsion of Sicilians over the 1992 murders of Mafia-fighting judges Giovanni Falcone and Paolo Borsellino helped to weaken the Mafia's grip on public opinion, its greatest weapon, and dented the age-old code of silence, or *omerta*. This, coupled with tougher laws and greater police determination, has exposed organised crime as never before.

Pentiti ("the penitents"), as Mafia turncoats are called, grew from a handful in 1992, when Falcone was killed, to 500 a year later. Dozens of dons, including the "boss of all Mafia bosses", Salvatore "Toto" Riina, the Godfather of Corleone, and his deputies, Giovanni Brusca and Leoluca Bagarella, have been jailed.

Women's work

The Mafia, once obsessed with tradition, is also changing. In 1995 it fell into debt, as income fell (fewer public works and confiscation of Mafia property) and costs rose (mainly legal fees). As the old Mafia guard languish in jail, their women, once tied to the home, are often forced to take up the "family business". If they still do any laundering, it is as likely to be of their husbands' money as of their shirts.

To fill the power vacuum, a "criminal mastermind" is thought to be reforming the Mafia, with the help of Cosa Nostra in the US, into a quieter, more secret and sophisticated organisation, based on "old Mafia values". The new generation of gangster is likely to be as ruthless on the stock exchange floor as on the streets of Palermo, be armed with a computer, and be adept at surfing the Internet – the favoured new medium for laundering money.

Adroitly, the Mafia is also believed to have learned how to exploit the phenomenon of *pentitismo,* infiltrating bogus turncoats, and

weaving false evidence, including that of Mafia involvement of institutional figures, together with genuine evidence. The aim is to stall cases, discredit *pentitismo*, and sow uncertainty.

The resulting confusion has hampered investigations into the suspected involvement of "Third Level" or key national and intelli-

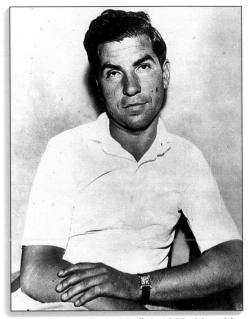

gence interests in the Mafia's 1992–3 bombing campaign, and assessing the legitimacy and evidence of would-be *pentiti* like Giovanni Brusca.

The uncertainty has also played havoc in major trials based on turncoat evidence, such as that of Giulio Andreotti, the seven-times former prime minister accused of being a mafioso. The trial's key witness, Baldassare Di Maggio, was found to have resumed his life as a boss while participating in a state's witness programme. Now re-arrested, he is suspected of playing a major role in forming the New Mafia.

Along with drugs, extortion and property speculation, Mafia activities now include trading arms, nuclear and conventional, between Eastern European and Middle Eastern and other embargo-covered countries. Investment features as much in Moscow as it does in Palermo.

Romantic treatment of what is arguably Italy's biggest blight and its second largest company pins its origins to medieval times and a mysterious religious sect, the Beati Poli, whose hooded members lurked, armed with pikes and swords, in underground passages below Palermo. Some say the word Mafia first appeared in the mid-1600s, meaning a witch; others say it derives from dialectical or Arabic words meaning "protection", "misery" or "hired assassin". What is certain is that the Mafia as we know it began to take shape in the early 19th century, in the form of brotherhoods, formed to protect Sicilians from corruption, foreign oppression and feudal malpractice. Criminal interests quickly seeped in, corruption became the preferred milieu, and before long the brotherhoods were feeding on the misery from which they pretended to defend their members.

Judges were soon said to be secretly protecting them; nobles to be backing them. The brotherhoods' principal manifestation was as the *gabelotti*, organised minders of the land holdings of an often absent nobility, who distributed jobs and land and policed the countryside.

Support for Garibaldi

When Garibaldi set off from Sicily with his redshirts, he did so thanks to the brotherhoods, which lent the support of some 20,000 men. Many were said to be cut-throats, eager to cash in on the spoils of a campaign. Turned back by the troops of Turin, they reorganised to oppose the redistribution to private landlords of nearly half a million acres (200,000 hectares) of Church land in Sicily. These were known as the "agrarian mafiosi".

As early as 1838, the brotherhoods infiltrated every walk of Sicilian public life. After 1863 the word Mafia became common parlance thanks to a comedy on prison life – *I Mafiusi della Vicaria* – which filled the theatres of the day. By 1875 the Mafia had infiltrated the Bourbon household in Palermo. Any investigator who delved too deeply into the brotherhoods was

THE FAMILY BUSINESS

The Mafia's annual turnover has been estimated at £12 billion (US$20 billion).

likely to be stripped of his case, then his job. The same year, the word Mafia was first mentioned in a parliamentary committee report.

Central to the so-called "Southern Question" was severe economic misery. Between 1872 and World War I, poverty and the defeat of agrarian trade unions forced 1.5 million Sicilians to emigrate. Most went to the Americas. There, many joined brotherhoods based on those back home and the foundations of Cosa Nostra were laid. Elements willing to cash in on illegal activity found a springboard with prohibition.

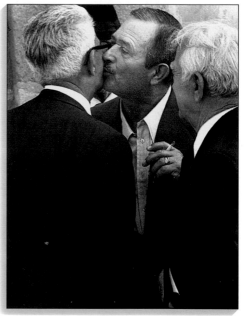

American bootlegging marked the Mafia's graduation from rural bands to a sophisticated urban gangster organisation.

In 1925, Mussolini, appalled at the Mafia's new importance as a surrogate state, set out to bring it to its knees. He sent his prefect Cesare Mori to Sicily, with almost unlimited powers. By 1927, victory was proclaimed for Mori's heavy-handed tactics. Called the "surgical precision of Fascism", they entailed throwing thousands into prison, and laying siege to towns to flush out the Mafia bosses. But Mori was also a threat to powerful agrarian mafiosi. Soon Sicily's landed interests struck a deal with the Fascists, and Mori left the island. In return, the agrarian mafiosi saw to it that Sicily's more

LEFT: Lucky Luciano, who forged links between the Sicilian and American mafias. **RIGHT:** the "kiss of death", often used as a signal.

criminal Mafia elements were almost wiped out.

They won a reprieve in 1943, when they were given the job of clearing the way for the Allied invasion. Fearing the effects which war between the US and Italy would have on their interests, Italian and American mobsters such as Lucky Luciano had struck a deal with US authorities in 1940. In return for their help they were to be left alone. The operation, overseen by Don Vito Genovese, a Naples thug wanted for murder in the US, went well: the Allies hardly fired a shot.

Local mafiosi, re-armed with weapons taken from Italian forces, and their dons – such as Don Calogero Vizini (39 murders, six attempted murders) – were installed by the Allies as mayors of key Sicilian towns.

Changing fortunes brought Sicilian and American Mafia elements to cities such as Milan and Naples; Naples, ruled by the less organised local Mafia, the Camorra, became a fiefdom of Cosa Nostra, and was chosen by American gangsters as the site of Italy's first heroin refinery. In Sicily, organised criminals began supporting the pro-separatist movement backed by agrarian interests. Together with the authorities, the Mafia joined in the suppression of banditry, which had made inroads into its territory during the Fascist siege.

10 COMMANDMENTS OF THE MAFIA

The Cosa Nostra rules on marital fidelity are rigid: Thou shalt not commit adultery. If cuckolded, thou shalt "wash thy shame in blood" or lose thy honour. Thou shalt not seek a divorce. Thou shalt not wed the daughter of someone separated or divorced. Thou shalt not court relatives of the police. Thou shalt not covet another mafioso's wife. Thou shalt not speak ill of another mafioso's wife. Thou shalt not indulge in homosexual relations. Thou shalt not use the services of prostitutes. Thou shalt not exploit prostitution. Mobsters who transgress face suitable punishment, including death.

Sicily's "Americanised" Mafia achieved its quantum leap in the late 1950s with the introduction of drugs. In 1957, after a crackdown in the US against organised crime, American bosses entrusted to their Sicilian counterparts the importation of heroin into America.

The move was built on roots laid down by Lucky Luciano, Frank "Three Fingers" Coppola, at the centre of the new Sicilian-US connection, and his protégé Luciano Liggio, who won his stripes by black marketeering during the war.

Clan warfare

Liggio, who died in the mid-1990s, launched his Corleonese family to the top of the heroin trade and to the pinnacle of the Cosa Nostra pecking order by breaking almost the entire codex of Mafia laws. After he was jailed in 1974 he was eclipsed as head of the Mafia by his lieutenants, Toto Riina, called the Wild Beast, and Bernardo "The Tractor" Provenzano.

The tactics of the Corleonesi were simple: the removal of any mafioso who coveted power or caused trouble. The Mafia clan war of the early 1980s left Palermo's streets strewn with blood and the Corleonesi undisputed victors. Riina's name has been linked to some 1,000 murders.

Not all concerned mafiosi. In response to the drugs trade which had prompted the carnage, a parliamentary anti-Mafia committee had been established; in response, the Mafia instituted a campaign of terror in which top officials, the police and politicians were targeted.

The list of corpses began with Palermo's chief prosecutor Pietro Scaglione in 1971, allegedly murdered by Liggio, Riina and Provenzano. In answer to the 1982 killing, with his wife, of General Carlo Alberto dalla Chiesa, the *carabiniere* who had vanquished terrorism before being sent to Palermo as chief prefect, the government pushed through a law to get at Mafia assets – a law proposed by Pio La Torre, Sicilian regional Communist Party leader, gunned down 100 days before dalla Chiesa.

Dalla Chiesa had begun digging into the island's huge construction industry, an easy area in which to invest profits from drugs, and is thought to have stumbled on a minefield: the "Third Level" question of who in the country's highest political circles protected, or possibly also issued orders to, the Mafia. The Mafia's chief supergrass, Tommaso Buscetta, claimed in 1993 that Giulio Andreotti, seven times prime minister, ordered the mob to kill dalla Chiesa and a journalist, because he knew too much.

Buscetta's evidence led to "maxi-trials" in the 1980s, where hundreds of mafiosi sat in the dock, and launched Giovanni Falcone, a Mafia-fighting magistrate, on the road to success.

Failure to use his weight to overturn a guilty verdict concerning the same "maxi-trial" in a supreme court decision in February 1992 is believed to have been the reason for Salvo Lima's killing by the Mafia a month later. Lima, a former Palermo mayor, an MP and a Euro MP when he died, was the most powerful Christian Democrat in Sicily and the island's representative of the party faction headed by Giulio Andreotti. He was later named as a mafioso.

His murder was the first in a new campaign of terror that saw the assassination of Falcone and his wife in May, victims of a car bomb. Falcone's colleague Paolo Borsellino, and five bodyguards were murdered two months later. The terror continued in 1993 with bombs in Milan and Rome which killed bystanders and devastated churches; an explosion at Florence's Uffizi Gallery destroyed minor masterpieces.

But the Mafia miscalculated. The assassination of the two Palermo judges and the attempt to destroy the nation's cultural treasures only served to tighten the resolve of the Italians and their government against the Mafia.

A rash of killings in Naples in 1998 and 1999, largely the result of battles between rival bands of the Camorra, have been exceptions to what has otherwise been several years of relative peace. As its activities face increasing pressure from aggressive prosecutors and the strong regulations of a united Europe, the question that remains is whether the Mafia is slowly being marginalised, or if it only seems so as it slips deeper into the fabric of Italian culture. ❑

LEFT: a threatening gesture is made during one of the "maxi-trials". **RIGHT:** former Prime Minister Giulio Andreotti, allegedly connected to the Mafia.

CONTEMPORARY ITALY

Tradition and rebellion, conformity and individuality, chaos and over-regulation ... Italian life is riddled with paradoxes

taly is a constellation of large families, whether ideological, political, professional or criminal – the Church, the business community, the trade unions, the professions, state bureaucracies and the Mafia." According to Sergio Romano, a political journalist on *La Stampa*, "Each family strives for sovereignty", acting as a fierce lobby group and dooming most national reforms to failure.

Curiously, Italian society combines anarchy and cosiness in equal measure, making it both chaotic and stultifying. At the simplest level, Italians create a cosy little world of "their" baker, dressmaker, or picture-framer, conveying the social status of a patron rather than of a mere consumer. Personal recommendation is everything. Yet beyond lies the arbitrary world of bureaucracy, in which citizens feel powerless in the face of state indifference. Many commentators conclude that Italy would be a paradise if it could only reinvent the relationship between citizen and state. Yet without political chaos and conflicting social groups, the Italians would cease to be Italians and become Swiss.

The political picture

"It is not impossible to govern Italians, it is pointless." Mussolini's judgment has been borne out by recent events. In the late 1990s, the country faced secessionist threats, a budgetary crisis, a wave of organised crime and a tide of refugees. Nonetheless, after the corruption scandals of the early 1990s, probity was the basic requirement of the new administration. The prime minister, a professor from Bologna with little taste for mud-slinging, defended himself from the circus of scandals: "I haven't heard anyone calling me a thief or a liar and all the rest is child's play." Italy's ruling centre-left coalition consolidated its power in sweeping victories in the 1997 local elections but faced a spanner in the works from one of its partners, the hardline Communist splinter group.

LEFT: keeping up with the latest news.
RIGHT: a demonstration by supporters of Lega Nord.

To make Italy more governable, there are moves to reduce the power of fringe parties that hold the country to ransom. Yet the Italian mindset precludes a modern democracy, favouring an abyss between the state and its citizens. The people swing between political disaffection and an obsession with politics. Fortunately, how-

ever, they also have an innate talent for brinkmanship, coupled with an ability to conjure compromise out of conflict.

In 1996 the secessionist Lega Nord (Northern League) marched to the symbolic River Po and in Venice declared independence for "the Republic of Padania". In a gesture of rejection of Rome and centralised bureaucracy, protesters waved republican flags and tossed their state television licences into the waters. In response, the Italian president called the country "one and indivisible", while addressing reforms that would allow for greater regional autonomy.

In the late 1990s, the country positioned itself as the new Italy, turning its back on a baroque

IN GOOD FAITH?

Curiously, the phrase often used to bemoan declining standards is, "There's no religion left any more". Jonathan Keates describes the Italian attitude to religion as, "a lackadaisical Catholicism taken out of mothballs at christenings, first communions, weddings and funerals; the religion of photo-opportunity". Increasingly, Italy's practising Catholics prefer to take their cue not from the Pope but from personal conscience or the liberal wing of the Church. Strive as the Church might, civic culture, regional pride and fierce individualism form the real Italian faith today.

political structure steeped in *clientelismo* (nepotism). Yet Italy remains deeply old-fashioned, despite its faddism. It is a paradox that, although priding themselves on their free-spirit, the people live in an over-regulated society. Protectionism has limited the growth of supermarkets. It is also illegal for shops not to issue a receipt (*ricevuta fiscale*): a customer without one can be charged with abetting tax evasion.

Milan is the business capital, a sophisticated modern metropolis dedicated to money-making and pleasure. Most wealth is still created in northern and central regions, such as Lombardy, the Veneto and Emilia-Romagna. However, although the Agnelli, Berlusconi and Armani

fiefdoms are well-known abroad, most Italian companies are family-run businesses. Specialised small companies provide more than two-thirds of industrial employment, from textiles in Tuscany to shoe-makers in the Marches, and mechanical engineering firms in Emilia. Nonetheless, economic patterns are complex, and high unemployment and low consumer demand mask a thriving black economy and tax evasion. In the workplace, industrial action is commonplace. The Italian art of conjuring compromise out of conflict in industrial relations is rooted in the social contract, a corporatist pact between government, unions and industry that has historically dominated labour relations.

Privatisation, restrictive employment practices and preparation for European Monetary Union have been the major economic issues. Privatisation of the public utilities in the late 1990s was considered overdue but did not end state interference. Given the traditional monopoly of top jobs in state companies by the political parties, politicians remain reluctant to give up their power. However, the country plans to privatise the motorways, Milan stock exchange, shipyards, state television and the national airline. IRI, the vast state holding company set up by Mussolini, should be sold off by the year 2000.

A complex but coherent society

The Italian social system is a rich landscape, not calibrated on class, success or wealth but on more subtle distinctions. In conventional terms, a class system exists but has different connotations. The aristocracy thrives, thanks to its adaptability. Many *marchesi* (marquesses) are entrepreneurs, carving niches in fashion, art, and the wine and food industry. The Strozzi are big in banking; the Tuscan Frescobaldi and Sicilian Tasca are successful wine dynasties; the Pucci fashion empire thrives in Florence.

Although class consciousness and accent are essentially immaterial, the *borghesi* (middle classes) form a recognisable group, as do the *contadini* (encompassing peasants and farmers). Whatever one's profession, honorific titles are important, especially in the South: an engineer is addressed as "*ingegnere*"; *dottore* (doctor) is a mark of respect bestowed on anyone with the

LEFT: a cheese seller in Marsala.
RIGHT: a performance of Ponchielli's opera, *La Gioconda* (*Mona Lisa*), in Verona's Roman Arena.

right gravitas. Politics rarely impinge on social divisions: a member of the PDS, the former Communist party, may be a Catholic, don Ferragamo shoes and have a Filipina maid.

Apart from the North–South divide, the most important distinction is between *statali*, who are government employees or civil servants, and *non-statali*, the rest. Civil servants are seen as utterly cosseted; virtually impossible to fire, they enjoy such privileges as protected pensions, including the right to retire early as "baby" pensioners. Ranged against the civil servants are the *dipendenti* (company employees), *autonomi* (self-employed), *imprenditori* (entrepreneurs)

and, lastly, the *liberi professionisti* (professionals). The *dipendenti* (company employees) claim the moral high ground, charging civil servants with exploiting the system, and accusing the self-employed and some professionals of tax evasion. In truth, this is a strange Italian stalemate in which private sector workers (*non statali*) justify tax evasion on the grounds that their taxes would only perpetuate the bloated state bureaucracy and southern incompetence.

Popular culture and the arts

Both in the art world and in the broader cultural arena, Italian genius thrives on dissension,

GUARDIANS OF SO MANY TREASURES

Italians are justifiably proud of their heritage. Italy possesses more UNESCO cultural heritage sites than any other country, matched by an impressive half of the world's artistic wealth.

Clearly, the burden of conservation is great for the authorities. Art fraud is commonplace, a situation compounded by illegal excavations, thefts from churches and the export of priceless artefacts, with penalties ridiculously light. In recent years, the state has been faced with a terrorist attack on Florence's Uffizi Gallery, mysterious and devastating fires at Venice's La Fenice opera house and Turin Cathedral, and earthquake dam-

age to San Francesco in Assisi. Monuments can be closed for years and masterpieces hidden from view. But, in future, the proceeds from the state lottery each Wednesday will be devoted to cultural investment.

Most collections are publicly owned, and the state offers little support to the private owner. Princess Corsini, who has the last 17th-century Florentine collection remaining in private hands, says such owners are treated as "over-privileged people who have to be kept in line like schoolchildren". As for the sale of art treasures, owners are secretive because selling abroad usually entails breaking Italian regulations.

diversity and unbridled rivalry. From an outsider's point of view, however, music and the performing arts are more dynamic than the literary scene. Contemporary fiction is an acquired taste, with writers often engaged in navel-gazing, esoteric concerns or petty politicking. The classical music scene is not restricted to the great opera houses. Italy boasts some of the best musical festivals in Europe, from the operatic cycles performed in the Roman Arena at Verona to the Puccini Festival

> ### STREET THEATRE
>
> Italian traffic police combine the country's passions for football and opera: officers in epaulettes and white gloves gesture operatically, using their piercing whistles like football referees.

at his lakeside home in Tuscany's Torre del Lago. The Macerata opera festival hit the headlines in 1995 when the firing squad in *Tosca* used real bullets and accidentally shot the tenor. In the case of the festival at Pesaro, Rossini's birthplace, the director bemoans Italian conservatism: "The public has no desire for opera to become theatre but only wants it to be about singing and tradition."

Popular culture is dominated by television and the competing claims of media magnates Silvio Berlusconi and Vittorio Cecchi Gori. With a few exceptions, the output is devoted to political propaganda, poor-quality American imports, and platitudinous game shows. Despite a suspended sentence for fraud in 1997, Berlusconi maintains his media empire, political role and chairmanship of AC Milan. His rival, Cecchi Gori, also plays the political game on and off the pitch. The centrist politician and chairman of Fiorentina football club inherited a huge film production company which now includes the Videomusic and TeleMonte-Carlo channels. Although due for privatisation, the RAI's three public channels remain political pawns, generating propaganda thinly disguised as programmes.

Football, like opera, is a national obsession and thrives on classic regional and city rivalries: Milan and Rome boast two teams apiece, with Berlusconi's AC Milan a rival to Fiat and Agnelli's Juventus at Turin. The public image of city and owner are inextricably linked to the fortunes of the football team. After Fiorentina were relegated in 1992, Cecchi Gori, the club chairman, had to avoid the wrath of fans by leaving the ground disguised as a fireman. And when Napoli won the championship in 1987, they were still celebrating a decade later.

Spectacle, sociability, conformity

Foremost among the reassuring rituals of modern Italian life is the love of spectacle. During the opera season, La Scala's marbled and mirrored lobby is awash with Milanese matrons in furs. Yet the deep-seated Italian love of display cuts across all regional and social divides, from the chic Venice carnival to the smallest Sardinian festival.

Tellingly, there is no Italian term for privacy. The emphasis is on the everyday values of sociability, simplicity and pleasure. The essence of Italian sociability is the *passeggiata*, the evening parade or dating ritual, with pauses for preening, chatting, flirting and gossiping.

Social life is neatly ordered, even underpinned by excessive planning. Commenting on the cloying social packaging of Italian life, writer Tim Parks says, "Cappuccino until ten, then espresso; *aperitivo* after twelve; your pasta, your meat, your *dolce* in bright packaging; light white wine, strong red wine, *prosecco*; baptism, first communion, marriage, funeral". ❑

LEFT: a traffic policewoman in her stylish uniform.
RIGHT: the *passeggiata* in Alghero, Sardinia.

THE UNITED STATES OF ITALY

The diversity of Italian culture spans native Ligurian, Celtic, Etruscan and Roman civilisations and is nurtured by proud regional loyalties

Nationhood is an abstraction to most Italians until it comes to football, cuisine or foreign travel. What counts is *campanilismo* – a love of one's town and its traditions. Until recently, simply by moving from one town to the next, a visitor to Italy could observe marked differences – in clothes, the pronunciation of vowels, even the cooking of pasta. The writer Gore Vidal, who chose Italy as his second home, has complained: "Towns that were once different to the point of hostility are now all unified by TV, Fiat, festivals and soccer matches." Yet deep cultural divisions persist. The Venetian is sardonic and self-contained, the Roman more aggressive, the Florentine aloof. The Piedmontese have a dignified conceit that betrays French influence; the Milanese are renowned for their strong commercial instincts; while Neapolitans are as superstitious as they ever were.

ONE NATION, SO MANY FACES

The Italian look defies simple definition. The Mediterranean type – dark, with olive skin and brown eyes – prevails, but the Latin "Julius Caesar" strain can be found in the mountains around Rome; Arab and Norman features are noticeable among Sicilians; while the farmers of the Veneto, near the border with the former Yugoslavia, have strong Slav traits. The Goths, Lombards and other Germanic conquerors left traces of their physical characteristics in Lombardy and Piedmont. There are Albanian and Greek areas in Calabria and Sicily; and there is a former Austrian province, South Tyrol, within the frontiers of the republic.

△ **TRULLI DIFFERENT**
Trulli, strange dome-roofed houses in whitewashed limestone, are found only in Apulia, near Alberobello.

▷ **HABSBURG LEGACY**
Germanic influences are clear in bilingual South Tyrol (Alto Adige), part of Austria until 1919.

▷ **A WORLD APART**
Venice is still separated from the Italian mainland – both geographically and by its impenetrable dialect.

◁ WELL MATCHED

At a traditional wedding in Naples, where ritual has a strong appeal, white doves are released after the ceremony. The southern Italian male still wants to be obeyed, but Neapolitan women often rule the roost.

▽ OLD VALUES

In parts of the Sicilian interior, poverty is prevalent and attitudes generally conservative. The role of women has hardly changed in a hundred years.

ARISTOCRATIC ENTREPRENEURS

Italians are not naturally snobbish, but a title and an established reputation in the region still count for much. As most Italian firms are family-run, it is no surprise to find aristocrats engaged in enterprise. Building on their traditional bases in banking, textiles and wine, they have infiltrated the state sector, tourism and even the media. Piero Antinori (*above*) is a scion of one of the most reputable Tuscan wine and food dynasties, centred on the family's Florentine palace. In Sicily, Count Tasca d'Almerita, an ardent patriot, flies the Sicilian flag over his ancestral home and runs Regaleali, the family wine estate and cookery school. Near Turin, the Ermenegildo Zegna dynasty controls an exclusive textile and men's fashion concern. As for Tuscan fashion, despite the loss of Marchese Emilio Pucci, the family still runs a fashion empire from the medieval Palazzo Pucci. All over Italy, crumbling palazzi are being restored by entrepreneurial contessas with funds from foreign visitors or paying guests.

▽ FASHION MECCA

Window shopping in Milan. The cosmopolitan commercial hub of the North rivals Paris as a fashion centre. A key to its success has been its ability to attract and foster talented designers.

△ NORTH-EAST FRONTIER

The spectacular Dolomites on the Austrian border, formed from an ancient coral reef, were the front line of battle during World War I.

▷ SWISS ROLE

The Swiss Guard, a corps of 120 men, all Catholic, all Swiss, is charged with protecting the Vatican.

THE ITALIANS

Individualism, a sense of survival and natural ebullience are qualities
almost all Italians share – but there the similarities end

It has been said that Italians do not exist, that those who are thought of as Italian regard themselves as Piedmontese, Tuscan, Venetian, Sicilian, Calabrian, and so on. No one has ever classified the Italians convincingly: to be born in Palermo, Sicily or in Turin, Piedmont is a classification by itself. And sometimes fellow-countrymen can seem like foreigners. In Pietro Germi's film *Il Cammino sella Speranza (The Path of Hope)*, a peasant woman says: "There's bad people in Milan, they eat rice."

According to the writer Ennio Flaiano, being Italian is a profession – except that it doesn't require much studying: one just inherits it. Generations of Italians have learned the art of *arrangiarsi*, of getting along in all kinds of difficult situations. Adjusting to political change and foreign conquest has generated a flexible mentality and a detached attitude towards political institutions and regimes, all of which are considered ephemeral. The forest of rules, statutes, norms, regulations, many hundreds of years old, others of obscure interpretation, has engendered distrust of the state. The popular saying *fatta la legge, trovato l'inganno* (a law is passed, a way past it is found) is almost a national motto.

North versus South

"Southerners tend to make money in order to rule, northerners to rule in order to make money," declared the writer Luigi Barzini. The conflicting values of North and South reflect different cultures and history. Compared with the industrialised, progressive North, the agrarian, conservative South experienced feudalism, oppression, corruption, poverty and neglect. Known as the *Mezzogiorno,* the region has suffered grandiose white elephants, called "cathedrals in the desert", steelworks sited in remote places with no proper infrastructure. Cut off

PRECEDING PAGES: street games in the backstreets of Naples; Venice carnival-goer in the mask of Janus, the Roman god of the New Year, who looks both backwards and forwards. LEFT: a stylish resident of prosperous Parma. RIGHT: handicraft in Tuscany.

from the progress and markets of northern Europe, southerners left for their own survival. Before 1914, more than 5 million emigrated to North America alone. Although emigration is on the wane, the South still suffers from depopulation, perceived backwardness, and a great gap between rich and poor. Southerners, termed

meridionali, often encounter prejudice, with northerners resenting "subsidising" the South through taxation. Indeed, some northerners see such aid as pouring their hard-earned money into the pockets of the Camorra in Naples or the Mafia, who are concentrated in western Sicily. The North–South divide, in all its tragicomic aspects, remains at the heart of Italian life.

Politics and individualism

At election time, a higher proportion of people go to the polls in Italy than in most other European countries. Yet the average person in the street expresses a revulsion for politics: *"La politica è una cosa sporca"* ("politics is a dirty thing") is a typical riposte. This is based on a belief that all parties are the same, and that politics work only for politicians – an understandable view in the light of the corruption and political scandals that shook Italy in the 1990s.

The Italians remain sceptical of the state. It is no surprise that they cannot conceive of abstract solutions or trust in ideologies. Even left-wing intellectuals have given up on ideology. And it is widely held that things would be better if everything were left to the common sense of those "who work and produce".

Behind such opinions there is often an unrestrained individualism that denies social respon-

sibility. Yet hand in hand with such entrepreneurship, there is often a nostalgic yearning for "the strong man", whose power and will is stamped on his face, whose voice captures the needs and desires of the nation. It was a wave of such nostalgia that swept Alessandra Mussolini, grand-daughter of Benito, into parliament in 1992. Similarly, in northern Italy, in the wake of the scandals of the early 1990s, many Christian Democrat supporters were won over by the oratory of Umberto Bossi, leader of the Northern League, a right-wing autonomy movement.

Centuries of authoritarian political and religious structures, which oppressed the values

THE LANGUAGE

The Italian language is the closest to Latin of any of the so-called Romance languages. Modern Italian owes much to writers such as Dante and Manzoni, who assumed as their standard the educated language of Tuscany. Today the best form of speech is said to be *la lingua toscana in bocca romana* (the Tuscan tongue in the Roman mouth).

Italian is considered the most musical language in the world: in the 16th century, the Holy Roman Emperor, Charles V, is said to have spoken Spanish with God, French with men, German with his horse, but Italian with women since it can express many subtleties of thought

and feeling. Italian can be as precise as any other language, yet the style of newspaper editorials, art criticism and political speeches in particular is often abstract and obscure.

Until recently, more than 1,500 dialects existed alongside the official Italian language, most of them virtually incomprehensible outside their own village. Many contained a large number of foreign words imported by foreign occupiers. Dialect is still spoken among old people in the countryside, but is fading away among younger generations. The advent of television has done much for linguistic unification.

and needs of individuals have, by forcing people to fall back on cunning and self-reliance, paradoxically produced an overblown ego. The strong sense that Italians have of their own existence is evident in their refusal to queue up at the windows of government offices, or at the bus stop.

Self-regard is reflected in the way the Italians dress. Shoes, ties, beautiful fabrics, and liberty of the imagination all contribute to the "costume". The same fastidious care is lavished

A SENSE OF BELONGING

Italians have an abiding attachment to their home, family and town. According to novelist Tim Parks,"When an Italian leaves a place, it's almost always with the intention of returning victorious and vindicated."

of the Vatican, Italy has the lowest birth rate in Europe. Catholicism has a stronger hold in the South and in the Veneto than in the "red belt" of Emilia-Romagna, Umbria and Tuscany. According to a recent survey, more than 85 percent of Italians claim to be Catholics. However, only about a quarter of them attend Mass regularly. Nonetheless Catholicism still plays an important role in Italian rituals, from first holy communion to the marriage ceremony and Christian burial.

on cars, which are seen as extensions of the personality.

"In Italy there are no angels nor devils, only average sinners," said Giulio Andreotti, seventimes premier. This tolerant Roman Catholic society is nurtured on the concept of original sin, universal temptation and redemption, so penitence can erase sins, including crimes.

Despite an authoritarian Pope, abortion and divorce are legal and artificial contraception is widely accepted. Indeed, much to the chagrin

LEFT: making music through speech in Syracuse.
ABOVE: a monk in an increasingly secular society.
RIGHT: sex roles are still very traditional in Italy.

Sex and the family

The image of the Italian man as the Latin lover – passionate, impetuously sentimental, and powerful in bed – is a myth. The principal male characteristic is an attachment to his mother which goes far beyond the natural tie to a parent. Its residue is always there, even late in life: the need to feel loved and understood, the wish to receive affection while giving little in return. The classic Italian mother, generous, over-protective and intrusive, reinforces this image. While the family remains the bedrock of traditional Italian society, *mammismo*, the cult of the mother, is its cornerstone. The iconic image of the mother pervades the male approach to courtship and his choice of bride. Once married, however, male infidelity is often quietly condoned, provided that the family is supported and appearances preserved. Yet, within the home, the wife is traditionally the dominant figure.

While women's increasing economic independence is gradually changing the domestic balance, the limitations of Italian feminism are clear. Official forms are not designed for equal partners or female flat-sharers: the imprimatur of the *capo di famiglia* (head of the household) is required. Staying together for the sake of appearances, *separati in casa*, is a typically civilised compromise: the couple live under the

same roof but lead separate lives. In terms of morality, a North-South divide prevails, with southern values more traditional and northern mores similar to those of northern Europe.

Yet even here, appearances are more important than reality. A slick young Milanese banker may dress like the proverbial preppy but attaches as much importance to family ties as does the humblest Calabrian peasant. His female counterpart, a Florentine designer, may act like the last of the yuppies but would not dare miss Sunday lunch with her parents. As for sex, discretion counts for much, and provided premarital relationships are not flaunted, family honour is maintained. However, tolerance

rarely extends to relationships openly conducted under the family roof. Since students tend to live at home, and Italian offspring are equally reluctant to leave the family nest until marriage, romantic assignments can take on the complexity of a Pirandello farce. High rents are a deterrent to leaving home; male offspring may also rely on a doting mother to act as a domestic drudge. But feminism is beginning to seep into family life, and mothers, particularly in northern and central Italy, increasingly expect a career outside the family business.

At least in the urban North, the stereotype of the roly-poly Italian *mamma,* with one eye on the baby and the other on the pasta, is losing its appeal. Indeed, Italy has a declining birthrate, with large families restricted to the South.

In career terms, women in the cities have made great strides in all fields, even politics and the law. Women have always been an important force in education, with the southern upper classes using higher education as a way of escaping strictures against working women. Nonetheless, it is still fair to say that in Italian male eyes, one is a woman first and a person second. To outsiders, Italy may seem a deeply patriarchal society but innate ingenuity and the importance placed upon good relations ensure that compromises are readily reached.

A style of life

How can one judge the national life of the Italians? Many would say that the Italian style of life is a failure because of the persistence of many seemingly insoluble problems. So many things, from the traffic in Rome to the cumbersome paperwork attached to the simplest official action, restrict and frustrate. And Italians seem unable to believe in the possibility of constructive change. For them, life is not about work and progress, but survival and individualism. On the other hand, and perhaps for that reason, Italian life sparkles with a brilliance unmatched anywhere else in Europe. The Italians have perfected a style of life that may be short on efficiency but is long on enjoyment. Simple things, such as eating a meal, taking a walk, watching the world go by, become special in Italy. Life is enjoyed to the fullest, with a flair gained over centuries of practice. ❏

LEFT: sign-language lives on. **RIGHT:** true friends in Portofino.

THE ITALIAN LOOK

*Supreme visual sense, a feeling for fashion and a creative twist
on classic lines form the essence of the Italian look*

Only an Italian fashion editor could be so sweeping: "The Versaces and Armanis are our modern-day Michelangelos, helping dress our dreams. Anything else isn't *moda* – it simply serves to cover us." In other words, from the Renaissance to Romeo Gigli is but a small step, preferably taken in Ferragamo footwear, La Perla lingerie and a Fendi fur coat. In a country where appearances are all, even the Mafia is not immune. According to a recent survey, the successful mafioso teams an Armani suit with a Moschino waistcoat and Pollini shoes; while in prison, he insists on Fila and Tacchini sportswear.

Secret conformists

Italians pride themselves on their individuality and exhibitionism. However, dressing appropriately for the season and occasion is more important than dressing to please oneself or one's mood. To be accidentally over-dressed for a visit to a park or pizzeria can be a cardinal sin; equally, a mere "stroll" can be code for parading in one's finery. If in doubt, the look of deluxe anonymity is the safe sartorial badge. Not that designer labels, hip fashion accessories and superior models of cars pass unnnoticed in the social stakes.

Instinctive grace and elegance are insufficient protection against conformity. In such a clannish society, each social group wears its subtle uniform with pride. Off-duty, a young right-winger favours a country gentleman's Barbour jacket and Timberland boots while his left-wing counterpart chooses a checked shirt, jeans, long pullovers and a Loden coat. Italy may be a victim of faddishness but some trends seem more durable than others. Predictably, this nation of consummate conversationalists boasts more mobile phones than any other European country.

In a country that worships visual display, conformity is inevitable, yet so too is competitiveness and creativity. This is the joyous paradox of the irrepressible Italian spirit. Style is there-

fore an emblem of high seriousness, with great attention accorded to the simple purchase of a picture or a place mat. Design is an all-inclusive philosophy involving creative alchemy and a crafts-based aesthetic, brain-storming and problem-solving skills, allied to a talent for interpreting mass culture. The world remains in awe

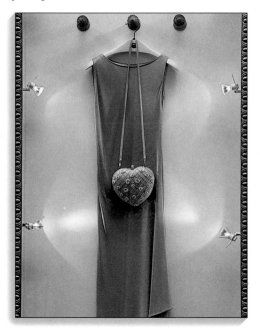

of Italian taste, inviting native talent to style American furniture, Japanese cameras, German limousines and French family cars. As a result, the inimitable character of *la linea italiana*, Italian style, has a continuing impact on international design.

Milan: fashion mecca

For fashion and design cognoscenti, Milan has a monopoly on "the Italian look". As the design capital, Milan is a well-tailored, cosmopolitan city that knows how to put on a show. During fashion week, the *modelari*, the louche men who chase models, are encased in leather trousers and regulation shades. At a Dolce &

Gabbana party, foreign stars gather by fountains overflowing with rose petals and pick from silver platters piled with pomegranates. Yet this picture of the city at its most hedonistic is only a party snapshot.

Milan's worldwide reputation for fashion has developed not by chance but by design. An innovative industrial culture and sound mass-production techniques set the city on its present successful course, particularly after World War II, when the burgeoning design industry came into its own. The Triennale, the prestigious design institute, is now in the 1940 premises which pioneered mass-production of household objects. It also boasts an exhibition of Italian design, from vintage scooters to early Olivetti computers.

Today, Milan still dominates the fashion and design calendar, from international trade fairs to the spring and summer couture and ready-to-wear collections. The city hosts Salone del Mobile, the furniture trade fair, and fairs dedicated to lighting and home and office design. The fashion and design showrooms are located between the Brera and Piazza San Babila in the *quadrilatero* or "golden triangle". Here, the Japanese buy swathes of Gucci belts or ten Prada bags apiece to offer friends back home.

THE FASHION SCENE

The contribution of fashion to Italy's balance of payments is second only to tourism. Commercially, the industry is more successful than its French counterpart, with the Milan collections considered more wearable and contemporary than those of Paris.

Italian fashion thrives on a long craft tradition, a ready supply of home-grown talent and a contemporary feel, essentially a creative twist on classic lines. Its deep design roots lie in medieval craftsmanship, traditional skills which are prized in haute couture (*alta moda*) as well as in the making of quality fabrics, jewellery, bags and shoes. Native designers also have a highly developed aesthetic sense dating back to the Renaissance.

Valentino, the Roman couturier, is probably the most highly regarded among Italians. Abroad, however, accolades are accorded to Armani, the master of deconstruction, with his sloping shoulder-lines and minimalist colours, and Versace, his sartorial polar opposite – vulgar, glamorous and sexually explicit – who died in 1997. Despite the loss of the creative genius, the firm thrives under his sister, Donatella. But in the late 1990s, such pre-eminence was challenged by Prada, Gucci, Dolce & Gabbana and Moschino.

A sense of style and design is in the Italian genes. In 1946, the Italian architect Ernesto Nathan Rogers stated that design should be all-embracing, "from the spoon to the city". Italian designers dutifully filled our world with high-tech telephones and computers; office furniture in fluid shapes; sleek chrome kitchen appliances and twirly pasta quills. Giandomenico Belotti's Spaghetti Chair was literally inspired by squiggly pasta.

Italian design encompasses the austere, the provocative, the classically restrained and the kitsch. The roll-call of honour includes the Olivetti typewriter and the Artemide lamp, as well as the Ferrari, a symbol of national pride. Italy has a reputation for inspired car and motorbike design, from exclusive Ferraris to basic Vespa scooters *(see pages 94–5)*. In reply, the fashion world fields designers with the aspirations of Renaissance princelings: Armani's fluid lines clash with Versace's camp eroticism, Romeo Gigli's romantic fantasies, and Dolce & Gabbana's Sicilian kitch.

Aesthetically, Italy is known for its smooth, streamlined objects, from washing machines to motorbikes. Creatively, however, the country moves with the times: designs can be functional or futuristic, elitist or democratic. Designers confidently switch fields, from interior to industrial or graphic design.

Design diversity

The design field has traditionally cultivated creative cross-fertilisation between the craftsman and architect, designer and artist. Giò Ponti, the century's greatest Modernist, believed that Italy had been created half by God and half by architects. He detested the superfluous and favoured practical, perfect forms such as his Superleggera, the consummate chair, a sculpted light-weight piece. Ponti designed Milan's Pirelli Tower (1956) as well as creating the espresso machine, founding the magazine *Domus* and establishing the Milan Triennale, Europe's major design exhibition.

The highlights of Italian design history reveal both its readiness to innovate and its essential classicism. In the 1950s, the Modernists abhorred meretricious designs but eclectic designers were eager to experiment. The 1960s avant-garde relished visual disorder and inflatable fantasies. Yet even during the Pop Art period and Swinging Sixties, designers did not abandon their love of craftsmanship or use of high quality materials, such as leather. The

LEFT: the late Gianni Versace at a show in 1991.
ABOVE: "beauty for its own sake" even extends to food.

1970s represented the high point of Italian minimalism, with austere tubular steel chairs. In the 1980s, designers equipped domestic kitchens as if they were for professional chefs. In the 1990s, many designers returned to minimalism, following the "less is more" approach of Mies van der Rohe.

The belief in *bellezza*, beauty for its own sake, means that even high-tech must be aesthetically pleasing. Olivetti is one of many high-profile companies that have always treated their designers as creative artists. The Olivetti typewriter is a design classic, its shape emblazoned over the company headquarters near Turin.

Olivetti launched Italy's first portable typewriter in 1950, with Marcello Nizzoli's Lettera 22. Nizzoli's successors, Ettore Sottsass and Mario Bellini, pioneered ergonomic keyboards and the use of textured plastics and colour.

The Milanese apartment might be a temple of minimalism, decorated with white tubular sofas, stainless steel shelving, and glass-topped dining tables with an unusual number of legs. However, domesticity *all'italiana* comes in a range of styles. Just as few Post-Modernist architects choose to live in their own houses, so few Italian designers practise what they preach. Versace was the high priest of vulgarity yet filled his opulent mansions with antiques. In a grand *salotto* (living room), the clinical effect of modernist design may be offset by rich Venetian velvets or Florentine brocades. Even in a modern setting, there is a place for family heirlooms, with regional rustic chests or walnut dressers dotted with Venetian vases. Climate, tradition and taste reject carpets in favour of tiles, terracotta or marble flooring dotted with loose rugs. As for superior furniture, the firm of Poltrona Frau make hand-crafted designs out of seasoned beechwood and leather. Their comfortable Art Deco leather armchair, Vanity Fair, has been in production since 1930.

High-tech in the home also has a distinguished pedigree, with cult objects by Aldo Rossi, Ettore Sottsass and Robert Venturi, including coffee pots, chairs and trays in severe metallic designs. Particularly prized are stainless steel kettles by Alessi, or Achille Castiglioni cutlery and his elegant, curiously shaped lamps. The Italians broke the mould of lighting design: "Light does not simply illuminate, it tells a story," says Sottsass. The modern lighting heyday was the 1970s, but certain lamps, from 18th-century Murano chandeliers to Pietro Chiesa's Art Deco funnel lamps, stand the test of time.

Temples of consumerism

Milan may be the design showcase but most cities are citadels of good taste, with smart shops and shiny people committed to sophisticated consumerism. Writer Jonathan Keates refers to the town of Modena as "Middle Italy incarnate, the most unrelentingly consumer-oriented society in Europe". Yet even in poorer southern cities, rampant consumerism is common. If the authentic article is too costly, then dedicated shoppers will settle for a fake: appearances are everything. Naples is the capital of counterfeit culture, where painted marzipan fruit looks finer than real peaches. This is the place for ersatz French cognac or Scotch whisky, Lacoste shirts or Gucci handbags.

Conspicuous consumption is only part of the public picture. An Italian city is a stage for preening and posturing. Whether dressed in Como silks and Armani suits or in the preppy uniform of shades, loafers and designer jeans, Italians make immaculate fashion victims. ❑

LEFT: an exquisite early design by the Murano workshops in Venice. **RIGHT:** Versace outfit in blue velvet.

THE LOOK OF THE CENTURY

Furniture, clothes, cars, typewriters, even kitchen appliances – the influence of Italian design has permeated the way we live and work today

Italian designers bask in their reputation for refinement, innate good taste and eye for colour and line. "Quite simply, we are the best," boasts architect and cultural commentator, Luigi Caccia. "We have more imagination, more culture, and are better mediators between the past and the future. That is why our design is more attractive and more in tune with the times than in other countries." Italian design is nothing if not inclusive. The traditional distinction between architect and industrial designer is blurred, with practitioners dabbling in fields as diverse as factory building and furniture design, office lighting and graphics. In the words of Ettore Sottsass, one of the most influential designers, "Design should be a discussion of life, society, politics, food and the design itself."

MODERNISM TO POP ART

Since the turn of the century, Milan has led industrial design, reaching its apogee in the 1970s and 1980s. The Italians produced seminal designs for cars and lamps in the 1930s, matched by radios and motorbikes in the 1940s. Milan also pioneered innovative design in the 1950s, with the mass production of household appliances, from cookers and washing machines to kitchen utensils. Italian modernism supplanted the post-war European taste for the safe, hand-crafted homeliness of Scandinavian design. Stylish kettles and coffee percolators became cult objects in the 1960s, followed by quirky Pop Art furniture and the fashion designer chic of subsequent decades, from cool Armani to pared-down Prada. The inimitable character of *la linea italiana*, Italian style, still sets the standard for international design values.

△ FERRARI FORMULA
The Ferrari Spider (1993 model) is in a long line of fabulous cars from the most admired Italian manufacturer. Enzo Ferrari (1898–1988), the firm's founder, was also a noted racing car designer.

▽ WINDOW SHOPPING
A highly structured Prada suit adorns Milan's fashion district. Prada is the fashion company that best captures the *Zeitgeist* of the 1990s. Its designs made it the most copied (faked) label on the city streets.

▷ WASHED OUT
Zanussi's rigorous designs, streamlined look and user-friendly features have long made it a European market leader in the field of washing machines, refrigerators and other "white goods".

CLASSIC CAR STYLE

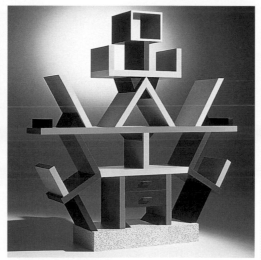

△ PLASTIC FANTASTIC
Post-Modernist bookcase in laminated plastic, a bold design for the Memphis studio by Sottsass (1981). Memphis was the design event of the 1980s, a playful and much-imitated school inspired by Bob Dylan's song, *Memphis Blues*.

◁ TALKING POINT
Italian design often takes ideas to their extreme, as in these eye-catching New Tone sculptural sofas by Atrium. This is subversive, unconventional, avant-garde living.

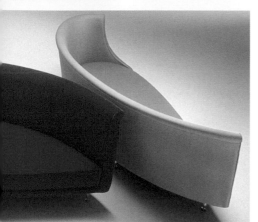

> DESIGN CLASSIC
The Piaggio Vespa ("wasp"), first produced in 1946, became the symbol of freedom for the post-war generation. The Vespa Lifestyle bag (*above*), part of a trend for brand recognition and product diversification, is an austere, minimalist offering from the Piaggio stable.

Ever since the 1930s, Italian car design has been characterised by stylistic restraint, versatility and timeless elegance. At one end of the scale, the Italians still produce some of the greatest status symbols in the world. In the 1950s, the beautiful Alfa Romeo convertibles spelt playboy raffishness; Ferrari's Spider, the ultimate in glamour, was produced from 1966 to 1992, making it the only sports car to boast a longer production run than Germany's Porsche 911.

Yet the Italians have also had great success with Fiat's bland but eminently practical models. Topolino ("the little mouse") was launched to great acclaim in 1939, and continued into the 1950s. Giovanni Agnelli studied American mass production techniques and from the 1950s the family dynasty had a captive market, with customers eager for the inexpensive Fiat 500.

The car industry is based in the North, with Fiat in Turin, Alfa Romeo in Milan and Ferrari in Modena. The huge Fiat Lingotto plant was set up near Turin in the 1920s. Still today, the city fortunes are inextricably linked to Fiat.

The Italians also design for foreign manufacturers, including Mercedes and Rolls Royce.

ITALIAN CUISINE

*Each region has its own cuisine, from the rich dishes of Emilia-Romagna
to the sparse, intensely flavoured diet of the South*

For Italians, a meal is a celebration of life itself – less of man's art than of nature's wondrously bountiful providence. A deep respect and admiration for ingredients is found throughout the country, although both history and geography have played their part in making the cooking of Italy so strongly regional.

One of the secrets of Italian cuisine, impossible to replicate elsewhere, lies in Italy's soil. After making pulp of Mexico, the Spanish conquistador Hernando Cortés returned to the Old World laden with strange new fruits and vegetables, among them a humble, fleshy yellow sphere smaller than a ping-pong ball which, in 1554, the Italians dubbed the *pomo d'oro* (golden apple). Two hundred years on, thanks to the rich Italian soil, these jaundiced cherries had become huge, lush tomatoes in deep ruby hues; moreover, their relatively demure taste (the contemporary writer Felici had described the original fruit as "more good-looking than good") had been transformed into a piquant yet tantalisingly sweet sensation.

These days, as well as being a key ingredient in many more elaborate Italian dishes, tomatoes are stuffed with beans or rice, offered as an *antipasto* with alternating slices of fresh mozzarella cheese, or simply served lightly dressed in olive oil and topped with sprigs of basil.

A savoury past

Until the Renaissance, the history of Italian cooking largely corresponded with Italy's military fortunes. In the 9th century, the Arabs invaded Italy, introducing Eastern sherbets and sorbets, originally served between courses to refresh the palate. Sicily, where Arab influence was most entrenched, is still noted for its sorbets and sumptuous sweets, including *cassata siciliana*, sweet sponge filled with ricotta cheese or pistachio cream and decorated with almond paste and candied fruit. Two hundred years after the Arabs left mainland Italy, the Italians set off

LEFT: cutting the *parmigiana* in a restaurant in the Italian Lakes. **RIGHT:** olive oil from a small producer.

on their own holy wars. Their return was sweetened by the presentation of sugar-cane which they had discovered in Tripoli. They called it "Indian salt" and for almost a century used it as a condiment for meat and vegetables, not suspecting its natural affinity with dessert.

Some time in the late Middle Ages, pasta

appeared. Nobody knows exactly how it was invented, but the legend of Marco Polo bringing it back from Cathay is firmly refuted by Italians. The Roman gastronome Apicius, writing in the 1st century AD, describes a *timballo* (a sweet or savoury pie made with pasta). Later, in the Middle Ages, Boccaccio recommended the combination of macaroni and cheese.

It was during the Renaissance that cooking became a fine art and evolved along the lines familiar to us today. Bartolomeo Sacchi, a Vatican librarian also known as Platina, composed a highly sophisticated cookbook entitled *De Honesta Voluptate ac Valetudine* (Concerning Honest Pleasures and Wellbeing); within three decades the volume had seen six editions. Florentine merchants spent huge sums on establishing schools for the promotion of culinary knowledge.

Consolidation of the Venetian Spice Route led to fragrant innovations. New pastry cooks invented macaroons, *frangipane* (filled with cream and flavoured with almonds) and *panettone* (a spicy celebration brioche incorporating sultanas). Conquistadors bombarded the Old World with its first potatoes, pimentoes and, of course, tomatoes. When Catherine de' Medici, a keen gourmet, married Henry II of France, she took with her to France her Italian cooks, thus laying the foundations for French cuisine. Until then, France had no cuisine of its own. Even *Larousse Gastronomique* honours Italy as the "mother" cuisine.

Regional flavours

The concept of an Italian national cuisine is highly treacherous. Italy offers the world 23 regional cuisines, a diversity reflecting the country's pre-unification history and the importance of locally available produce (for example, hare, boar, rabbit and chestnuts in Tuscany; pork and truffles in Umbria; mozzarella, squid and *polpo* – octopus – in Naples). Distinctive culi-

OLIVE OIL

Olives, which were first brought to Sicily by the Ancient Greeks, are grown throughout Italy, which produces an abundance of olive oil with marked variations in flavour, fruitiness and colour – from pale gold to a rich green. The oil tends to be heavier and stronger further south, but the location of the grove and the weather during the growing season affect its characteristics.

The first "cold pressing" by stone or steel rollers produces the best, most expensive oils; the residue is then pressed using heat for maximum yield. Quality is measured by acid content: the finest, "*extra vergine*", has a maximum 1 percent acidity.

nary identities evolved as naturally as particular painting styles or costumes. Even more influential than political boundaries were natural variations in soil type, climate and proximity to the sea.

But the single inescapable territorial distinction is that between the North and the South. There are two important culinary differences between the two regions. Firstly, northerners eat flat pasta shaped like a ribbon while southerners eat round pasta shaped like a tube. Northern pasta is usually prepared at home with eggs and eaten almost immediately, often *alla Bolognese*, the classic pasta sauce made with lean veal and tomatoes and seasoned with carrot, celery, *prosciutto*, lemon zest and nutmeg. Southern pasta, on the other hand, is manufactured in factories (the first factories opened in the 19th century), does not contain eggs and is purchased dry, a tradition stemming from the days when it was dried in the warm sea breezes around Naples. The classic sauce in the South is *napoletana*, based on pork.

The second difference between North and south concerns the lubrication used for cooking. North of Emilia-Romagna, Italians line almost all pots and pans with butter when making a meal, whereas south of Bologna, it is olive oil which sets the pans sizzling.

Zuppa di pesce, which is more of a stew than a soup, is a stalwart of many menus and usually served in an enormous tureen. Luxury versions include *buridda alla Genovese*, incorporating octopus, squid, mussels, shrimps and clams.

Anchovies and sardines are classic Mediterranean fish. *Pasta con sarde*, a speciality of Palermo, is *rigatoni* with a sauce of wild fennel, pine nuts, raisins and fried sardines. A more intricate dish, often found as an *antipasto*, is sardines stuffed with capers, pine nuts, pecorino cheese (from Sardinia), bread and eggs.

Italy also produces some of the finest meats in the world, which may explain why the Ital-

Situated between the Adriatic and the Tyrrhenian seas, Italy hauls in well over 320 million kg (700 million pounds) of fish a year. Wonderful fish abound in Emilia-Romagna. Alpine streams make the Adriatic significantly less salty than most oceans, and it is therefore an ideal habitat for rombo, "the pheasant of the sea", and gobies, derived from the Latin *gobius pagenellus* (little pagans). It is said that when St Anthony of Padua came to Rimini in 1221, he preached a sermon for which all the fish, save the gobie, lifted themselves from the water.

LEFT: the abundant wares of a Naples grocer.
ABOVE: fresh fish for sale on the Adriatic coast.

ians don't find it necessary to add sauce to their national specialities. Tuscany's Chianina cattle are alabaster in colour and grow to weigh 1,814 kg (4,000 lb). Chianina beef is used to best advantage in *bistecca alla Fiorentina* – a recipe in which the steak is marinated in a little olive oil, wine vinegar and garlic, then rapidly grilled. Baby lamb and kid is popular in hilly regions.

Game birds are also used extensively (Italians are said to eat anything which flies, however small), and warbler, bunting, lark, quail and pheasant are favourites on regional menus. Thrushes and larks are eaten whole, bones as well. *Piccioni* (wild pigeon), served fresh rather than hung, attains new gustatory heights in Italy.

Look out for *piccioni alle olive*, pigeons wrapped in bacon, roasted and served with green olives.

Of all Italy's provinces, Rome has the most festivals, and Rome's cuisine comes nearest to that associated with feasting. Suckling pigs and suckling lambs are mouth-watering specialities. The justly famous *saltimbocca alla romana* (a thin slice of veal wrapped around a slice of *prosciutto* and a sage leaf, browned in butter and simmered in white wine) lives up to its name – "jump into the mouth". Romans also thrive on *gnocchi* – feathery dumplings incorporating butter, eggs, nutmeg and Parmesan – while their

poor relation, *polenta*, a pudding or cake of yellow maize flour, is popular in Lombardy.

Emilia-Romagna, long celebrated for its gastronomy, has splendid natural resources. Moreover, the entire province has always had one of the world's best road systems, ensuring rapid distribution of ingredients. *Prosciutto* (air-cured ham) is synonymous with Parma, though Tuscany and Umbria also produce a good *prosciutto* rubbed with a garlic and pepper mixture before curing. It is often served with sliced melon or fresh figs. Emilia-Romagna is also the place for sausage. Bologna, the capital of Italian cuisine, lies in the heart of Emilia-Romagna. It is from here that *mortadella*, described by one

connoisseur as "the noblest of pork products", originates. *Mortadella* is made from finely hashed pork, generously spiced and forced into a casing made from suckling pig skin.

Bologna is also the home of *tortellini,* rosebud shaped pasta filled with spinach and ricotta cheese. "If the first father of the human race was lost for an apple, what would he not have done for a plate of *tortellini*?", goes a local saying. Legends as to tortellini's origins abound. One version gives credit to a young cook of a wealthy Bolognese merchant who modelled the curiously shaped pasta on the navel of his master's wife whom he had seen sleeping naked.

As well as being *polenta* country, Lombardy also boasts the most modern methods of food production in Italy. It produces more rice than any other European region and the famous *risotto alla milanese*, seasoned with saffron, does justice to the native grain, which, as the great cookery writer Elizabeth David pointed out, is ideally suited to slow cooking. Variations on the risotto theme, in which rice is cooked in a broth to absorb its flavour, include *risotto nero*, in which the rice is coloured black by cuttlefish ink.

One way to transform a plain risotto into a dish fit for a king is to shave a little truffle over the top. The truffle, a superior – and extremely fragrant – type of mushroom which grows beneath the soil around tree trunks, is prized for its unique flavour and texture. White truffles are found in Piedmont, where they are sniffed out by specially trained dogs. Black truffles are associated with Umbria.

Bread and pizza

Naples is the place to eat pizza baked over wood in a brick-lined oven – traditionally, *pizza napoletana* (tomatoes, mozzarella, anchovies and oregano), *pizza Margherita* (topped with mozzarella, tomatoes and basil leaves) and *pizza marinara* (topped with tomatoes, garlic, clams, mussels and oregano). A good pizza should be moist and fragrant with a raised rim known as *il cornicione* (large frame).

Bread, eaten without butter, accompanies every meal and is used to mop up juices and olive oil. Every region, even every town, in Italy has its own varieties and the different shapes alone are said to number 1,000. In Tuscany, bread (rough, white and with a floury top) is saltless to counteract the saltiness of the food;

in the South bread comes in large crusty wheels. Favourite speciality breads include *pane alle olive* (a Genoese bread incorporating olives) and *focaccia*, a flat bread drizzled with olive oil and sprinkled with salt, or, in a more elaborate version similar to pizza, topped with olives or onions. Sardinia is noted for its *carta da musica* (music-paper bread), a wafer-thin unleavened bread, which is crunchy and long-lasting. Shepherds traditionally took it with them on long expeditions into the hills with their flocks.

BIG CHEESE

Most Parmesan cheese is Parmigiano-Reggiano, produced around Parma, Reggio nell'Emilia and Modena.

ably similar order. The first course (*il primo*) invariably consists of a pasta or rice dish (especially in the North) or soup. (*Antipasti*, such as toasted bread with olive oil and garlic, seafood salad or grilled vegetables, are generally served only in restaurants or at banquets.) The second course (*il secondo*), comprising meat or sometimes (especially on Friday) fish, complements or elaborates the theme begun by the first. For example, if the first course was *tortellini* filled with parsley and ricotta, the second would probably be some-

The ritual of the meal

Wherever you are in Italy, the rituals surrounding food and eating remain the same. Devotion to any repast, however humble, is evident in the time Italians spend at the table. In many regions work still stops for a full two hours at midday, and everyone, from the poorest to the richest, is expected to go home and eat. Often the midday meal is the most important event of the day, the time when families swap stories and adventures.

Though their specialities differ greatly, all regions eat their particular dishes in a remark-

LEFT: making pizza in Naples, where it all started.
ABOVE: the best cakes are from Milan, some say.

thing light – such as a sautéed chicken dish with lemon and a little more parsley, echoing the first course. The second course is usually enhanced by at least one, often two or three vegetable dishes, such as *funghi trifolati* (mushrooms sautéed with garlic and parsley), *fave in salsa di limone* (broad beans in lemon sauce) and *cicoria all'aglio* (chicory with garlic sauce).

Afterwards, a light green salad is generally served to cleanse the palate, and to prepare the tastebuds for the grand finale – anything from an exotic pastry (*dolce*) to one of Italy's many cheeses, perhaps served with fruit. Needless to say, each course is washed down with ample quantities of wine. ❑

WINE IN ITALY

In Italy, wine exists primarily to turn everyday meals
and family get-togethers into hugely pleasurable social occasions

Wine is part of the cultural furniture in Italy. It goes on the table along with salt, pepper and olive oil – and it is made to be drunk with food. This means that the flavours of Italian wine are often both more subtle and more demanding than those of wines from countries where the link is less strong.

Just as there is hardly any such thing as Italian cooking, so the wines of Italy, too, are intensely regional. Vine-growing echoes the North–South divide, largely for climatic reasons. Wines from a delimited region are designated Denominazione di Origine Controllata (DOC). Most DOC wine (which accounts for one in every eight bottles) is produced north of Rome: as one travels south, the grape varieties, and the tastes, become increasingly exotic. Italy grows more grape varieties, and makes more wine (nearly a fifth of the world's total) than any other country. Not all of it is good, but much of it is exciting. Be prepared to take a risk: you will usually be amply rewarded.

Light but quaffable

Soave and Valpolicella illustrate a useful principle. These light white and red wines are produced on a vast industrial scale. The Veneto region – from Venice to Lake Garda, from the Yugoslavian Alps to the flat Po Valley – is the largest producer of DOC wine. Soave, by far the country's biggest selling dry white DOC, can be as memorable as muzak or waiting-room wallpaper. But for those who are prepared to pay a little more, for Soave Classico made on a small scale by first-rate producers, it can be very good indeed. Any Valpolicella billed as *ripasso* will have more character than straight Valpolicella. Recioto Amarone and Recioto Amabile (made from dried grapes) have extra depth and flavour; the former is dry, the latter sweet and reminiscent of port. Recioto Soave is the white equivalent, a golden, gently honeyed wine.

To the north and east of Venice, Friuli-

Venezia Giulia is a source of much crisp, fresh white wine from a long list of grape varieties.

Up above Lake Garda, in the mountain air of Trentino-Alto Adige, the vineyards cling to precipitous slopes under peaks that are snow-covered until well into the spring. The Alto Adige, or South Tyrol, was once part of Austria, and

many growers have distinctly unItalian names. Reds from here can be chewy and plummy, or strawberry-fresh; whites are as crisp as the mountain air, light and ethereal.

Piedmont, Italy's other sub-alpine wine region, is a wonderful place to visit in autumn, when the early morning fog that hangs over the vineyards clears slowly, and the streets of Alba smell of white truffles. The fog, or *nebbia,* gives its name to the main red grape variety, Nebbiolo, which ripens very late; its thick skin enables it to survive the humidity and rot that would threaten thinner-skinned varieties.

The thick skin is also responsible for the wine's deep colour, and for mouth-puckering

LEFT: a variety of fine wines for sale. **RIGHT:** traditional methods in Tuscany.

tannins that make Barolo and Barbaresco such big, powerful, long-lived wines. They are both DOCG, a step up from DOC. These wines are to be taken seriously: wines for long, companiable dinners that stretch well into the night, not wines for an *al fresco* lunch. A glass of sweet, sparkling Asti, aromatic and irresistably quaffable, is more welcome at lunchtime, followed by one of the lighter local reds, such as Nebbiolo d'Alba.

Chianti country
Tuscany challenges Piedmont as producer of the country's most aristocratic wines. Some of the

TOP TEN WINE PRODUCERS
You can always rely on **Allegrini** for serious Valpolicella; **Anselmi** for starry Soave (go for the *cru* and *recioto*); and **Antinori** for quality Chianti, *vino da tavola* Tignanello and stupendous white Castello della Sala. For wonderful Barolo, try **Clerico**, both **Conterno** brothers or **Bruno Giacosa** (also recommended for Barbaresco). **Angelo Gaja** has great Barbaresco at great prices. **Isole e Olena** produce elegant Chianti. **Pieropan's** Recioto di Soave is rich beyond the dreams of avarice (as you'll have to be, too); and **Regaleali** use local grape varieties to produce quality Sicilians with wacky flavours.

families in the business today (Antinoris and Frescobaldis, for example) have been making wine since before the Renaissance. Chianti is the staple, Italy's best known red wine, made mostly from the Sangiovese grape. The "blood of Jove" manifests itself in varying forms, from light and fruity to capable of ageing in the bottle. Standards of winemaking in the region have improved so that most Chianti is gratifyingly better than it used to be, even a decade ago.

Brunello di Montalcino and Vino Nobile di Montepulciano, both Sangiovese-based, both super-expensive, have traditionally represented the heights to which Tuscan reds could aspire. But Super-Tuscans, a loose-knit family of brilliant but quirkily named *vini da tavola* that burgeoned in the 1980s, are now some of Tuscany's greatest stars. Each has its individual style: they sprang from the desire of certain winemakers to produce their dream wine outside the often stultifying law of the time. They have snappy names like Sassicaia or Solaia, and are pricey, but with inimitable richness and complexity.

Dry white wines from Tuscany are less exalted. Galestro is a brave attempt to show that Italy's high-yelding Trebbiano grape can turn into something tasty, especially when blended with Sauvignon Blanc, Chardonnay and others. Vernaccia, from the medieval town of San Gimignano, is made in more traditional style. Tuscany's classiest whites, however, are sweet, made from dried grapes and called Vin Santo.

In Emilia-Romagna, where dishes are gloriously rich and sticky, Lambrusco is the natural partner. Most of it is red, some is dry, and the bubbles vary from a mere prickle to a full-blown sparkle. Much of it, too, is an improvement on the coloured sweet pop that floods the export market. Look for Lambrusco di Sorbara to get a taste of the real thing.

Further south
Most of the best wines of central and southern Italy are red. Those from the South tend to be cheaper, but don't be fooled: a wine-making revolution has taken place in these sun-baked villages, and wines such as Apulia's Copertino and Umbria's Sagrantino offer tremendous flavours of spices, earth and dried fruit. Montepulciano d'Abruzzo, too, is good, juicy red, with a typically Italian bite.

The whites of the centre and South have their virtues, but character is not always among them.

HOW TO READ AN ITALIAN WINE LABEL

Denominazione di Origine Controllata (DOC) is a delimited wine region, the equivalent of the French Appellation Contrôlée. Not all DOC wines are very good and some top wines are in fact not DOC; the producer's name is often a surer guide. DOCG (the G standing for *c garantita*) is meant to be a better wine than a straight DOC. Indicazione Geografiche Tipici (IGT) is a classification between DOC and *vino da tavola*, which embraces the two ends of the scale – cheap everyday wine and some high quality, expensive wines made by producers dissatisfied with DOC restrictions. *Classico* refers to the heartland of a wine region, often producing the best wine. Other words to look for are *abboccato* (semi-sweet); *amabile* (sweet); *secco* (dry); *frizzante* (pétillant); *spumante* (sparkling), which may be made by the *metodo classico* (Champagne method). *Passito* is sweet wine made from semi-dried grapes; *recioto* sweet or dry wine made from dried grapes; and *ripasso* a rich red wine fermented in the barrels previously used for a *recioto*. In Valpolicella, *amarone* is a dry wine of great character made from dried grapes. *Riserva* is wine given extra ageing in the barrel.

All too many are clean, fresh, well made, but bland; often because they are designed for washing down food without drawing attention to themselves.

Exceptions are Orvieto Classico, from Umbria, which can have good nutty fruit, and Frascati, which at its best has an attractive sour-cream tang. But if Frascati did not have Rome on its doorstep it would probably not have achieved the fame it has. Most of it is Trebbiano-based and quaffable, but the better producers use Malvasia.

LEFT: a vineyard and *trulli* house near Alberobello in Apulia. **ABOVE:** decanting an old vintage in Tuscany.

Sweet wines

Sweet, sometimes fortified whites, however, are another matter. The southern half of the country abounds in these, as do the islands, and very good they are too – although calling them whites seems perverse when most age to a rich tawny colour. Look for the names of the Malvasia or Moscato grapes on the label.

In Tuscany, try the Vin Santo ("holy wine") made from grapes which have been hung to dry for months or even years. Traditionally, this was offered to favoured guests as refreshment, along with little sweet almond biscuits, but it can equally well be drunk after dinner – or after lunch if you want to snooze all afternoon. ❑

MUSIC AND OPERA

*Italy's contribution to music is unparalleled. And where better
to enjoy the art of opera than where it began and flourished?*

Italy is rightly known as the home of music, and Milan's image is inextricably bound up with La Scala. When opera houses burn down, as they still tend to do in Italy, people cry in public and the country grieves. Fortunately, the country still has more major opera houses than it deserves. However, Italy's contribution to Western music goes beyond operatic rococo interiors and impassioned outpourings of Verdi.

A monk, Guido d'Arezzo, devised the musical scale, while a Venetian printer, Ottavino Petrucci, invented a method of printing music with moveable type. The language of music remains resolutely Italian, including such terms as *soprano*, *drammatico* and *soprano lirico*. Italy also gave us the piano, the accordion and the fabulous Stradivarius and Guarneri violins and cellos. Cremona has been the capital of violin masters since the 16th century. Indeed, it is not too fanciful to see the curves of violins echoed in the spiral cornices of city palaces.

The food of love

Without the Italian sensibility, the world of music would be without the nobility and intensity of Verdi or the seductive strains of Vivaldi. The lush strings of Albinoni perfectly chime with the public's taste for haunting baroque music, while opera-lovers are rewarded with Rossini's *Il Barbiere di Siviglia*, a comic masterpiece, Bellini's ravishing melodies, or the dramatic flow of Puccini's *Tosca* and *Turandot*. Other musical keynotes are *bel canto*, the traditional Italian art of singing, and Neapolitan love songs, as much part of the passionate city as spicy pizza and Mount Vesuvius. Yet Italian music also embraces Scarlatti sonatas, memorable madrigals, Palestrina's solemn melodies and the purest Gregorian chant – not to mention Mina's soulful pop ballads and Mediterranean rock. Of the old-school balladeers, often witty as well as romantic, Gino Paoli, Francesco de

PRECEDING PAGES: a glittering gala at Milan's La Scala.
LEFT: Verdi, great opera composer and Italian patriot.
RIGHT: Claudio Monteverdi, the "father of opera".

Gregori, Lucio Dalla and Claudio Baglioni deserve mention. Gianna Nannini is an out-spoken firebrand of Sienese feminism and Mediterranean rock, while some of the fusion bands from the South are tinged with North African and Arab notes, a reminder of the Moorish legacy in Sicily and Campania. Eros Ramazotti,

the king of Italian easy listening music, has achieved great sales in continental Europe and is designated "the Pavarotti of pop".

Opera was Italy's greatest musical achievement, a rousing art form which came into being in 14th-century Florence and was perfected by Monteverdi. In his opera *Orfeo*, the title role was taken by a *castrato,* a male soprano or contralto with an unbroken voice. *Castrati* were in great demand during the 17th and 18th centuries, thanks to their strong, flexible yet voluptuous voices. Farinelli (1705–82) was the most famous, a soprano whose singing and stage presence caused women to faint from excitement. Italian divas have also graced the stages of the great *teatri lirici* (opera houses), including Cecilia Bartoli in the present day, the mezzo-soprano acclaimed for her interpretations of Mozart. Italy, which gave the world Enrico Caruso and Beniamino Gigli, also boasts a clutch of talented tenors, from Luciano Pavarotti to the romantic Roberto d'Alagna, raised in Paris by Sicilian parents.

The world's their stage

Composers such as the modernist, Luciano Berio, also enjoy international renown, experimenting with sound in all its forms, from electronic and rock music to folk, jazz and classical.

La Scala recently honoured him with a premiere of his opera *Outis*. Gian Carlo Menotti, the founder of the Spoleto Festival, set in a ravishing Roman theatre, is acclaimed for his operas as well as his skills as an impresario. As for conductors, this has been an Italian forte since Toscanini, whose first public performance at the age of 19 was *Aida*, conducted from memory after stepping in at short notice. Riccardo Muti now conducts at Milan's La Scala and runs the Ravenna music festival, close to his home. Muti's respected predecessor, Claudio Abbado, directs productions around the world, as well as in Ferrara. Conductors Daniele Gatti, Riccardo

THE WORLD'S MOST FAMOUS TENOR

Luciano Pavarotti has legendary status, regularly singing with Carreras and Domingo as the "Three Tenors". He is as happy singing Neapolitan love duets as he is crooning with international rock stars, such as Sting, U2 and Tina Turner. The Maestro credits the longevity of his career to his father, who is still singing and recording in his eighties, and credits his musical gift to the female members of his family: "I probably owe my way of singing to them – the lyricism, the softness, the affection". More startlingly, Pavarotti attributes his singing technique to his wet-nurse, who breast-fed both him and the accomplished soprano Mirella Freni. As a five-

year-old, he was singing *La donna è mobile* for sweets, but his career was launched only with the winning of a Welsh choral competition.

A connection is often made between the bulkiness of "Big Luciano" and the best cuisine in Italy, boasted by his home region of Emilia-Romagna. Certainly, the world's most famous tenor remains close to his earthy roots and stages charity concerts and show-jumping events in his native Modena. Pavarotti is sanguine about his future: "They say that I'll sing until 2001, when I celebrate 40 years of my tenor career, but it's not true – I'll sing while I have the voice."

Chailly and Giuseppe Sinopoli have also found fame abroad, notably at Amsterdam's Concertgebouw, London's Covent Garden and the Dresden opera house.

Conductors working abroad are probably relieved to escape their knowledgeable but critical audiences back home. Italian audiences are hard task-masters, with applause led by the official clapping societies that are present in the major houses. Yet if the opera falls short of perfection, the *loggionisti*, those in the gods, are ready to rain down abuse on fallen divas, with booing and hissing commonplace. Brave visitors who wish to show their appreciation can

lies the key to Italian opera. It is essentially sensual and lush, appealing more to the emotions than the intellect.

The bookends of Italian opera's golden age stand clear: on the one side, the 1815 production of Rossini's classic *opera buffa* (comic opera), *Il Barbiere di Siviglia*; and, on the other, the posthumous 1926 opening of Puccini's last and unfinished opus, *Turandot*. Between the two lies more than a century of operatic triumphs.

During the 19th century, when Giocchino Rossini, Gaetano Donizetti, and Vincenzo Bellini dominated the scene, Italian opera

shout "*bravo*" for tenors, "*brava*" for sopranos and "*bravi*" for all. Ultimately, as long as the opera provides a spectacle, of people-watching or, perish the thought, of mellifluous music, then an Italian audience usually goes home happy, whether the fat lady sings or not.

Opera's golden age

Giacomo Puccini once said of himself, "I have more heart than mind". In these characteristics

---

LEFT: an animated 19th-century audience in San Carlo Opera House in Naples.
ABOVE: composer Vincenzo Bellini.
RIGHT: self-portrait by Gaetano Donizetti.

became infused with vitality, and Europe once again looked towards Italy for operatic innovation. All three composers, born within a decade of one another, shared much in style, and their careers followed similar paths and detours.

Rossini is probably most celebrated for his productions of *Il Barbiere di Siviglia* and *Guillaume Tell*, while Donizetti's masterpieces are *Lucia di Lammermoor* and *La Fille du Régiment*. Bellini is celebrated for his *semi seria* works, *La Sonnambula*, *Norma* and *I Puritani*. These operas are part of standard repertoires constantly performed throughout the world.

The three composers shared a small-town background, and all enjoyed great success at an early age, although Bellini was already 22 years old when he made his operatic debut. Each faced the voracious demands of impresarios and the finicky tastes of leading performers, and they all worked with remarkable speed, producing new works in the space of a few weeks. Not surprisingly, there was a fierce and jealous rivalry between them. Upon hearing that Rossini had composed *Il Barbiere di Siviglia* in 13 days, Donizetti shrugged proudly and concluded, "No wonder – he is so lazy."

They acquired gold and glory all over Europe, but, tragically, all three burnt themselves out. Bellini and Donizetti died young, the latter a

Giorno di Regno (1840), met with lacklustre receptions at La Scala premieres, rave notices for the epic *Nabucco* (1842) marked the beginning of a long and distinguished career. From then on, Verdi saw success after success, highlighted by *Rigoletto* (1851), *Il Trovatore* (1853), *La Traviata* (1853), *La Forza del Destino* (1862), *Don Carlo* (1867), *Aida* (1871), and *Otello* (1887). With premieres in London, Paris, St Petersburg and Cairo, along with those in the theatres of Italy, Verdi was a composer of true international stature.

It was a reputation well deserved. Verdi's sharp, almost brutal dynamism freed Italian

crazed syphilitic, and Rossini's last triumph was achieved before he reached 40. They were followed by the brightest light in Italian opera.

The brightest star

Giuseppe Verdi was born in 1813 (the same year as Richard Wagner) in Le Roncole, a small village 17 km (12 miles) from Parma. His father was a semi-literate peasant, and the family had no history of talent, musical or otherwise, but young Giuseppe made a mark as the local church organist. In 1832, he was denied admission to the prestigious Milan Conservatory. But the young Verdi was persistent, and, although his first two productions, *Oberto* (1839) and *Un*

opera from the lingering vestiges of empty conventions. Verdi also refused to tailor his works to the whims of individual singers, something that no composer had dared do in the past. His independence extended to his personal life. In a very conservative and religious society, he openly lived with his mistress, the soprano Giuseppina Strepponi, for more than a decade before taking her to the altar in 1859.

If Verdi was permitted artistic and personal freedom, he was still constrained by the political realities of his day. Censorship was a constant impediment in an Italy dominated by foreign powers. Verdi was himself an ardent nationalist. His historical works were charged with analogies of the Italians' plight – allusions that were not lost upon native audiences. A dear friend of Count Cavour, Verdi briefly served in the new chamber of deputies after unification. On his death in 1901, Verdi was mourned not only as a composer but also as a patriot.

The best-loved tunes

Although operas of fine quality continue to be composed today, the golden age of Italian opera drew to a close with the career of Giacomo Puccini, who was inspired by Verdi's *Aida* to become an operatic composer. Others contended for the mantle of Verdi, but Puccini had

the advantage of the blessing of the old man himself. "Now there are dynasties, also in art," lamented rival Alfredo Catalani, "and I know that Puccini 'has to be' the successor of Verdi … who, like a good king, often invites the 'crown prince' to dinner!" A dynasty it may have been, but one clearly based on merit. Puccini's success lay as much in his great gift for melody as in his unerring sense of theatre. *La Bohème* (1896), *Tosca* (1900), and *Madama Butterfly* (1904) are today among the best-loved works of opera. ❏

LEFT: curtain call at La Scala.
ABOVE: Giacomo Puccini, composer of *La Bohème*.

ITALY'S OPERA HOUSES

Beyond their gilt and stucco interiors, Italy's glittering opera houses (*teatri lirici*) are mostly neoclassical theatres rebuilt after numerous fires. Historically, the rivalry of noble courts gave birth to countless private opera houses, which gradually opened their doors to the public – the first was in Venice in 1637. The fashion for opera spread, and by the 18th century there were 20 in Venice alone. Most historic opera houses are in Lombardy and Emilia-Romagna, linked to great courts such as Cremona, Parma and Mantua.

Milan's La Scala is the premier opera house. All the great Italian composers have written for La Scala, notably Rossini, Donizetti, Bellini, Puccini and Verdi. It underwent a period of glory with performances of Verdi's patriotic works and spent the early 20th-century under Toscanini's direction. The historic building, a symphony of red, cream and gold, opened in 1778 with a performance of an opera by Antonio Salieri (who is best known today for being an adversary of Mozart). The theatre, which seats 2,000, has a superb acoustic, but is closed for restoration until the centenary of Verdi's birth in January 2001. In the interim, opera-goers may attend performances elsewhere in the city.

San Carlo in Naples enjoys a reputation second only to La Scala. Rebuilt in 1816, it won a name as a "singer's theatre", where vocal gymnastics and artistic rivalry were pre-eminent. While there are major opera houses in Florence and Rome, La Fenice (the Phoenix) in Venice enjoys greater prestige, despite its tragic history. Venice's "Phoenix" lived to rue its name after fires in 1836 and 1996. Australian diva Joan Sutherland mourned the loss of "the most beautiful opera house in the world; singing in La Fenice felt like being inside a diamond". The red and gold rococo confection is being rebuilt exactly as before, but until the year 2000 chic opera-goers must tolerate a tented affair. On the next rung down in terms of size, but not necessarily in scope, are Parma, Genoa, Bergamo, Modena and Turin.

Opera houses have been buffeted by strikes, budgetary cuts and even arson attacks: La Fenice's last fire, in which it was completely gutted, was a suspected Mafia attack. On a more positive note, Palermo's Teatro Massimo reopened recently after 25 years, during which it had opened its doors only once – ironically to allow the filming of *The Godfather*. In response to excessive bureaucracy and a funding crisis, the government announced the privatisation of all opera houses in 1997, with La Scala being the first.

ITALIAN CINEMA

*As windows of the nation's soul, Italian films showed
a vital resurgence, once freed from the fictions of Fascism*

Italian cinema has always flickered between epic spectacles and unabashedly intimate emotions. Before the outbreak of World War I, Italian directors had already filmed *The Romance of a Poor Young Man* and several versions of Bulwer-Lytton's monumental novel *The Last Days of Pompeii*.

When the Alberini-Santoni production company released *La Presa di Roma* in 1905 the Italian feature film was born. The subject is the 1870 rout of the pope by Garibaldi's troops. In its most famous scene, Bersaglieri rallies his forces to breach the wall at Rome's Porta Pia. Because so much of it was shot on location, the film anticipates two dominant currents in Italian film history: realism and historical spectacle.

However, Italian cinema skipped several steps in the development of international cinema. In England, America and France, early directors associated themselves with vaudeville and music halls and so motion pictures tended to be classed as "low entertainment". By contrast, Italy's first feature film-makers were the most learned and aristocratic in the world, creating what was dubbed a "cerebral cinema". At a time when most other countries still saw film as an amusing novelty, Italy was using it to express the meaning of life.

Early extravaganzas

Early in the 20th century, two directors, Enrico Guazzoni and Piero Fosca, revolutionised Italian films. Both directors' historic and melodramatic tastes perfectly complemented Italy's burgeoning nationalism; and both thrived on glorifying the martial exploits of Ancient Rome.

But Guazzoni's significance derives as much from his commercial innovations as from his conceptual ones. *Quo Vadis?* (1913), which established his reputation, ran for two hours and used the world's first gargantuan sets. Guazzoni limited distribution to first-class theatres, and

LEFT: Marcello Mastroianni, Italy's most sophisticated leading man. **RIGHT:** Maciste, an earlier heart-throb.

in New York *Quo Vadis?* received the first personality-spangled premiere. His shrewd marketing enabled future producers to raise unprecedented financial backing. However, *Quo Vadis?* masks any complexity of character with busy sets and costumes; and escapist addiction to costume drama haunts Italian cinema to this day.

Piero Fosca's contribution was more aesthetic and more influential. His grand opus, *Cabiria* (1913), details the adventures of virtuous maidens, strong men, gruesome villains and romantic generals during the wars between Ancient Rome and Carthage. Fosca was one of the first to pan cameras across vast scenes, and introduced live orchestras at screenings. More importantly, *Cabiria* showed it was possible to include subtle characterisation within the epic form.

After the successes of *Quo Vadis?* and *Cabiria*, the world woke up to film's great potential. Industrialists saw opportunities of making money. Also intrigued was the aristocracy, the source of many of Italy's film-makers and patrons. (Luchino Visconti, first generation neo-realist, was the heir of an aristocratic Sicilian family; a Roman countess provided Rossellini with the money to begin filming *Roma, Città Aperta*.)

The support of the nobility is one explanation for the high production standards of early Italian cinema. While directors in France and the United States were still pinning up painted backdrops, Italians hired the nation's finest

BIRTH OF AN EPIC

Hollywood drew inspiration from Italy for its own epics. Fosca's *Cabiria* had a direct influence on D.W. Griffith's 1915 *Birth of a Nation*.

able films. Directors who had ideological credibility were eligible for up to 60 percent state financing. Particularly patriotic endeavours, such as *Scipione l'Africano*, often received total backing from the government.

The final blow to creative competition was dealt by the new National Body for Importation of Foreign Films). It decided which films could be imported, then insisted they be dubbed into Italian. Unable to compete economically, Italy's better directors went into hibernation.

architects to design and construct full-scale sets. Furnishings in historical dramas were often borrowed from the personal collections of descendants of the depicted heroes; and if a film included aristocrats, authentic aristocrats were invited to make guest appearances.

This so-called Golden Age of Italian cinema hardly had time to blossom before the Fascists came to power. Mussolini instituted several organisations to regulate cinema, so convinced was he of the power of the medium. The Direzione Generale per la Cinematografia became an official department of the Ministry of Popular Culture. In addition, the Banco del Lavoro helped provide finance for politically accept-

Neo-realism

In 1944, while the Germans were still retreating from Rome, Roberto Rossellini, who had launched his career by filming for Mussolini a patriotic panegyric on dashing navy pilots, made *Roma, Città Aperta*, a film whose unflinching confrontation with truth unnerves audiences to this day. The film follows the lives of several Resistance workers. Every scene, except those set in the Gestapo headquarters, was shot on location. *Roma, Città Aperta* has a rough visceral throb that was revolutionary for the time. Some sequences seem to be documentary footage; the camera jerks and twists; shots break off suddenly.

Despite the unprecedented, relentless immediacy, *Roma, Città Aperta* has a complex symbolic structure. The film elevates drug addicts, priests, German lesbians and Austrian deserters to levels of wider symbolic import without sacrificing their unique personalities. Pina (Anna Magnani), for example, an agonised mother leading a mob of matriarchs to plunder exploitative bakeries in the neighbourhood, is utterly convincing, yet she also symbolises the desperate plight of Italian housewives during the war.

Federico Fellini, who helped Rossellini write the script for *Roma, Città Aperta*, summarised the atmosphere following World War II that pro-

remarkable homogeny Italy achieved just after World War II, with the widespread conviction that Fascism was wrong. Neo-realist directors spoke from and for an Italy which could confess, if not to chaos, at least to contradictions.

But, as the Cold War set in, Italian cinema came under fire. The government accused the best neo-realists of blackening Italy's image to encourage communism.

Resurgence

During the 1960s and early '70s, economic prosperity triggered a resurgence of Italian film, dominated by Federico Fellini, Michelangelo

duced neo-realism: "We discovered our own country ... we could look freely around us now, and the reality appeared so extraordinary that we couldn't resist watching it and photographing it with astonished and virgin eyes."

For the next few years, Rossellini, along with Visconti, Vittorio de Sica and Alberto Lattuada, developed a cinema characterised by rapid, seemingly spontaneous juxtaposition. Neo-realism remains the core of what is considered modern in film. The movement arose from the

LEFT: Anna Magnani in the neo-realist classic, Rossellini's *Roma, Città Aperta* (Rome, Open City).
ABOVE: Federico Fellini on the set.

Antonioni and Francesco Rosi – though this was also the period of Luchino Visconti's *The Damned*, Bernardo Bertolucci's *The Conformist* and Paolo Pasolini's *The Decameron*. Rosi was born in Naples, and southern Italy is a dominant theme in his films, in which the emphasis is on realism and social concerns. Antonioni's exploration of existential themes and individual crises reached a climax with *Blow Up* (1967). The tireless Fellini, arguably the greatest Italian director, produced a string of classics.

In many ways, Fellini can be viewed as the triumphant culmination of neo-realist philosophy. His characters are torn between the desire to realise their true selves and the urge to conform.

ITALY IN THE MOVIES

Rome, Tuscany, Sicily and Venice provide the main backdrops to the cinematic illusion of Italy. Such is the power of the movie myth that Sicilian Mafia murders and Tuscan costume dramas are equally convincing. Fellini, who had a virtual monopoly on Roman sensibility, loved to satirise his fellow-citizens on film: "The Roman is like a grotesque, overgrown child who has the satisfaction of being continually spanked by the Pope". In *La Dolce Vita* (1959) and *Roma* (1972), he held a distorting mirror to Roman reality. Of foreign directors, Peter Greenaway's *Belly of an Architect* (1987) arguably best captures the elusive character of the Eternal City.

Tuscany is a favoured location for foreign films, with the Merchant-Ivory *Room with a View* (1985) both a classic and a cliché, shot in villas in Florence and Fiesole. More quirky are Jane Campion's *Portrait of a Lady* (1996), shot near Lucca, and Tarkovsky's *Nostalgia* (1983) shot in Bagno Vignone, fabulously moody Roman baths south of Siena. Although best-known for *The Last Emperor* (1987) Bertolucci returned to Tuscany to shoot *Stealing Beauty* (1996), a Chiantishire tale, set in a rustic villa and idyllic wine estates. The Taviani brothers, from San Miniato, fully exploit Tuscan settings in *The Night of San Lorenzo* (1982) and *Elective Affinities*, shot near Livorno.

Sicily has long drawn directors of the highest calibre, with Rossellini's *Stromboli* (1950) set on a volcanic island, and Visconti's hymn to faded grandeur and Sicilian decadence, *The Leopard* (1968). Coppola's gross yet engrossing *Godfather* trilogy was partly shot in Sicily.

Venice provides an ideal location for moody "art house" films and action pictures. One James Bond movie, *Moonraker* (1979), features a frenzied gondola chase with 007 discovering an enemy hide-out in St Mark's belltower. By contrast, Antonioni's masterpiece, *Identification of a Woman* (1982) shows Venice as a magical yet murky world. In a similar but more ominous vein, *Don't Look Now* (1973) by Nicolas Roeg brings Donald Sutherland and Julie Christie to a eerily deserted Venice shortly after the death of their child. David Lean's *Summertime* (1955) casts Katharine Hepburn as an American abroad who both falls in love and falls into a canal. But the undisputed Venetian masterpiece is Visconti's *Death in Venice* (1970), based on Thomas Mann's novella. Visconti wanted "the light of the *sirocco*, the pale, still pearl light" and, with his artistic decision to use dawn and night shoots, forced his stars into sleeplessness.

His heroes swing wildly between the need to be like no one and the need to be like everyone.

Fellini said that his films were a "marriage of innocence and experience", but they were also about fantasy and loss, tinged with irony, fun and sadness. In *Amarcord* (1975), Fellini's surreal flights of fancy turned Rimini, his home town, into a virtual reality world. It was sweet revenge on the "inert, provincial, opaque, dull" Adriatic seaside resort he left for Roman chic. In his 1954 masterpiece *La Strada*, he claimed to have based the central character on the lost innocence of his actress wife, Giulietta Masina, who also starred in the film. *La Dolce Vita*

(1960) was the first time Fellini worked with his male muse, Marcello Mastroianni, who was chosen for his candour, innocence and "normal face, a face with no personality". The filmic frolicking in Rome's Trevi Fountain turned Anita Ekberg, Mastroianni's co-star, into an international sex symbol.

In 1967, with *A Fistful of Dollars* and *The Good, the Bad and the Ugly*, Sergio Leone presented world cinema with a new genre: the spaghetti western. These witty and stylised films, which were made on surprisingly low budgets, became the Italian movie industry's most successful exports since Sophia Loren, Gina Lollobrigida and Claudia Cardinale.

Recent trends

In the 1980s the generation of angry young Marxists and Sixties radicals gave way to commercial producers eager to create pale imitations of Hollywood action pictures. Bernardo Bertolucci is an exception in being free to command Hollywood budgets for international blockbusters or to concentrate on more low-key work. Competition from the highly commercial Italian television networks has had a detrimental effect on feature films, as has the partial demise of Cinecittà, the Roman film studios, and former hothouse for young Italian directors. Since privatisation in 1996, the studios have

Many of the recent films that have done well on the foreign circuit are set in the rural South, and portray a nostalgic, slightly naive version of Italy. Among them are *Cinema Paradiso* (1988), set in Sicily, and *Il Postino (The Postman)*, in Campania. In 1998 Italian cinema received a boost with Roberto Benigni's *La Vita è Bella (Life is Beautiful)*. Benigni wrote, directed and starred in this story of a Jewish waiter who invents jokes and games to protect his child from the horrors of life inside a Nazi concentration camp. The film captured several Oscars, including Best Foreign Film and Best Actor for Benigni. ❑

focused on television and advertising, rather than on feature films.

Italy is still suffering from the loss of Fellini in 1993, the finest Italian director, and of the well-loved actor Marcello Mastroianni in 1996. However, there are some reasons for hope. Nanni Moretti, known as an Italian Woody Allen, is a witty maverick attempting to reinvigorate the Roman cinematic scene. Since the success of his quirky *Dear Diary* (1994), he has established a new cinema for experimental and less mainstream films in Trastevere.

LEFT: a young cinema-lover in *Cinema Paradiso*.
ABOVE: the title character from the 1996 hit, *Il Postino*.

"BEAUTY IS IN MY DNA"

All Italian film directors are influenced by their environments to an extraordinary degree. Asked why his films always looked so lush, Bernardo Bertolucci pointed to his upbringing in Parma: "Growing up in such a beautiful city is a kind of *dolce condanna*, a sweet prison sentence. Look at our local painter, Parmigiano, he was the most decorative of all the Mannerists, the least tortured. I think beauty is in my DNA." Federico Fellini may still be regarded as Italy's greatest director, but Bertolucci remains the more incorrigible romantic, an idealist with considerable power and artistry.

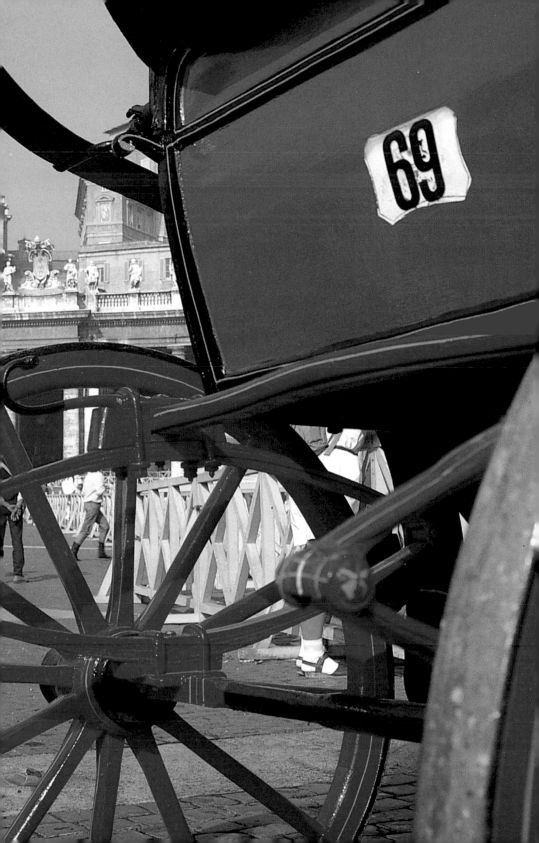

PLACES

*A detailed guide to the entire country, with principal sights
cross-referenced by number to the maps*

Negotiating the tangle of one-way streets in an Italian city takes years of experience. Often a helpful native will point the way, even take you personally to your hotel, restaurant or museum. But if no one materialises, don't panic, simply follow the tourist signs for Centro Storico (historic centre) and Duomo (cathedral), and remember that *senso unico* means "one way". Then find the first *parcheggio* (car park) and abandon your car, for most Italian cities are best explored on foot. If you arrive by train, the station will invariably be in the seedier part of town, so leave it behind for the greener pastures of the Centro Storico.

Modern life has stamped even small villages with a bar and a large population of motor-cycle-riding youths. Every town has its Duomo, but how different is the austere Romanesque cathedral of Apulia from the lavish baroque of the one in Turin. Every town has at least one piazza: in the South they are crowded with men smoking and playing cards; in the North, the men are still there, but so are the women and the tourists.

Our favourite places in Italy include many spots less frequented than the tried and true trio of Rome, Florence and Venice. We suggest that, after visiting Rome, you take an excursion east into Abruzzo or Molise, those hitherto remote regions whose architecture, parks, mountains and beaches rank among the most refreshing vacation spots in the country. Or, if you happen to be exploring the Bay of Naples, rent a car and continue down to Italy's heel and toe – Apulia, Basilicata, Calabria.

The North has Florence and Venice, of course, but also Milan and Turin, two very modern cities packed with art and history. You could follow the path of generations of travellers who, with Dante and Ariosto in hand, toured the cities of Lombardy, the Veneto, Emilia-Romagna and Tuscany. If you want to catch your breath and relax, retreat into the green hills of Umbria, home of Italy's beloved St Francis of Assisi. ❏

PRECEDING PAGES: Limone, on Lake Garda; St Peter's, Rome; Tricárico, in Basilicata.
LEFT: Castel Tirolo, in the Alto Adige.

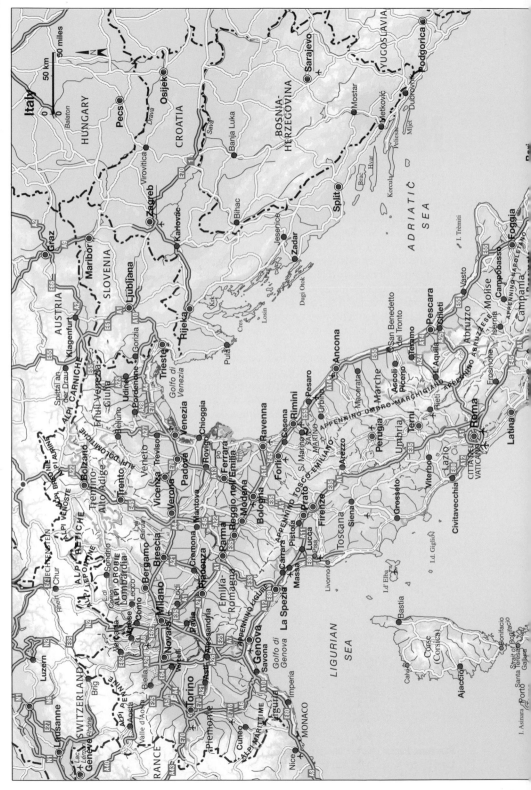

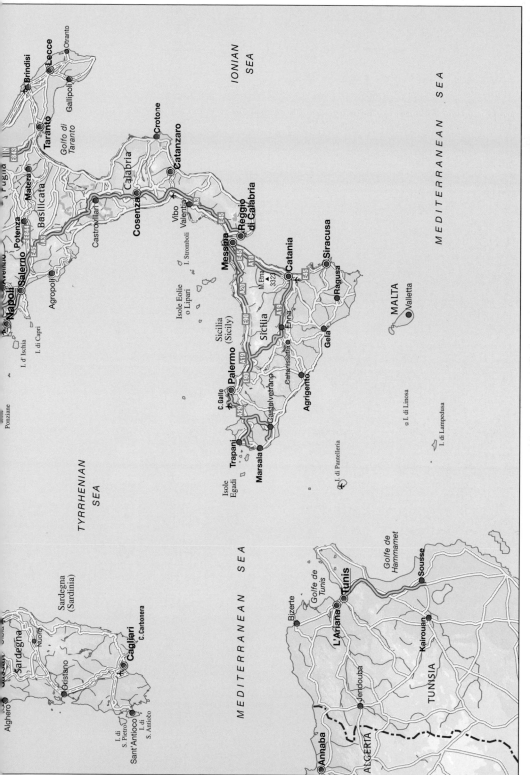

ROME

Follow in the footsteps of emperors and saints,
discovering the monuments and churches that mark Rome
as the capital of Italy and the ancient world

Map,
pages
132–3

ITALY
●Rome

Lord Byron gave **Rome** (Roma) the epithet "City of the Soul". Poetic hyper-
bole perhaps, but the description still strikes a chord among visitors to the
city. Though less efficient and sophisticated than Milan, less picturesque
and well-preserved than Florence or Venice, Rome remains, in Thomas Hardy's
words, "Time's central city". More than any other city, it helps us understand
ourselves, our "petty misery" (Byron) and the fragility of the world.

The Palatine Hill

The best introduction to Rome is not Piazza Venezia, the terrifying roundabout
at the centre of the modern city, but the more pastoral **Palatino** (Palatine Hill) **❶**,
believed by the ancients to be the home of Rome's mythical founder, Romulus.
Its claim to be the site of the original settlement is supported by the remains of
early Iron Age dwellings in the southwestern corner of the hill.

Close by are the remains of the **Tempio di Cibele**, picturesquely planted with
an ilex grove. The cult of the Eastern goddess of fertility, also known as Magna
Mater, was introduced to Italy during the Second Punic War (218–201BC).
Though its mystical rites – involving throngs of frenzied female worshippers,
priests committing self-mutilation, and bull sacrifices – were distasteful to old-
fashioned Romans, the cult spread widely during the
imperial era.

The name Palatine, said to be derived from Pales, the
goddess of shepherds, is the root of the word palace. In
Roman times this hill was celebrated for the splendour
of its princely dwellings. Earliest, and simplest, of these
was the Domus Augustana. A portion of it, erroneously
called the **Casa di Livia** (Livia was Augustus's wife),
is renowned for its *trompe l'oeil* wall paintings.

To the north, alongside the Palazzo di Tiberio (now
mostly covered by the Farnese Gardens) runs the **Crip-
toporticus**, a cool underground passage with a delicately stuccoed vault, built by Nero to connect the
palaces of Augustus, Tiberius and Caligula to his own
sumptuous Golden House on the Esquiline Hill. To the
southeast of this passage extend the remains of the
Domus Flavia, built at the end of the 1st century AD by
the Emperor Domitian. An infamous sadist, who took
pleasure in torturing everything from flies to senators,
Domitian suffered from an obsessive fear of assassination. According to the ancient historian Suetonius, an
entertaining if not entirely trustworthy source, the
emperor covered the walls of the peristyle (the section
with an octagonal maze) with reflective moonstone so
that no assassin could creep up on him unobserved.
Next to the peristyle lie the remains of a splendid ban-
queting hall, hailed by contemporaries as "the dining
room of Jove". Its buckling pavement, still covered with

LEFT: Bernini's
Fontana del Tritone.
BELOW: an umbrella
pine shades the
ruins of the
Palatine Hill.

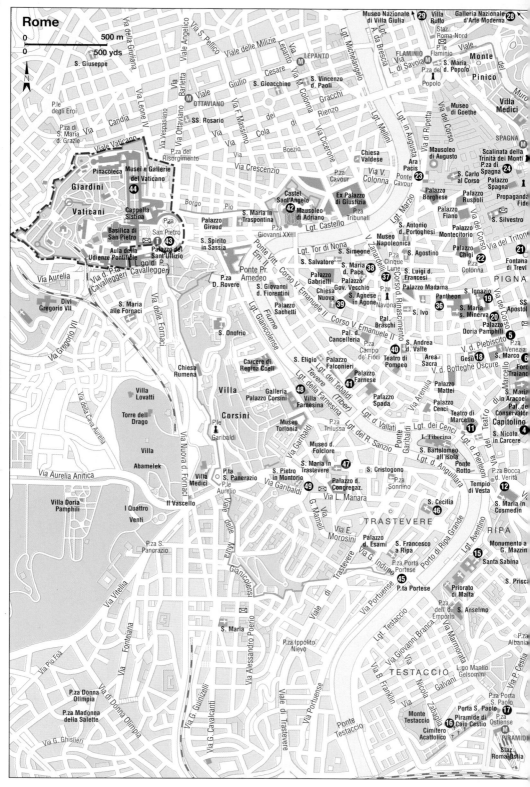

Rome

pink and yellow marble, gives some sense of its former grandeur. To the south lie the extensive remains of the Domus Augustana and the Stadium.

Following the fortunes of the city as a whole, the imperial palaces fell into disuse during the Middle Ages. Monks made their home among the ruins and the powerful Frangipani family built a fortress here. During the Renaissance, when there was a surge of new building throughout the city, Cardinal Alexander Farnese bought a large part of the Palatine and laid out the gardens on the slope overlooking the Forum. The lush **Orti Farnesiani** are delightful, with their formal landscaping, the sounds of fountains and birds, and good views over Rome.

For lovers of the picturesque, the ruins of the Palatine are hard to beat. Even archaeological excavations cannot deprive this location of its wild charm. It is the last place in Rome where you can find a landscape as it might have been drawn by Piranesi or Claude Lorraine. Roses, moss and poppies growing amidst the crumbling bricks and shattered marble give it a romantic rather than an imperial splendour. It is the perfect place in which to wander, sketch or picnic.

ABOVE: letters in stone in the Forum.

The Roman Forum

The Clivus Palatinus leads from the domestic extravagances of the emperors down into the **Foro Romano** (Forum) ❷ (open daily till 1½ hours before sunset; Sun till 1pm; special night viewings in summer; entrance fee), the civic centre of Ancient Rome. This area, once a swamp used as a burial ground by the original inhabitants of the surrounding hills, was drained by an Etruscan king in the 6th century BC. Until excavations began in the 19th century, the Forum – buried under 8 metres (25 ft) of debris – was known as the "Campo Vaccino" because smallholders tended their herds among the ruins. Today it reveals a stu-

BELOW: Casa delle Vestali (House of the Vestal Virgins).
BELOW RIGHT: view over the Forum.

pendous array of ruined temples, public buildings, arches and shops. The overall effect is impressive, but identifying individual buildings can be hard work.

At the bottom of the Clivus Palatinus, the **Arco di Tito** (Arch of Titus) commemorates that emperor's destruction of Jerusalem and its sacred temple in AD 70. This event marked the beginning of the Diaspora and the shift from the Temple in Jerusalem to local synagogues as the focus of Jewish worship. Until Israel was founded in 1948 and the return to Palestine became possible, pious Jews refused to walk under this arch.

The Via Sacra leads past the three remaining arches of the **Basilica di Costantino**, a source of inspiration for Renaissance architects. Bramante said of his design for St Peter's: "I shall place the Pantheon on top of the Basilica of Constantine". The **Tempio di Antonino e Faustina**, also known as San Lorenzo in Miranda, is a superb example of Rome's architectural layering. Originally a temple erected in AD 141 by the Emperor Antoninus Pius, it was converted into a church in the Middle Ages. During the 17th century a baroque facade was added, as was the case with so many Roman churches.

Across the Via Sacra is the lovely, round **Tempio di Vesta** (Vesta was the goddess of the hearth), where the six vestal virgins took turns tending the sacred fire. The punishment for allowing the fire to die down was a whipping by the priest. Service was for 30 years and chastity was the rule. Few patricians were eager to offer their daughters and the Emperor Augustus had to pick girls by lot. Laxity about vows was common and the Emperor Domitian resorted to the traditional punishment of burying errant virgins alive and stoning their lovers to death. Living in the lovely **Casa delle Vestali** was some compensation for this demanding life. The ruins remain a rose-scented haven.

The Vestals had seats of honour in the circus and theatre, and, in the city, where wheeled vehicles were forbidden, they alone had the right to travel in a carriage.

BELOW: Arch of Titus.

BELOW: Temple of Castor and Pollux.
BELOW RIGHT: Palazzo Senatorio in Piazza del Campidoglio.

Like 20th-century Americans, the Ancient Romans were keen litigants. Walk past the three elegant columns of the Temple of Castor and Pollux to the **Basilica di Giulio** (on the left of the Via Sacra), where trials were held, as many as four at a time. The acoustics were terrible and on one occasion the booming speech of a particularly loud lawyer was applauded by audiences in all four chambers. In cases where an advocate wanted a little extra help, professional applauders, called "supper praisers", could be hired. When not employed, these claqueurs would loiter on the steps of the basilica and play games. Their roughly carved boards can still be seen. The Senate met across the way in the Curia, the best preserved building in the Forum. Its sombre, solid appearance fits the seriousness of its purpose.

At the western end of the Forum rises the famed **Rostra**, where the orator Cicero declaimed to the Roman masses. After his death, during Octavian's anti-Republican proscriptions, Cicero's hands and head were displayed here. Opposite the Rostra is the single **Colonna di Foca** (Column of Phocas). For centuries the symbol of the Forum, it was described by Byron as the "eloquent and nameless column with the buried base". Unburied and named, it is still, as the Italians say, *molto suggestivo*. To the right is the **Arco di Settimio Severo**.

At the end of the Via Sacra, in the shadow of the Capitoline Hill, rise the eight Ionic columns of the **Tempio di Saturno**. The god's festival, called the Saturnalia, marked the merriest occasion in the Roman calendar, when gifts were exchanged and distinctions between master and slave forgotten. Occurring in the middle of winter, this was the feast that Christians later transformed into Christmas. Behind the temple are, from left to right, the Temple of Vespasian and Titus, and the Temple of the Concordia.

Outside the Forum excavations, across from Pietro da Cortona's Chiesa di Santi Luca e Martina, is the **Carcere Tulliano** (Mamertine Prison; open daily, closed 12–2pm; donation) ❸, home of some of Rome's most famous prisoners. A plaque on the wall lists how they met their unhappy ends: strangulation, starvation, torture or decapitation was their usual fate. According to legend, this dank, gloomy dungeon was where St Peter converted his pagan guards. Miraculously, a fountain sprang up so that he could baptise the new Christians.

Map, pages 132–3

The Capitoline Hill

From the **Capitoline Hill** ❹, the Temple of Jupiter Capitolinus (dedicated 509 BC) watched over the city. It was also here that modern Italians raised their tribute to Italy's unification after 1,400 years of fragmentation. The **Vittoriano** (Victor Emmanuel Monument), completed in 1911 and dedicated to Italy's first king, captures the neoclassical bad taste of the 19th century. Natives and visitors alike claim to despise this "typewriter" or "wedding cake".

Throughout Rome's history hopes for Italy's future have centred on this hill. In 1300, the poet Petrarch was crowned laureate here; in 1347 Cola di Rienzo roused the Roman populous to support his shortlived attempt to revive the Roman Republic; in the 16th century Michelangelo planned the elegant Campidoglio, thus restoring the Capitoline's status as the architectural focal point of the city; and it was here that the historian Edward Gibbon drew inspiration for *The History of the Decline and Fall of the Roman Empire* (published between 1776 and 1788).

If you're feeling energetic, climb the 124 steps to the medieval **Santa Maria in Aracoeli** (if you happen to be here at Christmas, come for the midnight mass). The weak-kneed will probably prefer Michelangelo's regal staircase (known as

Vercingetorix, leader of the Gauls, was executed in the Mamertine Prison after Julius Caesar defeated his forces in 52 BC.

MAMERTINUM
LA PRIGIONE dei SS APOSTOLI
PIETRO e PAOLO
IL PIÙ ANTICO CARCERE di ROMA
XXV SECOLI di STORIA

BELOW: the *Dying Gaul* in the Museo Capitolino.

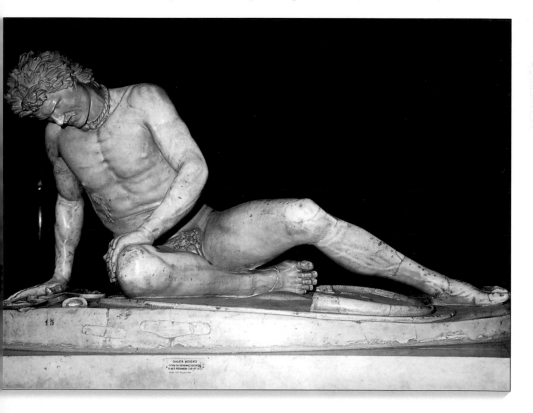

Wine, fish, spices, flowers, shoes, silk – anything could be bought at Trajan's Market.

BELOW: Trajan's Column, celebrating his victories in Romania early in the 2nd century AD.

the **cordonata**), flanked at the top by monumental statues of Castor and Pollux. In the back of the Campidoglio Palazzo Senatorio surmounts the ancient Tabularium, dating from Republican times. On the right of Palazzo Senatorio rises **Palazzo dei Conservatori**, on the left, **Palazzo del Museo Capitolino**, each housing art collections (open Tues–Sun 9am–7pm; entrance fee). For an insight into the Ancient Roman character, study the busts of emperors in the Sala degli Imperatori in the Museo Capitolino. Realistic portraiture was Rome's greatest contribution to the art of sculpture.

Mussolini's legacy

Piazza Venezia 5, at the foot of the Vittoriano monument, marks the centre of contemporary Rome. You may feel you risk your life by crossing its wide expanse but usually the torrents of traffic will part to allow a pedestrian passage. The Palazzo di Venezia, Rome's first great Renaissance palace (built in 1455), dominates one side. This was Mussolini's headquarters from 1929. Some of his most famous speeches were delivered from the balcony. The light burning in his bedroom at all hours of the night reassured the Italians that the "sleepless one" was busy solving the nation's problems (though according to Luigi Barzini the light was often left on when Mussolini was not there). Now the palace contains the **Museo del Palazzo di Venezia** (open Tues–Sun 9am–1.30pm; entrance fee) with a collection of paintings, sculptures and tapestries.

"Ten years from now, comrades, no one will recognise Italy," proclaimed Il Duce in 1926. One of the most dramatic changes the Fascists wrought on Rome was the Via dei Fori Imperiali. Mussolini cut down old neighbourhoods (reminders of Rome's decadent period) in order to excavate the fora and build the road. By such brutal means he hoped to create a symbolic connection between Rome's glorious past and his own regime.

West of the Imperial Fora is **Trajan's Forum 6**, dominated by its famous column. Behind are the splendidly preserved **Mercati di Traiano** (open Tues–Sun 9am–1.30pm; entrance fee), a favourite haunt of Rome's ubiquitous *gatti* (cats). In ancient times the five storeys of the market were abundantly stocked with exotic fare. The top floor contained two fishponds, one of which received water from an aqueduct, while the other held sea water brought all the way from Ostia. Cunning vendors attracted customers by displaying monkeys whose antics proved to be an effective magnet.

Augustus and Nerva both built their fora to accommodate Rome's growing population and passion for litigation. Statues of them stand opposite their fora.

Finally, at the end of all this ruined splendour, rises the **Colosseum 7** (open daily 9am–6pm, 7pm in summer; entrance fee), stripped of its picturesque wildflowers and weeds, surrounded by buses and snack stands, encircled by a swirling moat of traffic. This symbol of the Eternal City is less splendid than it was in its marble-clad, imperial days and less picturesque than it was in its tumble-down Romantic period; but, scientifically excavated, much of it roped off to ensure the safety of both visitor and building, it remains one of the key sights of Rome.

The Colosseum was built in AD 79 when the Emperor Vespasian drained the lake of Nero's **Domus Aurea** (Golden House) ❽. The message was clear: where Nero had been profligate, emptying the coffers of the empire to construct his own personal pleasure palace, the Flavian prince built a public monument. Also close to the Colosseum is the **Arco di Costantino** (Arch of Constantine)

Architectural layer cake

From the Colosseum, Via di San Giovanni in Laterano brings you to **San Clemente** ❾, one of Rome's most interesting churches. There are three levels of building. A 12th-century basilica descends to a 4th-century basilica, which in turn leads to a 1st-century Roman apartment building containing, in its court-yard, a Mithraic temple honouring one of the popular cults of imperial Rome. The excavations are extremely well documented in the church guide.

A little further along, Via di San Giovanni opens up into **Piazza di San Giovanni in Laterano** ❿, containing some of the most important buildings in Christendom. The **Obelisk** is the tallest and oldest in Rome and a suitable marker for the Church of Rome, **San Giovanni in Laterano**, founded by Constantine the Great. Not surprisingly, such an important church is a hodge-podge of build-ing styles, from the exquisite 4th-century baptistry to the peaceful medieval cloister and the majestic baroque interior. The **Palazzo Laterano** was the home of the popes until the Avignon exile in 1309. The pious may want to ascend the nearby **Scala Santa** (on their knees of course) (open daily 7am–noon, 3.30–7pm, 6pm in winter) said to be the steps Christ walked down after being condemned by Pontius Pilate. Constantine's mother, St Helena, retrieved them from Jerusalem.

Map, pages 132–3

TIP

Museum opening times in Rome are subject to change. It's always a good idea to check with the tourist office before planning your day.

BELOW: boy scouts on a cultural excursion.

ABOVE: the Bocca della Verità.

BELOW: fragments of columns in the Terme di Caracalla, and (**RIGHT**) visitors explore the ancient baths.

The ghetto

Rome's old ghetto lies on the western side of the Capitoline Hill, near the ruins of the **Teatro di Marcello ⓫**. The city has had a substantial Jewish community since the Republican era, but its isolation dates from the Counter-Reformation and the papacy of Paul IV (1555–59). From then on, the gates to the ghetto were locked from sunset to sunrise, Jewish men had to wear a yellow hat, the women a yellow scarf, and most professions were closed to Jews. "The iron of persecution and insult is every day driven into their souls," wrote one outraged 19th-century American. At that time the Jews were forced several times a year to listen to a tirade from a Dominican friar in the nearby church of Sant'Angelo in Pescheria.

Wandering through the narrow streets or visiting the Synagogue on the Tiber, one gets little sense of those years of confinement. A plaque on Via Portico d'Ottavia, however, is a reminder that just over 50 years ago more than 2,000 Roman Jews were deported to a Nazi concentration camp.

The Via del Teatro di Marcello leads south to **Piazza Bocca della Verità ⓬**, which yokes together two Roman temples (the Tempio di Portuno and the round Tempio d'Ercole), a baroque fountain and the medieval church of Santa Maria in Cosmedin. In the portico of this church, which uses the Byzantine-rites, is the **Bocca della Verità**, a marble slab resembling a human face and considered to be one of the world's oldest lie detectors. If a perjurer puts his hand in the mouth, so the legend goes, it will be bitten off. In fact, the slab's origin is sadly prosaic: it once covered a drain.

The oldest and largest of the famed Roman circuses, the **Circus Maximus ⓭**, lies in the valley between the Aventine and the Palatine Hills. It once seated

250,000 people. In addition to the main event, vendors, fortune tellers and prostitutes plied their trades beneath the arcades.

If the circus has earned the Ancient Romans a bad reputation, their public baths have inspired great praise. In addition to the three pools (hot, warm and cold), the **Terme di Caracalla** ⓮ (open Tues–Sat till 6pm, till 3pm in winter; till 1pm Sun & Mon; entrance fee) offered exercise rooms, libraries and lecture halls, for the improvement of mind and body. But less salubrious activities also went on here, especially when mixed bathing was permitted. Some took their cleanliness to an extreme. Emperor Commodus is said to have taken eight baths a day. But, for the most part, the baths represent a triumph of the Roman public spirit, demonstrating that cleanliness was not limited to those rich enough to have private facilities.

The affluent Aventine

For a contrast to the dusty and barren remnants of the circus and baths, visit the Aventine, one of modern Rome's most desirable residential neighbourhoods. As you climb the Clivo dei Publicii the smell of roses wafts down from the pretty garden at the top of the hill. Via S. Sabina leads to **Santa Sabina** ⓯, a perfectly preserved basilican church of the 5th century. Inside, shafts of Rome's golden sunlight light up the immense antique columns of the nave. Outside, in the portico, are some of the oldest wooden doors in existence (5th-century).

On the other side of the Aventine, in the shadow of the Piramide Cestio, lies the **Cimitero Acattolico** (Protestant Cemetery) ⓰ (open Thur–Tues; donation), one of the most picturesque spots in Rome. Scores of unfortunate travellers who fell fatally ill on a wedding trip or Grand Tour are buried here. In the old part of

Map, pages 132–3

ABOVE: the Piramide Cestio, 2,000 years old. **BELOW:** interior of Santa Sabina.

TIP

The Protestant Cemetery is divided into two parts: the oldest section, containing the tomb of Keats, lies to the left of the entrance.

the graveyard is Keats's tomb. Its sad epitaph reads: "Here lies one whose name was writ in water".

The modern part of the cemetery contains Shelley's heart. His body was burned on the shore near Pisa. As his dear friend Lord Byron put it: "All of Shelley was consumed, except his heart, which could not take the flame and is now preserved in spirits of wine."

Outside the **Porta San Paolo** ⓱ is the basilica of **San Paolo fuori le Mura**, one of the major basilicas of Rome. It is believed to house the tomb of St Paul.

Marble, gilt – and flesh and blood

Exuberant, awe-inspiring and outrageous, baroque architecture offers such an over-profusion of detail, painting, gilt and marble that it often overwhelms. But what pleasure there is in discovering a particularly winning putto winking at you from an architrave, in craning to see a fantastic ceiling by Pietro da Cortona or Andrea dal Pozzo, in calculating the time and expense spent on covering every inch of a building in marble, gilt and precious metals, and in seeing saints and biblical figures made flesh and blood by Caravaggio or Bernini.

The baroque style dominates in Rome and the best place to start appreciating it is the **Gesù** ⓲. The church was started in 1568 for the recently approved Jesuit order, champions of the Counter-Reformation. The Council of Trent (1545–63) laid down the rigorous principles for strengthening the Catholic Church against the Protestant heretics. Originally, the Gesù was meant to be austere; its baroque makeover was performed in the late 17th century. By this time, the Counter-Reformers had discovered art's role as a means of making the intangible more accessible to the faithful. Baroque art also impressed upon the masses the

BELOW: San Paolo fuori le Mura.

ROME AND THE BAROQUE

The baroque (1600–1750) was born in Rome, and nurtured by a papal campaign to make the city one of unparalleled beauty "for the greater glory of God and the Church". One artist to answer the call was Caravaggio (1573–1610), whose early secular portraits of sybaritic youths revealed him to be a painfully realistic artist. His later monumental religious painting entitled *The Calling of St Matthew,* in San Luigi dei Francesi, shocked the city by setting a holy act in a contemporary tavern.

The decoration of the interior of St Peter's by Gianlorenzo Bernini (1598–1680) was more acceptable to the Romans: a bronze tabernacle with spiralling columns at the main altar; a magnificent throne with angels clustered around a burst of sacred light at the end of the church; and, for the exterior, the classically simple colonnade embracing the piazza (1657).

Bernini's rival was Francesco Borromini (1599–1667), whose eccentric designs were the opposite of Bernini's classics. Many of Borromini's most famous designs hinge on a complex interplay of concave and convex surfaces, which can be seen in the undulating facades of San Carlo alle Quattro Fontane, Sant'Ivo, and Sant'Agnese in Piazza Navona (1653–63).

immense power of the Church. Andrea dal Pozzo's altar to St Ignatius in the
Gesù is particularly sumptuous.

Map,
pages
132–3

But it is the Gesù's ceiling, with Il Baciccia's painting *The Triumph of the
Name of Jesus*, that shows what baroque is all about. White statues cling to the
gilt vault, some supporting the central painting which spills out of its frame.
Here is the characteristic baroque blend of architecture, painting and sculpture,
all working to reinforce the role of a church as a place between this world and the
next. The vault of the church seems almost to dissolve into the vault of heaven.

Another Jesuit church, **Sant'Ignazio ⓭**, this time with a ceiling by Andrea
del Pozzo, is also an impressive example of baroque. To appreciate its fantastic perspective, stand in the middle of the nave and look heavenwards: the vault
seems to disappear as an ecstatic St Ignatius receives from Jesus the light he
will disperse to the four corners of the earth. Pozzo also painted a fake dome,
since the Jesuit fathers were unable to afford a real one.

Carnival Corso

Via del Corso stretches from Piazza Venezia to Piazza del Popolo, a distance
of almost 1.5 km (1 mile). Lined with elegant palaces and crowded with shoppers, this central artery has always been a good place in which to take the pulse
of the city. In ancient times it was the main route north, known as the Via Lata
(Wide Way), which gives an idea of how very narrow most ancient streets were.
Between the 18th and 19th centuries, it was the scene of the Roman Carnival,
when aristocrats and riff-raff alike used to pelt one another with flowers bons-
bons and confetti. Masked revellers abandoned all discretion and temporary balconies were attached to palaces to facilitate the ogling of ladies and the hurling

ABOVE: the Gesù.
BELOW LEFT: Via del
Corso.
BELOW: ceiling of
the Gesù, painted
by Il Baciccia.

of missiles. This chaotic setting provided a dramatic background for the climax of Hawthorne's *The Marble Faun* (1860). Alas, Rome has sobered up since it became the nation's capital, and for Carnival you must now head for Venice.

First stop on a tour of the Corso is **Palazzo Doria Pamphili ⓴** (open Fri–Wed 10am–5pm; entrance fee), home of the Galleria Doria Pamphili. The collection is superb (paintings by Titian, Caravaggio and Raphael), but nothing is labelled, so unless you're a connoisseur of 16th- and 17th-century art, buy a catalogue. The star of the collection is Velazquez's portrait of *Pope Innocent X*. Via delle Muratte, to the right off the Corso, leads to the most grandiose and famous of Rome's baroque fountains: the **Fontana di Trevi** (Trevi Fountain) ㉑ where the voluptuous Anita Ekberg frolicked in Fellini's film *La Dolce Vita* (1960).

But the ancient city rears its head even in the most up-to-date places. **Piazza Colonna ㉒**, about halfway down the Corso, is home to the Column of Marcus Aurelius (AD 180–93). Sixtus V (1585–90) crowned this column with a statue of St Paul and Trajan's Column with one of St Peter. (Sixtus was always eager to appropriate Roman triumphal symbols to Christianity: he placed many fallen, forgotten obelisks in front of churches.)

Two particularly impressive relics of the Augustan era, cleaned up and reassembled during the Fascist era, are the **Mausoleo di Augusto** (closed to the public) and the **Ara Pacis Augustae ㉓** (between the Corso and the Tiber) (open Tues–Sat 9am–6pm, Sun 9am–1pm; entrance fee). The emperor's funeral pyre burned in front of the mausoleum for five days. In the Middle Ages the ill-fated Cola di Rienzo was cremated there. For centuries the Ara Pacis, built from 13–8 BC to celebrate peace throughout the Empire, was in pieces. Fragments were to be found as far away as the Louvre in Paris and the Uffizi in Florence. Finally, in 1983, the altar was reconstructed with fragments and copies of missing parts.

ABOVE and **BELOW:** Egyptian obelisk in the Piazza del Popolo, from the 12th or 13th century BC.

The gate of Rome

Everyone – from emperors in triumph to pilgrims on foot – used to enter Rome through the **Porta del Popolo** (Porta Flaminia). On the east rises the lush green of the Pincian hill where, in the Middle Ages, the Emperor Nero's ghost was believed to wander. According to legend, a walnut tree infested with crows sprang from Nero's final resting place. In the 11th century, however, Pope Paschal II dreamt that the crows were demons and that the Virgin Mary wanted him to cut down the tree and build her a sanctuary. The existing church of **Santa Maria del Popolo** dates from the late 15th century and contains splendidly decorated chapels of different periods, with works by Pinturicchio, Raphael (the Chigi Chapel) and Caravaggio (the *Conversion of St Paul* and the *Crucifixion of St Peter*).

Take Via del Babuino, on the left of the twin baroque churches, south to **Piazza di Spagna ㉔**. The piazza is shaped like an hour glass. In the southern section is the Palazzo di Spagna, the seat of the Spanish embassy to the Vatican, which gives the square its name. But it is in the northern part that the famous **Scalinata della Trinità dei Monti** (Spanish Steps) rises. Neither New York's Times Square nor the Champs-Elysées in Paris provides a better location for watching the world go by.

Caricaturists sketch tourists; old women sell roasted chestnuts or coconuts; gypsy children solicit *lire*, often with the help of an accordion or an endearing kitten; tired sightseers rinse their hands in Pietro Bernini's fountain; backpackers sunbathe on the steps; hippies play guitars; and shoppers crowd the windows of the elegant shops below. Off this piazza stretch the most fashionable shopping streets in Rome: Via Condotti, Via Frattina, Via Borgognona. Underneath the Pincian, the quiet Via Margutta is the place to buy art.

Years ago this area was inhabited by English and American expatriates. John Keats died in the house overlooking the steps, which contains a cluttered collection of memorabilia. The **Keats and Shelley Museum** (open Mon–Fri 9am–1pm, 3–6pm, Sat 11am–2pm, 3–6pm; entrance fee) is a must for all romantic ghost seekers. Keep an eye out for plaques marking the past residences of famous foreigners. Henry James stayed in Hotel Inghilterra; Shelley in the Via Sistina and Via del Corso; George Eliot in the Via del Babuino; Goethe at 20 Via del Corso, where you can visit a museum devoted to the poet's travels in Italy (open Wed–Mon 11am–6pm; entrance fee). One of the most grandiose plaques marks James Joyce's residences at 50/52 Via Frattina. Joyce, it says, "made of his Dublin, our universe".

The bones and the bees
The street between Trinità dei Monti and Santa Maria Maggiore was cut by Sixtus V, a pope bent on improving Rome and glorifying his own name. The view down the length of the road is dramatic – culminating in the obelisk which Sixtus raised in front of Santa Maria Maggiore. Once called Strada Felice, the street now changes its name three times as it cuts through the tangled Roman streets.

Map, pages 132–3

ABOVE: Trevi Fountain. **BELOW LEFT:** the Spanish Steps. **BELOW:** detail of the Ara Pacis.

ABOVE and **BELOW:** temples in Villa Borghese park.

The first leg, Via Sistina, leads down to **Piazza Barberini** ㉕, in the centre of which is Bernini's magnificently sensual **Fontana del Tritone** (*see page 130*). The musclebound sea creature blows fiercely on a conch shell while a geyser of water shoots above him. In the base is the unmistakable coat of arms of the Barberini family: three bees. The family palace nearby is the work of, among others, Carlo Maderno, Bernini and Borromini. In the 19th century, William Wetmore Story, a second rate neoclassical sculptor from Boston, was able to rent a 50-room suite in the palace for a song, but today the Palazzo Barberini houses the **Galleria Nazionale di Arte Antica** (open Tues–Sat 9am–7pm, Sun 9am–1pm; entrance fee). Don't miss Pietro da Cortona's *The Triumph of Divine Providence*, a baroque celebration of the Barberini Pope Urban VIII – a pope who quarried the ruins of Ancient Rome so extensively that he inspired the witticism: "What the Barbarians didn't do, the Barberini did".

Via Veneto swoops off the Piazza Barberini. Before strolling along its wide streets or retiring to one of its cafés, stop at the unique and slightly disturbing **Chiesa dei Cappuccini** (open Fri–Wed 9am–noon, 3–6pm; donation) to see its cemetery. According to Catholic legend, a group of artistically and ghoulishly inclined friars decided to put the dead brothers' bones to a cautionary use. Four rooms of rococo sculptures contain a playful filigree of hip bones, a garland of spines and an array of skulls stacked as neatly as oranges and apples on a fruit vendor's stall. In case anyone should forget these are bones and begin to look on them as mere elements in an elegant design, there are also a few rotting corpses, still swathed in their humble brown robes.

The **Via Veneto** became famous after World War II as the centre of Rome's "Dolce Vita", but today it seems more sleazy than glamorous. Buy a magazine, put on your dark glasses and adjourn to one of the streetside cafés for refreshment, then move on to the Villa Borghese where you can picnic or visit the **Giardino Zoologico** ㉖ (open daily 9am–6pm; entrance fee). Near the Via Veneto entrance to the park is the **Galleria Borghese** ㉗ (daily 9am–6pm, visits by reservation only, tel: 06-32810), with many works by Bernini, Caravaggio and Raphael. If you are also interested in Italy's more recent artistic achievements, visit the **Galleria Nazionale d'Arte Moderna** ㉘ (open Tues–Sat 9am–7pm, Sun 9am–1pm; entrance fee).

To the north of the Villa Borghese is another aristocratic palace built for Julius III. The **Villa Giulia** ㉙ (open Tues–Sat 9am–7pm, Sun 9am–2pm; entrance fee) has a beautiful Renaissance garden and, inside, the fascinating Museo Nazionale di Villa Giulia, full of pre-Roman art. The Etruscan terracotta sculptures are particularly interesting. Also well worth seeking out are a touching sarcophagus of a husband and wife and a magnificent statue of Apollo.

Bernini and Borromini

From the intersection of **Via delle Quattro Fontane** (the extension of Via Sistina) and Via XX Settembre you can admire the drama of Roman urban planning: in three directions obelisks scrape the sky. The Via XX Settembre contains a number of splendid baroque churches. First is **San Carlo alle Quattro Fontane** ㉚, also

known as San Carlino. This tiny church, whose interior is the same size as one of the piers under the dome of St Peter's, was designed by Francesco Borromini (1599–1667). The undulating facade is characteristic of this eccentric architect's style. The all-white interior is a fantastic play of ovals. The financially pressed monks who commissioned the church were impressed by Borromini's ability to keep down the costs of the church – by using delicate stucco work rather than marble or gilt – without in any way lessening the beauty of the interior.

Up Via del Quirinale, off the other side of Via delle Quattro Fontane, is another oval gem by Borromini's arch rival, Gianlorenzo Bernini (1598–1680). **Sant' Andrea al Quirinale** ● offers quite a contrast to its neighbour. Every inch of this church is covered with gilt and marble. Putti ascend the wall as if in a cloud of smoke. Yet the architect's masterful, classical handling of space creates a marvellous sense of simplicity.

For another Bernini masterpiece head in the other direction to **Santa Maria della Vittoria** ●, in Largo Santa Susanna (off Via XX Settembre). Here is Bernini's sculpture of the 17th-century Spanish mystic St Theresa of Avila. The artist captures her at the moment when she was being struck by the arrow of divine love.

In order to get a sense of the size of the Roman baths, visit **Santa Maria degli Angeli** ● (near Piazza della Repubblica), a church Michelangelo created from the tepidarium of the **Terme di Diocleziano**, the largest baths in Rome, constructed between AD 298 and 306. The baths also once housed the **Museo Nazionale Romano**, but this great collection of ancient art has now moved to the newly restored **Palazzo Massimo** and **Palazzo Altemps** (open Tues–Sat 9am–7pm, Sun 9am–2pm; entrance fee), nearby in Piazza dei Cinquecento. The

Map, pages 132–3

ABOVE: gilded door-knob in Santa Maria della Vittoria.
BELOW: Bernini's *Ecstasy of St Theresa.*

collection includes such sculptures as the *Venus of Cyrene*, two copies of Myron's *Discobolus* and the Ludovisi throne. Roman wall painting is seen at its best in the delicate frescoes from the dining room of the Villa of Livia. They depict a refreshing garden scene with fruits, trees and birds, designed to sooth the digestion of the empress and her guests.

Mary and Moses

The Italian reverence for mothers perhaps explains why Rome has more churches dedicated to the Virgin Mary than to any other saint. The largest and most splendid of these is **Santa Maria Maggiore ❸** (open daily 7am–7pm), one of the four patriarchal churches of Rome. Here the mélange of architectural styles is surprisingly harmonious: early Christianity is represented in the basilican form and in the 5th-century mosaics above the architrave in the nave (binoculars are a must if you want to decipher them). Medieval input includes the Campanile (largest in Rome), the Cosmatesque pavement and the mosaic in the apse. But the overwhelming effect is baroque. The coffered gold ceiling was supposedly gilded with the gold Columbus brought from America.

If your head is spinning with the excess of gilt and marble, head down the Via Cavour to **San Pietro in Vincoli ❸**, where you will find Michelangelo's massive and dignified *Moses*. Originally the statue was to form part of an enormous freestanding tomb for Pope Julius II, but politics and constrained finances curtailed Michelangelo's imagination. Of this one statue Giorgio Vasari, artist and biographer of artists, said: "No modern work will ever approach it in beauty". Moses sits 3 metres (10 ft) high, every inch the powerful lawgiver.

ABOVE: torso of a centurion in the Museo Nazionale Romano. **BELOW:** Michelangelo's *Moses* in San Pietro in Vincoli.

The living city

During the Middle Ages, most of Rome's population was crowded either into the region between Via del Corso and the Tiber (Campus Martius to the ancients) or into Trastevere (*see page 159*) across the river. While wandering through the cobblestoned streets of these areas, especially late at night, it is easy to imagine the Rome of the medieval tyrant Cola di Rienzo, or of Pope Julius II, or even of Byron – at least until the spell is broken by the roar of a speeding scooter. An even better time to tour Trastevere or the Campo Marzio is the early morning, when you will be able to admire the facades of buildings alone, enter churches with only the faithful as companions, and watch the Romans starting their day. Windowless shops give directly onto crooked, narrow streets and workers leave their doors open for light and air. Look in and you will see bakers kneading loaves of *casareccio* bread, furniture restorers rubbing down wood with strong smelling waxes, and cobblers hammering heels onto worn boots. Children walk to school and women drag metal carts to market. Occasionally a door glides open in the side of a crumbling stucco facade to release a shiny black Fiat.

Have a *cornetto* (an Italian croissant) and a cappuccino in Piazza della Rotonda and admire the outside of the **Pantheon ❸** (open Mon–Sat 9am–6.30pm; Sun 9am–1pm; free) – the best preserved of all Ancient Roman buildings. For those who question the greatness of Roman architecture and dismiss it as inferior to Greek, the Pantheon is an eloquent answer. This perfectly proportioned round temple proves how adept the Romans were in shaping interior space. Rebuilt by the Emperor Hadrian, its architectural antecedents are not the Republican round temples – such as the one in the Forum Boarium – but the round chambers used in the baths. Western architecture owes the Romans an enormous debt for their skilful work with vaults and domes. The only light is provided by a large hole set in the centre of the dome – the *oculus* – and this means that the building has been open to the elements for nearly 2,000 years.

Near the Pantheon, in front of **Santa Maria Sopra Minerva** (closed Thurs pm), Bernini's much-loved elephant carries the smallest of Rome's obelisks. Inside the church (the only one in the Gothic style in Rome) are a chapel decorated by Fra Filippo Lippi and, to the left of the main altar, Michelangelo's statue of *Christ bearing the Cross*. Other ecclesiastical treasures are just a few blocks away. Caravaggio frescoes adorn both **San Luigi dei Francesi** (*The Calling of St Matthew, St Matthew and the Angel* and *The Martyrdom of St Matthew*) and **Sant'Agostino** (*The Madonna of the Pilgrims*). Borromini's **Sant'Ivo** is tucked into the courtyard of Palazzo Sapienza. Like San Carlino, this church's interior is dazzlingly white. Most startling, however, is its spiralling campanile.

Even the crowds of people milling around eating ice cream, the artists sitting on collapsible chairs hoping to sell their paintings, and Roman youths zooming through on their motorbikes cannot mask the elegance of **Piazza Navona** ㊲. This totally enclosed space was once the Stadium of Domitian, parts of which can still be seen outside the northern end. Hagiographers claim that when the youthful St Agnes was exposed naked in the vaulted areas of the circus beneath

Map, pages 132–3

ABOVE: oculus of the Pantheon. **BELOW LEFT:** Piazza Navona. **BELOW:** Santa Maria Maggiore marble.

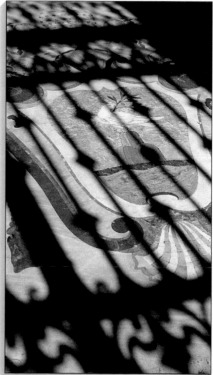

Map, pages 132–3

the church that bears her name, her hair grew to shield her. Agnes had refused to marry because she had vowed to be a virgin bride of Christ. In another version of her martyrdom, she was banished to a brothel where her chastity was miraculously preserved; a subsequent attempt to burn her was also unsuccessful; finally, she was beheaded.

The church of **Sant'Agnese in Agone** has another curvaceous facade by Borromini. His rival, Bernini, designed the **Fontana dei Quattro Fiumi** in the centre of the piazza. A popular tale claims that the statue of the Nile which faces Sant'Agnese is covering its eyes for fear the church will collapse.

Stony words

Close by, **Piazza di Pasquino** contains a battered statue that once functioned as the underground newspaper of Rome. The papal censors allowed so little criticism that irrepressible commentators attached their writings to statues in the city. The most famous satirist was Pasquino, hence the word "pasquinade".

Near the piazza is the elegant little church of **Santa Maria della Pace** ㊳. The facade and piazza may be all you can see, since the church is rarely open. If you do make it inside there are frescoes by Raphael and a beautiful cloister. To the north, Via dei Coronari is lit with torches every night. The picturesque street is full of expensive antique stores.

ABOVE: Palazzo della Cancelleria.
BELOW: fountain in Piazza Navona.
RIGHT: Via Giulia.

At the end of Via dei Cornari, take a left turn and you will soon arrive at the **Chiesa Nuova** ㊴, dedicated to St Philip Neri, without question one of the most *simpatico* saints in the calendar. He arrived in Rome in 1533 and spent the rest of his life gently trying to reform the population of this sinful city. He invited young men off the streets and into his room for informal discussions of the Gospel, prayers and song. From this simple beginning arose his oratory. St Philip refused to withdraw from the world or condemn it, preferring to work steadily and with great humour to save souls. He once advised an overly zealous penitent to wear his hairshirt on the outside of his clothes.

The baroque splendour of the Chiesa Nuova was never intended by this humble man, who had a weakness for practical jokes. But for fans of the style, Pietro da Cortona's interior is sumptuous. Behind the altar are three paintings by Rubens.

The last baroque church on this tour is perhaps the most ornate. Puccini chose **Sant'Andrea della Valle** ㊵ as a setting for the opening act of *Tosca*. Act II takes place at the nearby **Palazzo Farnese** ㊶, most splendid of Renaissance palaces and suitably intimidating as headquarters for the villainous Scarpia.

The palace is now the French Embassy and, alas for the visitor who would like to pop in to see Annibale Carracci's frescoes, it is closed to the public. Other palaces in the neighbourhood include **Palazzo della Cancelleria**, and **Palazzo Spada** (open Tues–Sat 9am–7pm, Sun 9am–1pm; entrance fee) which has a handsome gallery.

Act III of *Tosca* takes place on the west bank of the Tiber, in the notorious **Castel Sant'Angelo** prison (*see page 155*). Visiting this fortress takes us from Rome into the Vatican City, the world's smallest state, with an area of a mere 0.4 square km (100 acres). ❑

THE COLOSSEUM: BREAD AND CIRCUSES

"While the Colosseum stands, Rome shall stand;
when the Colosseum falls, Rome shall fall;
when Rome falls, the world shall fall."

The Venerable Bede's 8th-century prophecy has been taken to heart and the Colosseum shored up ever since. The ancient amphitheatre is the city's most stirring sight, a place of stupendous size and spatial harmony. The Colosseum was begun by Vespasian, inaugurated by his son Titus in AD 80, and completed by Domitian (AD 81–96). Titus used Jewish captives from Jerusalem as masons. The Colosseum had 80 numbered, arched entrances, allowing over 50,000 spectators to be seated within ten minutes. "Bread and circuses" was how Juvenal, the 2nd-century satirist, mocked the Romans who here sold their souls for free food and entertainment.

FALL AND RUIN

With the fall of the empire, the Colosseum fell into disuse. During the Renaissance, the ruins were plundered to create churches and palaces all over Rome, including Palazzo Farnese, now the French Embassy. Quarrying was only halted by Pope Benedict XIV, in the 18th century, and the site consecrated to Christian martyrs. The Colosseum was still neglected on the German poet Goethe's visit in 1787, with a hermit and beggars "at home in the crumbling vaults". In 1817 Lord Byron was enthralled by this "noble wreck in ruinous perfection", while Edgar Allan Poe, another Romantic poet, celebrated its "grandeur, gloom and glory".

During the Fascist era, Mussolini, attracted to the power which the Colosseum represented, demolished a line of buildings to create a clear view of it from his balcony on Palazzo di Venezia. An ambitious restoration programme is currently underway to make the Colosseum fit for Holy Year in the year 2000.

△ ALL AT SEA
Renaissance historians believed that, in ancient times, Roman arenas were sometimes flooded to stage mock naval battles, but there is scant evidence to suggest such a display ever took place in the Colosseum.

▽ GLADIATORIAL COMBAT
The price of failure: the Gate of Life was reserved for victorious gladiators, with vanquished gladiators doomed to the Gate of Death.

△ BEHIND THE SCENES
From the higher tiers stretch views down to the arena and a maze of passages. The arena was encircled by netting to prevent beasts escaping. The moveable wooden floor was covered in sand, the better to soak up the blood. Below, the subterranean section concealed the animal cages and sophisticated technical apparatus, from winches and mechanical lifts to ramps and trap doors.

▽ SOCIAL STRATA
Although supremely public, the Colosseum was a stratified affair. The podium, set on the lowest tier, was reserved exclusively for the emperor, senators, magistrates and Vestal Virgins. Above them sat the bourgeoisie, with the lower orders restricted to the top tier, and the populace on wooden seats in the very top rows.

◁ IMPERIAL COINAGE
Bearing the head of Emperor Vespasian, the coin depicts no grape-sucking degenerate but a professional soldier who consolidated Roman rule in Britain and Germany. As the founder of the Flavian dynasty and emperor between AD 69 and 79, he began the stadium.

◁ ROMANTIC ROME
This 18th-century view by Giovanni Volpato reflects the nostalgic sensibility of the Romantic era. Visitors on the Grand Tour were beguiled by the ruins bathed in moonlight or haunted by the sense of a lost civilisation. In Byron's words, "Some cypresses beyond the time-worn breach/Appeared to skirt the horizon, yet they stood/Within a bowshot – where the Caesars dwelt".

ENTERTAINMENT FOR THE MASSES

The Roman appetite for bloodshed was legendary, with the barbaric *munera*, or blood sports, introduced as a corrupt version of Greek games. The animals, mostly imported from Africa, included lions, elephants, giraffes, hyenas, hippos, wild horses and zebras. The contests were also a way of eliminating slaves and proscribed sects, Christians and common criminals, political agitators and prisoners of war. Variants included battles involving nets, swords and tridents, mock hunts and freak shows with panthers pulling chariots or cripples pitted against clowns. Seneca, Nero's tutor, came expecting "fun, wit and some relaxation" but was dumbfounded by the butchery and cries of: "Kill him! Lash him! Why does he meet the sword so timidly?"

In AD 248, the millennium of the founding of Rome was celebrated by contests involving 2,000 gladiators and the slaying of tame giraffes and hippos as well as big cats. Although convicted criminals were routinely fed to the lions, Christian martyrdom in the arena is less well documented. However, St Ignatius of Antioch, who described himself as "the wheat of Christ", was dutifully devoured by lions in AD 107. Gladiatorial combat was banned in AD 404, while animal fights ended in the following century.

THE VATICAN AND TRASTEVERE

From the spirituality of St Peter's, with its
extensive museums and magnificent art treasures,
to the earthiness of Rome's medieval quarter

Map,
pages
132–3

The west bank of the Tiber offers contrasting experiences. Cheek by jowl with the Vatican, with all its papal pomp, is the working-class district of Trastevere, with its tenements, narrow streets, and lively street life.

As you cross the Tiber using Ponte Sant'Angelo, it is not the domed heart of the Vatican you see first, however, but the almost windowless walls of the medieval citadel, the **Castel Sant'Angelo** ❷ (open daily, except 2nd and 4th Tues of month, 8am–10pm; entrance fee). Back in AD 139, this was the site of the mausoleum of the Emperor Hadrian. Later it became a fortress and prison, then a residence to which the popes could flee in times of turbulence. Today it is a museum full of 16th-century furnishings and frescoes. Puccini's heroine, Tosca, plunged to her death from the parapet where visitors now come to admire the views. Towering over the battlements is a gigantic statue of St Michael, the war-like archangel after whom the castle is named.

The Vatican City

From Castel Sant'Angelo, Via della Conciliazione leads to St Peter's, at the heart of the Vatican City. If size were the only measure of a nation's power or importance, the Vatican would warrant hardly any attention at all. Yet the Vatican serves as an exception to the rule that tiny nations are famous for little more than their postage stamps.

For centuries the Vatican was the unchallenged centre of the Western world. Its symbolic significance, both past and present, and its enduring international role, as both a religious and a diplomatic force, have put this tiny city-state on a par with nations many million times larger. No matter how secular our world has become, divine authority seems still to count and to make the Vatican much more than a geographic oddity, much more than the academic footnote it might otherwise be.

Covering a total area of slightly more than 40 hectares (100 acres), Vatican City is by far the world's smallest independent sovereign entity. What other nation is as small as New York's Central Park? What other nation can lock its gates at midnight, as the Vatican's door-keepers do each night, opening them only at the ring of a bell? What other nation can be crossed at a leisurely pace in well under half an hour?

In Imperial Roman days, the lower part of what is now Vatican City was an unhealthy bog, an area famous among caesars and consuls for its vinegary wine, snakes and diseases. But in the 1st century AD, the dowager empress Agrippina had the Vatican Valley drained and planted with imperial gardens. Under Caligula and Nero, the area was turned over to the circus. Chariot racing and executions – including that of St Peter – were regular events on what later became St Peter's Square.

LEFT: view from St Peter's.
BELOW: Swiss Guards enjoying some time off.

The Lateran Treaty of 1929, concluded between Pope Pius XI and Benito Mussolini, established the present territorial limits of the Vatican. The city is roughly trapezoidal in shape, bounded by medieval walls on all sides except on the corner, where the opening of St Peter's Square marks the border with Rome and the rest of Italy. Of the six openings to the Vatican, only three are for public use: the Piazza, the Arco delle Campane (south of St Peter's Basilica), and the entrance to the Vatican Museums. Pius XI had a special Vatican railway station built in the early 1930s, a facility which no paying passenger has ever used (even popes use it very infrequently). A heliport has been built on a spot where British diplomats whiled away their days during World War II.

Aside from an impressive array of palaces and office buildings, there is also a Vatican prison, a supermarket, and the printing press, which churns out the daily *L'Osservatore Romano* and scripts in a wide range of languages, from Coptic to Ecclesiastical Georgian to Tamil. In short, the Vatican is much more than an oversized museum.

Apart from the area enclosed by the Vatican walls, the Vatican State comprises several other buildings in Rome, plus the Pope's summer residence southeast of the city, Castel Gandolfo.

Piazza San Pietro

Bernini's spectacular, colonnaded **Piazza San Pietro** ❸ is, according to one's viewpoint, either the welcoming embrace of the Mother Church or her grasping claws. The Via della Conciliazione, constructed in 1937 to commemorate the reconciliation between Mussolini and Pope Pius XI, changed the original impact of the space. Before this throughfare provided a monumental approach to St Peter's, the entrance was by way of smaller streets, winding through the old Borgo and arriving, finally, in the enclosed open space, with the biggest church in the world at one end and an enormous Egyptian obelisk in the centre.

BELOW: a public Mass draws thousands to St Peter's Square.

Subjects of the Holy See

To be one of the 400 or so citizens with a Vatican passport is to belong to one of the world's most exclusive clubs – the privilege of citizenship hinges on a direct and continuous relationship with the Holy See; when ties are severed, the privilege is lost. The pope himself carries passport No. 1 and he rules absolutely over Vatican City.

The word "pope" comes from the Greek *pappas*, meaning "father". Despite two millennia having passed since St Peter first assumed the mantle, the pope's role remains paternal, alternating between concern for humanity and stern warnings against theological or spiritual deviation. John Paul II, elected in 1978, has asserted his moral authority vigorously. His 1993 encyclical (a letter to all Roman Catholic bishops) denounced contraception, homosexuality and other infringements of the faith as "intrinsically evil".

The facts and figures

There have been 262 popes. The shortest reign of a pope was that of Stephen II, who died four days after his election in March 752. At the other extreme, the 19th-century's Pius IX, famous for his practical jokes and his love of billiards, headed the Holy See for 32 years. The youngest pope on record, John XI, was just 16 when he took the helm in 931; the oldest, Gregory IX, managed to survive 14 years after his election in 1227 at the age of 86.

While the great majority have been of either Roman or Italian extraction, Spain, Greece, Syria, France and Germany have all been represented, and there has been at least one of African birth (Miltiades, 311–314), and one hailing from England (Hadrian IV, 1154–59). John Paul II is the first Pole to lead the Catholic Church. At least 14 popes abdicated or were deposed from office. Ten popes met violent deaths, including a record three in a row in the 10th century.

The process of electing a new pope is necessarily unique, as the papacy is the world's only elective monarchy. Members of the Sacred College of Cardinals, a largely titular body of 120 bishops and archbishops, are sealed into the Sistine Chapel soon after the death knell tolls in the Vatican Palace. They cannot leave until a new successor has been chosen. Voting can proceed by acclamation, whereby the cardinals all shout the same name at the same time; by scrutiny, in which four ballots are cast daily until one candidate has captured a two-thirds majority plus one; or, as a last resort, by compromise.

All modern popes have been selected by the second method. Paper ballots are burned after each tally, and onlookers watch the chapel's chimney for dark smoke, which indicates an inconclusive vote, or white plumes, which denote a winner (electors are provided with special chemicals so that there can be no mistake). Finally the cardinal dean announces to the faithful, "Habemus Papam", and the chosen cardinal appears in one of three robes (sized small, medium and large) kept on hand for the occasion. The coronation takes place on the following day.

RIGHT: part of the substantial gardens behind St Peter's and the Vatican Museums.

ABOVE: decorative marble in the Vatican Museums.

BELOW: Roman torso in the Vatican's Chiaramonti Museum.

Church, museum, mausoleum; the Basilica di San Pietro, **St Peter's** (open daily 7am–7pm, except during papal audiences (some Wed mornings); modest dress code) is all three. No other temple surpasses it in terms of historical significance or architectural splendour. Some may feel the immensity of the interior is more suited to moving commuters through a railway station than to inspiring the intimate act of prayer, but the many architects and patrons of St Peter's intended the building to symbolise worldly power as much as spiritual piety. Just about every important Renaissance and baroque architect from Bramante onwards had a hand in the design of St Peter's. The idea for rebuilding the original 4th-century basilica had been around since the mid-5th century but not until Julius II became pope did a complete reconstruction get underway. Bramante was succeeded by Raphael, Baldassare Peruzzi, Michelangelo (usually credited with the dome), Giacomo della Porta and Bernini.

The vast size of the interior is offset by its proportions: thus the cherubic putti are actually 2 metres (6 ft) tall, as are the mosaic letters of the frieze that runs around the church. On the right, as you walk in, is Michelangelo's *Pietà*, an inspiration to beholders ever since the sculptor finished it in 1500, at the age of 25. At the end of the nave is the bronze statue of *St Peter*, its toe worn away by the kisses of pilgrims.

Over the high altar, which is directly above the tomb of St Peter, rises Bernini's garish bronze *baldacchino*, resembling the canopy of an imperial bed. Pope Urban VIII stripped the bronze from the Pantheon. But Bernini outdid himself in the design for the *Cathedra Petri* (the Chair of St Peter) in the apse. Four gilt bronze figures of the church fathers hold up the chair.

Above, light streams through the golden glass of a window crowned by a dove (symbol of the Holy Ghost). The chair bears a relief of Christ's command to Peter to "feed his sheep". Thus the position of the pope is explained and bolstered by Christ's words and the teachings of the Church fathers, and blessed by the Holy Ghost.

Further confirmation of the pope's sacred trust is found in Christ's words inscribed on the dome: "You are Peter and on this rock I will build my Church and I will give you the keys to the kingdom of heaven".

The Vatican Museums

The **Musei e Gallerie del Vaticano** 🄬 (open summer: Mon–Fri 10am–4pm, Sat 10am–1pm, winter: Mon–Sat 10am–1pm; entrance fee) merit a lifetime's study. But for those who have only a few hours, some sights shouldn't be missed. The **Museo Pio-Clementino** contains the pope's collection of antiquities. Be sure to visit the Belvedere Courtyard, home of the celebrated and cerebral *Apollo Belvedere* and the contrasting muscle-bound, sensual *Laocoön*. The Vatican **Pinacoteca** contains superb paintings including Raphael's *Madonna of Foligno* and *Transfiguration*. There are also rooms covered in frescoes: the Stanze di Raffaello comprise three rooms painted by Raphael. Downstairs, colourful frescoes by Pinturicchio decorate the Appartamento Borgia.

But the triumph of fresco painting, not only of the Vatican Palace, but of the entire world, is the **Cappella Sistina** (Sistine Chapel). The walls are covered in paintings by Botticelli, Pinturicchio and Ghirlandaio, but the breathtaking star of the show is Michelangelo's ceiling, begun in 1508 and completed by 1512. It is a shallow barrel vault divided into large and small panels tracing the history of the Creation.

No reproduction can ever do justice to the interplay of painting and architecture, to the drama of the whole chapel, alive with colour (considerably brighter since the controversial cleaning of the frescoes in the 1980s) and human emotion. "All the world hastened to behold this marvel and was overwhelmed, speechless with astonishment," Vasari wrote. The astonishment is no less today than it was in the Renaissance.

Trastevere

The heart of medieval Trastevere, literally "across the Tiber", is southeast of the Vatican City. Here you can find many reasonably priced restaurants and, at **Porta Portese** ⑮, a popular flea market on Sunday. Traditionally, Trastevere has been a working-class neighbourhood with strong communist leanings.

South of Viale di Trastevere are two churches worth visiting. **Santa Cecilia** ⑯ was built on top of the house of a Christian martyr whom the Roman authorities attempted to scald to death in her own *caldarium* (hot bath). When this failed, she was sentenced to decapitation, but three blows failed to sever her head and she lived for a further three days (enough time to consecrate her house as a church). Carlo Maderno's touching statue of the saint curled in a foetal position was inspired by his observations when her tomb was opened in 1599.

Map, pages 132–3

ABOVE: stained glass in the Vatican Museums. **BELOW:** *Fire in the Borgo*, in the Stanze di Raffaello.

Map,
pages
132–3

*Bramante's
Tempietto, next to
San Pietro in
Montorio, was built
in 1502. It was the
first High
Renaissance
building in Rome,
and an important
homage to antiquity.*

BELOW: Castel
Sant'Angelo. **RIGHT:**
inside St Peter's.

A contrastingly sublime statue of a woman in her death throes is Bernini's *Blessed Luisa Albertoni* in nearby **San Francesco a Ripa**. This late work of the master captures even more powerfully than his St Theresa the conflict between joy and sorrow felt by a woman who is between this world and the next.

In the piazza of the same name, **Santa Maria in Trastevere** ❼ is one of the oldest churches in Rome. It boasts some beautiful mosaics illustrating the life of Mary (this was the first of many Roman churches to be dedicated to the Virgin).

After these sobering places of worship, preoccupied with the horrors of this world and the glories of the next, it is a relief to come to the **Villa Farnesina** ❽ (open Tues–Sat 9am–1pm; entrance fee), a jewel of the Renaissance, worldly and pagan. A ceiling fresco by Raphael details the love of Cupid and Psyche. The figures are robust, fleshy, almost Rubenesque. Breasts and buttocks are unabashedly displayed in a rollicking sea of banqueteers. In the next room, Raphael's *Galatea* captures the moment when the nymph, safe from the clutches of the cyclops Polyphemus, looks round.

Upstairs, Baldassare Peruzzi, who designed the entire villa, devised a fantastic *trompe l'oeil*. The room seems to open upon a restful village scene. In the bedroom is Sodoma's erotic painting *The Wedding of Alexander and Roxanne*.

To reach another important Renaissance monument, this time ecclesiastical, climb the steps up the Gianicolo to **San Pietro in Montorio** ❾. In the courtyard is Bramante's Tempietto, a circular church that marks what was once mistakenly believed to be the site of St Peter's martyrdom. Climb a little further to the Fontana Paola, an impressive baroque monument that is now a busy car wash.

The shady **Passeggiata del Gianicolo** provides panoramic views over the city. You should be able to pick out some of your favourite monuments. Easiest to spot are the flat dome of the Pantheon, the twin domes of Santa Maria Maggiore and the Victor Emmanuel Monument.

Into the bowels of the earth

Visitors with more time in Rome should try to see remains from the early Christian era. The secretive beginnings of Christianity are recalled in **Sant'Agnese fuori le Mura** ❺⓪, about 2 km (1¼ miles) beyond Michelangelo's Porta Pia on the Via Nomentana. Beneath the church run extensive catacombs where the martyred Roman maiden St Agnes was buried.

Also in the complex is the incomparable Santa Costanza, the mausoleum of Constantine's daughter. The ambulatory of this elegant round building is encrusted with some of Rome's most beautiful mosaics.

And for those not averse to tortuous tunnels winding endlessly past burial niches dusty with disintegrated bones, there are countless catacombs outside the walls of Rome. The best way to see them is to spend a day on the picturesque Via Appia Antica. You can picnic amid the remains of the Villa of the Quintilii or an unnamed crumbling edifice overrun with wildflowers and lizards. Above ground sits what Byron called the "stern round tower" of the Tomba di Cecilia Metella. Below spread the **Catacombs of St Callisto**, the most famous in Rome (open Thur–Tues 8.30am–noon, 2–5pm; entrance fee) and those of Saints Sebastian and Domitilla. ❏

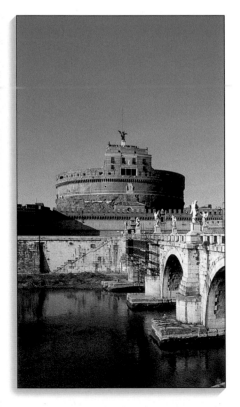

ROME'S ENVIRONS

Explore ancient towns, villas set among beautiful gardens and a reconstructed monastery, then visit the Etruscan tombs to gain a vivid insight into a vanished world

The Fascists boasted that they represented the continuation of Ancient Rome. The official art of the regime appropriated forms of Roman grandeur. Mosaics in the style of Ancient Roman floors pave the avenue and decorate the walls of the **Foro Italico** ❶, the ambitious sports centre created in 1931 northwest of the capital. Bulky square columns support the Palazzo della Civiltà del Lavoro – commonly called the "Square Colosseum" – at EUR (**Esposizione Universale di Roma**) ❷, an area south of Rome. Sixty colossal statues of athletes adorn the Stadio Olimpico in the Foro Italico. Stark lines and impressive bulk characterise the church of SS Pietro e Paolo at EUR. The aesthetic of the regime did succeed in creating some striking effects, but mostly the result was phony grandeur. In the city itself, urban planners ruthlessly drove roads through areas of historical importance, tearing down medieval quarters, which they considered an inheritance of dark times, and ripping through the very heart of Rome a triumphal way for the new eagles of the regime.

From this point of view, EUR, an area undeveloped before the Fascist era, is the least offensive of Il Duce's efforts in town planning. In 1938 Mussolini undertook to build, with the designs of Marcello Piacentini, a magnificent Third Rome which would be the natural successor to Imperial Rome and the Rome of the Renaissance. Plans for an exposition in 1942 to commemorate 20 years of Fascism were overtaken by World War II, and the overall design was only partially completed. In the 1950s new buildings were added, government offices and museums moved here and EUR evolved into a residential quarter.

Apart from architectural interest, the EUR has a number of interesting museums, including the **Museo Nazionale Preistorico ed Etnografico** (Prehistorical and Ethnographic Museum; open Tues–Sun 9am–1pm; entrance fee) and the **Museo della Civiltà Romana** (open Tues–Sat; Sun till 1pm; entrance fee), devoted to the history of Rome. The latter contains the famous *plastico di Roma*, a reconstruction of the city in the time of Constantine.

Ancient apartment dwellers

The town of **Ostia Antica** ❸ (open daily 9am–1 hour before sunset; entrance fee) was founded around the end of the 4th century BC as a fortified city to guard the mouth of the Tiber. Later it developed into the commercial port of Rome as well as its naval base. By the time of Constantine, Ostia had turned into a residential town for middle- and lower-class Romans. Ostia's ruins rival those of Pompeii for showing the layout of an ancient Italian city. Houses unearthed in Ostia offer valuable insights into the type of dwellings the same classes presumably had in Rome. Each block contained

LEFT: the Teatro Marittimo, at Hadrian's Villa, near Tivoli. **BELOW:** statuary in EUR's Museo della Civiltà Romana.

ABOVE: sculpture in the Insula dei Dipinti, Ostia Antica.

a four-storey house with numerous rooms, built in brick, reaching a maximum height of 15 metres (49 ft). Each room had a window, covered in mica rather than glass. The *domus*, the typical Pompeiian residence built for the very rich, usually on one floor only, was very rare in Ostia. The Roman theatre, enlarged in the 2nd century by Septimius Severus to hold 2,700 people, houses the summer season of the Teatro di Roma.

The **Lido di Ostia** ❹ is an overcrowded but popular seaside resort. Naturists can drive about 8 km (5 miles) south to the laid-back beaches of Tor Vaianica.

Palestrina

The ancient **Praeneste** (modern Palestrina) ❺ is one of the oldest towns of Latium. According to myth, it was founded by Telegonus, son of Ulysses and Circe. The town was flourishing in the 8th century BC and it wasn't until the 4th century that it became a subject of Rome. Later, during the civil war between Marius and Sulla, Marius fled to Praeneste, which was besieged by Sulla's troops and eventually destroyed. But Sulla wanted to make amends and so ordered the reconstruction of the sanctuary of Fortuna Primigenia, containing an oracle. The temple, which occupied an area of about 32 hectares (79 acres), was one of the grandest of antiquity. It comprised a series of terraces on the slopes of Mount Ginestro connected by ramps. Its cult lasted until the 4th century AD when the temple was abandoned. In the Middle Ages a new town rose on its ruins. In 1944 bombs destroyed the part of the town which stood on the third terrace, bringing the temple to light and prompting excavations. The **Museo Nazionale Archeologico Prenestino** (open Mon–Sat 9am–6pm; Sun 9am–1pm; entrance fee) houses many of the local finds including the incomparable Barberini Mosaic.

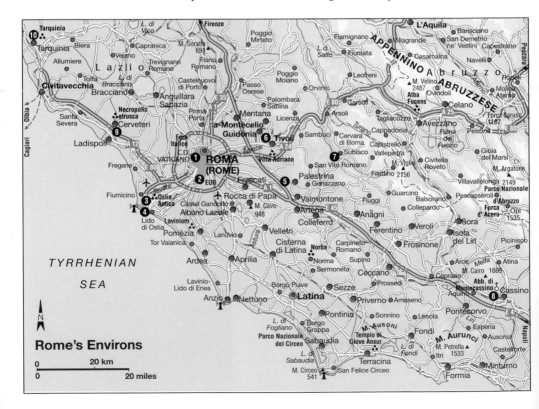

Rome's Environs

Tivoli

At the height of the Roman Empire, the ancient site of **Tibur** (Tivoli) , on the lower slopes of the Sabine Hills, was a favourite retreat for poets and Rome's wealthier citizens. The lavish villas scattered around sacred woods and scenic waterfalls attracted such famous visitors as Horace, Catullus, Maecenas, Sallust and the Emperor Trajan. In the year AD 117 the Emperor Hadrian began building his luxurious retirement home on the gently sloping plain below the foothills on which Tivoli stands. **Hadrian's Villa** (open daily 9am–1 hour before sunset; entrance fee), which occupies 73 hectares (180 acres), was the largest and richest in the Roman Empire. Hadrian wanted to recreate the monuments and places which had impressed him most during his extensive travelling in the East (the peaceful Canopus, for example, was modelled on a sanctuary of Serapis near Egyptian Alexandria), but Hadrian's overall conception goes beyond mere imitation. The endless succession of terraces, water basins and baths is a joyful reaction against functionality and common sense, but the design doesn't resort to extravagant artifice. Instead, it is a rigorous, geometrical, classical controlling of nature.

The building standing at the heart of the complex, which a romantic archaeologist previously labelled Teatro Marittimo, is a good example of this. It is a circular building with a columned portico and a moated island in the middle. The effect is metaphysical. It suggests escape from reality, retreat into the memory, even the lucid contemplation of death.

The spirit which pervades Tivoli's **Villa d'Este** (open daily 9am–1 hour before sunset; closed Mon in winter; entrance fee), the sumptuous residence which Cardinal Ippolito d'Este had the skilful Pirro Ligorio transform from a Benedictine convent, is very different. The palace is light and gay; with its facade overlooking the park and rooms decorated with frescoes, it is a typical Renaissance mansion. Ippolito, one of the Dukes of Este, was more absorbed by mundane business than spiritual cares. But the real splendour here lies in the symmetrically terraced garden which slopes down the surrounding hillside, covered with luxuriant vegetation, and the unrestrained play of water.

Water here is the prime element. Long, quiet pools, escorted by rows of elegiac cypresses extending into the distance, suggest infinity. Water spouts from obelisks or gurgles from the mouths of mythological creatures and monsters, or gaily springs from the nipples of a sphinx or the multiple-breasted Artemis of Ephesus. In this monument, dedicated to the ephemeral, in this superb triumph of theatricality, are the beginnings of the baroque.

Monastic foundations

Subiaco already existed when the Emperor Nero began building his villas overlooking one of the three artificial lakes he had created from the waters of the River Aniene. The slaves employed in the construction of the dam and villa founded the town. Five centuries later a rich young man from Norcia, named Benedict, came here in search of a place for meditation and prayer. He stayed for three years, living in a cavern, now known

ABOVE: stone mask in Ostia's theatre, and (**BELOW**) mosaic in the ancient baths.

ABOVE: entrance mosaic for Villa d'Este, and (**BELOW**) the villa's gardens and frescoes.

as the Sacro Speco (Holy Grotto). Subiaco, considered the birthplace of Western monasticism, now comprises a series of convents with their numerous cloisters and churches, bell towers, chapels decorated with frescoes and grottoes hewn out of the mountainside, all connected by picturesque stairs. The complex is one of the most interesting sights in the region.

Around AD 529 Benedict and his faithful monks left Subiaco and moved to **Montecassino** ❽ (open daily 9am–12.30pm, 3.30pm–sunset) to continue their mystical experience. Here they established one of the most important religious and cultural institutions of the Middle Ages. Five centuries after Benedict's death in 543, the abbey he had founded was one of the richest in the world. The illuminated manuscripts, frescoes and mosaics were so skilfully executed that they became models for others throughout the rest of medieval Europe.

During World War II, Montecassino rose to prominence once more. After the American forces entered Naples, Montecassino became the German's front-line (the so-called Gustave Line) designed to defend the environs of Rome. When repeated attacks by the Allies failed to penetrate the powerfully strengthened bulwark, a decision was made to bomb. It resulted in the total destruction of Montecassino. The ancient abbey was swept away. What one sees today is a faithful, loving reconstruction of what existed before the catastrophe.

Cerveteri

Before Rome was the capital of Italy, capital of the popes, or capital of the world, Italy had a highly refined civilisation: that of the Etruscans. Their zest for life and emphasis on physical vitality has fascinated many, including D.H. Lawrence, who saw them as a happy contrast to the puritanical Romans.

The small medieval town of **Cerveteri** ❾, north of Rome on the Via Aurelia, was built on the site of the Etruscan town of Caere. In the 6th and 5th centuries BC, Caere was one of the most populated towns of the Mediterranean. It had strong ties with Hellenic lands, the influence of whose merchants and artists made Caere the centre of a lively and sophisticated cultural life. Its decline began in AD 384, when Pyrgi harbour, its main port, was devastated by a Greek incursion. Eventually the rude, haughty, still barbaric strength of rising Rome blindly wiped away what had been a refined and joyous civilisation. Nothing remains today of the ancient town of Caere, bar a few walls.

Caere's necropolis occupies a hill outside the city proper. From here it could be seen from the ramparts of the city, gay with painted houses and temples. The oldest tombs (8th century BC) have a small circular well carved into the stone where the urns containing the ashes of the dead were placed. (Two modes of burial, cremation and inhumation, continued side by side for centuries.) The first chamber-tombs, also cut into the stone and covered with rocky blocks and mounds (*tumuli*), appeared as early as the beginning of the 7th century BC. The noble Etruscans were either enclosed in great sarcophagi with their effigies on top, or laid out on stone beds in their chamber tombs.

Excavations of the tombs not already rifled – the Romans were the first collectors of Etruscan antiquities – revealed goods of gold, silver, ivory, bronze and ceramic. The vases show strong Greek influence as well as the excellent quality of the Etruscan craftmanship. Much of this material is now on display in the **Museum of Cerveteri** (open Tues–Sun 9am–7pm; free), housed in the Ruspoli Castle, in the Museo di Villa Giulia in Rome, and in the Vatican Museums (*see page 158*).

ABOVE: decorative waterspout at Villa d'Este. **BELOW:** Roman statue on the canal at Tivoli.

Tarquinia

The Etruscan town of **Tarquinia** ❿ stood on a hill northwest of the picturesque medieval town bearing the same name. The town existed as early as the 9th century BC and two centuries later was at its height. In 1924 the **Museo Nazionale Tarquinese** (open Tues–Sun 9am–7pm; entrance fee) was founded. In it are many Etruscan treasures, including the famous terracotta winged horses.

The **Necropolis of Tarquinia** (open Tues–Sun 9am–1 hour before sunset; entrance fee), together with that of Caere, is the most important Etruscan necropoli. It stands on a hill south of the original town, occupying an area 5 km (3 miles) long and 1 km (⅔ mile) wide. Some tombs are painted with frescoes that are not only the most important example of Etruscan painting but also a precious document of the life of the Etruscans, their costumes and beliefs. Horizontal ribbons of bright colours frame the animated scenes below: the banqueters and musicians in the Tomba dei Leopardi; the hunters in the Tomba del Cacciatore; the erotic scenes in the Tomba dei Tori; the prancing dancers, diving dolphins and soaring birds of the Tomba della Leonessa; the beautiful maiden from the Velcha family in the Tomba di Polifemo o dell'Orco. Ironically, visitors often leave these dusty houses of death feeling shored up by a renewed faith in life and its many joys and mysteries.

THE NORTH

Above all the sense of going down into Italy – the delight of seeing the North melt slowly into the South – of seeing Italy gradually crop up in bits and vaguely latently betray itself – until finally at the little frontier village of Isella, where I spent the night, it lay before me warm and living and palpable ...

—HENRY JAMES (from his *Letters*, Vol. 1, ed. Leon Edel)

For centuries most travellers arrived in Italy from the north. They crossed the mountains from Switzerland or France and often, if physically fit and romantically minded – as was the young Henry James – they made part of the journey on foot. This way Italy came into focus gradually, as they left the cold north behind and made their way south from the lakes to Milan. From there, the cities of the Po Valley beckoned.

If possible, this is still the best way to approach northern Italy. Rather than rush through, with your eyes on the train schedule and your mind checking off each town you have "done", see fewer cities, but see them well. Each one is so rich in history and art that it merits weeks. After all, this is the Italy of Shakespeare – *Romeo and Juliet* (Verona), *The Taming of the Shrew* (Padua) – and of medieval communes and Renaissance princes. The great families – the Visconti in Milan, the Gonzaga in Mantua, the della Scala in Verona – are still remembered for the artistic triumphs, as well as the political scandals, of their courts.

In this section of the book we pass from Byzantine Venice to the great cities of the Veneto – Padua, Verona and Vicenza – magnets for university students since the Middle Ages; and then to Milan, the style and shopping capital of Italy, via the magnificent glaciated landscapes of the Alps and the Italian Lake District.

Northern Italians, though generally more aloof and self-contained than the more gregarious southerners, are always pleased to answer questions and make suggestions, always willing to spare a moment to give a stranger a little-known fact or their personal opinion on a historical personage. Quite possibly that native will bear more than a slight resemblance to the figures in the 15th-century frescoes of the local *duomo* – in these regions, the past is always present. ❑

PRECEDING PAGES: brightly painted houses on the Venetian island of Burano.
LEFT: a snow-fed waterfall in the Valle d'Aosta.

VENICE

… out of the wave her structures rise
As from the stroke of the Enchanter's wand
—LORD BYRON *Childe Harold's Pilgrimage* (1812)

Maps,
pages
190 & 174

When Lord Byron arrived in Venice in 1810, the "Queen of the Adriatic" had been in decline for many years. Though nonetheless enchanted by the beauty of the city, the poet describes her palaces as "crumbling to the shore". The seeds of decline were sown at the turn of the 15th century when the Portuguese stripped Venice of its monopoly of the spice trade. A decade later the League of Cambrai put an end to Venice's hold on crucial cities on the mainland. But even if Venice has been on a downward trend for more than five centuries, it remains one of the most spectacular urban displays in the annals of cultural history. It is not only tourists who are captivated by its charms. For centuries the city has lifted poets, painters and writers to new heights of inspired vision. Proust, James, Waugh and Hemingway are just a handful of the writers who have found her irresistible; few other cities in the world have a more prolific and talented school of painters, from Bellini and Giorgione through Titian and Tintoretto to Tiepolo and Guardi.

Built on over 100 islets, supported by millions of wooden stakes and linked by 400 bridges, Venice is the only city in the world which is built entirely on water. The greatest advantage of this, apart from the obvious aesthetic appeal, is the absence of cars. The biggest disadvantage is the fact that the city is prone to problems of flooding. The sense of precariousness, associated with the city for centuries, inevitably adds to the fascination for the visitor. There is always a feeling that once you turn your back on all this fragile but vibrant glory, the islands, once inhabited by refugees fleeing the hordes of Attila the Hun, will crumble and disappear like a mirage into the sea.

However, Venice's most recent devastation was not caused by water but by fire. In January 1996 La Fenice, its historic opera house – where Verdi's *La Traviata* and *Rigoletto* were first performed – was razed to the ground. Its slow, painstaking rebuilding – which will be as far as possible a replica of the old opera house – is taking some years and consuming funds which would otherwise have been spent on saving the city from the pollution and floods. Ironically, the opera has burned down and been rebuilt before – *fenice* means phoenix.

St Mark's Square

The heart of Venice is the vast **Piazza San Marco ❶**. Described by Napoleon as the most elegant drawing room in Europe, this is the great architectural showpiece of Venice. With its pigeons, café bands and exotic shops under the arcades, it is also the hub of tourist Venice. At one end of the piazza, crouching like an enormous, dark amphibious reptile, the great Basilica di San Marco (St Mark's Basilica) invites visitors to explore its mysterious depths.

LEFT: the ornate Torre dell'Orologio.
BELOW: a gondolier.

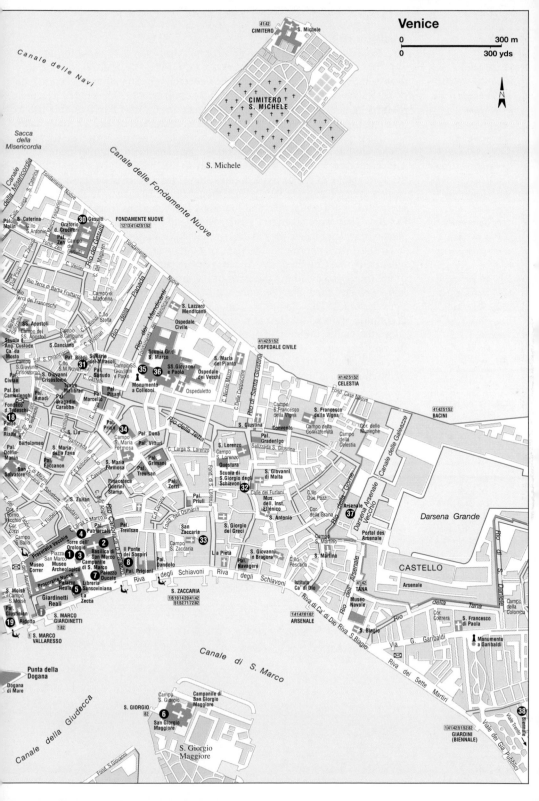

Venice

0   300 m

0   300 yds

N

Canale delle Navi

Sacca
della
Misericordia

Canale delle Fondamente Nuove

41.42 CIMITERO   S. Michele

CIMITERO
S. MICHELE

S. Michele

FONDAMENTE NUOVE
12 13 41 42 51 52

Canale delle Fondamente Nuove

S. Caterina
Pal. Molin
S. Antonio
C.llo
S. Antonio

Oratorio
d. Crociferi
Pal. Zen
Campo
dei
Gesulti

30 Gesulti

Fond. Toscani

Rio dei Gesulti

Rio dei Magbani

C. Venier

Rio Terra di Barba Fruttarol

Campo d.
Madonna

Rio della Panada

C.llo
Stella

S. Lazzaro
Mendicanti

Ospedale
Civile

OSPEDALE CIVILE
41 42 51 52

Scuola Gr. di
S. Marco

SS. Giovanni
e Paolo

S. Maria
del Pianto

Ospedale
dei Vecchi

Ospedaletto

35 36

Monumento
a Colleoni

CELESTIA
41 42 51 52

Fond. delle Case Nuove

BACINI
41 42 51 52

SS. Apostoli
Campo dei
SS. Apostoli
Scuola
Ang. Custode
Ca' da
Mosto

S. Canciano
Campo S. Canciano

C. Widman

Rio dei Mendicanti

C. Nicolo Massa

Campo
S.Francesco
della Vigna

S. Francesco
della Vigna

Cor. delle
Muneghe

Canale delle Galeazze

Campo
S. Giovanni
Crisostomo

Pal. Boldu
S.M. Nova?
S. Maria
dei Miracoli

Pal. Sanudo
C. Castelli

SS. Giovanni
e Paolo

C. Delle Cappuccine

S. Giovanni
Crisostomo
Ca' Civran

31

Rio di S. Caterina

Teatro
Malibran
C. Pali
Bragadin
Caraba

Pal. Priuli
Pal. Sanudo

Pal.
Pisani

S. Maria
del Pianto

Rio di Santa Giustina

Fondaco
d. Tedeschi
18
Ponte
di
Rialto

Pal. dei
Camerlenghi
Pal.
Amadi

S. Lio

34

Pal. Donà
Pal. Vitturi

Campo
S. Maria
Formosa

Convento

Campo della
Celestia

Campo
della
Celestia

Bartolomeo
Pal.
Dolfin-Manin

S. Maria
della Fava
Pal.
Faccanon

Pal.
Marcello

Pal.
Grimani

S. Giustina

Questura

Portal des
Arsenale

Darsena Grande

San
Salvatore
C. d. Merceria
Merceria 2 April S. Salvatore

S. Antonio
C. Cassellaria

Pal.
Trevisan

Pinacoteca
Querini
Stamp.

Campo
S. Lorenzo

C. Larga S. Lorenzo

S. Lorenzo

Pal.
Gradenigo
Salizzada S. Giustina

Cor. delle Galeazze

Darsena Arsenale
Vecchio

37

CASTELLO

S. Zulian

Pal.
Zorzi

Scuola di
S. Giorgio degli
Schiavoni
32

S. Giovanni
di Malta

Calle dei Furlani

Mus.
dell. Inst.
Ellenico

Cor.
della Grana

C.llo
Due Pozzi

Arsenale

Canale dell'Arsenale

Torre dell'
Orologio
Basilica di
San Marco
Campanile
di S. Marco

2

Pal.
Priuli

C.Ilo Colpa
Rio di S. Lorenzo
Fond. dell' Osmarin

San
Zaccaria

S. Giorgio
dei Greci

S. Antonio

Cor.
del Forno

Arsenale

Procuratie Vecchie
Piazza
San Marco
1 3
Museo
Correr
Museo
Archeologico

4

Il Ponte
dei Sospiri

Pal.
Patriarcale

Pal.
Trevisan

33

Campo
S. Zaccaria

La Pietà

S. Giovanni
in Bragora

TANA
41 42

Cor. della Tana

Rio della Tana

Campo
della
Colomba

Procuratie Nuove
Palazzo
Reale

Museo
Correr
Libreria
Sansoviniana

8

Pal.
Ducale
Pal. Prigioni

Pal.
Dandolo

Pal.
Navagero

S. Giovanni
Museo
Navale

S. Martino

S. Martino

S. Moisè
Campo
S. Moisè

5

La
Zecca

7

Riva

degli

Schiavoni

S. ZACCARIA
1 6 10 14 20 41 42
51 52 71 72 82

Riva

degli

Schiavoni

C.llo
Pescaria

Istituto
Ca' di Dio

Riva di Ca' di Dio Riva S. Biagio

S. Biagio

S. Francesco
di Paola

Pal.
Giustinian

Giardinetti
Reali

S. MARCO
GIARDINETTI
1 82

ARSENALE
1 41 42 61 62

Via   G. Garibaldi

Monumento
a Garibaldi

Biennale

38

19

Ridotto

1 S. MARCO
VALLARESSO

S. Moisè

Riva   dei   Sette   Martiri

Viale Trento

Viale dei Gia. Pubblici

Punta della
Dogana

Canale   di   S. Marco

Dogana
di Mare

S. GIORGIO
82

Campo
S. Giorgio

Campanile di
San Giorgio
Maggiore

6

GIARDINI
(BIENNALE)
1 41 42 51 52 82

Canale della Giudecca

San Giorgio
Maggiore

S. Giorgio
Maggiore

Fond. S. Giovanni

I stood in Venice, on the 'Bridge of Sighs'; A Palace and a prison on each hand: I saw from out the wave her structures rise As from the stroke of the Enchanter's wand: A thousand Years their cloudy wings expand Around me, and a dying Glory smiles O'er the far times, when many a subject land Look'd to the winged Lion's marble piles, Where Venice sat in state, throned on her hundred isles!

– *Lord Byron*: Childe Harold's Pilgrimage

Basilica di San Marco

The **Basilica di San Marco** ❷ (open Mon–Sat 9.45am–4.30pm, Sun 1–4.30pm; entrance fee to Sanctuary, Pala d'Oro and Treasury) is named after the evangelist St Mark whose remains were recovered (or stolen, depending on your viewpoint) by the Venetians from Alexandria in the 9th century. The then ruler of Venice, Doge Giustiniano Participazio, built a church on this site to house the remains. The original church was destroyed by fire a century later, and was replaced in the late 11th century by the huge ornate edifice we see today.

The sumptuous facade has five portals decorated with shimmering mosaics. The only original mosaic – in the doorway to the far left – gives a good idea of the appearance of the basilica in the 13th century. Above the main portal are replicas of the famous bronze horses, thought to be Roman or Hellenistic works of the 3rd or 4th century AD and looted by the Venetians from Constantinople in 1204. They were taken to Paris by Napoleon in 1797 and returned in 1815, and are now kept inside the basilica, protected from pigeons and pollution.

The basilica's interior, in the shape of a Greek cross, is thought to have been inspired by the Church of the Apostles in Constantinople. Above the columns of the minor naves, lining the arms of the cross, are the women's galleries or *matronei*, designed in accordance with Greek Orthodox custom, which separates the sexes. The sumptuous atmosphere of the interior is enhanced by the decoration of the walls: marble slabs cover the lower part, while golden mosaics adorn the vaults, arches and domes. Following a complex iconographic plan, the mosaics cover 4,000 sq. metres (43,000 sq. ft), which is why St Mark's is sometimes called the Basilica d'Oro (Church of Gold). For a brief explanation of the mosaics, join one of the groups that tour the basilica.

Among the many gems housed in the church are the **Pala d'Oro**, a jewel-studded gold and enamel altarpiece dating from the 10th century. The **Treasury** also houses a priceless collection of gold and silver from Byzantium. The **Marciano Museum** (same hours as Basilica; entrance fee), reached by steep steps from the entrance narthex, affords fine views of the interior as a whole, while the open-air terrace beyond the museum gives a bird's-eye view of Piazza San Marco. It was here that the Doge and other dignitaries gathered to watch celebrations taking place below.

Map, pages 174–5

A panoramic view

A striking feature of the square is the soaring **Campanile** ❸ (open daily 9.30am–3.45pm, 10pm in summer; entrance fee), a faithful replica of the original tower that collapsed in 1902. Inside, a lift – or, for the energetic, a stairway – ascends 100 metres (327 ft) to the top for a sweeping panorama of the city and lagoon. The piazza's other tower is Coducci's intricate **Torre dell'Orologio** (Clock Tower) ❹, designed in 1496 (currently closed for restoration). On the top two mechanical bronze Moors strike the hour.

Adjoining the piazza and extending to the waterfront is the **Piazzetta San Marco**. On the right as you face the lagoon is the 16th-century **Libreria Sansoviniana** ❺ (open only for special exhibitions). Palladio, Italy's greatest 16th-century architect, considered this structure, with its finely sculpted arcades and detailed figures, one of the most beautiful buildings ever constructed since ancient times. Today it houses the **Archaeological Museum** (closed for restoration), the National Library of St Mark and the Venetian Old Library – a collection of treasures from the city's golden years.

ABOVE: mosaic of Christ in St Mark's.
LEFT: St Mark's.
BELOW: Doge's Palace.

ABOVE: sculptures of Adam and Eve by Antonio Rizzo on the facade of the Palazzo Ducale.
BELOW: weather-vane with a figure of Fortuna, near Santa Maria della Salute.

At the lagoon end of the Piazzetta stand two large 12th-century columns, one crowned with a winged lion, the symbol of Venice, the other with a statue of St Theodore, the original patron saint of the city. Originally a market place, the area later became known as a gathering place for politicians waiting to attend meetings. Public executions also used to take place between the two columns.

Across the water lies one of Venice's great landmarks – the majestic **Church of San Giorgio Maggiore** ❻ (open daily in summer 9am–12.30pm, 2.30–6pm; winter 10am–12.30pm, 3–5pm; entrance fee for Campanile) on the little islet of the same name. This classical masterpiece by Andrea Palladio has a huge white stone interior with works of art by Tintoretto and a campanile (entrance fee) with views that, on a clear day, extend as far as the Alps.

The Doge's Palace

The **Palazzo Ducale** ❼ (open daily; entrance fee) flanks the eastern side of the Piazzetta. This "vast and sumptuous pile", as Byron described it, is the grandest and most conspicuous example of Venetian Gothic in the city. The official residence of the Doge and the seat of government during the republic, it stands today as eloquent evidence of the power and pomp of Venice in its heyday.

Inside, the three wings of the palace reveal a seemingly endless series of grandiose rooms and halls. The largest of these is the Sala del Maggior Consiglio (the Great Council Chamber) which could accommodate all 480 (and later 1,700) of the Venetian patricians who sat on the council. The art collection here gives a foretaste of the countless artistic treasures scattered throughout the city, particularly the works by the two Venetian giants – Tintoretto and Veronese. One painting, *Paradise,* painted by Tintoretto in 1588–92, was for many years the largest painting in the world (7 metres x 22 metres/23 ft x 72 ft). Veronese's *Apotheosis of Venice*, in the same room, is another compelling masterpiece, though his finest work in the palace is *The Rape of Europa* in the Anticollegio.

Adjoining the palace is the former prison. Once tried and convicted in the palace, prisoners were led across sthis slender covered bridge to their cell. Since the windowed bridge offered the captive his last glimpse of freedom, it was called **Il Ponte dei Sospiri** ❽ (the Bridge of Sighs). However grim its original purpose, it has a romantic air, and is favoured today by young lovers who believe that if they kiss under the bridge (presumably in a gondola) their love will last. A tour of the ducal palace is best rounded off with a coffee break in the piazza. The most famous cafés are **Florian**, for years a rendezvous of fashionable Venetian society, and **Quadri** (opposite) which was favoured by the Austrians when they occupied Venice in the 19th century.

The Grand Canal

"The great street of Venice", as Henry James prosaically described the **Canal Grande** (Grand Canal), winds for some 3.5 km (2 miles) through the city. This splendid shimmering thoroughfare is flanked by pastel-coloured palaces in a mixture of Byzantine, Gothic, Renaissance and baroque styles, built mostly between the 13th and the 18th centuries.

The best way to see the canal is from a boat. If you are feeling flush, hire a gondola from the San Marco waterfront. Thomas Mann, who commented that the gondolas of Venice were "black as nothing else on earth except a coffin", nonetheless found their seats "the softest, most luxurious, most relaxing in the world". Far cheaper, though less romantic and more noisy, is the No. 1 public waterbus (*vaporetto*) which plies the length of the canal at frequent intervals.

Starting from San Marco, the entrance of the canal is marked on the left bank by the great baroque church of **Santa Maria della Salute ❾**, designed by the 17th-century baroque architect Baldassare Longhena, and erected in thanks for the city's deliverance from the plague of 1630. To the enamoured James, the church was "like a great lady on the threshold of her salon … with her domes and scrolls, her scalloped buttresses and statues forming a pompous crown, and her wide steps disposed on the ground like the train of a robe."

On the same side is the one-storeyed **Palazzo Venier dei Leoni ❿** (open Wed–Mon 11am–6pm; entrance fee), housing the **Guggenheim Collection** of modern art. The artworks in the palace and gardens belonged to the late Peggy Guggenheim. When the American patron of the arts lived there, it is rumoured that the prominent and erect penis on the nude equestrian statue (by Marino Marini), in the courtyard facing the canal, was removed from time to time – presumably to spare the blushes of her more sensitive visitors.

On the right bank opposite is **Ca'Grande ⓫**, a three-storey Renaissance residence by Sansovino, now the office of the city magistrate. The first bridge that spans the canal is the wooden **Ponte dell'Accademia ⓬**, built in 1932 as a temporary structure but retained through popular demand. It is named after the nearby **Galleria dell'Accademia ⓭** (openTues–Sat 9am–7pm, Sun–Mon

Map, pages 174–5

The Guggenheim Collection includes works by Picasso, Mondrian, Brancusi, Miró and Pollock, among others.

BELOW LEFT: interior of Santa Maria della Salute.

BELOW: detail from Veronese's *Feast in the House of Levi*, in the Accademia.

9am–2pm; entrance fee) housed in the former Scuola della Carità. This contains the world's finest collection of Venetian paintings, with works by Mantegna, Bellini, Giorgione (*The Tempest*), Carpaccio, Titian, Tintoretto, Veronese, Tiepolo, Guardi and Canaletto, all arranged in chronological order.

Further down the canal on the same side stands the imposing baroque palace of the **Ca' Rezzonico** ⓮, housing a museum of 18th-century Venice (closed for restoration). The stately rooms are richly decorated with period paintings, furniture and frescoes. It was here that the poet Robert Browning died in 1889.

Richard Wagner was staying at the second of the two Gothic **Palazzi Giustinian** on the left bank when he composed the second act of *Tristan and Isolde* during 1858–59. Next door, **Ca' Foscari** ⓯ is a 15th-century palace in the Venetian Gothic style, named after the family of the great 15th-century doge who masterminded large Venetian conquests on the Italian mainland.

Beyond the Sant'Angelo landing stage, on the right bank, **Palazzo Corner Spinelli** ⓰ was designed during the early Venetian Renaissance in the Lombardic style by Coducci. Beyond the next side canal, the **Palazzo Grimani** ⓱ now the Court of Appeal, is a late Renaissance masterpiece by Sanmicheli. In front of you, Venice's most famous bridge, **Ponte di Rialto** ⓲, arches over the canal. The former wooden drawbridges built across the canal at this point all collapsed, necessitating the erection of a more weighty stone structure. Antonio da Ponte, one of many eminent contenders for the commission, supervised its construction between 1588 and 1592. The single-span, balustraded bridge has two parallel rows of tightly packed shops selling jewellery, leather, masks, silk and souvenirs. As one of only three bridges across the Grand Canal, it is of course a good spot from which to view the canal and its traffic.

Ca' d'Oro

The most beautiful Gothic palace in Venice, the **Ca' d'Oro** (open daily 9am–1pm; entrance fee) appears on the right at the first landing stage beyond the bridge. When built in 1420 by the wealthy patrician Marino Contarini, it was covered in gold leaf, hence the name "House of Gold". Inside, the Giorgio Franchetti art gallery comprises a varied collection of paintings, frescoes and sculpture. Further along, on the left bank, the enormous baroque **Ca' Pesaro** ❷⓿ is another masterpiece by Longhena; this one houses the Galleria d'Arte Moderna (temporarily closed) and the Museo Orientale (open Tues–Sun till 2pm; entrance fee). The last building of note before the railway station is **Palazzo Vendramin-Calergi** ❷❶, one of the finest Renaissance palaces by Mauro Coducci (1440–1504). Wagner died here in 1883. Today it is the winter quarters of the city's casino.

The six districts of Venice

It is impossible to list all of Venice's architectural and artistic treasures; perhaps the greatest experience the city can offer to the inquisitive visitor is the maze of tiny alleys, the narrow silent canals and the pretty squares and courtyards only minutes away from **San Marco**, the most central of the six districts (*sestieri*) of Venice. Leading north from the Piazza San Marco, starting at the clock tower, is the **Merceria dell'Orologia**. This ancient commercial thoroughfare is still one of Venice's busiest streets, flanked by small shops and boutiques.

Dorsoduro is the most southerly section of historic Venice – an excellent area to stay if you are looking for a quiet *pensione* within easy access of central Venice. To the south, the area is bounded by the **Zattere**, a long, broad and surprisingly peaceful quayside whose cafés and restaurants afford splendid views across the water to the island of Giudecca. East of the Accademia Gallery, the Dorsoduro is quiet and intimate, characterised by pretty canals, small shops, galleries and chic residences.

Northwest of the Accademia, the area around San Barnaba was traditionally the quarter for impoverished Venetian nobility. Today it is the scene of cafés, artisans and one of the last surviving vegetable barges. Further west, the church of **San Sebastiano** ❷❷ (entrance fee; enquire at tourist office about a cumulative ticket for church visits) was the parish church of Veronese and the interior is covered with many of his early works. The area becomes increasingly shabby towards San Nicolò dei Mendicoli, erstwhile home of sailors and fishermen. The charming Romanesque church of **San Nicolò dei Mendicoli** ❷❸ was expertly restored by the British Venice in Peril Fund in the 1970s.

The island of **Giudecca**, across the Giudecca Canal, is a quiet working-class area of narrow streets and tightly packed apartments. The main landmark on its waterfront is Andrea Palladio's **Redentore** church ❷❹ (entrance fee), built in gratitude for the city's deliverance from plague in 1576. On the third Sunday in July, the city commemorates this event by building a bridge of boats from the Zattere to the Redentore, where a special mass is held. That night, a firework display lights up the sky over the Giudecca Canal.

Map, pages 174–5

TIP

The sign-posted routes between St Mark's, Rialto and Accademia can get very crowded. For respite from the hordes of tourists, just turn off onto any side canal, where you will find equally attractive buildings and a glimpse of genuine Venetian life.

BELOW: Tiepolo's *Abraham visited by the Angels* in San Rocco.

San Polo

The *sestiere* of **San Polo** lies within the large bend of the Grand Canal, northwest of San Marco. The quarter around the **Rialto**, the oldest inhabited part of mainland Venice, became the gathering place of merchants from the east and thence the commercial hub of the city. It is still a bustling area, with shops and market stalls. Fruit and vegetables are laid out under the arcades of the Fabbriche Vecchie while the mock-Gothic stone loggia of the Pescheria marks the site of the morning fish market. Arrive early, as the market begins to close by noon.

The major church of San Polo is the majestic brick Gothic **Santa Maria Gloriosa dei Frari** ㉕ (open Mon–Sat 9am–6pm, Sun 1–6pm; entrance fee), usually referred to as the Frari. The interior houses some of Venice's finest masterpieces, including an exquisite *Madonna and Child* by Giovanni Bellini, Titian's celebrated and sublime *Assumption* (crowning the main altar) and – another masterpiece by Titian – the *Madonna di Ca' Pesaro*. Buried in the Frari are the composer Claudio Monteverdi, the sculptor Canova (who lies in a pyramidal tomb he designed as a monument to Titian) and several doges.

Close to the Frari, the **Scuola Grande di San Rocco** ㉖ (open daily in summer 9am–5.30pm; restricted hours in winter; entrance fee) is celebrated for its series of religious works by Tintoretto, painted on the walls and ceilings in 1564–87. The dramatic scenes from the *Life of Christ* culminate in *The Crucifixion,* of which Henry James wrote: "Surely no single picture in the world contains more human life, there is everything in it including the most exquisite beauty. It is one of the greatest things of art."

Santa Croce ㉗, lying north and west of San Polo, is for the most part a relatively unexplored district. Its core is a maze of covered alleyways lined by peeling facades and criss-crossed by canals barely wide enough for the passage of a barge. Its squares are pleasingly shabby, bustling with local life. The only real concession to tourism is the **Piazzale Roma**, the uninspiring arrival point for those coming by road.

The origins of the Ghetto

Cannaregio is the quietest and most remote district in Venice. Its name derives from *canne* (reeds), for this area was once marshland. The *sestiere* forms the northern arc of the city, stretching from the railway station to the Rio dei Mendicanti in the east. At its heart lies the **Ghetto** ㉘: its name originated from an iron foundry (*getto*) which once stood here. This was Europe's first ghetto, an area for the exclusive but confined occupation of Jews. Built in the early 16th century, it gave its name to isolated Jewish communities throughout the world. It remained a ghetto until Napoleonic times. Though very few Jews still live here, the synagogues, tenements and kosher restaurants lend a distinctive Jewish air, and the area's history is well documented in the **Museo Ebraico** (open Sun–Fri 9.30am–9.30pm; entrance fee), a small museum in the main square.

The northern part of Cannaregio is the most remote and the area around the lovely Gothic church of the **Madonna dell'Orto** ㉙ (entrance fee) the most appealing. Tintoretto was born here and lived at No. 3399, near the Campo dei Mori. Forming the northern border of

Venice's scuole *were a cross between professional guilds and charitable societies. Some of them became very wealthy and commissioned fine artists to decorate their headquarters.*

BELOW: Renaissance gateway to the Arsenale, built in 1460 by Antonio Gambello.

Cannaregio, the Fondamente Nuove is the main departure point for ferries to the northern islands. Across the water you can see the walled cemetery on the island of San Michele. Back from the main quayside, the baroque church of the **Gesuiti** ❸ has an outrageously extravagant green and white marble interior. The prize work of art is Titian's dramatic *Martyrdom of St Lawrence*.

To the east of Cannaregio, it is worth exploring the warren of alleys and canals. With luck, you will stumble upon the church of **Santa Maria dei Miracoli** ❸ (entrance fee). Designed in the 1480s by Pietro Lombardo and members of his workshop, it is one of the loveliest Renaissance churches in the city. Decorated inside and out with marble, it is often likened to a jewel-box.

Castello

Castello, the city's western section, varies in character from the busy southern waterfront near San Marco to the humble cheek-by-jowl residences of the north. The area behind Riva degli Schiavoni is worth exploring for its pretty canals, quaysides and elegant faded palaces. Essential viewing for those interested in art is the frieze of paintings by Carpaccio in the **Scuola di San Giorgio degli Schiavoni** ❸ (open Tues–Sat 10am–12.30pm, 3–6pm, Sun 10am–12.30pm; entrance fee), and Coducci's 16th-century church of **San Zaccaria** ❸.

The **Campo Santa Maria Formosa** ❸ (entrance fee) is a pleasantly lived-in market square with a handsome Renaissance church, which is home to Palma il Vecchio's splendid *St Barbara and Saints* of 1510. The spiritual heart of Castello is the **Campo Santi Giovanni e Paolo** ❸, better known in Venetian dialect as San Zanipolo. Standing prominently in this spacious square is Andrea del Verrocchio's masterly bronze equestrian statue of the fierce mercenary Bar-

Map, pages 174–5

ABOVE: Murano vase.
BELOW: the Casa Bepi on Burano.

Map, pages 174–5

tolomeo Colleoni. Presiding over the square is the majestic Gothic church of **Santi Giovanni e Paolo** ⑯, where 46 Doges are buried. Many of their tomb monuments are magnificent, as is Paolo Veronese's *Adoration of the Shepherds* in the Cappella del Rosario.

Part of eastern Castello is occupied by the **Arsenale** ⑰, the great shipyard of the republic where Venice's galleys were built and refurbished. It is now largely abandoned and inaccessible to the public, but you can see a small part from the No. 52 public waterbus and there is an excellent **Naval Museum** (open Mon–Sat 8.45am–1pm; entrance fee) alongside the main entrance gate. To the east of the public gardens is the site of the **Biennale** ⑱, an international exhibition of modern art, film and music (held sporadically; check with the tourist office).

Island excursions

There is plenty to see away from the historic centre of Venice. The lagoon was settled over a long period from the 5th century AD and you can still see the remains of the very first Venetian community on the tiny island of Torcello. Frequent ferry services link Venice to the main islands.

ABOVE: relaxing on the Lido. BELOW: Burano. RIGHT: Palladio's San Giorgio Maggiore.

The island of **San Michele**, just north of Venice, is occupied by the cemetery and the early Renaissance church of San Michele in Isola, designed by Coducci. Napoleon, who forbade burials in the historic centre, established the cemetery here. Ezra Pound and Igor Stravinsky are two of the eminent visitors to Venice who are buried here.

Further north, the island of **Murano** is spread over five islets criss-crossed by canals, which make it seem like a mini-Venice. In the late 13th century Murano became the centre of Venice's ancient glass-blowing industry, as factories were moved from the city centre for fear of fire. The **Museo Vetrario** (open daily in summer 9am–7pm, 9am–5pm in winter; entrance fee) in the Fondamenta Giustinian has exquisite examples of glasswork.

Venice's justly famous lace industry is based in **Burano**, northeast of Venice. This is a colourful island where canals are lined by brightly painted houses and stalls selling lace and linen. Prices in Burano can be cheaper than elsewhere in Venice, but beware of imitation Venetian lace from factories in the Far East.

Torcello, the most remote of these islands (an hour by ferry), is the least populated and, for many, the most interesting. This rural, marshy island was the site of the original settlement in the Venetian lagoon. Still standing is the magnificent Byzantine cathedral, dating from the 7th century but rebuilt in the 11th century. A large striking mosaic of *The Virgin*, standing above a frieze of apostles, decorates the chancel apse of the church, while the entire western wall is covered by a huge and elaborate mosaic depicting *The Last Judgement*.

To the south of Venice, on a different route, lies the **Lido**, where Thomas Mann's unhappy von Aschenbach loitered too long, feasting his tired eyes on Tadzio, and died of cholera. The Lido is no longer the fashionable resort depicted in *Death in Venice* but in the hot summer months, when the city and its sights can be overwhelming, the sands and sea air usually provide a welcome break. ❑

LIFE AS A MASQUERADE

Carnival in Venice is supreme self-indulgence, a giddy round of masked balls and private parties suggesting mystery and promising romance

Carnival in Venice is a 10-day pre-Lenten extravaganza, culminating in the burning of the effigy of Carnival in Piazza San Marco on Shrove Tuesday. As an expression of a topsy-turvy world, carnival is a time for rebellion without the risk of ridicule. The essence of the "feast of fools" lies in the unfolding Venetian vistas: masked processions heading towards Piazza San Marco past shimmering palaces, with surreal masqueraders tumbling out of every alley. As the revellers flock to Florian's café in Piazza San Marco, the air is sickly-sweet with the scent of fritters and the sound of lush baroque music. Carnival capers include costumed balls, firework displays and historical parades, all staged by the carnival societies.

SPIRIT OF RESISTANCE

Carnival is often dismissed as commercialised and chaotic but Venetian traditionalists view it differently. The leader of a venerable carnival company sees the event as saving his city: "Life in Venice is inconvenient and costly. With the carnival, we give a positive picture and show the pleasure of living here. Carnival is a form of resistance. By resisting the temptation to leave, we are saving the spirit of the city for future generations."

▽ THE GREAT LEVELLER

A mask makes everyone equal. Masqueraders are addressed as *"sior maschera"* (masked gentleman) regardless of age, rank or even gender. One way of preserving some individuality is face-painting.

△ SELECT CARDS

A select group of Venetians still appears as *tarocchi*, fortune-telling tarot cards. These famous cards supposedly reached Europe from the East, through Venice. The star of the pack is the Queen of Swords, her costume rich in silver cabalistic signs.

▽ WINDOW DRESSING

Masks originally allowed the nobility to mingle incognito with the common people in *casini* (private clubs), but are now an excuse for all-purpose revelry. This shop window displays fantasy masks, which are creative rather than authentic, and appeal to individual tastes.

MASTERS OF DISGUISE

Mask-makers had their own guild in medieval times, when a *mascheraio* (mask-maker) helped a secretive society run smoothly. Modern masqueraders must choose between masks in leather *(cuoio)*, china *(ceramica)* or papier-mâché *(cartapesta)*. Papier-mâché and leather masks are the most authentic.

Antique masks are rare since neither material readily stands the test of time or the Venetian climate. Authentic mask-makers both reinterpret traditional designs and create new ones. In the case of papier-mâché masks, the pattern is made from a fired clay design, which generates a plaster of Paris mould. Layers of papier-mâché paste are used to line the mould and thus create the mask. When dry, the glue gives the mask a shiny surface akin to porcelain. Polish and a white base coat are applied before the eye holes are cut and decorative detail added. This painting process can be simple or highly artistic.

The alternatives to papier-mâché include leather masks, which are hard to fashion, or ceramic designs, ideal as hand-held masks or wall decorations, often adorned with fine fabrics. Places to browse include Laboratorio Artigiano Maschere (Barbaria delle Tole) founded by a family of puppet-makers, and the bohemian workshop of Ca del Sol (Fondamenta dell'Osmarin).

△ THE NOBLE LOOK

Costumes can be historical, traditional or simply surreal. The classic Venetian disguise of the 17th and 18th centuries was known as the *maschera nobile*, the patrician mask. The carnival companies wear noble Renaissance and rococo costumes *(left)* as a matter of course.

▽ VOLTO FACE

The patrician *maschera nobile* and witty *commedia dell'arte* masks are among a number of authentic disguises. While this cumbersome ruff is pure fantasy, the white mask looks to the past for inspiration: it is a modern variant on the slightly sinister *volto*, the traditional Venetian mask.

THE VENETO

*Two cities with links to Shakespearean heroines
and a chance to surfeit on the buildings of
Italy's greatest Renaissance architect*

Shakespeare called Italy's second oldest university city "Fair Padua, nursery of Arts" and described it as a place where Renaissance Englishmen came to "suck the sweets of sweet philosophy". Dante and Galileo both lectured at **Padua** (Padova) ❷, and in the mid-17th century, a learned woman earned a doctorate here, the first woman in Europe to do so. (Padua's most famous daughter is, without a doubt, Katherina, Shakespeare's tamable shrew.)

But long before the university was established in 1222, Padua was an important Roman town, believed by Virgil to have been founded by the brother of the Trojan King Priam, after the fall of Troy – though, in fact, it had been a settlement of pre-Roman tribesmen. (The Roman historian Livy was born in the nearby hills and was always proud to call himself a Paduan.)

Padua is also a magnet for the faithful. Every June, pilgrims come from all over the world to honour St Anthony of Padua, a 13th-century itinerant preacher whose spell-binding sermons packed church pews throughout Italy. The **Basilica di Sant'Antonio** (open daily 7am–7pm), built over his remains between 1232 and 1307, celebrates his sanctity handsomely, with works by Donatello (who lived in Padua from 1443–53), Sansovino and Menabuoi. **Venice** ❶ is, of course, very close to Padua, and Venetian influence is evident in the church's

BELOW: Donatello's *Gattamelata.*
BELOW RIGHT: Caffè Pedrocchi.

design. Byzantine domes, an ornate facade and two high, thin bell towers give the exterior an oriental appearance. The interior also has Byzantine decorative details. The chapel of St Anthony, containing the revered tomb, is a 16th-century design by Biosco.

Padua's piazzas

In **Piazza del Santo**, to one side of the basilica, stands a famous equestrian statue of Erasmo da Narni, called *Gattamelata*, by Donatello. This sculpture of the great Venetian *condottiere* (mercenary) is believed to be the first great bronze cast in Italy during the Renaissance. Also in the piazza is the **Oratorio di San Giorgio** (open 9.30am–12.30pm, 2.30–5pm; entrance fee), originally a private mausoleum for the prominent Soranzo family. The oratory is decorated with beautiful frescoes by Altichiero and Avanzo. On the corner of the piazza is the entrance to the **Scuola di Sant'Antonio** (open daily in summer 9am–12.30pm, 2.30–7pm, till 5pm in winter; entrance fee) which houses paintings by Bellini, Titian and Giorgione, amongst others.

The Via Belludi leads to another notable square, the **Prato della Valle,** fronted by the **Basilica di Santa Giustina**. A small park at its centre is reached by crossing one of the four stone bridges over a circular moat. In the park, a circle of statues represents famous past citizens of Padua.

The city centres on the crowded **Piazza delle Erbe**, one of its three market squares. Here stands the **Palazzo della Ragione** (open in summer Mon–Sat 9am–6pm, 9am–12.30pm, 3–6pm in winter; entrance fee) called locally **Il Salone**, a massive medieval structure. The interior is decorated with fine frescoes and houses a large wooden horse copied from Donatello's bronze masterpiece.

TIP

The upstairs rooms at the Caffè Pedrocchi are used for concerts and other events. The rooms are worth seeing for their extravagant Egyptian, Moorish, Greek and other decor.

BELOW: the Prato della Valle and Basilica di Santa Giustina.

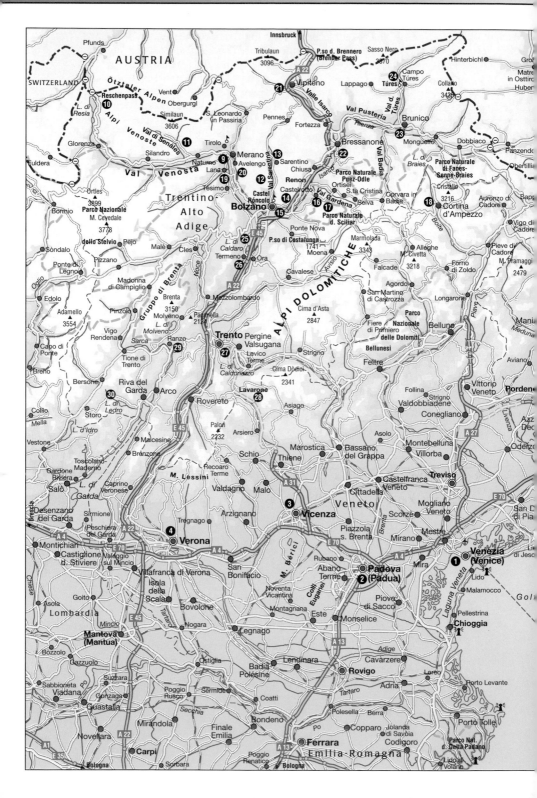

Behind Il Salone is a large coffee bar, **Caffè Pedrocchi**, famous throughout Italy as a gathering place for intellectuals. During the Risorgimento, liberals from the nearby university met here to discuss the founding of the new nation.

From here it is only a short walk through **Piazza dei Signori** to Padua's **Duomo**. Although the cathedral was designed by Michelangelo, many alterations were made to his plans and the result is rather disappointing. The most interesting corner of the church is the frescoed baptistry (open daily in summer 9.30am–1.30pm, 3–7pm; till 6pm in winter; entrance fee).

Miser's Madonna

To the north of the university lies the **Cappella degli Scrovegni** (open daily in summer 9am–7pm; till 6pm in winter; entrance fee), also known as the Arena Chapel on account of the nearby ruins of an amphitheatre. Enrico Scrovegni commissioned this richly decorated chapel in 1303 to atone for his father's miserliness and usury. It contains a cycle of frescoes by Giotto depicting the history of Christian redemption. The panels rank among Giotto's masterpieces. The solidity and emotional depth of the figures marked a turning point in Western painting. "In my opinion," wrote Giorgio Vasari in the 17th century, "painters owe to Giotto, the Florentine painter, exactly the same debt they owe to nature, which constantly serves them as a model and whose finest and most beautiful aspects they are always striving to imitate and reproduce."

It is lucky for art lovers that the Arena Chapel escaped the fate of the nearby **Eremitani** church whose apse, covered with precious Mantegna frescoes, was bombed during World War II – Italy's greatest art loss of the war. This barewalled church stands in poignant contrast to the rich collection of paintings, frescoes, bronzes and mosaics in the **Eremitani Museum** (open daily in summer 9am–7pm; till 6pm in winter; entrance fee) alongside, which contains outstanding works of art, such as Bellini's *Portrait of a Young Suitor*.

Vicenza

Andrea di Pietro, nicknamed Palladio, and the most prominent architect of the Italian High Renaissance, worked for most of his life (1508–80) in **Vicenza ❸**. Rich and eager to decorate their city with new buildings, the local gentry gave Palladio many opportunities to use his talents. As a result, there is hardly a street in central Vicenza not graced by a Palladian mansion despite the destruction of 14 of Palladio's buildings during World War II.

In **Piazza dei Signori**, at the city's heart, stand two of Palladio's master-pieces. The **Basilica**, his first major work, is not a church but a remodelling of a Gothic courthouse (called *basilica* in the Roman sense – a place where justice is administered). Palladio's elegant design features two open galleries, the lower one with Tuscan Doric columns and the upper one with Ionic columns. Facing the Basilica is the **Loggia del Capitaniato**, a later Palladian work commissioned in 1571 to honour the victory over the Turks at Lepanto. This triumphant occasion called for an ornate style, hence the garish details and extravagantly balustraded windows.

The city's Gothic-style **Duomo** stands just behind behind the Basilica. It was badly bombed during World War II but has since been completely rebuilt. The interior is unremarkable. A Palladian cupola tops the roof.

North of the Duomo is **Corso Palladio**, the city's main street, lined with many fine villas. Number 163 is the so-called **Casa del Palladio**. With its classic lines and precise geometric proportions, it is a typical example of Palladio's work. Another excellent example of the Palladian style is the **Palazzo Chiericati**, in the Piazza Matteotti, at the end of Corso Palladio. This beautiful building houses the **Museo Civico** (open Tues–Sun 9am–12.30pm, 2–5pm; closed Sun pm in

Palladio's addition of open galleries to the Basilica was not just a way of embellishing the market square – the galleries were designed to strengthen the older building, which was suffering from subsidence.

BELOW: Palladio's Villa Rotonda, outside Vicenza.

winter; entrance fee) and the city's art collection. Tintoretto's *Miracle of St Augustine* and several fine works by Flemish artists are on permanent display.

Palladio wasn't the only great architect to work here. The younger Scamozzi, who learned much from Palladio, designed the **Palazzo del Comune** on the Corso Palladio; it reflects his strict interpretation of classical architecture.

The finest example of Scamozzi and Palladio's joint work is the **Teatro Olimpico** (open Tues–Sun 9am–12.30pm, 2–5pm; closed Sun pm in winter; entrance fee), said to have been the first covered theatre in Europe when it was built between 1580 and 1582. Palladio died before its completion and Scamozzi took over. The theatre is a wood and stucco structure with a permanent stage set of a piazza and streets in perfect perspective. In 1585, the first play performed here was Sophocles's *Oedipus Tyrannus*. The theatre is still in regular use today.

Excursions from Vicenza

Monte Berico, a forested hill visible from all parts of Vicenza, is well worth a visit. Take a bus from the Piazza Duomo, or walk for approximately one hour to reach the **Madonna del Monte**, a 17th-century rebuilding of a chapel that commemorated the site of two apparitions of the Virgin. The final section of the approach is covered by a portico with 150 arches and 17 chapels. Inside, the basilica is spacious and airy, and works of art include a *Pietà* by Montagna. During World War I, the mountains beyond Vicenza were the scene of many great battles. The **Piazzale della Vittoria**, a few yards from the church, is a memorial to all the Italians who died close to here.

To the southeast of the town centre is the **Villa Rotonda** (open mid Mar–end Oct: Wed 10am–noon, 3–6pm; gardens open Tues–Thur same hours; entrance

Map, pages 190–1

ABOVE: Verona.

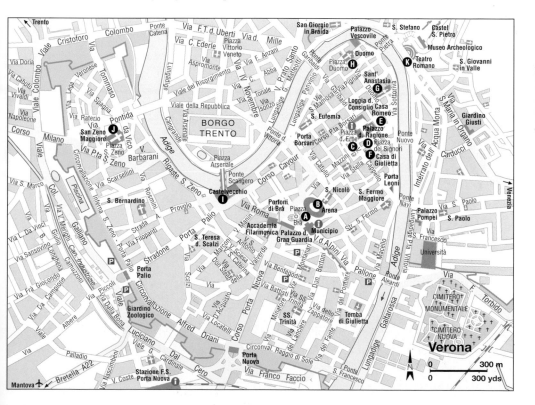

Verona's Giardino Giusti, a superb example of a Renaissance garden, is dotted with statuary.

BELOW: the Ponte Scaligero in Verona.

fee), a famous belvedere built by Palladio in 1551 with a distinctive circle within a cube design. Another fine villa nearby was built in 1688 by Antonio Muttoni. Known as the Villa ai Nani (Villa of the Dwarfs) on account of the statues of comical figures topping the garden wall, it is decorated with the delightful illusionistic frescoes of father and son, Giambattista and Giandomenico Tiepolo.

Verona

Built in the distinctive local pink marble, **Verona** ❹ has a rosy hue, as if the sun were constantly setting. In actuality, there is nothing faded about this misty, atmospheric city, now at the peak of its glory. What was once a thriving Roman settlement is today one of the most prosperous and elegant cities in Italy.

The **Piazza Brà** ❹ is where the Veronese gather day and night to talk, shop and drink together. They sit or stroll in the shadow of the glorious 1st-century Roman **Arena** ❸ (open Tues–Sun 8am–6.30pm; 8am–1.30pm in opera season, July–August; entrance fee), the third largest structure of its kind in existence. The highest fragment, called the Ala, reveals the Arena's original height. The Veronese have taken an interest in the Arena's preservation since the 16th century. It is often used for city fairs and, in summer, up to 25,000 people at a time fill it to attend performances of popular Italian opera – notably Verdi's *Aida* (if you are fortunate enough to get tickets, take a cushion and do not drink for several hours beforehand – the loos are impossible to reach).

The Roman Forum was located in what is now **Piazza delle Erbe** ❻, off the **Via Mazzini**. This large open space has a quirky beauty due to the variety of palazzi and towers that line its sides. Among the most impressive is the baroque **Palazzo Maffei**, next to the **Torre del Gardello**, the tallest Gothic structure in

Map, pages 193

the square. The palace with the attractive double-arched windows on the corner of **Via Palladio** is the medieval guild house – the **Casa dei Mercanti**.

The adjoining **Piazza dei Signori D** is more formal than its neighbour. The **Palazzo della Ragione**, a massive structure with heavy exterior decoration, stands on the border of the two squares. The interior courtyard has a delicate Gothic stairway. Opposite rises the **Loggia del Consiglio**, considered the finest Renaissance building in the city. Nearby are the tombs of the della Scala family (the Scaligeri), one-time rulers of Verona. The elaborately sculpted monuments stand outside the tiny church of Santa Maria Antica, surrounded by a wrought-iron fence featuring the family's staircase motif (della Scala means "of the stairs").

Verona is, of course, the city of *Romeo and Juliet*. Though the Capulet and Montague families immortalised by Shakespeare did actually exist, the story of the star-crossed lovers was entirely fictional. However, what is now a rather seedy bar on the Via delle Arche Scaligeri was allegedly the **Casa Romeo E**. Rather better maintained is **Juliet's House F** (open Tues–Sun 8am–6.30pm; entrance fee)at No. 23 Via Cappello, near Piazza delle Erbe, a medieval townhouse complete with balcony and recently opened museum. It is also possible to visit Juliet's purported final resting place. The "tomb" is several miles out of the centre on the Lungoadige Capuleti.

If your taste runs to the Gothic, head for **Sant'Anastasia G**, which, behind its brick facade, houses a magnificent painting by Pisanello of St George, as well as frescoes by Altichiero and Turone. Verona's **Duomo H** is nearby. Inside is Titian's *Assumption of the Virgin*.

ABOVE: relief in the Castelvecchio.
BELOW: "Juliet's House".

The **Castelvecchio I** (open Tues–Sun; entrance fee; free on first Sunday of the month) on the River Adige is a reminder of one of the grimmer chapters in the history of "fair Verona". The castle was first built in 1354 by the hated tyrant Can Grande II della Scala for protection if a rebellion occurred. But he met his end not at the hands of the mob but through the treachery and ambition of his own brother, who stabbed him. As elsewhere in Italy, this fortress, its closets crammed with skeletons, is now an excellent museum with works by Veronese, Tiepolo, Bellini and others.

A saint and a prophet

In addition to a benevolent or malevolent ruling family, every Italian city must have a patron saint, and Verona is no exception. Little is known about St Zeno, a 4th-century holy man, though it seems he was a fisherman. His most famous miracle is depicted by Nicola Pisano on the porch of the **Basilica di San Zeno J** (entrance fee), Verona's most beautiful church. According to the story, the saint was out fishing when he saw a man being dragged into the Adige by crazed oxen. St Zeno made the sign of the Cross, exorcised the devils and the man continued safely on his journey. The bronze doors of the church are of splendid workmanship though the artists are unknown.

There is no question that most people are drawn to Verona because of *Romeo and Juliet*, and this and other Shakespeare plays are frequently performed in the **Teatro Romano K**, an ancient construction of perfect proportion and superb acoustics. ❑

ITALY
●Rome

FRIULI-VENEZIA GIULIA

*The influence of successive invaders has given Italy's
northeastern corner a cosmopolitan feel,
combining flavours of Italy, Austria and Slovenia*

*While living in
Trieste, James Joyce
finished* Dubliners,
*wrote the final draft
of* Portrait of the
Artist as a Young
Man, *and conceived*
Ulysses.

BELOW: the Grand
Canal in Trieste.

S ince the 2nd century BC – when the Romans took over the northeastern corner of the Italian peninsula – Friuli-Venezia Giulia has been a victim of foreign invasions. The Visigoths poured into the area in 403 AD; Attila the Hun earned his nickname "the Scourge of God" here in 452; and in 489 came Theodoric and the Ostrogoths. Many of the most gracious modern towns, including Cividale del Friuli, began as barbarian outposts. As a result, Cividale has an outstanding collection of sculpture, jewellery and weapons from this period, displayed in the **Museo Archeologico** (open daily 8.30am–2pm; entrance fee), and the **Museo Cristiano** in the cathedral (open daily 9.30am–noon, 3–6pm). Subsequent invaders – the Venetians and the Austrians – left their mark, adding to the cosmopolitan flavour of this region which shares a convoluted border with Slovenia. The border runs through the heart of the bilingual city of **Gorizia**, which has a fascinating museum (open Tues–Sun 9.30am–12.30pm, 3–7pm; till 5pm in winter; entrance fee) devoted to both world wars.

Trieste

Of all Friuli's foreign "invaders", perhaps the best known is James Joyce, who arrived in **Trieste ❺** in March 1905. He may not be Trieste's favourite son – he

was constantly in debt, often drunk, and given to shouting in the theatre – but the city was to become his home for the following 10 years.

Today the city has an air of faded elegance. Once Venice's rival for trade on the Adriatic, later the gateway to the sea for the Austro-Hungarian empire, Trieste is now a port without a hinterland, a city that history left behind. In the Città Nuova, long, straight avenues flank a Grand Canal where tall ships once anchored. Southwest of the canal is the **Piazza dell'Unità d'Italia** – said to be the largest piazza in Italy – with cafés where visitors can watch the passing scene. At the head of the piazza stands the ornate **Municipio**, of 19th-century Austrian inspiration. At the foot of the piazza, across the railroad tracks, stretches the long quay with its **Acquario Marino** exhibiting fish from the Adriatic Sea.

Map, pages 190–1

The old city

Behind the Municipio are the narrow, winding streets of the **Città Vecchia**. Stairs by the **Teatro Romano** (closed to visitors) ascend steeply to the 6th-century **Duomo di San Giusto**. Two 5th-century basilicas were here combined into a single four-aisled structure in the 14th century. At the top of the hill here – also named San Giusto after the city's patron saint – rises a 15th-century Venetian **Castello** (open daily; entrance fee), with a sweeping view of the city and the harbour. The **Museo Civico** (open Tues–Sun 9am–1pm; entrance fee) inside the castle has exhibits of early weapons plus a small art collection. On your way back down the hill, you may want to stop at the **Museo di Storia ed Arte** (open Tues–Sun 9am–1pm; entrance fee), which features relics from the various invaders and inhabitants of Friuli-Venezia Giulia. Also worth a visit is the **Basilica of San Silvestro** on the hillside, dating from the 12th century.

Seven km (4 miles) west of Trieste, set in lush green gardens, is the fairytale **Castello di Miramare**, near the seaside town of **Barcola ⑥**. Built between 1856 and 1860, this mock medieval fortress was the summer home of Archduke Maximilian. A museum (open daily; entrance fee) honours the ill-fated archduke, who later became emperor of Mexico and died in front of a revolutionary firing squad.

The Romans based their Northern Adriatic fleet at **Aquileia ⑦** which now lies several miles inland. Here you can see the ruin of a once-vast harbour, dating from the 1st century AD. Best of all is the **basilica**, begun in AD 313, with its vivid and well-preserved floor mosaics.

Udine ⑧ has an appealing style all its own. Echoes of Venetian rule are everywhere: the 16th-century **Castello** that towers over the city was built as the residence for Udine's Venetian governors and now houses the city's art and archaeology museums. At the foot of the castle hill, lining the monumental Piazza della Libertà, are elegant buildings, Venetian in style, including the graceful **Porticato di San Giovanni**, built in 1523, and the **Loggia del Lionello**, the city hall constructed in the 15th century. This building shows a distinct Venetian influence, with its layered pink and white masonry and windows and arches with pointed tops.

Tiepolo, the greatest Venetian baroque painter, did some of his best work here. The city's **Duomo** has three chapels decorated by him in golds and pinks. ❑

BELOW: Piazza della Libertà in Udine, with the 15th-century Palazzo del Comune.

TRENTINO-ALTO ADIGE

*The limestone peaks of the Dolomites frame an area
of castles, lakes and ancient spas, with its own distinctive
mix of Italian and German culture*

Map,
pages
190–1

ITALY
●Rome

This mountainous region, which stretches north to the Italian-Austrian border, first came to the attention of tourists in the English-speaking world in 1837 when John Murray, the London publisher, brought out a handbook for travellers. The book's description of the Dolomites sparked interest particularly among mountaineers who had conquered the Swiss Alps and were looking for new challenges: "They are unlike any other mountains, and are to be seen nowhere else among the Alps. They arrest the attention by the singularity and picturesqueness of their forms, by their sharp peaks or horns, sometimes rising up in pinnacles and obelisks, at others extending in serrated ridges, teethed like the jaw of an alligator."

Today, Trentino-Alto Adige (also known as the South Tyrol) is a popular holiday retreat for hikers, skiers and water sports enthusiasts. It is marked by contrasts, in the landscape as well as in the culture. Here it is possible to hike around a secluded alpine lake in the morning, sample wine in an Italian vineyard at noon, stroll along the palm-lined promenade of a Continental spa in the afternoon and then slip into bed in a medieval castle at the end of the day.

Trentino-Alto Adige actually consists of two different provinces. Trentino, historically a part of Italy except for a period during the 19th and early 20th centuries when it was ruled by Austria, has a definite Italian flair. Alto Adige, on the other hand, was a part of the Austrian Tyrol for six centuries, first becoming an Italian domain in 1919 when the Austro-Hungarian empire was carved up and the European borders were redrawn.

Forced assimilation

The Germanic traditions, culture and language have remained, despite post-World War I efforts by Mussolini to stamp them out. The dictator Italianised not only the names of the towns, mountains and rivers but even went so far as to force the South Tyrolean people to adopt Italian family names. Schools were forbidden to teach in German and huge numbers of Italians were sent into the region to run both the government and industries as well as to tip the ethnic balance within the population.

The South Tyroleans, however, insisted on clinging steadfastly to their cultural heritage, turning, in the 1960s, to acts of terrorism in an attempt to gain more autonomy for the province. Today, the atmosphere is once again peaceful as Italians and Germans live side by side, accepting and even appreciating each other's differences. The province is officially bilingual.

The mix of cultures is just one of the factors which makes Trentino-Alto Adige so diverse. The landscape in the east and north is marked by the awe-inspiring peaks of the rocky Dolomites, while the rolling green hills of the south central region are blanketed with vine-

LEFT: the majestic landscape of the Dolomites.
BELOW: Germanic traditions are still flourishing.

ABOVE: a medieval belfrey in Graun.

yards and orchards. The castles, of which there are more than 350, vary from crumbling overgrown ruins reminiscent of the one described in *Sleeping Beauty* to those that have been comprehensively restored and now house restaurants, hotels or well-appointed museums documenting the region's history.

Merano

The sleepy spa town of **Merano** (Meran) ❾, with its palm-lined promenades, exclusive shops, fine restaurants and grand old hotels, offers the visitor a taste of old Europe. The largest and most renowned spa in the Alps, Merano has played host to the great and the gracious for well over a century. Those who can afford it come to relax and take the cure in a Mediterranean-like climate. The city owes its famously mild climate to its position in a deep basin, protected to the north by the massive Alpine peaks and opening to the Etsch Valley in the south. Merano flourished between the late 13th and early 15th centuries, when it was the capital of the Tyrol. Thereafter, it passed into relative insignificance until its value as a spa was discovered.

Just a short distance north of Merano is the **Castel Tirolo**, one of the only castles in the world to have lent its name to an entire region. During the summer, concerts are performed in the castle. Just down the hill is the **Castel Brunnenburg**, where Ezra Pound (1885–1972) spent the last years of his life.

BELOW: view from the Stelvio Pass, near Venosta Valley.

To the west of Merano, the **Venosta** (Vinschgau) Valley extends all the way to the Swiss/Austrian/Italian border. The route leading over the **Reschen Pass** ❿ was first constructed during Roman times as an important link between Augsburg and the Po Valley. Vinschgauer bread, a speciality of the region which is baked in small flat loaves and flavoured with aniseed, is worth sampling.

The **Val di Senales** (Schnals Valley) , which branches to the north, just past Naturno, passes through the region of the Similaun glacier. It was here that the 5,000-year-old "Similaun Man" was found by hikers in the autumn of 1991. This frozen corpse, complete with tools, weapons and clothing, has provided valuable new insights into life in the Bronze Age.

In the central part of Alto Adige is the **Val Sarentina** (Sarn Valley) ⑫, a region where time seems to have stood still. The simple lifestyle of the farmers in this valley presents a direct contrast to the wealth and splendour of Merano. Old farms perch precariously on the mountainsides, wild rushing brooks carve deep gorges through the mountain walls and the people themselves, celebrating traditional festivals dressed in colourful national costumes, all combine to give a feeling of yester-year. The ancient craft of *federkielstickerei*, or embroidering with peacock quills, is still practised here. The quill is split lengthways with a razor-sharp knife into thin threads. These are then used to embroider leather goods such as shoes, braces, handbags and book covers. In **Sarentino** (Sarnthein) ⑬ you can watch the craftsmen at work.

The road leading out of the valley towards the provincial capital of Bolzano winds through numerous tunnels before emerging at **Castel Róncolo** (Schloss Runkelstein) (open Mar–Nov Tues–Sat; entrance fee) ⑭, built on a towering cliff in 1250 and today housing a museum with Gothic frescoes.

Bolzano

Bolzano (Bozen) ⑮ itself provides one of the most vivid examples of the coexistence of Italian and Germanic cultures. The old part of the city, gathered around Piazza Walther and the arcades of the Via dei Portici, is marked by patrician

Map, pages 190–1

ABOVE: bi-lingual road sign.
BELOW: fresco in Castel Róncolo.

houses and German Gothic architecture. Adjacent to Piazza Walther is the impressive Gothic Duomo, built in the 13th and 14th centuries and reputedly the oldest hall church in Alto Adige. On the other side of the Talfer river, in "New Bolzano", the Italian influence is seen in the austere buildings constructed during the Mussolini era. As a part of the Italianisation effort after World War I, the city was industrialised and today Bolzano, outside of the old town, is an unattractive mass of factories and fume-spewing smoke-stacks.

From Bolzano a cable car takes visitors on a scenic journey up to the **Renón** (Ritten) **Plateau**, a popular resort area. On a clear day, the views of the Dolomite formations are spectacular. On the way up, at l'Assunta (Maria Himmelfahrt), you can see a group of earth pyramids, giant conical piles of sand, resembling termite nests, with a slab of stone perched on the top of each. These impressive natural features are the result of centuries of erosion.

Just east of Bolzano is the **Sciliar** (Schlern) massif, towering like a great stone fortress above the surrounding area. At its base is the **Alpe di Siusi** (Seiser Alm), Europe's largest expanse of mountain pastureland, comprising almost 50 sq. km (20 sq. miles) and offering an abundance of hiking and ski trails.

Following the road from Sciliar to **Castelrotto** ⑯, one emerges in the **Val Gardena** (Grödner Valley) ⑰ with the popular ski resorts of **Ortisei** (St Ulrich), **Santa Cristina** and **Selva** (Wolkenstein). This valley is also famous for its woodcarvers. From **Wolkenstein**, the Sella Joch Pass winds its way between the jagged peaks of Mount Langkofel and the majestic Sella massif. Travellers through this pass enjoy a panoramic view of Mount Marmolada, the region's highest mountain, standing at 3,343 metres (10,965 ft). This route connects with the Great Dolomite Road which leads east to **Cortina d'Ampezzo** ⑱, the site of

TIP

The Alto Adige produces some good wines. Try the white wines, such as Pinot Grigio or aromatic Gewürztraminer, or the light red wines, which are very good chilled.

BELOW: the Gothic Duomo in Bolzano. **BELOW RIGHT:** Lake Carezza.

the 1956 Winter Olympics and today a popular winter resort, and west over the **Costalunga** (Karer Pass) to Bolzano. The road towards Bolzano passes the **Catinaccio** (Rosengarten) massif. During the twilight hours, the rose-coloured rays of the setting sun bathe the cliffs of the Rosengarten (literally "rose garden") in a sea of red, reminding visitors of the aptness of the name.

Lana ⑲, located between Bolzano and Merano, is the centre of the apple-growing region. The parish church in **Niederlana** contains Alto Adige's largest late-Gothic altarpiece, over 14 metres (46 ft) in height. Across the valley is **Avelengo** (Hafling) ⑳, home of the famous Hafling breed of horses.

In central Alto Adige, the **Isarco** (Eisach) **Valley** has, for the past 2,000 years, served as the major route connecting the German north to the Latin south via the Brenner Pass. The former commercial importance of **Vipiteno** (Sterzing) ㉑, the northernmost town on this route, is still evident today in its patrician houses.

Bressanone

Bressanone (Brixen) ㉒, the region's oldest settlement, was a bishopric from 990 until 1964, when the bishop moved to Bolzano. Interesting sights include the prince-bishop's palace and the baroque Duomo. The latter has impressive marble work on the walls as well as lovely ceiling frescoes. A stroll through the Gothic cloisters adjacent to the Duomo is well worthwhile. The frescoes in the cloisters, dating from 1390 to 1509, are among the best examples of Gothic painting in the Alto Adige. The late Romanesque chapel of St John, located at the southern end of the cloisters, was built as a baptismal church.

Just north of Bressanone, stretching to the east, is the **Pusteria Valley**. The valley's main town is **Brunico** (Bruneck) ㉓ with its lovely main street lined

Above: decorative sign in Vipiteno.
Below: grazing under the Rosengarten massif.

with houses from the 15th century. West of Brunico, the **Badia Valley** (Gadera), where the Ladin language is still spoken, branches to the south. From Brunico, the **Túres Valley** leads north to **Campo Túres** (Sand in Taufers), site of **Castle Túres ㉔**. The castle has been restored with many of its original furnishings and is open to the public (for information on guided tours check with the regional tourist office). The Pusteria Valley is the gateway to the Sexten Dolomites where the majestic Three Pinnacles and the Sexten Sundial formations are located. The latter was used by early astronomers as a point of orientation.

Trentino and the Adige Valley

In direct contrast to the rugged mountainous north, the **Adige** (Etsch) **Valley** in south central Alto Adige is marked by a more tranquil landscape. The fertile hills are blanketed with vineyards while orchards stretch across the plains. In addition to the wealth of castles, this region is also the site of numerous aristocratic residences dating from the late 16th and early 17th centuries when it was the fashion among the Tyrolean nobility to build country houses in the Italian Renaissance style. Many of these now serve as luxurious hotels and restaurants. **Lago di Caldaro** (Lake Kalterer) **㉕**, nestled between vineyards and a waterfowl preserve, is one of the warmest lakes in the Alps. Further south is **Termeno** (Tramin) **㉖**, home of the world-famous Gewürztraminer grape.

The capital of the province of Trentino is **Trento ㉗**, site of the Council of Trent which was held intermittently between 1545 and 1563. It was during these sessions, called by the Catholic Church to discuss the rising threat of Lutheranism, that the seeds for the Counter-Reformation were sown. Noteworthy sights include the **Duomo**, built between the 13th and 14th centuries in an aus-

The Adige is one of Italy's longest rivers. It rises on the border with Switzerland and Austria, and flows down through Trentino and the city of Verona, before emptying into the Adriatic at Chioggia.

BELOW: in the garden in Castelrotto.
BELOW RIGHT: a baroque church in Tesido, east of Brunico.

Map, pages 190–1

tere Romanesque-Gothic style, and the **Castello del Buonconsiglio** (Castle of Good Counsel), the residence of the prince-bishops who ruled the city for centuries. Located at the edge of the old part of town, the castle consists of several palazzi enclosed by a wall. Today it houses a museum of local art (open Tues–Sun; entrance fee).

The region of **Lavarone** ㉘ is located to the southeast of Trento. Here one finds dark green forests, mountain pastures, lakes and caves full of stalactite and stalagmite formations. The lakes invite meditative thought. It was on the shores of the small **Lago di Lavarone** that Sigmund Freud, the father of psychoanalysis, liked to stroll while letting his mind wander in its search for the relationship between the psyche and human behaviour.

The **Paganella mountains**, considered by many to be the most beautiful in Italy, range to the north of Trento. At the foot of this massif are the lakes of **Terlago**, **Santo** and **Lamar**. Further south is **Lago Toblino,** with a short hiking path leading to **Ranzo** ㉙, a small village with a breathtaking panorama over the valley of the lakes. More ambitious trekkers can follow the *translagorai* route through the wild **Catena dei Lagorai** in the eastern part of the province, passing by numerous serene alpine lakes.

Visitors interested in history might want to visit **Lago di Ledro** ㉚, just west of **Lago di Garda**, where the remains of a Bronze Age stilt village can be seen, as well as a museum with tools, canoes and other relics excavated from the former village. The northern tip of Lake Garda is located within Trentino. Although many towns on the lake have, in the past, been obliged to close their beaches due to pollution, the northern waters remain uncontaminated and are well worth exploring (*see page 225*). ❑

ABOVE: a spring bouquet.
BELOW: exploring Termeno, or Tramin.

MILAN

Map, page 210

For Henry James, Milan's reserved northern European flavour made it more "the last of the prose capitals than the first of the poetic". But there is poetry in Milan in spite of its modernity

ilan (Milano) is one of the world's fashion capitals, and home to both Leonardo's *Last Supper* and the world's premier opera house, La Scala. Above all, Milan is the centre of business in Italy and it is here and in provincial Lombardy that the demand for federalism – embodied by the right-wing Northern League – is strongest. The prosperous Milanese are courteous but reserved towards visitors and preoccupied with their own lives. Female tourists receive little of the unasked-for attention that is common further south.

There is no better place to begin a tour of Milan than at its spiritual hub, the **Duomo ⓐ** (open daily 9am–5.30pm; till 4.30pm in winter), described by Mark Twain as "a poem in marble". This gargantuan Gothic cathedral (the third largest church in Europe) was begun in 1386 but not finished until 1813. Decorating the exterior are 135 pinnacles and over 2,245 marble statues from all periods. The "Madonnina", a beautiful 4-metre (13-ft) gilded statue, graces the top of the Duomo's highest pinnacle.

Inside the Duomo

The English novelist D.H. Lawrence called the Duomo "an imitation hedgehog of a cathedral", because of its pointy intricate exterior. But inside, the church is simple, majestic and vast. Five great aisles stretch from the entrance to the altar. Enormous stone pillars dominate the nave, which is big enough to accommodate some 40,000 worshippers. In the apse, three large and intricate stained-glass windows attributed to Nicolas de Bonaventura shed a soft half-light over the area behind the altar. The central window features the shield of the Visconti, Milan's ruling family during the 13th and 14th centuries. It was Duke Gian Galeazzo Visconti, the most powerful member of the family, who commissioned the Duomo.

A gruesome statue of the flayed St Bartholomew, carrying his skin, stands in the left transept. In the right transept is an imposing 16th-century marble tomb made for Giacomo di Medici by Leone Leoni after the style of Michelangelo. The crypt contains the tomb of the Counter-Reformation saint Charles Borromeo. This 16th-century Archbishop of Milan epitomised the Lombardic virtues of energy, efficiency and discipline. Ascetic and rigorously self-denying, he expected no less from his flock. His unbending character led to frequent battles with the lay authorities, especially when he tried to ban dancing, drama and sport.

Outside, a lift will take you up to the roof of the Duomo, among the pinnacles and carved rosettes. The view from the top is spectacular; on a clear day it stretches as far as the Alps.

PRECEDING PAGES: high fashion meets high church. **LEFT:** Galleria Vittorio Emanuele. **BELOW:** the Pirelli Building, built in 1959.

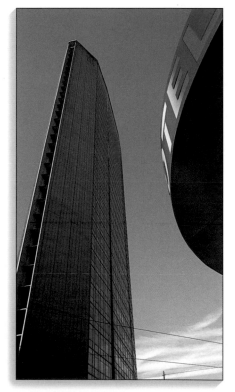

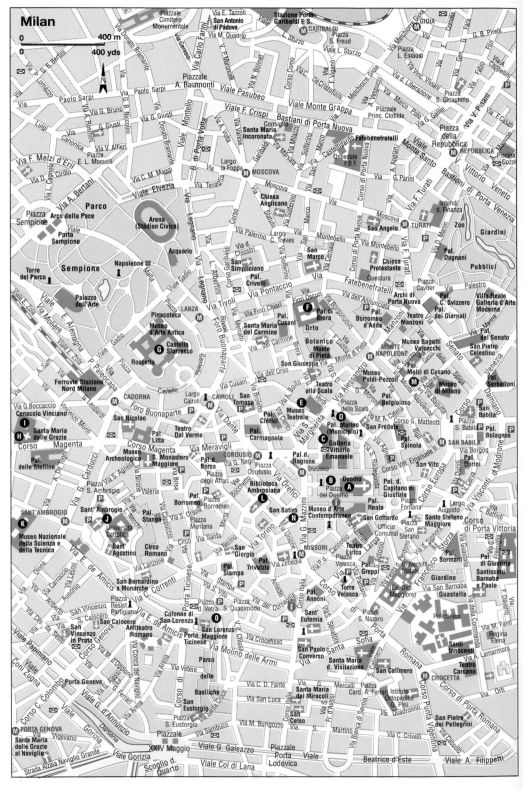

Come down into the **Piazza del Duomo** **B** where Milan's many worlds converge. The large equestrian statue standing at one end of the square honours Italy's first king, Victor Emmanuel (after whom major boulevards in cities throughout Italy are named). On two sides the piazza is lined with porticoes, where Milanese of all ages and styles love to gather. To the north is the entrance to the **Galleria Vittorio Emanuele** **C**, Italy's oldest and most elegant shopping mall. Its four-storey arcade is full of boutiques, offices, bars and restaurants. But, before you sit down to watch the world go by, be forewarned: the cafés here are pricey.

At the other side of the Galleria is **Piazza della Scala** **D**, site of the famed **La Scala** opera house, built between 1776 and 1778. The theatre suffered serious damage during Allied bombings in World War II, but has since been carefully restored. It was here that Verdi's *Otello* and Puccini's *Madama Butterfly* were first performed.

The interior of the opera house is elegantly shabby. The walls are covered in red damask and trimmed with gilt. Crystal chandeliers provide light for a capacity audience of 3,000 people. Next door, the **Museo Teatrale alla Scala** **E** (open daily 9am–noon, 2–6pm; closed Sundays in winter; entrance fee) next door will appeal to opera lovers. Memorabilia include original scores by Verdi, Liszt's piano and portraits of plump prima donnas and beefy tenors. There are even composers' death masks and casts of their hands.

Follow the Via Verdi from La Scala to the **Palazzo di Brera** **F** (open Tues–Sat 9am–5.30pm, Sun 9am–1pm; entrance fee), home of one of Italy's finest art collections. Paintings of the 15th to 18th centuries are especially well represented in the Pinacoteca di Brera. Famous works included in the collection are Mantegna's *The Dead Christ* (viewed from the pierced soles of His feet), Caravaggio's *Supper at Emmaus*, and the restored 15th-century *Madonna and Saints* by Piero della Francesca. Raphael's beautiful *Betrothal of the Virgin (Lo Sposalizio)*, a masterpiece of his Umbrian period, was his first painting to show powers of composition and draughtsmanship far in advance of his biggest influence, Perugino.

A despot's dwelling

Off the Piazza del Duomo is Via Mercanto. From there, Via Dante leads to the **Castello Sforzesco** **G** (open Tues–Sun 9.30am–5.30pm), stronghold and residence of the Sforza family, the despotic rulers of Milan in the 15th century (*forza* means strength in Italian). The greatest of the Sforzas was Francesco, a mercenary general who became the fourth Duke of Milan. To design his stronghold, Francesco employed a local architect, Giovanni da Milano, but the decoration of the principal tower was undertaken by Filarete, a Florentine.

The residential part of the castle, the Corte Ducale, contains a magnificent collection of sculpture, including Michelangelo's *Rondanini Pietà*, an almost abstract work charged with emotion. Michelangelo worked on this pietà until within a few days of his death in 1564.

Three blocks west of the castle stands the church of **Santa Maria delle Grazie** **H**, begun in 1466 but expanded in 1492 by Bramante, who also built the

See map opposite

ABOVE: bust of Verdi, in the Museo Teatrale alla Scala. **BELOW:** fortune telling.

ABOVE: fashion shop on the Via della Spiga.

BELOW: ceiling fresco in the Castello Sforzesco, and (**RIGHT**), the castle's Ponticella with a loggia by Bramante.

exquisite cloister. Next door, the **Cenacolo Vinciano**  (open 8am–10pm daily; entrance fee), once a refectory for Dominican friars, is home to Leonardo's famous *Last Supper* (1495–7). Partly because Leonardo did not use the proper fresco technique – as an experiment he worked on the plaster in oil instead of fresco – the painting has deteriorated considerably. The ongoing restoration cannot completely counteract the effects of time and damp.

Although it is considerably faded, the *Last Supper* remains a powerful and moving work. It is far larger than expected, some 9 metres (30 ft) wide and 4.5 metres (15 ft) high. Not all the expressions on the disciples' faces can be discerned, but the careful composition of the work remains completely clear. On either side of Jesus sit two groups of three apostles, linked to each other through their individual gestures and glances. It vividly captures the moment when Jesus announces that one of them is about to betray Him. This painting was seminal to the perception of the artist as a creative thinker rather than just an artisan.

From Santa Maria delle Grazie, proceed to the church of **Sant'Ambrogio** on Via Carducci. This is the finest medieval building in Milan. To enter, step down from street level and cross an austere atrium. The church is dark and low, but compelling in its antiquity. Founded between 379 and 386 by St Ambrose, then bishop of Milan – it was he who converted St Augustine – the basilica was enlarged first in the 9th century and again in the 11th. The brick-ribbed square vaults that support the galleries are typical of Lombardic architecture.

Down Via San Vittore from the basilica is the **Museo Nazionale della Scienza e della Tecnica** (open Tues–Fri 9.30am–5pm, Sat–Sun 9.30am–6pm; entrance fee). Although the large section devoted to applied physics will probably be of interest only to specialists, everyone will enjoy the huge room filled

Map, page 210

with wooden models of Leonardo's most ingenious inventions, some bearing more than a passing resemblance to modern machines. Don't miss the reconstruction of Leonardo's famous flying machine.

Return in the direction of the Duomo to the **Biblioteca Ambrosiana** , a library founded by Cardinal Federico Borromeo and built by Lelio Buzzi from 1607–9. It now houses a small but exquisite collection of paintings dating from the 15th to the 17th century (open Tues–Sun 10am–6pm; entrance fee). Most notable among the works is Leonardo's *Portrait of a Musician*.

Fashion avenue

For a break from sightseeing and a glimpse of an important and more contemporary aspect of Milanese life, stroll down the **Via Monte Napoleone** ⓜ, which extends off Corso Vittorio Emanuele between the Duomo and Piazza Santa Babila. This is the most elegant shopping street in Milan. You will find all the star names of Italian fashion here (or on the adjoining Via della Spiga and Via Sant'-Andrea) – Armani, Moschino, Valentino, Romeo Gigli, Krizia and Versace to name a few – as well as the latest in household design and contemporary art.

If you have time on your visit to Milan, there are two more churches which are worth seeking out. In the Via Torino, near the Piazza del Duomo, stands **San Satiro** ⓝ, built by Bramante in 1478–80. Inside, the architect cleverly used stucco to create an illusionistic effect, giving the impression that the church is far larger than it actually is. **San Lorenzo Maggiore** ⓞ, quite nearby on Corso di Porta Ticinese, attests to Milan's antiquity. The basilica was founded in the 4th century and rebuilt in 1103. Martino Bassi restored it in 1574–88, but its octagonal shape and many beautiful 5th-century mosaics are original. ❑

TIP

For a gruesome glimpse of the past, venture down into the crypt of Sant'Ambrogio to see the skeletal remains of St Ambrose, Milan's patron saint, along with those of two early Christian martyrs.

BELOW: fresco in Sant'Ambrogio.

CONSPICUOUS CONSUMPTION

Visitors come to Milan as much to shop and dine as to visit the much decayed *Last Supper* of Leonardo da Vinci. Following the exposure of institutionalised corruption and the imprisonment (albeit on suspended sentences) of some prominent Italian industrialists and politicians, getting a seat at La Scala, or a table at one of Milan's top restaurants, is no longer quite so difficult as it used to be. Even so, you should book well in advance if you plan to eat at a top establishment, such as the very grand Savini (Galleria Vittorio Emanuele II, tel: 7200 3433) where you can try the definitive *risotto alla Milanese*, or the Michelin-starred Ristorante Peck, at Via Victor Hugo 4, where you can enjoy a reasonably priced six-course gastronomic menu (tel: 876 774). Impoverished visitors need not feel left out: you can always shop for picnic ingredients at Gastronomia Peck, choosing from the huge and enticing selection of cheeses, meats and pastries on display.

Neither need shopping in Milan cost an arm and a leg. Though you need deep pockets to buy designer goods in the Golden Quarter (Quadrilatera d'Oro), there are also many factory outlets selling seconds or last season's goods, especially in the north of the city (the city guide available from Milan's tourist office has further details).

LOMBARDY

Beneath is spread like a green sea / The waveless plain
of Lombardy, Bounded by the vaporous air, Islanded by cities fair
— PERCY BYSSHE SHELLEY

F rom the heights of the central Alps to the low-lying plains of the Po Valley, the province of Lombardy is remarkably diverse. Contrasts abound in this land named after the Lombards, one of the barbarian tribes that invaded Italy in the 6th century. Its cities, renowned for their elegance since Renaissance times, are complemented by dramatic scenery. The Italian Lakes jut into the heart of a steep mountain range, offset by fertile farmlands and fields of gently swaying poplars.

An easy day trip from **Milan ❶**, or a stop-over on a longer journey south, is the **Certosa di Pavia ❷** (Charterhouse of Pavia; open Tues–Sun 9–11.30am, 2.30pm–1 hr before sunset; donation). This world-famous church, mausoleum and monastery complex, founded in 1396, is a masterpiece of Lombardic Renaissance architecture, complete with relief sculpture and inlaid marble. The interior of the church is Gothic in plan, but highly embellished with Renaissance and baroque details. Inside stand the tombs of Ludovico Visconti and his child-bride, Beatrice d'Este. Their bodies are not actually buried here, but life-sized effigies on top of the tombs portray them in all their life-time splendour.

Behind the Certosa is a magnificent Great Cloister where Carthusian monks, who had taken vows of silence, once lived in individual dwellings. Each cottage is two-storeys high with two rooms on the ground floor and a bedroom and loggia above. Each monk, living in seclusion, took delivery of his food through the small swing portal at the right of his doorway.

Nowadays, Pavia is a country backwater, but between the 6th and 8th centuries it was the capital city of the Lombards. Pavia's fame was augmented in 1361 when the university was founded, and to this day it remains a prestigious centre of learning.

On the Via Diacono, in the old centre of town, is the church of **San Michele**, consecrated in 1155. Here the great medieval Lombard leader, Frederick Barbarossa, was crowned king of Italy. Look for the carefully sculpted scenes of the battle between good and evil above the three doorways. Inside, San Michele is plain and sombre; only the columns are highly decorated.

Eclectic and electric

To reach the **Duomo**, follow the Strada Nuova from San Michele. This cathedral is an eclectic mixture of four centuries of architectural styles. The basic design is Renaissance (Bramante and Leonardo worked on it), but the immense dome is a late 19th-century touch and the facade was added in 1933. The rest of the exterior is unfinished.

If you continue on the Strada Nuova you will arrive at the **Università**, where 17,000 students currently attend classes. One of Pavia's most famous past graduates was

LEFT: the cloister of the Certosa di Pavia, and (**BELOW**) sculpture on its facade.

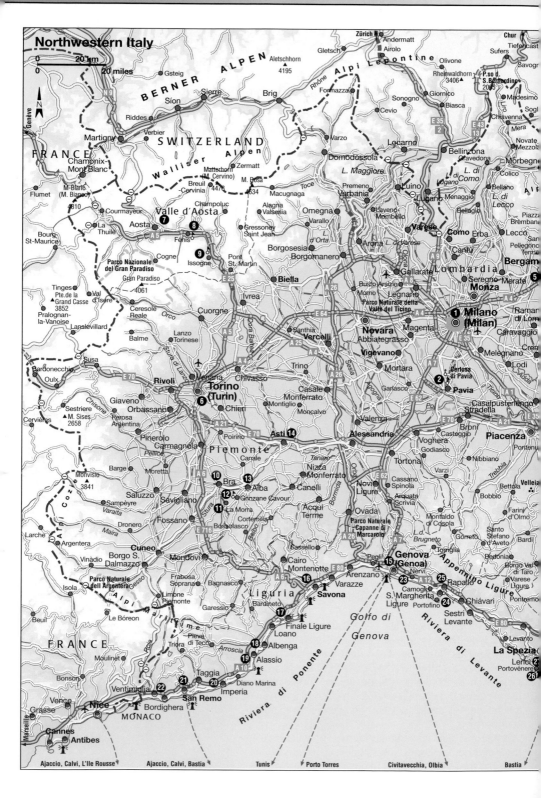

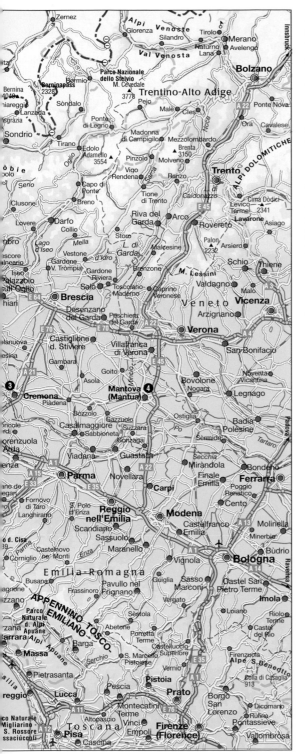

Alessandro Volta, the physicist who discovered and gave his name to electrical volts. His statue stands in the left-hand court of the university complex.

At the end of the Strada Nuova stands the **Castello Visconteo**, an imposing square fortress built in 1360–65. Today, the castle is the home of the **Museo Civico** (open Tues–Sun 9am–1pm; entrance fee). Included in the museum's collection are many fine Lombardic Romanesque sculptures and remnants of Roman Pavia – inscriptions, glass and pottery.

Go west from the castle to reach **San Pietro in Ciel d'Oro**, a fine Lombardic Romanesque church, smaller than San Michele, but quite similar. A richly decorated Gothic arch at the high altar is said to contain the relics of St Augustine.

Before leaving Pavia, have a bowl of the town's speciality, the hearty *zuppa alla pavese*, a recipe said to have been concocted by a peasant woman for Francis I of France. The king was about to lose the Battle of Pavia (1525) to the Spanish when he stopped for a bite to eat at a nearby cottage. His hostess wanted her humble minestrone to be fit for a king, so she added toasted bread, cheese and eggs.

Cremona

About two hours' drive from Pavia lies the city of **Cremona ❸**, a world-famous centre of violin making and a pleasant market town on the banks of the Po River. The greatest of Cremonese violin makers was Antonio Stradivari (1644–1737) whose secret formula for varnish may account for the beautiful sound of a Stradivarius violin. Some of these glorious instruments are on display at the 13th-century **Palazzo del Comune** (open Tues–Sat 8.30am–6pm, Sun 9am–noon, 3–6pm; entrance fee) on Corso Vittorio Emanuele and the modern **International School of Violin Making** nearby.

The **Duomo** at Cremona is a pink marble structure in the Lombardic Romanesque style. Although it was consecrated in 1190, it was not completed until much later. Inside the church, 17th-century tapestries on the *Life of Samson* surround some of the heavy columns.

Try to visit Mantua on a Thursday, when Piazza delle Erbe, Piazza Mantegna and nearby streets become an enormous market.

BELOW: outside a violin workshop in Cremona.

Mantua

Because **Mantua** (Mantova) ❹ lies on a peninsula in the Mincio River, surrounded by a lagoon on three sides, it is known as Piccola Venezia (Little Venice). But history has given the city a more resonant name: "Ducal Mantua", because from 1328–1707 the enlightened but despotic Gonzaga family ruled the town from its sombre fortress. Mantua has a slightly musty medieval atmosphere about it. Wandering through the cobble-stoned streets at night, a visitor might easily imagine being challenged by a couple of comic characters from a Shakespearean play, or happening upon one of the trysts between the unfortunate Gilda and the philandering Duke of Mantua from Verdi's *Rigoletto*.

During the Renaissance, the Gonzaga court was one of the bright lights of Italian culture, especially under the influence of the Marchioness Isabella d'Este (1474–1539), who modelled her life on *Il Cortegione*, a textbook for courtiers and ladies written by Castiglione. She even gave Castiglione a palace in Mantua. Nor was her patronage limited to literary geniuses, since she also hired Raphael, Mantegna and Giulio Romano to decorate the Reggia dei Gonzaga (**Palazzo Ducale**), once the largest palace in Europe. The public can visit a selection of the palace's 500 or more rooms by joining a tour (open Tues–Sat 9am–1pm, 2.30–5pm, Sun–Mon 9am–1pm; entrance fee). Particularly worth seeing are the nine tapestries in the Appartamento degli Arazzi that were made in Flanders from drawings by Raphael. The Camera degli Sposi (the matrimonial suite) is decorated with frescoes by Mantegna depicting scenes from the lives of the Marquess Ludovico Gonzaga and his wife, Barbara of Brandenburg.

Across town is **Palazzo del Tè** (open Tues–Fri 9am–5.30pm, Mon 1–5.30pm; entrance fee), the Gonzaga summer residence. Designed by Giulio Romano in

1525, this palace is delicate and pleasing. Many rooms are decorated with frescoes of summer scenes and there is a lovely garden, though the lime trees (*tigli*) that gave the palace its name are long gone.

Mantua's **Duomo**, located near the Reggia, has a baroque facade added in 1756. Inside, the cathedral has a Renaissance design and stucco decoration by Giulio Romano. Also worth a visit is the **Basilica di Sant'Andrea** in Piazza Mantegna. The Florentine L.B. Alberti designed most of Sant'Andrea, starting in 1472, but the dome was added in the 18th century. Inside, Sant'Andrea is at once both simple and grand. The frescoes that adorn the walls were designed by Mantegna and executed by his pupils, among them Correggio.

Map, pages 216–7

Bergamo

If you want to escape from the hot stillness of "the waveless plain of Lombardy", there is no more restful or picturesque town than **Bergamo** ❺, too often bypassed by tourists racing along the autostrada between Milan and Venice. Bergamo is, in fact, two cities: Bergamo Bassa and Bergamo Alta.

The modern **Bergamo Bassa**, where the railway station is, though pleasant and spacious, is less dramatic than its parent town which rises upon a rough-hewn crag. Beneath its shadow runs Via Pignola lined with elegant palaces built between the 16th and 18th centuries. But the real treasure of Bergamo Bassa is the **Accademia Carrara** (open Wed–Mon 9.30am–noon, 2.30–5.30pm; entrance fee). Where else but in Italy can you find, in a small city, a collection of paintings that the grandest metropolis would be proud to have? In this case, it is thanks to the good taste of the 18th-century Count Giacomo Carrara. There is no need to queue to look at paintings by Pisanello, Lotto, Carpaccio, Bellini and Mantegna since the museum is deserted except for the cordial guards.

ABOVE: window of Bergamo's Santa Maria Maggiore.
BELOW: the Palazzo Ducale in Mantua.

If you enjoy mountain climbing, take the creaking funicular to **Bergamo Alta**, a medieval town built in a warm brown stone. The inhabitants keep their ancient town in beautiful condition. The best spot in which to sit and admire it is the central **Piazza Vecchia** – a good place to find the local speciality *polenta con gli uccelli* (polenta with quail). The piazza is flanked by the 17th-century Palazzo Nuovo and the 12th-century Palazzo della Ragione. Beyond the medieval building's arcade is the small Piazza del Duomo packed with ecclesiastical treasures: the Romanesque **Santa Maria Maggiore** and the Renaissance Colleoni Chapel (open daily in summer 9am–12.30pm, 2–6.30pm, Tues–Sat till 4.30pm in winter), designed by Amadeo who contributed to the Certosa di Pavia, and with an 18th-century ceiling by Tiepolo. The chapel is dedicated to the Bergamesque *condottiere* Bartolomeo Colleoni. The mercenary fought so well for the Venetians that he was rewarded with an estate in his native province, which, at that time, was under Venetian rule.

Music lovers will want to visit the **Istituto Musicale Donizetti** (open Tues–Sun; entrance fee). The composer was born in 1797 in Bergamo to a seamstress mother and pawnbroker father. He died here in 1848, quite insane, having composed 75 operas, of which the best known today is *Lucia di Lammermoor*. ❑

THE LAKES

*Although close to the Alps, the Italian lakes enjoy cool summers
and mild winters which make the region ideal for hikers,
windsurfers, or anyone who enjoys magnificent landscapes*

Map,
pages
222–3

T he Italian lakes have long been a retreat for romantics. Writers drawn to their shores include Pliny the Younger, Shelley, Stendhal and D.H. Lawrence. "What can one say of Lake Maggiore, of the Borromean Islands, of the Lake Como, except to pity people who do not go mad over them?" wrote Stendhal. Today, they are also a playground for the rich, as well as a popular destination for tourists and honeymooners from all over the world, drawn to their ravishing scenery. But despite the number of visitors, and the lakes' proximity to Milan's international airport (Lake Como, for instance, is a 90-minute drive away), the region has lost none of its allure.

There are five major lakes in the Italian Lake District (from west to east: Lakes Maggiore, Lugano, Como, Iseo and Garda), and each lake has its own character, though all are the result of the same geological processes. The lakes were formed during the last Ice Age, which ended around 11,000 years ago, and are the result of glaciers thrusting down from the Alps and gouging out deep valleys wherever softer rock created an easy pathway for the ice. Later, as the ice melted, the lakes were formed in the valley bottoms. All run roughly north to south and all enjoy sheltered microclimates that make them warm and mild in winter (especially on the southern shores which benefit from winter sunshine – the northern shores tend to be overshadowed by Alpine peaks).

Another phenomenon, which makes the lakes popular with sailors and windsurfers, is the dependable offshore wind, caused by temperature and air pressure differences between the warmer water and the cooler surrounding mountains. Sunbathers on the shores of the lake can bask in warm still air, whilst a stiff wind blows on the lake itself.

LEFT: Bellagio, on Lake Como.
BELOW: statue in the garden of Villa Pallavicino.

Lake Maggiore

The westernmost lake, **Lago Maggiore ❶**, has a special attraction: the **Borromean Islands ❷**, named after their owners, a prominent Milanese family whose members included a cardinal, a bishop and a saint. **Isola Bella**, the most romantic of the three islands, was a desolate rock with just a few cottages until the 16th century when Count Charles Borromeo III decided to civilise the island in honour of his wife, Isabella. With the help of the architect Angelo Crivelli, Charles designed the splendid palace and gardens.

Isola dei Pescatori is, as the name suggests, a fishing village. Another Borromeo palace and elaborate botanical gardens decorate **Isola Madre**. All three islands are served by ferries from the main lakeside towns.

The most famous and liveliest settlement on the shores of Lago Maggiore is **Stresa ❸** (put on the

ABOVE: ceiling decoration in Como's cathedral. The building was started in 1396 and only completed in the 18th century.

literary map by Hemingway's *A Farewell to Arms*) with its many beautiful *belle époque* villas. Two famous villas adjoining the landing stage are the **Villa Ducale**, residence of the philosopher Antonio Rosmini (1797–1855), and the **Villa Pallavicino** (open Mar–Oct daily; entrance fee), remarkable for its fine gardens. From Stresa, it's a short drive to the summit of **Monte Mottarone**, from where there is a stunning view of the Alps, the lake and the town below.

  Baveno ❹, northwest of Stresa, is a small quiet town near the islands and the site of many villas, among them the **Castello Branca** where the British Queen Victoria spent the spring of 1879. The drive south from Stresa to **Arona ❺** along the Lungolago is especially pretty: the road is tree-lined, the views of the lakes and islands spectacular. Arona itself is a rather unremarkable resort town, but it does contain a number of attractive 15th-century buildings.

Lake Lugano

On the map, **Lago di Lugano ❻** (Lake Lugano) looks like a crudely drawn cartoon animal with a very long tail. Much of the lake lies within Swiss territory; only the very eastern tip of the tail is Italian, plus the enclave of Campione d'Italia, a little lakeside town that remains proudly and typically Italian, whilst being entirely surrounded by Swiss territory (and using Swiss currency and postage stamps). Visitors come to Campione for the Casino and its nightlife.

Lake Como

Lago di Como ❼ (Lake Como) is the most dramatic of the lakes. It is 31 km (19 miles) long and up to 5 km (3 miles) across. At many points the shore is a sheer cliff, and the Alps (providing year-round skiing on the glaciers) loom like

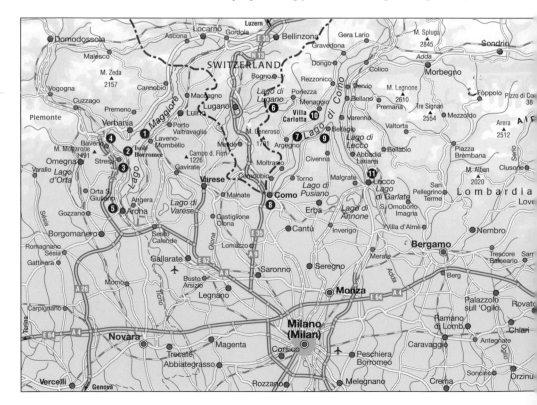

a wall at the northern end of the lake. **Como** ❽ itself is an historic yet thriving town. Silk weaving, which for many years was confined to homes and small workshops in Como, is now concentrated in several factories.

Como's **Giardini Pubblici** is a pleasant place to relax and look over the lake. In the midst of these gardens stands the Tempio Voltiano, a classic rotunda dedicated to Alessandro Volta, who gave his name to the volt. Many of the instruments he used in his electrical experiments are on display.

It's an easy walk across the town to **Santa Maria Maggiore**, Como's 14th-century marble cathedral. The intricately carved portal is flanked by statues of the two Plinys, who were among the earliest admirers of Lake Como. "Are you given to studying, or do you prefer fishing or hunting or do you go in for all three?" the younger Pliny asked a friend and boasted that all three activities were possible at Lake Como. Some 2,000 years later, Como still offers sports to athletically inclined visitors, relaxation to harried city dwellers and inspiration to artists and poets.

The 11th-century church of **Sant'Abbondio** on the outskirts of Como will transport you back to Como's pre-resort days, when it was a pious and prosperous medieval village. Chances are that you will have this solemn Lombardic church to yourself. The 14th-century frescoes of the *Life of Jesus*, in the apse, make it worth the trip.

Although the distance between the two cities is not great as the crow flies, it takes an hour of driving on narrow, twisting roads to reach **Bellagio** ❾ from Como. Going by public boat from Como's pier is a more pleasant way of getting there. Bellagio sits on the point of land that divides Lago di Como into three parts. From here you can see the entire expanse of the lake and enjoy a spectac-

Map, see opposite

The southeastern spur of Lake Como is known as the Lago di Lecco.

BELOW: sculpture by Canova in Villa Carlotta, across the lake from Bellagio.

Lecco is a good base
for hikers. It also has
good rail connections
with Milan and
Bergamo.

ular view of the Alps. "Sublimity and grace here combine to a degree which is
equalled but not surpassed by the most famous site in the world, the Bay of
Naples," wrote Stendhal in *The Charterhouse of Parma*. The Frenchman set the
opening scenes of his novel in the **Villa Carlotta** ⑩ (across the lake from Bellagio) after staying here as a guest. Today the villa (open mid-Mar–Oct daily;
entrance fee), originally built by a Prussian princess for her daughter, and its
idyllic gardens provide the perfect setting for a picnic lunch.

Lecco ⑪, a pleasant city at the southeastern end of Lago di Como, is famous
as the setting of Alessandro Manzoni's *The Betrothed*, a 19th-century novel
which is a classic of Italian literature, and a revealing piece of social history.
The author was a native of Lecco and a political activist instrumental in bringing about Italy's unification. Visitors can explore his childhood home, the **Villa
Manzoni** (open Tues–Sun 9.30am–2pm; entrance fee).

Among the more antique attractions of the city is the **Basilica** with its fine
frescoes from the 14th century depicting the Annunciation, the Deposition and
the Life of San Antonio. The oldest monument in the city is the bridge spanning
the Adda river, the **Ponte Azzone Visconti**, built between 1336 and 1338.

BELOW: the baroque
church of Madonna
di Monte Castello,
on the west side of
Lake Garda.
BELOW RIGHT: the
Rocca Scaligera.

Lake Iseo

Lago d'Iseo ⑫ (Lake Iseo) is the fifth largest of the lakes, measuring 24 km
(15 miles) long by 5 km (3 miles) wide. Views of the lake all focus on the large
island that sits in the middle: graphically named **Monte Isola** (Mountain Island),
this is the largest island of any European lake, and it typifies the rugged mountainous appeal of this lake and its surroundings. Northeast of the lake, the town
of **Capo di Ponte** makes a good base for exploring the **Val Camonica**,

renowned for its prehistoric rock carvings and designated a UN World Heritage Site. Some 158,000 rock carvings have been found, 75 percent of them in the Capo di Ponte area; dating from as far back as 8,000 years ago, they are a record of the hunting and farming activities of the local Camuni tribe. The local tourist office sells guides to the **Parco Nazionale delle Incisioni Rupestri** (National Rock Engravings Park; open Tues–Sun 9am–sunset; entrance fee) with five colour-coded trails.

Southeast of the lake is Lombardy's second city, **Brescia** ⓭. The highlights of the city are clustered together on the Cydnean Hill at the heart of the city, and they include the remains of a Roman temple, a **Roman Museum** (open in summer Tues–Sun 10am–5pm; 9.30am–1pm, 2.30–5pm in winter; entrance fee) containing the fine bronze figure of *Victory* which once stood on the temple pediment, a small zoo, a 15th-century castle and the fine 12th-century church of San Pietro, all set in attractive parkland. Down in the town is the 12th-century Old Cathedral, and its 16th-century replacement, a domed baroque building clad in white marble. The early Christian heritage of Brescia is celebrated in the **Museum of Christian Antiquities** (hours as for Roman Museum), including a magnificent 8th-century silver cross encrusted with precious jewels. The **Museo delle Armi** houses Italy's finest collection of antique weapons (open Tues–Sun; closed 12.30–3pm; entrance fee).

Lake Garda

Lago di Garda ⓮ (Lake Garda) is the cleanest and largest of the Italian lakes. It is especially popular with northern European tourists, who come to sail and water-ski. Its equable climate is responsible for Soave and Valpolicella wines.

ABOVE: lily from Gardone Riviera.
BELOW: church in Bardolino, on Garda.

On the shores of this lake is a garish remnant of the Fascist era – **Il Vittoriale** – the home of the flamboyant Italian poet and patriot Gabriele d'Annunzio which was given to him by his greatest admirer, Benito Mussolini (open in summer Tues–Sun 9am–8pm; 9am–12.30pm, 2–5.30pm in winter; entrance fee). Located in **Gardone Riviera** ⓯, at one time Lake Garda's most fashionable resort, Il Vittoriale is more than a house, it is a shrine to d'Annunzio's dreams of Italian imperialism. Included in the estate is the prow of the warship *Puglia,* built into the hillside. In the auditorium, the plane d'Annunzio flew during World War I is suspended from the ceiling. Mussolini subscribed to d'Annunzio's ideas whole-heartedly and accorded him a place of honour in Fascist Italy.

From Salò and Gardone Riviera it takes no more than an hour to reach **Sirmione** ⓰, a medieval town built on a spit of land extending into the lake. The **Rocca Scaligera** (open Tues–Sun 9am–6pm; till 1pm in winter; entrance fee), a fairytale castle, dominates the town's entrance. It was originally the fortress of the Scaligeri family, rulers of Garda in the 13th century, and it is said that they entertained the poet Dante here. An enjoyable hour or two can be spent exploring the local shops, dipping into churches and following the footpath that leads to the tip of the peninsula, with its extensive ruins of a Roman spa, the **Grotte di Catullo** (open Tues–Sun 8.30am–6pm; till 4pm in winter; entrance fee). ❏

PIEDMONT, VALLE D'AOSTA AND LIGURIA

Maps, pages 216 & 228

If it is not so Italian as Italy it is at least more Italian than anything but Italy.—HENRY JAMES

Piedmont (Piemonte) may strike today's visitor, as it did Henry James, as not very Italian. The bordering nations of France and Switzerland have contributed much to the cultural life of this northwestern region. More-over, the Alpine landscapes of Piedmont, especially in the dramatic Valle d'Aosta, are very different from scenery elsewhere in Italy. But the particular Piedmontese twist on Italian life is not unappealing. It's as if the cool mountain breezes have bestowed a calming effect on the people. No wonder that it was a Piedmontese king, Victor Emmanuel, and his Piedmontese advisor, Count Camillo Cavour, who guided Italy to independence.

Turin ❻ (Torino), the capital of Piedmont, is a genuinely Italian city, but its proximity and century-old ties to France give it a strong Gallic flavour. During the Middle Ages, it was part of a Lombardic duchy, but in the 16th century it became the capital of the French province of Savoy. Following the Risorgi-mento, it was the capital of united Italy from 1861 to 1865.

Today, Turin is headquarters for some of Italy's most successful industries, including the Fiat automobile company. It is also a centre for the chemical and confectionery industries, metal working and industrial design. But the factories of Turin are a long way from the city's gracious centre, with its wide streets and beau-tiful squares, gardens and parks where visitors can soak up the sun and sample the spirit of this most modern of Italian cities.

LEFT: the dome of San Lorenzo in Turin. **BELOW:** the city's Royal Garden.

Historic town centre

The centre of civic life in Turin is the fashionable **Via Roma**, an arcaded shopping street that connects the **Stazione Porta Nuova ❶** with **Piazza Castello ❷**, a huge rectangular Renaissance square planned in 1584. In the centre stands **Palazzo Madama**, a 15th-century castle that houses the **Museo Civico di Arte Antica** (Museum of Ancient Art), unfortunately closed indefi-nitely for restoration. Included in this museum's col-lections is a copy of part of the famous *Book of Hours* of the Duc de Berry, illustrated by Jan van Eyck.

Another fine building on the Piazza Castello is the baroque church of **San Lorenzo**, once the royal chapel. The royal residence was the 17th-century **Palazzo Reale ❸** (open Tues–Sun till 2pm; booking essential, tel: 011-436 1455; entrance fee) in the nearby piazza of the same name. From its balcony, Prince Carlo Alberto declared war on Austria in March 1848. In the same square is the **Armeria Reale** (Royal Armoury).

Behind the Palazzo Reale, in **Piazza San Giovanni**, are the **Duomo ❹** and **Campanile**. The former is a

Turin

Renaissance construction designed by the Tuscan, Meo del Caprino; the Campanile is the work of a baroque architect. The cathedral was damaged by fire in April 1997, but fortunately the flames did not consume the **Cappella della Sacra Sindone** (Chapel of the Holy Shroud) – a work of Guarino Guarini. It contains the famous Turin Shroud, for centuries believed to be the shroud in which Christ was wrapped after the Crucifixion.The cloth is imprinted with the image of a bearded man crowned with thorns. Carbon dating, conducted by three universities in 1989, suggests that the shroud is the work of clever medieval forgers. For four centuries the royal House of Savoy owned the shroud, but on his death in 1983, the exiled king, Umberto, left the relic to the Vatican. It will, however, remain in Turin, but is not generally on view.

See map opposite

The Piedmontese capital may seem an unlikely centre for the study of Egyptian art, but there is a rich **Egyptian Museum** (open Tues–Sat 9am–10pm, Sun 9am–6pm; entrance fee) in the **Palazzo dell'Accademia delle Scienze** ❺, off Via Roma. The collection was assembled by Carlo Emanuele III, and includes the fascinating tomb of the architect Kha. The same palazzo also contains a good picture collection on the second floor in the **Galleria Sabauda** (open Tues–Sat till 2pm; also Sun till 10pm; entrance fee). There are several beautiful Flemish and Dutch works, and many paintings by Piedmontese masters.

For a taste of France, visit the agreeable **Parco del Valentino**, on the bank of the Po, which contains miles of paths, a botanic garden and the **Castello del Valentino** ❻ (open Tues–Sun 10.30am–4pm; entrance fee), a 17th-century palace built in the style of a French château. In 1884, Turin was the site of a great international exhibition for which the park's **Borgo Medioevale** (a pseudo-medieval town) was erected.

ABOVE: vintage car in the Museo dell' Automobile. **BELOW:** medieval castle in the Valle d'Aosta.

It is not surprising that the automobile capital of Italy should have a fine museum of cars. It can take hours to explore **Carlo Biscaretti di Ruffia Museo dell'Automobile** ❼ (open Tues–Sun 9am–12.30pm, 3–7pm; entrance fee). Exhibits include the earliest Fiat, the Itala that won the world's longest automobile race (between Peking (Beijing) and Paris in 1907) and an elegant Rolls-Royce Silver Ghost.

Across the Po, a small hill, the **Monte dei Cappuccini** ❽, is crowned by a Capuchin church and convent. After visiting this, take a bus or the rack railway to **Superga**, to see the **Basilica di Superga**, a "great votive temple" (Henry James) by Juvarra which houses the tombs of the kings of Sardinia and the Princes of Savoy. This basilica sits on a high hill commanding a splendid view of the natural amphitheatre of the Alps.

Valle d'Aosta

For anyone who wishes to get away from the city, the beautiful Alpine valleys of Piedmont have much to offer. This was the venue for the World Alpine Skiing Championship in 1997. During July and August the thrills of winter sports give way to the calmer delights of hiking and touring in an area noted for its glaciers, hilltop castles, clear mountain lakes and streams, pine forests and green meadows.

The most striking part of this area is called Valle d'Aosta. In 1947, this valley acquired political auton-

omy and became a region in its own right. Here rise Europe's highest mountains: Mont Blanc, Monte Rosa, and the Cervino (Matterhorn). The capital, **Aosta** ❼, was an important city in Roman times and has many interesting Roman ruins. Roman walls surround the city, and the ruins of the **Roman Theatre**, in the northwest corner of Aosta, include the well-preserved backdrop of the stage. Emperor Augustus, nicknamed Aosta the "Rome of the Alps", and it is the Arch of Augustus that guards the main entrance to the city.

Dating from Aosta's medieval period are the cathedral and several smaller churches. Among the latter group, the **church of Sant'Orso** (outside the walls on Via Sant'Orso) is the most interesting. The architecture is a strange mix of Gothic and Romanesque. St Orso – he converted the first Christians in the Valle d'Aosta – is buried beneath the altar. Be sure to visit the cloister, which dates back to the 12th-century and is known for its unusual carved pillars.

The courtyard of the castle at Fénis has a vivid fresco of St George and the Dragon.

The valley southeast of Aosta contains many fine castles, in particular those at **Fénis** ❽ (open daily 10am–5pm; till 7pm in summer; entrance fee) and **Issogne** ❾ (open daily 10am–5pm; entrance fee), which were used as both residences and fortresses. The lord of Verrès, Giorgio de Challant, commissioned the castle at Issogne in 1497. Today you can stroll through the former seigneurial apartments to see the collection of tapestries, jewellery and furniture.

BELOW: Gran Paradiso National Park, south of Aosta.

Southeast of Turin, Piedmont turns into a region of rolling hills and long valleys. In some ways it is reminiscent of Tuscany, and like Tuscany it is an excellent wine-growing area. From Turin head towards Alba along the autostrada. If you have time, make a stop at **Bra** ❿ to see a fine baroque church, **Sant' Andrea**, and an attractive Gothic building called the **Casa Traversa**. The hills surounding the small town of **La Morra** ⓫, 10 km (6 miles) from Bra, are the

source of one of Italy's greatest wines, Barolo. In **Grinzane Cavour** , between La Morra and Alba, is the Castello Cavour, an imposing 13th-century fortification which houses a wine museum (open Wed–Mon am; also pm in summer; closed Jan; entrance fee).

Alba ⓭ has long been a favourite with gourmets. It sits at the centre of an area famous for white truffles. These treats are a principal attraction at the city's October fair. Alba also has a fine late 15th-century Gothic cathedral, with a 16th-century inlaid wooden choir.

For more taste treats, proceed to **Asti** ⓮, a city at the centre of a valley that produces Asti Spumante and other famous wines. The city's Gothic cathedral is a splendid edifice with three ornate portals and circular openings above. The nearby baptistry of San Pietro, dating from the 12th century, is the most interesting of the city's medieval monuments.

The region of Liguria

A narrow strip of coastline sandwiched between sea and mountains, Liguria curves and twists in an east-west arch from the French border to Tuscany. Known as the Italian Riviera, the region is favoured by a year-round mild climate, excellent beaches, and the dramatic Maritime and Ligurian Apennines, which plunge in sheer cliffs or slope gradually to the sea. It is an area of sudden contrasts, not merely between rocky shores and deep green-blue water, but between cosmopolitan resorts and isolated villages, bustling ports and quiet inlets.

Genoa ⓯ (Genova) rises above the sea like a great theatre. Its tiers are elegant palazzi and its pit is a noisy, strong-smelling port, the most important in Italy. La Superba, as the city was known in its heyday, rose to prominence between the 11th and 15th centuries, growing rich on trade with the East, and economic and cultural control of Liguria and the island of Corsica.

Immediately behind the docks, the lower city begins. Here streets are ancient and narrow with twisting alleys – called *carrugi* – nowadays lined with exotic shops. The afternoon *passeggiata* in Genoa takes place on the elegant **Via Luccoli** Ⓐ, a *carrugio* of slightly wider proportions than most. Strolling along with the prosperous Genoese, you can decide for yourself whether Mark Twain was right to consider the Genoese women the most beautiful in Italy.

Not far from the dock that serves large luxury liners is the **Stazione Principe** Ⓑ, an open airy building facing a small square with a striking statue of Christopher Columbus, the most famous Genoese of all time. From the railway station follow the Via Balbi, an avenue lined on both sides with sombre Renaissance palazzi. Stop at No. 10, the 17th-century **Palazzo Reale** Ⓒ, famous for its mirror gallery and its art collection (open Sun–Tues 9am–2pm, Wed–Sat 9am–7pm; entrance fee).

Continue towards the centre on Via Balbi until it becomes **Via Garibaldi** Ⓓ. This street splits Genoa in two; to your right are the twisting alleys of the old town, and to the left are the newer sections on the hillside. No. 11 Via Garibaldi is one of the most magnificent of Genoese palaces: **Palazzo Bianco** Ⓔ (open Tues–Sun 9am–1pm; Wed, Sat, Sun till 6pm;entrance fee). This

ABOVE: door knocker in Genoa's Palazzo Ducale.
BELOW: Genoa harbour.

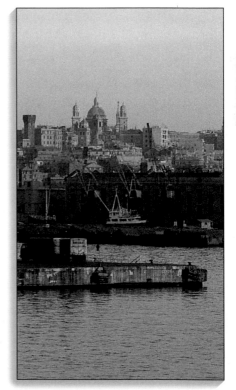

Maps, pages 216 & 232

16th-century structure was originally white, but the stone has darkened considerably with time. The facade is baroque, due to major remodelling in the early 18th century. Inside, an art collection features many extraordinary works by Flemish masters.

Across the street is the **Palazzo Rosso** ❻ (hours as above; entrance fee); in this case time has wrought few changes in the colour. Go inside to see the beautiful courtyard. Most of the other Renaissance residences on Via Garibaldi are privately owned and can only be admired from the outside. The Romanesque-Gothic **Duomo** ❻ (12th–14th century) was, according to legend, founded by St Lawrence in the 3rd century. History, however, dates the building to 1118. One of its Gothic portals bears a relief sculpture of the Roman saint's gruesome martyrdom. While being burned alive, St Lawrence is supposed to have said to his tormentors: "One side has been roasted, turn me over and eat it."

The doors open onto a severe interior, simply decorated with black and white marble in the central nave and galleries. At the end of the left nave is the entrance to the **Treasury**, a museum of the cathedral's artefacts (open Mon–Sat 9am–noon, 3–6pm; entrance fee). Among the sacred relics of the church is a basin of green Roman glass which, according to tradition, was used at the Last Supper. Some people believe it to be the true Holy Grail.

The Doria family, who ruled Genoa in the Middle Ages, built their houses and a private church around the **Piazza San Matteo** ❻, lying just behind the cathedral. Each of the buildings on this small, elegant piazza has a black and white facade. Between San Matteo and the port lies the most beguiling part of old Genoa, best explored by day. Also near the cathedral is the 16th-century **Palazzo Ducale** ❶, once the seat of government and now a cultural centre.

BELOW: Palazzo San Giorgio in Genoa.

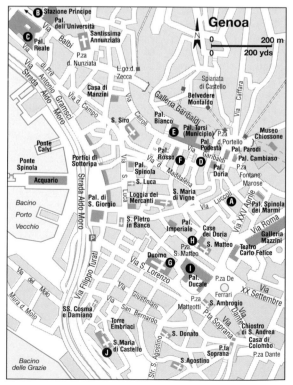

To reach another fine Genoese church, go down Via Chiabrera to Piazza Embriaci. Follow the precipitous Salita della Torre degli Embriaci up to **Santa Maria di Castello ❿** (open Mon–Sun 9am–noon, 3.30–6pm, Sun 3.30–6pm; entrance fee), an elegant church with a complex of chapels, courtyards and gardens. This was the site of a Roman camp, and several Roman columns have been incorporated into the Romanesque design of the nave. When you're tired of churches and palaces, head down to the bustling waterfront for a plate of *trenette* with *pesto alla genovese* – pasta with a sauce of basil, garlic and cheese.

The Italian Rivieras

Flanking Genoa on either side are two famous and beautiful coasts; each offers ample doses of sand, sun and sea, but they are quite different. The **Riviera di Ponente**, stretching from Genoa to the French border, is the longer of the two, and the one with more popular resorts. The **Riviera di Levante** is characterised by rocky cliffs and promontaries and has a large naval port at La Spezia.

Heading towards France from Genoa, the first city you'll pass is **Savona ⓰**, a port and industrial centre. With the exception of a small art gallery on Via Quarda Superiore, Savona offers little of interest to the tourist. The town of **Finale Ligure ⓱**, a 30-minute drive further on, is a more inviting place. Visit the **Church of San Biagio**, which has an octagonal Gothic bell tower adjoining.

The most important town on the Riviera di Ponente, from the artistic and historic point of view, is **Albenga ⓲**. The Romans founded a port on this site in 181 BC, but over the centuries the topography has changed and today the old centre is about a mile from the beach. Surrounding the town is a well-preserved medieval wall and three large 17th-century gates. The cathedral of **San Michele** dates back to the 5th century. Even older are the Roman aqueduct and the ruins of a Roman amphitheatre. In addition to the historic monuments are fine facilities for swimming and boating.

The nearby resort of **Alassio ⓳** has long been popular with celebrities and ordinary Italian tourists alike. **Caffè Roma** in the centre of town has a wall – the **Muretto** – decorated with tiles bearing the signatures of, among others, Ernest Hemingway, Sophia Loren and Sir Winston Churchill.

Imperia ⓴ was once two separate seaside towns: Oneglia and Porto Maurizio. It was Mussolini's idea to unite the two and name the city after a nearby river. **Corso Matteotti**, a wide boulevard with magnificent views of the coast, links the two town centres. **Oneglia**, in the east, known for its olive oil and pasta production, is the more industrial and modern sector. A large cathedral, **San Maurizio**, towers over the narrow streets of **Porto Maurizio**.

The Edwardian Age lives on at **San Remo ㉑**, a large international resort that was once a gathering spot for European aristocracy. Although there is a sense that San Remo's best days have passed, the city offers two enjoyable diversions: walking along the famous palm-lined promenade and gambling at the casino.

Near the tourist office at the city's centre is an authentic Russian Orthodox church, the **Chiesa Russa** (open daily 9.30am–12.30pm, 3–6pm) recognisable by its

Maps, pages 216 & 232

TIP

Visitors interested in ancient and modern maritime history should head for the Museo Navale Internazionale del Ponente Ligure, near Porto Maurizio's cathedral. The museum is open 4–7.30pm, Wednesday to Saturday.

BELOW: the harbour at Portofino.

Map, pages 216–7

San Remo's Russian Orthodox church.

BELOW: villa in Santa Margherita. **RIGHT:** relaxing in Borghetto d'Arróscia, inland from Albenga.

onion domes and gilded cross. The church was built by a colony of exiled Russian nobles in the 1920s. Another landmark is the art nouveau **Villa Nobel**, where Alfred Nobel (1833–96), inventor and philanthropist, spent his last years.

The gateway to France is nearby at **Ventimiglia ㉒**, a centre of flower cultivation and a pleasant city with a fine medieval quarter. The major architectural attraction is the 11th-century **Duomo**. Of great natural beauty is the **Giardino Hanbury** (open daily in summer 10am–6pm; till 4pm in winter; entrance fee), located in the village of Mortola, about 6 km (4 miles) from Ventimiglia, where you will find the colourful flora of five continents.

Riviera di Levante

Among the eastern suburbs of Genoa is **Quarto dei Mille**, famous as the starting point of Garibaldi's daring 1,000-man expedition that liberated Sicily and led to the unification of Italy. Nearby **Nervi ㉓** is the oldest winter resort on the eastern coast. Here you can take hot sea baths, or follow a 3-km (2-mile) cliff walk which is the city's pride.

After Camogli, take the branch off the main road that leads to **Portofino ㉔** via **Santa Margherita** and **Paraggi**. Of these three resorts, Portofino is by far the most interesting. A tiny waterfront village of extraordinary concentrated beauty, it was discovered by wealthy visitors after World War II. Once, only fishing boats docked in the narrow, deep-green inlet, edged on three sides by high cliffs, but it is now a berth for luxurious yachts. Part of Portofino's attraction is its size. There are no beaches, and few large shops and restaurants. The pleasures of the port are visual – the reflection of brightly painted houses in the clear water, the ragged edges of stone heights set against the brilliant blue sky.

Rapallo ㉕ is a family-style resort, with a large beach and many moderately priced hotels. Other attractions include the 17th-century **Collegiata**, and the 16th-century church of **San Francesco**, which houses several fine paintings by Borzone, a local artist. Nearby **Chiávari**, a wealthy shipbuilding centre, once had close links with South America.

The Gulf of La Spezia has been praised so often by poets – Dante, Petrarch, Byron and Shelley, to name just a few of them – that it is often called the Golfo dei Poeti. On its western point the elongated orange and yellow houses of **Portovenere ㉖** stretch up the precipitous mountain. The resort atmosphere here is friendly and relaxed as natives exchange gossip and tourists stroll alongside the pungent harbour, home to boats with names such as *Vergilia* and *Byron*.

Anglophiles and romantics should make a pilgrimage to the grotto – now littered with cigarette packets, drink containers and scantily clad lovers – from where the virile Lord Byron began his famous swim across the Gulf to visit Shelley in **Casa Magni**. If you take the 20-minute boat ride to **Lerici ㉗**, you will appreciate what a powerful swimmer the poet must have been to achieve such a feat. Shelley, alas, had less luck against the waves when his ship sank off the coast. The plaque, in Italian, on Casa Magni commemorates the tragedy: "Sailing on a fragile bark he was landed, by an unforeseen chance, in the silence of the Elysian Fields." ❑

CENTRAL ITALY

Subtle differences in art, cooking, fashion sense and attitude to life – even between neighbouring towns – help to form a destination that appeals both to the heart and the head

To many travellers, Central Italy is the true Italy – that is, the Italy they know from Merchant-Ivory films of E.M. Forster novels, or from the pictures that adorn all the tour brochures. Ironically, the people of this region are reluctant to admit to being Italian at all. They are Tuscan, Florentine, Sienese, Bolognese or Perugian – not a semantic distinction, but a deeply held conviction based on history, culture, and even tribal and genetic differences from the pre-Roman era. And this is an area where history is not the dry stuff of academic books, but a living part of the culture – for anthropologists, Central Italy has long been fertile ground for testing the belief that competition for resources leads people to emphasise their differences. If you want to see this process in action, visit any Umbrian or Tuscan town during its annual festivities – not to mention Siena during Palio, or Florence during Calcio in Costume (Football in Costume) – and feel the intense and elemental atmosphere of inter-parish rivalry.

Such rivalries are reflected in myriad ways that make exploring the region a delight for the sensitive and enquiring traveller. Food is an obvious indicator, whether it be the subtle differences between different sheep's-milk cheeses, the more emphatic distinctions between a crisp Orvieto wine and a soft, fruity Chianti, or whether it be the view firmly held by every seafront restaurant along the long Tuscan Riviera that theirs is the only authentic fish soup (*cacciucco*), and that it is far superior to anything the French produce.

Art and architecture is another indicator: labels, such as Florentine, Umbrian School, Lombardic or Pisan Romanesque at first seem designed to confuse the uninitiated, until continued exposure to some of the world's finest artistic creations leads you to the point where you can distinguish between the light-filled limpidity of the School of Perugino and the crisply delineated and boldly coloured frescoes of Benozzo Gozzoli – unmistakably Florentine even when encountered in the tiny Umbrian hilltown of Montefalco. ❑

PRECEDING PAGES: Siena's Piazza del Campo.
LEFT: a medieval street in Perugia, decorated for a festival.

EMILIA-ROMAGNA

The gastronomic heart of Italy is also noted for its medieval cities and the late-Roman mosaics of Ravenna – all of which are rewarding reasons for visiting this prosperous region

Map, pages 242 & 246

E milia-Romagna's winters are cold, wet and foggy, and its summers long and hot. Together with the rich soil of the Po Valley, this climate makes it one of Italy's most prosperous farming regions, famous for its succulent hams and flavoursome Parmesan cheeses.

Emilia-Romagna also has a rich cultural past. The Via Emilia, a road first built by the Romans, cuts through the centre of the region, linking Rimini, Bologna, Modena, Parma and Piacenza – all founded by the Romans as way stations along the road from the Adriatic to the interior. The other major cities of Emilia-Romagna, Ferrara and Ravenna, are off this main thoroughfare. In the Renaissance, Ferrara was home for the Este family whose court was a centre of culture and learning. Ravenna was a great international centre from the 4th to 8th century, originally as the last capital of the Western Empire then as the seat of the Byzantine emperors.

Bologna ❶, the capital of Emilia-Romagna, is a city of half a million people and famous for its university, its cuisine, its left-wing stance and its beautifully preserved historic centre. The old buildings are of a soft orange-red brick and have handsome marble or brick porticoes which shelter shoppers and pedestrians from inclement weather.

The old city evolved around two adjoining squares, **Piazza Maggiore ❹** and **Piazza del Nettuno ❸**. On the south side of the former stands **San Petronio ❻**, the largest church in Bologna. Originally, the Bolognese had hoped to outdo St Peter's in Rome, but church authorities decreed that some funds be set aside for the construction of **Palazzo Archiginnasio ❹** nearby. The design is by Antonio di Vincenzo, and although construction began in 1390, the facade is still unfinished. The completed sections are of red and white marble and decorated with reliefs of biblical scenes.

The interior of San Petronio is simple but elegant. Most of the bare brick walls remain unadorned. In the fifth chapel on the left is a spectacular 15th-century altarpiece of the *Martyrdom of St Sebastian* by Lorenzo Costa. At the east end of this aisle is a **museum** (open 10am–12.30pm, closed Tues and Thurs) which includes plans for the completion of the facade and the enlargement of the church.

LEFT: Piazza del Nettuno in Bologna. **BELOW:** delicacies on display in a Bologna deli.

Centre of learning

Behind San Petronio is the Archiginnasio, now the municipal library but once the seat of the university. The world's first lessons in human anatomy were given at Bologna University, and upstairs the 17th-century anatomical theatre survives.

The Piazza del Nettuno has many attractions. At its centre is the **Fontana di Nettuno ❺**, a 16th-century

Santo Stefano was originally a complex of seven churches; only four remain today. In the courtyard is a fountain in which Pontius Pilate is said to have washed his hands of the fate of Christ.

fountain with bronze sculptures by Giambologna of the muscle-bound Neptune surrounded by cherubs and mermaids. On its west side is the majestic **Palazzo Comunale ❻** (open Tues–Sun 10am–6pm; entrance fee), a medieval building remodelled in the Renaissance by Fieravante Fieravanti. The bronze statue above the gateway is of Pope Gregory XIII, a native of Bologna. To the left is a beautiful terracotta Madonna by Niccolò dell'Arca. Inside are grand public rooms and a fine collection of works by Giorgio Morandi (1890–1964).

Bologna's leaning towers

From Piazza del Nettuno follow the **Via Rizzoli**, a picturesque street lined with cafés, down to **Piazza di Porta Ravegnana ❼** at the foot of the **Due Torri**, the "leaning towers" of Bologna. In medieval days, 180 of these towers were built by the city's leading families; now only a dozen remain. Legend has it that the two richest families in Bologna – the Asinelli and the Garisenda – competed to build the tallest and most beautiful tower in the city. However, the Torre Garisenda was built on weak foundations and was never finished. For safety's sake it was shortened between 1351 and 1360, and is now only 48 metres (157 ft) high and leans more than 3 metres (10 ft) to one side. The Torre degli Asinelli is still standing at its original height of 97 metres (318 ft), but it too leans more than 1 metre (3 ft) out of the perpendicular.

The **Strada Maggiore** leads east from the two towers along the original line of the Via Emilia to the **Basilica di San Bartolomeo ❽**. Inside, look for the *Annunciation* by Albani in the fourth chapel of the south aisle, and a beautiful Madonna by Guido Reni in the north transept. Further down the Strada Maggiore is **Santa Maria dei Servi ❾**, a well-preserved Gothic church.

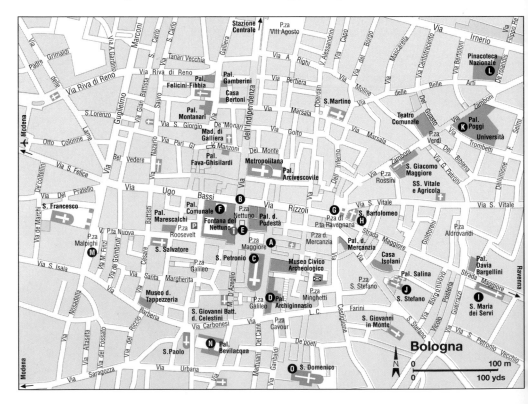

Bologna

The **Abbazia di Santo Stefano ❿** – a complex of churches all dedicated to St Stephen – is located off Via Santo Stefano, just south of the Casa Isolani, a well-restored 13th-century house. Of the several churches, the most interesting is **San Sepolcro**, where San Petronio, patron saint of Bologna, is buried near the striking Romanesque pulpit.

To the left is **Santi Vitale e Agricola**, the oldest church of the group, a 5th-century structure containing several Roman capitals and columns. In San Sepolcro is the entrance to the 12th-century **Cortile di Pilato**, "Pilate's courtyard", and beyond this open courtyard is the church of **Santa Trinità**, a dark, 13th-century building.

Bologna's **University**, the oldest in Italy, an institution founded in the 11th century and famous in its early days for reviving the study of Roman law, is located on **Via Zamboni**. Petrarch attended classes here, as did Copernicus. Today, although faculties are spread throughout the city, the official centre is the 16th-century **Palazzo Poggi ❾**.

Past the university, on the left, is the **Pinacoteca Nazionale ❿** (open Tues–Sun 9am–1pm; entrance fee), home of an interesting and varied collection of Italian paintings. The emphasis is on the development of Bolognese art from the Middle Ages through the 1700s, including works by Vitale da Bologna (especially the painting of *St George and the Dragon*) and Guido Reni. The stars of the collection are Raphael's great *Ecstasy of St Cecilia* (1515) and Perugino's *Madonna in Glory* (1491).

South and west of the Piazza Maggiore, Bologna has more architectural treasures. Follow the Via Ugo Bassi west to **Piazza Malpighi ❿**. On the west side of this piazza rises **San Francesco**, a church constructed between 1236 and 1263, with a design of French-Gothic inspiration. The larger of San Francesco's two towers and the surrounding decorative terracotta are the work of Antonio di Vincenzo. Though badly damaged in the war, the tower has been skilfully restored.

From San Francesco walk southeast until you reach **Palazzo Bevilacqua ❿**, a 15th-century building in the Tuscan style. Here, the Council of Trent met for two sessions after fleeing an epidemic in Trent. Nearby, **San Domenico ❿** is a church dedicated to the founder of the Dominican order. The tomb of St Dominic stands in a chapel off the south aisle.

Bologna has earned a number of epithets, "La Dotta" (the learned one), "La Turritta" (the turreted one), and finally "La Grassa" (the fat one), for here the rich cooking of Emilia-Romagna is at its best. Specialities are mortadella sausage, *tortellini*, and *tagliatelle*, said to have been invented for the marriage feast of Lucrezia Borgia and the Duke of Ferrara. These long, light-coloured noodles were inspired by the bride's lovely locks. The Bolognese dress their *tagliatelle* with *ragù*, which in its home town is an incredibly thick blend of beef, ham, vegetables, cream and butter.

Modena

Since the Romans conquered **Modena ❷** in the 2nd century BC, the city has thrived. In the past, the sources of Modena's wealth were the rich farmland of the Po

See map opposite

San Domenico contains several statues by Michelangelo.

BELOW: typical arcaded street in Bologna.

TIP

Motoring enthusiasts will enjoy a visit to the Galleria Ferrari at Via Dino Ferrari 43 in Maranello, south of Modena (0536-943204). Exhibits tells the history of the Ferrari company.

plateau that surrounds it, and its position on the Via Emilia. This famous Roman road still runs through the centre of Modena, but the city has new riches; the car factories where Maserati and Ferrari sports cars are manufactured.

Modena's massive and magnificent Romanesque **Duomo** sits right off the Via Emilia. It dates from the end of the 11th century when Countess Matilda of Tuscany, ruler of Modena, commissioned a cathedral which would be worthy to receive the remains of St Geminiano, patron saint of the city. Matilda engaged Lanfranco, the greatest architect of the time, to mastermind the project.

The partly Gothic, partly Romanesque belltower that stands to one side is the famous **Torre Ghirlandina**. It contains a bucket whose theft from Bologna in 1325 sparked off a war between the two cities. The poet Tassoni immortalised the incident in his celebrated poem *La Secchia Rapita* (*The Stolen Bucket*).

Frequently seen strolling around Modena are the smartly dressed students of the **Accademia Militare**, Italy's military academy, which is housed in a 17th-century palace in the centre of Modena. Another Modenese palace, **Palazzo dei Musei** (open Tues– Sun 9am–1pm; Tues, Fri, Sat till 7pm; entrance fee), contains an interesting art collection and the **Biblioteca Estense**, the library of the Este family, dukes of Modena as well as Ferrara. On permanent display in the library is a collection of illuminated manuscripts, a 1481 copy of Dante's *Divine Comedy*, and the stunning Borso d'Este Bible which contains 1,200 miniatures.

Parma

There is no better place to become a connoisseur of *parmigiano* (Parmesan), the hard, sharp-flavoured cheese, than in **Parma ❸**, where the cheese is made. It is a medium-sized city that enjoys a cooler, fresher climate than other towns in

BELOW: stone lion outside Modena's Romanesque Duomo. **BELOW RIGHT:** Piazza Grande in Modena.

Map,
pages
246–7

the muggy Po Valley. The history of Parma is full of interesting personalities. Napoleon's widow, Marie Louise, was ceded this city after her husband's death. Despite her reputation for immodest behaviour, she did good things for Parma, building roads and bridges and founding orphanages and public institutions. She also founded the picture gallery (open daily till 1.45pm; entrance fee) in the 16th-century **Palazzo della Pilotta**, containing four great canvases by Emilia's master painter, Correggio.

However, the main aesthetic attraction of Parma is the **Duomo** (open daily 9am–1.30pm, 3–7pm) and adjoining Baptistry. Its nave and cupola are decorated with splendid frescoes by Correggio. Contemporaries gushed over them: Titian said that if the dome of the cathedral were turned upside down and filled with gold it would not be as valuable as Correggio's frescoes. Vasari wrote of the *Assumption*: "It seems impossible that a man could have conceived such a work as this is, and more impossible still, that he should have done it with human hands. It is extraordinary in its beauty, so graceful is the flow of the draperies, so exquisite the expression on the faces."

The brilliantly restored **Baptistry** (open daily 9am–1.30pm, 3–7pm; entrance fee) is the work of Benedetto Antelami, who built this octagonal building in rich red Verona marble and then sculpted the reliefs that adorn both the interior and the exterior.

In the dome of **San Giovanni Evangelista**, another splendidly sensuous Correggio fresco can be seen. It depicts St John gazing up at heaven where the Apostles are gathered.

If you are driving northwest on the Via Emilia towards Piacenza, consider making a quick stop in **Fidenza ❹** to see another glorious Romanesque cathe-

BELOW: Parma hams.

PARMA HAM AND PARMESAN

Parma ham and Parmesan cheese (*parmigiano*) are intricately linked, because it is the whey – the waste-product from Parmesan production – that is used to feed the pigs that produce Parma ham. True Parma ham is branded with the five-pointed crown of the medieval Dukes of Parma, and is produced in the Langhirino hills, south of Parma. Here the raw hind thighs are hung in drying sheds for up to ten months. The air that blows through the sheds is said to impart a sweet flavour to the meat – unlike cheap, mass-produced *prosciutto crudo*, which is injected with brine and artificially dried to speed up the curing process.

Try it as a starter (*antipasto*) in any Parma restaurant, sliced into wafer-thin slivers for eating with bread, melon or figs; and end your meal, perhaps, with slivers of superior *Parmigiano-Reggiano*, the king of Parmesans, which is especially delicious partnered by apples, pears or a good red wine. A lower-quality Parmesan is known as *grana*.

Another speciality of the region is *aceto balsamico* (balsamic vinegar). Now widely popular, this is made from sweet grape juice, boiled slowly and reduced to a syrup, mixed with vinegar, and then aged in wooden casks for many years. It can be used in salads or as a marinade, or even drizzled over fresh berries or ice cream.

dral. Just beyond Fidenza is the turn off for the little town of **Róncole Verdi** ❺, where you can visit the humble cottage in which Giuseppe Verdi was born in 1813 (open Tues–Sun 9am–12.30 pm, 2.30–5pm; entrance fee).

In the revolutionary year of 1848, when Prince Charles Albert of Savoy called for Italians to assemble under his leadership and form an independent nation, the citizens of **Piacenza** ❻ were the first to respond in a plebiscite. This vote of rebellion was a remarkable event in Piacenza's otherwise peaceful history. Situated at the point where the Via Emilia meets the Po, Piacenza has been a lively trading post since 218 BC. Nothing remains of the Roman period, though there are many fine medieval and Renaissance buildings. At the centre of the city is the massive **Palazzo del Comune** (not open to the public), called "Il Gotico". This town hall was built during Piacenza's "Communal Period" (approximately 1200–1400) when the city was an independent and important member of the Lombard League that defeated Emperor Frederick II of Hohenstaufen in his bid to conquer Italy. Il Gotico, begun in 1280, is a remarkably well-preserved building of brick, marble and terracotta. In front of it stand two massive baroque equestrian statues of Piacenza's 16th-century rulers, the Farnese dukes. At the end of the Via Venti Settembre stands Piacenza's Romanesque **Duomo**. Although gloomy on the inside, the cathedral is worth a visit for the frescoes on the columns near the entrance.

Ferrara

A prosperous market town on the banks of the misty Po River, **Ferrara** ❼ seems at first glance peaceful and provincial. But the city has a colourful history and splendid treasures. At the southern end is a well-preserved medieval town, and

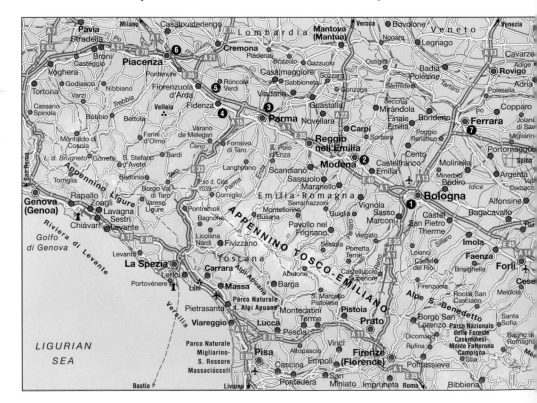

to the north are long broad avenues lined with Renaissance *palazzi* and carefully groomed gardens.

The Este family ruled Ferrara from the late 13th century until 1598, a time of prosperity when their court attracted poets, scholars and artists. The Renaissance, the city's golden age, is reflected in all the major monuments. Dominating Ferrara's skyline is the huge medieval **Castello Estense**, complete with moats, drawbridges and towers (open Tues–Sat 9.30am–5pm; entrance fee).

Just behind the castle is Ferrara's 12th-century cathedral. Among the noteworthy paintings in the Duomo and adjoining museum (open daily 10am–noon, 3–5pm; donation) are Cosimo Tura's *San Giorgio* and his *Annunciation,* and Jacopo della Quercia's *Madonna della Melagrana.* Across from the Duomo is the **Palazzo del Comune** (not open to the public), a medieval building with a beautiful Renaissance staircase. The piazza in front of this town hall is the hub of life in modern Ferrara. Not all Ferrarese are on foot, however – cycles are the rage in this town without hills.

Many of the medieval streets south of the cathedral are lined with fortified houses, and, stretching across the **Via delle Volte**, a narrow street near the Po, there are a number of elegant arches. At the beautiful **Palazzo Schifanoia** (open daily 9am–7pm; entrance fee), one of the Este family's summer residences, you can climb the steep stairs to the Salone dei Mesi, a large, high room decorated with colourful frescoes of the months. These were executed for the Duke of Borgo d'Este by masters of the Ferrarese school, including Ercole de' Roberti.

Down Via Mellone from Schifanoia is another, smaller Este palace, the **Palazzo di Ludovico il Moro** (open Tues–Sun 9am–2pm; entrance fee), designed by the famous Ferrarese Renaissance architect Biagio Rossetti.

See map opposite

Ariosto, Petrarch, Tasso, Mantegna and Bellini were just some of the great Italian poets and painters favoured by the Este family of Ferrara.

BELOW: the Castello Estense, built in the 14th century.

The Tempio Malatestiano contains the tombs of Sigismondo and his mistress and third wife, Isotta. There is also a fresco of Sigismondo praying at the feet of St Sigismond, by Piero della Francesca.

BELOW: on the beach in Rimini.

Although the plan of the building is actually simple and stark, the elaborate decoration gives the palazzo an ornate effect.

North of the Duomo, Ferrara is a city of broad avenues. Along one of the prettiest streets, Corso Ercole d'Este, is Rossetti's **Palazzo dei Diamanti** (open Tues–Sat 9am–2pm, Sun 9am–1pm; entrance fee), a large Renaissance structure with a unique facade. The diamond, emblem of the Este family, is repeated 12,600 times.

Rimini

Today **Rimini** ❽ is two cities: the old medieval and Renaissance town, and the ultra-modern beach resort a mile distant. In the skyscraper hotels that line Rimini's coast, you are more likely to hear German or English spoken than Italian, but the old centre retains its charm despite the influx of tourists.

The infamous ruler Sigismondo Malatesta has left his mark everywhere in Rimini. It was this anticlerical patron of art who presided over the transformation of a 13th-century Franciscan church into one of the most spectacular Renaissance buildings in Italy. The **Tempio Malatestiano** (open daily 7am–noon, 3.30–7pm; free) is considered more a personal tribute to Sigismondo's mistress, Isotta degli Atti (who later became his third wife), than a church. But perhaps that is what Sigismondo intended, since he and Church authorities were never the best of friends. Pope Pius II even went so far as to excommunicate the violent and sensual Sigismondo, and to condemn him publicly to Hell.

Sigismondo had better luck with women and artists. He was patron of such great artists as Piero della Francesca and Leon Battista Alberti, among others. It was Alberti who designed the exterior of the Tempio. (He found inspiration in the Roman Arch of Augustus which still stands at the gates of Rimini.) Note the wide classical arches on each side of the entrance. The interior rebuilding was supervised by Matteo de' Pasti, and although the simple, single-nave plan and wooden-trussed roof of the original Franciscan church remain, the side chapels (some added and others only redecorated) are opulent and intricate in design. Immediately on your right as you enter is Sigismondo's tomb. It is decorated with his initials intertwined with Isotta's.

To the left of the Tempio is **Piazza Tre Martiri**, which was named in honour of three Italian partisans hanged by the Nazis in this square in 1944. The piazza is also the site of the ancient Roman forum, whose columns now support the porticoes of the two eastern buildings.

Walk out of the piazza along **Corso di Augusto** for four blocks. At the end stands the **Arco di Augusto**, dating from 27 BC. With this archway the Romans marked the junction of the Via Emilia and the Via Flaminia, the primary road north from Rome to the Adriatic Sea.

Ravenna

When the unstoppable barbarians overran Rome in the 5th century AD, **Ravenna** ❾ benefited, gaining the honourable rank of capital of the Western Empire. This Adriatic port town continued as capital under the Ostrogoths, and the barbarian leaders Odoacer and Teodoric also ruled their vast dominions from here. Later, when the Byzantine emperor Justinian reconquered part of Italy, he too made Ravenna his seat of power, liking it for its imperial tradition under the barbarians and – perhaps more importantly – for its direct sea links to Byzantium.

Under Justinian's rule the Ravenna we know today began to take shape. New buildings arose all over the city, including a handful of churches that are among the wonders of Italian art and architecture. There is no preparation in their simple brick exteriors for the brilliant mosaics within. It is these mosaics that make modern Ravenna, if no longer capital of the Western world, at least a capital of the Western art world.

Start with **San Vitale** (open daily 9am–7pm; entrance fee), the city's great 6th-century octagonal basilica, famous for the mosaics in its choir and apse. These "monuments of unaging intellect", as the Irish poet W.B. Yeats called them, immediately draw the eye with their marvellous colours and intricate detail. Bright ducks, bulls, lions, dolphins and a phoenix intertwine with flowers and oddly angled corners of buildings to frame Old Testament scenes and portraits of Byzantine rulers with humour and exactitude.

In the dome of the apse a purple-clad and beardless Christ sits on a blue globe flanked by archangels and, at the far sides, St Vitalis and Bishop Ecclesius. Christ hands the saint (Ravenna's patron) a triumphal crown, while the bishop (who founded the church in 521) carries a model of the structure as it finally appeared many years after his death. Below stretch imperial scenes of Justinian with his courtiers and Theodora, his beloved wife, with hers.

San Vitale is not the only place to see mosaics in Ravenna. Nearly every church contains a pristine example of the art. Just north, another set may be seen

Map,
pages
246–7

TIP

Ravenna's medieval Piazza del Popolo is a good place to relax with a cup of coffee after seeing the mosaics.

BELOW: mosaic of the three magi in Sant'Apollinare Nuovo in Ravenna.

Map, pages 246–7

at the **Mausoleo di Galla Placidia** (open daily 9am–7pm; entrance fee). This interesting lady was born a Roman princess, sister to Emperor Honorius, but after she was captured by the Goths, she married their leader, Athaulf, and ruled with him. He, however, soon died, and she next married a Roman general to whom she bore a son. This son became Emperor Valentinian III. As Valentinian's regent, and a woman with connections in the highest barbarian circles, Galla Placidia played a powerful role in the world of "the decline". The building that houses her tomb has a simple exterior but inside the walls, floors, and ceiling are covered with mosaics.

Through the gate that lies between San Vitale and Galla Placidia are two Renaissance cloisters that now house the **Museo Nazionale** (open Tues–Sun 8.30am–7pm; entrance fee). The museum includes, as one might expect, many mosaics as well as other relics from Ravenna's past. There's glass from San Vitale to see and also fabrics from the tomb of St Julian at Rimini.

The baroque Duomo

A pleasant walk along Via Fanni, Via Barbiani and left on to Via d'Azeglio leads to Ravenna's **Duomo** – originally constructed in the 5th century but redone in baroque style in the 1730s. Far more attractive than the cathedral itself is the adjoining **Battistero Neoniano** (open daily 9.30am–6.30pm; entrance fee), a 5th-century octagonal baptistry that was once a Roman bath house. The interior combines spectacular Byzantine mosaics with marble inlay from the original.

Across Piazza Caduti from the cathedral complex is **San Francesco**, another 5th-century church almost completely redone in the baroque style. To the left stands the **Tomba di Dante** (open daily 9.30am–noon, 3.30–6pm), not a remarkable building architecturally, but of great historic interest. Dante, the author of *The Divine Comedy*, was exiled from his home in Florence for his political outspokenness and found refuge in Ravenna in 1317. He spent the remaining four years of his life here, putting the finishing touches to his great work.

BELOW: outside the church of San Vitale and (**RIGHT**) the apse, with a mosaic of Christ handing a crown to the martyr, Vitale.

After Dante's death, the repentant Florentines would dearly have loved to honour their famous son with a splendid tomb, but proud Ravenna refused to give up the poet's remains. The battle over the bones continued for hundreds of years. At one point in 1519, it looked as if Ravenna would lose. The powerful Medici of Florence sent their representatives to Ravenna with a papal injunction demanding the relics. The sarcophagus was duly opened, but the bones were not inside. Someone had been warned of the Florentine scheme and had removed the bones to a secret hiding place. They were not found again until 1865, and now rest within the sarcophagus that is on display. To this day, the city of Florence provides the oil for the lamp which burns on his tomb.

Down the Via di Roma from the troubled tomb is another church full of mosaics, **Sant'Apollinare Nuovo** (open daily 9.30am–6.30pm; entrance fee). The scenes are of processions, one of virgins and the other of martyrs who appear to be moving towards the altar between rows of palms. Above, the decorations depict episodes from the *Life of Christ*. ❏

FLORENCE

One of the world's great artistic centres, packed with aesthetic masterpieces, Florence is the essential destination for students of Renaissance art and architecture

Map, pages 254–5

F lorence (Firenze) is the city that gave birth to the Renaissance and many visitors come here to trace the development of this extraordinary outpouring of artistic talent in the 15th century. A huge number of Renaissance works have remained in the city where they were created; many paintings, statues and whole buildings, such as the Palazzo Pitti, were bequeathed to the people of Florence by Anna Maria Lodovica of the Medici family, whose death in 1743 brought an end to the dynasty that had ruled Florence since 1434.

Her far-sighted bequest ensured that the Medici collections remained intact and were not dispersed all over the globe. Napoleon stole a few choice pieces during his adventures in Italy (including the *Medici Venus*, now in the Louvre), and English collectors bought some splendid paintings very cheaply in the 19th century when the so-called "primitives" were out of fashion. Despite this, you can still see in Florence many of the paintings and frescoes that Vasari, the first art historian, mentions in his entertaining and anecdotal *Lives of the Artists*, first published in 1550. Many of these works have been superbly restored since the great flood of November 1966, and the bulletproof glass installed to protect the most important paintings in the Uffizi proved effective when a terrorist bomb exploded in May 1993, reducing some minor masterpieces to shreds.

LEFT: buy a postcard of the city's glories, or (**BELOW**) make your own sketch.

Where the Renaissance started

To see where the Renaissance began, it is traditional to begin with Piazza del Duomo. Approaching this massive square, now free of traffic thanks to a ban introduced in 1988, you file through sober streets lined with buildings presenting a stern defensive face. Suddenly the 19th-century face of the **Duomo** (cathedral) ❶ (open Mon–Sat 10am–5pm, Sun 1–5pm) is revealed, all festive in its polychrome marble – green from Prato, white from Carrara and red from the Maremma. The design echoes that of the tall **Campanile** (open daily 9am–5pm; till 6pm on summer; closed 8 September; entrance fee) alongside, designed by Giotto in 1331. You can climb the 285 steps of the belltower for intimate views of the cathedral dome and roofline, or simply enjoy the flamboyant exterior of the cathedral from one of the open-air cafés on the south side of the square.

The little octagonal **Battistero** (Baptistry) (open daily 1.30–6.30pm; entrance fee), to the west of the cathedral, dates to the 7th century, though the interior was re-designed and given its ceiling mosaics of the *Creation* and *Last Judgement* in 1300. The Baptistry has three sets of bronze doors and those to the north have an important place in art history. If it is possible to pin down the start of the Renaissance to a particular event, then it was the competition held in the winter of 1401 to choose an artist to design these doors. Of the six

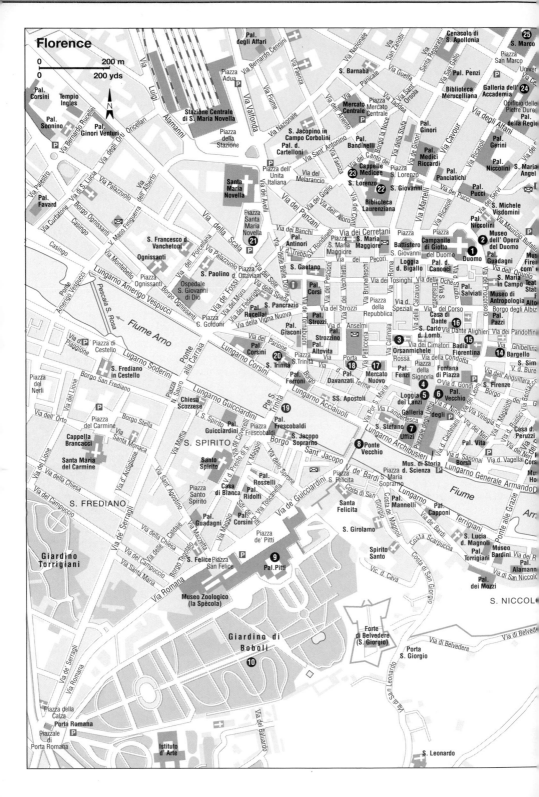

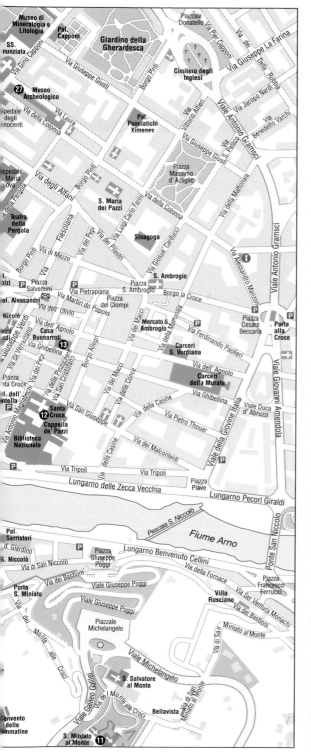

artists who entered the competition, Ghiberti and Brunelleschi were adjudged joint winners, but Brunelleschi, a fiery tempered genius, refused to work with Ghiberti and went off in a huff to Rome.

Ghiberti, left with sole responsibility for the doors, did not complete them until 1424, but the resulting work shows many of the key features that define Renaissance art: realistic depiction of people, fully worked-out perspective, and narrative clarity combined with dramatic tension. Ghiberti was immediately commissioned to design another set of doors, this time for the east portal, and these were unveiled in 1452 when Michelangelo hailed them as fit to serve as the "gates of Paradise"; they are known to this day as the Paradise doors. The third set of doors, to the south, are the work of Andrea Pisano (1339) and tell the story of John the Baptist, patron saint of the city.

Biggest dome in the world

Brunelleschi, meanwhile, spent his time in Rome studying Ancient Roman Architecture and he returned to Florence full of confidence that he could accomplish a task that had defeated other architects, namely to complete the cathedral by erecting the vast **dome**. In typically Florentine fashion, the city had decided to build the biggest dome in the world without actually knowing how to achieve it. If you enter the cathedral and climb the 436 steps to the top (dome open Mon–Sat 8.30am–5pm; entrance fee) you can study how the problem was solved – by building a light inner shell of interlocking brick which serves as the support for the outer roof of the dome.

Brunelleschi was hailed as a new Icarus (the mythical hero who similarly defied gravity by inventing flight) and the city passed an ordinance forbidding the construction of any building taller than the dome out of respect for his achievement; to this day, the massive dome rises supreme above the red roofs of the city, rising almost higher than the surrounding hills. Brunelleschi was also buried in the cathedral – an honour granted to him alone – and his tomb can be seen in the

Lorenzo Ghiberti took themes from the Old Testament for the East Doors (the "gates of Paradise") of the Battistero. This is a detail from the Battle with the Philistines.

BELOW: figure of a saint in an external niche of Orsanmichele.

crypt (open Mon–Sat 10am–5pm; closed religious hols; entrance fee), among the excavated ruins of Santa Reparata, the city's first (4th-century) cathedral.

Much of the rest of the cathedral is bare. There is an interesting fresco on the north aisle wall, painted by Paolo Uccello in 1436, depicting Sir John Hawkwood, the English mercenary who served as Captain of the Florentine army from 1377 to 1394. Otherwise, to see the cathedral treasures you must visit the **Museo dell'Opera del Duomo** ❷ (open Mon–Sat 9am–6.30pm; entrance fee) on the east side of Piazza del Duomo. This is full of outstanding sculptures, from Donatello's haggard *Mary Magdalene* carved in wood in the 1460s to the same artist's superb *cantoria* (choir gallery), decorated with angels and cherubs engaged in some frenzied ritual of music and song. The star exhibit here is Michelangelo's *Pietà*, begun around 1550. Michelangelo intended this for his own tomb, but left it unfinished (a pupil rather clumsily attempted to finish the work). Its magnetic hold over visitors derives from the fact that the tall hooded figure of Nicodemus, at the centre of the group, is Michelangelo's self-portrait.

Showpiece of the guilds

From the cathedral square, **Via dei Calzaiuoli** leads south. This was the principal street of Roman and medieval Florence and, having been restored after World War II bombing, it is lined with good shops. Part way down, on the right, is the church of **Orsanmichele** ❸ (a contraction of Orti di San Michele – the Garden of San Michele church, which once stood here). The niches around the exterior walls are filled with Renaissance statues sponsored by the guilds and depicting their respective patron saints. Of these, Donatello's *St George*, made for the Guild of Armourers, is the most important, and for that reason it has been removed to a place of honour in the Bargello museum (see below) and replaced by a copy.

The same fate befell Michelangelo's *David*, which once stood in the **Piazza della Signoria** ❹, just to the south. The original was moved to the Galleria dell' Accademia (*see page 262*) in 1873 but the copy that now stands in front of the Palazzo Vecchio is faithful to the original. David's companions are the rather constipated-looking figure of *Hercules* (1534 by Bandinelli), the mythical founder of Florence, and Ammannati's licentious *Neptune Fountain* (1575). Nearby, to the south of the square, the **Loggia dei Lanzi** ❺ shelters several Ancient Roman statues and Giambologna's *Rape of the Sabine Women* (1583).

Most of the statues gathered here are symbolic, not least David himself, carved by Michelangelo to represent the aspirations of the Florentine people not long after the citizens had declared themselves independent of all rulers except for God. The fledgling Florentine Republic was threatened by a number of tyrannical Goliaths, including the pope, the Holy Roman Emperor and the Medici. The combined forces of all three held the city to siege in 1530 and shortly afterwards Cosimo I was crowned Duke of Florence.

This Cosimo was a very different character from his earlier namesake, the humanist, classics scholar and patron of the arts, Cosimo il Vecchio, who ruled the city from 1434 to 1464 without ever holding office. Cosimo

Map, pages 254–5

I was a no-nonsense military man who set about conquering all those cities in the region not already ruled by Florence. Cosimo I created the Tuscany of today by this means and he set up an efficient administration to rule his dukedom, which remained in place until Tuscany joined the united kingdom of Italy in 1861.

That administration was based in the **Palazzo Vecchio** ❻ (open daily 9am–7pm except Thurs and Sun pm; entrance fee), which remains the town hall of Florence, and which was comprehensively redesigned during the reign of Cosimo I. Visiting the ancient town hall, you can see the delicately decorated entrance courtyard with its little fountain – Vasari's copy of the original *Putto and Dolphin* fountain made by Verrocchio in 1470. By contrast, the vast Salone dei Cinquecento (Hall of the Five Hundred) was originally intended as the council chamber of the 500 citizens who governed during the Republic. Cosimo I set his stamp on the chamber by commissioning a series of vast frescoes, painted by Vasari, which glorified his military triumphs. Other rooms of the palace contain mementoes of various prominent Florentines, such as portraits of the Medici popes Leo X and Clement VII. A small bust of Machiavelli is located in the little room that he used during his term of office as the Chancellor of Florence.

Under Cosimo I, the size of the Tuscan bureaucracy grew to the point where new offices were required to house the burgeoning army of lawyers and notaries, the guilds and the judiciary. Thus it was that the **Uffizi** ❼ (open Tues–Sat 8am–7pm, Sun 9am–2pm; entrance fee) came to be built alongside the Palazzo Vecchio, now a famous art gallery but intended to serve a more utilitarian purpose (the word *uffizi* simply means offices).

Vasari was the architect and he built a well-lit upper storey, using iron reinforcement to create an almost continuous wall of glass running round the long

ABOVE: copy of Michelangelo's *David* in Piazza della Signoria.
BELOW: the Duomo.

TIP

At the end of your visit to the Uffizi, stop in the museum's café terrace, where you can enjoy the view of the Piazza della Signoria.

inner courtyard of the Uffizi. It was this glass wall that caused so much damage when a terrorist bomb exploded near the west wing of the Uffizi in May 1993, sending splinters of glass everywhere and destroying a number of paintings in the process. In the 16th century, such lavish use of glass was novel and Cosimo's heirs decided that the airy upper corridor of the Uffizi would make a perfect exhibition space for the family statues, carpets and paintings.

Thus began what has grown to be one of the richest and most illuminating art collections in the world. It is arranged chronologically so that you can trace, almost in textbook fashion, the development of Florentine art from the formal style of the Gothic era (13th and 14th centuries), to the greater realism of the early Renaissance (15th century), and finally to the painterly use of exaggerated colours and the contorted poses designed to show off the artist's skill that is so characteristic of the High Renaissance and Mannerist periods (16th century).

The famous names and familiar works come thick and fast as you explore the collection; not to be missed are Botticelli's *Primavera* (1480) and the *Birth of Venus* (1485). You should also seek out the Medici family portraits gathered in the octagonal Tribune, including Bronzino's, *Portrait of Bia*, illegitimate daughter of Cosimo I (1542). The corridors of the gallery are lined with ancient Roman and Greek statues, of which the most famous perhaps is the boy removing a thorn from his foot, in the south corridor. Look out too for Michelangelo's influential *Holy Family* (*Doni Tondo*) (1506–8), Raphael's tender *Madonna of the Goldfinch* (1506) and Titian's erotic *Venus of Urbino* (1538).

When Vasari planned the Uffizi, he incorporated an aerial corridor (the Corridoio Vasariano) into the design. This consists of a continuous covered walkway linking the Palazzo Vecchio to the Pitti Palace, passing through the Uffizi and

BELOW: the Ponte Vecchio, built in 1345.

Map, pages 254–5

along the top of the Ponte Vecchio. The Medici dukes used this corridor to walk between their various palaces without having to mix with their subjects in the streets below. The corridor is difficult to visit (ask at the tourist office about making an appointment), but it is possible to follow the same route at street level. The corridor passes over the ancient **Ponte Vecchio 8**, with its jewellers, buskers and festive crowds. The bridge was built in 1345 and the workshops on the bridge were used by butchers and tanners until these noxious trades were banned by ducal ordinance in 1593. It is well worth browsing in the goldsmith's tiny shop windows to see the range of goods on display, from cheap trinkets to costume jewellery and from expensive antique pieces to modern creations.

Good shops line the route south of the bridge into the Oltrarno district where you will find the churches of **Santo Spirito**, an architectural masterpiece by Brunelleschi, and **Santa Maria del Carmine**, where the Brancacci Chapel contains Masaccio's fresco cycle on the *Life of St Peter*. The latter (open 10am–5pm, closed Tues, and Sun am; entrance fee) is one of the great works of the early Renaissance and the Brancacci Chapel is tiny, so there are likely to be queues at the entrance. Visits are limited to 15 minutes.

Residence of the Medici Grand Dukes

Space is not a problem at the vast and fortress-like **Palazzo Pitti 9**. This became the residence of the Medici Grand Dukes in 1550 and, like the Uffizi, it is stuffed with artistic treasures, housed in several museums, including the Palatine Gallery, the Modern Art Collection, the Argenti (Silver) Museum and the Costume Museum.

The most rewarding of these is the **Palatine Gallery** (open Tues–Sat 8.30am–7pm, Sun 8.30am–2pm; entrance fee), especially the richly decorated rooms with ceiling frescoes by Pietro da Cortona. These illustrate, in allegorical form, the education of a prince under the tutorship of the gods. In Room 1, the prince is torn from the arms of Venus (love) by Minerva (knowledge) and in subsequent rooms learns about science from Apollo, war from Mars and leadership from Jupiter. Finally the prince takes his place alongside Saturn, who, in ancient mythology, presided over the Golden Age.

Among the paintings displayed in these rooms are some wonderful portraits by Titian who even manages to turn the reformed prostitute, Mary Magdalene, into a delectable study of the delights of the female form. More disturbing is Rubens' celebrated masterpiece, the *The Consequences of War* (1638), an allegory of the Thirty Years' War. The artist explained in a letter that the figure in black represents "unfortunate Europe who, for so many years now, has suffered plunder, outrage and misery." Next to her, Venus is trying to restrain the war god, Mars, who is trampling over books, symbolising his disregard for civilisation.

The **Giardino di Boboli ⓾** (open daily 9am–1 hr before sunset; closed 1st and last Mon of month; entrance fee), behind the Pal-azzo Pitti, was laid out in the 16th century and is a wonderful example of the Renaissance garden style. Here you will find box hedges clipped into formal geometric patterns set

BELOW: the church of San Miniato rises gracefully above Florence.

The Bargello was built in 1255 and became a national museum in 1865.

BELOW: stroking the snout of the bronze boar in the Mercato Nuovo is meant to bring good luck.

against wild groves of ilex and cypress to create a contrast between artifice and nature. Dotted around the gardens are numerous grottoes, statues and fountains.

Jewel on the hill

On one of the hills above Florence sits **San Miniato** ⓫ (open daily 8am–noon, 2–6.30pm), a jewel-like Romanesque church. If you walk up to the church you can descend via Piazzale Michelangelo, a terrace set high above the city and dotted with reproductions of Michelangelo's famous works.

Prominent in the view, to the east of the city, is the massive church of **Santa Croce** ⓬ which features famously in E.M. Forster's novel (and the Merchant-Ivory film) *A Room with a View* (church: open Mon–Sat 8am–6.30pm in summer; 8am–12.30pm, 2.30–6pm in winter, Sun 3–5pm all year; free; cloister, Capella de'Pazzi and museum:Thurs–Tues 10am–12.30pm, 2.30–6.30pm in summer; till 5pm in winter; entrance fee). Here you will find frescoes by Giotto and his pupils and the tombs and monuments of famous Florentines, including Michelangelo, Machiavelli and Galileo (born in Pisa but protected by the Medici after his excommunication for holding the heretical view that the earth goes round the sun, rather than the other way around).

Weaving your way back from the church through the alleys of the Santa Croce district you pass the **Casa Buonarroti** ⓭ (open Wed–Mon 9.30am–1.30pm; entrance fee), a house owned by Michelangelo and now containing one of his earliest works, the *Madonna della Scala*. Call in at the **Bar Vivoli Gelateria**, in Via Isola delle Stinche, which – as everyone who samples it agrees – serves the best ice cream in Florence, if not the world. From here it is a short step to the **Bargello** ⓮ (open daily 8.30am–2pm; closed 1st, 3rd & 5th Sun and 2nd &

4th Mon each month; entrance fee), once a prison and place of execution but now a museum devoted to sculpture and applied art where you can see works by Donatello, Michelangelo, Cellini and Giambologna. Dante was born in this district and opposite the Bargello you can see the abbey church, the **Badia Fiorentina** ⓰, where the poet used to watch his beloved Beatrice attending mass. Round the corner, in Via Dante Alighieri, is the **Casa di Dante** ⓰ (open Thur–Tues 9.30am–1.30pm; entrance fee), the house in which the poet is supposed to have been born in 1265.

Continuing west, you will reach another important shopping street, Via Roma, which leads south into Via Calimala and the **Mercato Nuovo** ⓱ (open daily; closed Sun and Mon Nov–Mar). Despite its name, the "New Market" has been here since 1551 and was known as the Straw Market in the 19th century, on account of its specialising in raffia goods. Today it sells leather and tourist souvenirs. The little bronze boar, **Il Porcellino**, in the south side of the market, has a shiny nose because of the number of visitors who have rubbed it for good luck.

From the north side of the market, Via Porta Rossa will take you to the **Palazzo Davanzati** ⓲ (currently closed for restoration), a delightful 13th-century townhouse complete with frescoed walls and contemporary furnishings, that will give you a good idea of domestic life in late medieval Florence. You are now close to the **River Arno** and the bridge called **Ponte Santa Trìnita** ⓳, after the adjacent church. The bridge, which features statues of the *Four Seasons*, was blown up by the retreating Nazis in 1944 and dredged up from the river bed to be restored to its original design.

The church of **Santa Trìnita** ⓴ contains frescoes by Ghirlandaio showing the *Life of St Francis* set not in Assisi, the saint's home town, but against the

ABOVE: relief on a door at Santa Trìnita. **BELOW:** fresco by Gozzoli in the Palazzo Medici-Riccardi.

Map, pages 254–5

ABOVE: sculpture in the Accademia.
BELOW: atrium of the Annunziata.
OPPOSITE: along the Arno embankment.

background of Florentine buildings. North from here, **Via de' Tornabuoni** is lined with the chic boutiques of high-class couturiers, such as Salvatore Ferragamo and Gucci. At the top of the street, the Palazzo Antinori contains an excellent wine bar and restaurant, but if the prices are too steep you can sample the cheap Chinese restaurants in **Piazza Santa Maria Novella ㉑**, with a view of the church of the same name. The latter features in the opening stanzas of Boccaccio's great work, the *Decameron*, and contains colourful frescoes by Ghirlandaio on the *Life of the Virgin*. In the adjoining cloister you can see what remains of Paolo Uccello's masterpiece, the *Universal Deluge* fresco, depicting the flood that drowned all but Noah and his entourage, a fresco that was, ironically, badly damaged by the Florentine floods of 1966. In the Spanish Chapel you can also see frescoes that depict the Dominican monks as hunting dogs (the Dominicans were known as *Domini Canes* – Hounds of the Lord).

Popular market

Heading back to the heart of Florence, it is easy to get lost in the streets surrounding **San Lorenzo ㉒** because this is the venue of a crowded street market most days of the week. The popular market continues, despite official attempts to ban it, and is a good place in which to buy almost anything – from picnic food to souvenirs. At the back of San Lorenzo is the entrance to the **Cappelle Medicee ㉓** (open daily 8.30am–2pm; closed 1st, 3rd & 5th Mon and 2nd & 4th Sun each month; entrance fee), the mausoleum of the Medici family, for which Michelangelo carved two splendid tombs featuring the allegorical figures of *Night* and *Day, Dusk* and *Dawn*. The church itself, entered through the rough, unfinished facade, is an example of Renaissance rationalism in architecture, all cool whites and greys and restrained classical decoration. By contrast, the two huge pulpits carved by Donatello with scenes from the *Life of Christ* are full of impassioned emotion, and Michelangelo's staircase leading to the **Biblioteca Laurenziana** (Laurentian Library; open Mon–Sat 9am–1pm), off the cloister, is considerably more exuberant. Just off Piazza di San Lorenzo is the Palazzo Medici-Riccardi, the Medici family home.

Michelangelo's most famous work, *David*, is in the **Galleria dell'Accademia ㉔** (open Tues–Sat 8am–6pm, Sun 8am–2pm; entrance fee), two blocks away in Via Ricasoli. Queues for this museum can be long, although the entry price is steep for a museum that contains little else of great interest, apart from Michelangelo's unfinished works, the *Four Slaves*.

Instead, the nearby convent of **San Marco ㉕** (open daily 8.30am–2pm; closed 1st, 3rd & 5th Sun and 2nd & 4th Mon each month; entrance fee), which contains nearly every painting and fresco ever produced by the saintly artist, Fra Angelico, may prove more rewarding. On your return to the city centre you can also take in the **Piazza della Santissima Annunziata ㉖**, with its delicate Renaissance colonnade fronting the **Innocenti** orphanage, the work of Brunelleschi, and the **Archaeological Museum ㉗** (open Tues–Sat 9am–2pm, Sun 9am–1pm; entrance fee), with its ancient Etruscan and Egyptian treasures. ❑

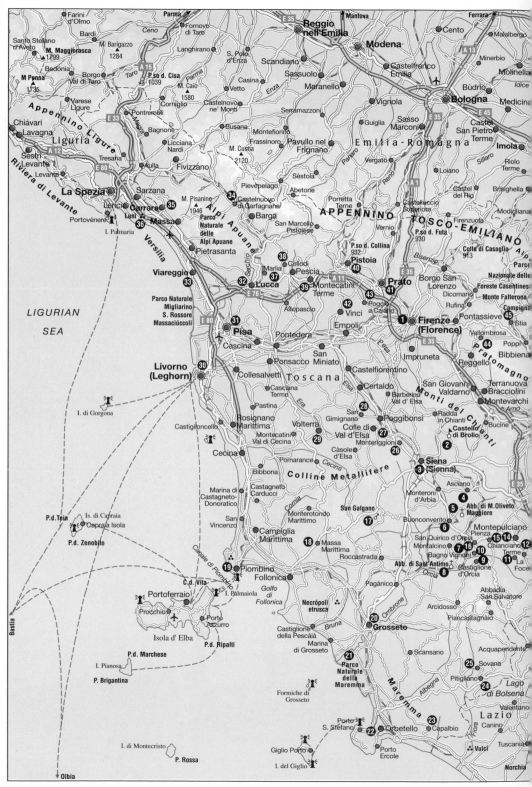

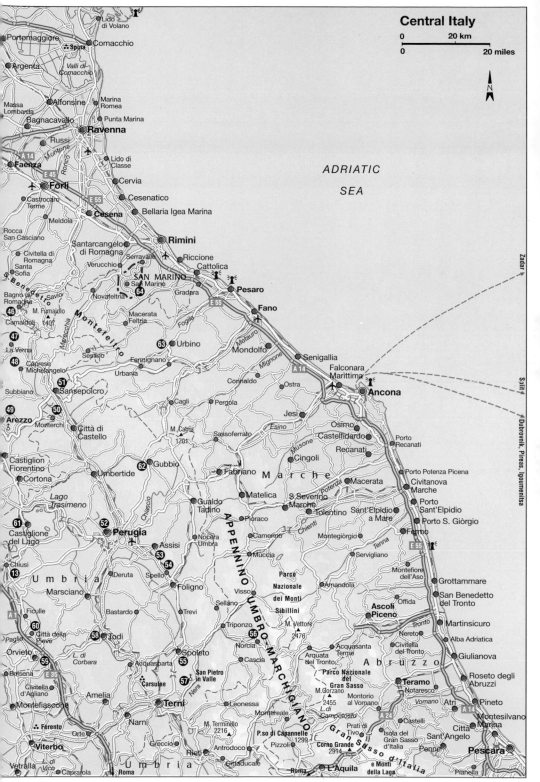

Central Italy

0 20 km

0 20 miles

N

ADRIATIC

SEA

Zadar

Split

Dubrovnik, Piraeus, Igoumenitsa

Lido
di Volano

Portomaggiore
Spina
Comacchio

Argenta
Valli di
Comacchio

Massa
Lombarda
Alfonsine
Marina
Romea

Bagnacavallo
Punta Marina

Russi
Ravenna

Faenza
Montone
Lido di
Classe

A 14
Ronco

E 45
Forlì
Cervia

Castrocaro
Terme
Cesenatico

Meldola
E 55
Cesena
Bellaria Igea Marina

Rocca
San Casciano

Civitella di
Romagna
Santa
Sofia
Santarcangelo
di Romagna
Rimini

Verucchio
Serravalle
Riccione

Bagno di
Romagna
Savio
SAN MARINO
Cattolica

46
M. Fumaiolo
1407
Novafeltria
San Marino
64
Gradara
Pesaro

Camaldoli
Macerata
Feltria
E 55

47
Sestino
Fano

La Verna
Urbania
Fermignano
63
Urbino

48
Caprese
Michelangelo
Metauro
Mondolfo

51
Sansepolcro
Corinaldo
Senigallia

Subbiano
Cagli
Ostra
A 14
Falconara
Marittima

49
50
Monterchi
Pergola
Ancona

Arezzo
Sassoferrato
Jesi

Città di
Castello
M. Catria
1701
Esino
Osimo

Castiglion
Fiorentino
Porto
Recanati

Cortona
Umbertide
62
Gubbio
Fabriano
MARCHE
Castelfidardo

Lago
Trasimeno
Cingoli
Recanati

Gualdo
Tadino
Matelica
Macerata
Porto Potenza Picena

61
52
Perugia
Pioraco
S.Severino
Marche
Civitanova
Marche

Castiglione
del Lago
Assisi
Nocera
Umbra
Tolentino
Porto
Sant'Elpidio

Chiusi
53
Camerino
Sant'Elpidio
a Mare
Porto S. Giòrgio

13
54
Deruta
Spello
Muccia
Montegiorgio
Fermo

Umbria
Marsciano
Foligno
Servigliano
E 55

A 1
Ficulle
Bastardo
Trevi
Parco
Nazionale
dei Monti
Sibillini
Montefiore
dell'Aso
Grottammare

60
Città della
Pieve
58
Todi
Sellano
M. Vettore
2476
Offida
San Benedetto
del Tronto

Paglia
Triponzo
Amandola
Ascoli
Piceno
Martinsicuro

Orvieto
59
L. di
Corbara
56
Norcia
Nereto
Alba Adriatica

Bolsena
E 35
Spoleto
55
Cascia
Acquasanta
Terme
Tronto
Giulianova

Civitella
d'Agliano
Acquasparta
57
San Pietro
in Valle
Arquata
del Tronto
Civitella
del Tronto
Abruzzo
Roseto degli
Abruzzi

Montefiascone
Carsulae
Nera
Parco Nazionale
del
Gran Sasso
M.Gorzano
2455
Teramo
Notaresco
Atri
Pineto

Ferento
Amelia
Terni
Leonessa
Montereale
Montorio
al Vomano
Castelli
A 14
Montesilvano
Marina

Viterbo
Narni
Greccio
Rieti
M.Terminillo
2216
L.di
Campotosto
Vomano
Penne
Città
Sant'Angelo

Orte
P.so di Capannelle
1299
Prati di
Tivo
Isola del
Gran Sasso
d'Italia
Pescara

Vetralla
Capranola
Roma
Antrodoco
Cittaducale
Pizzoli
Corno Grande
2914
Gran Sasso d'Italia
e Monti
della Laga
Pianella

Umbria
Roma
L'Aquila

TUSCANY

*Strong architecture, evocative landscapes, soft red wines
form an essential part of this region's appeal, and the cities of Siena
and Pisa have much to recommend them*

Map, pages 264 & 268

For those not fascinated by frescoes, the delights of Florence ❶ can quickly fade and the desire to escape the cauldron-like atmosphere of this hot, dry city can prove overwhelming, as it did in the case of the English writer Lauric Lee: "I'd had my fill of Florence, lovely but indigestible city. My eyes were choked with pictures and frescoes … I began to long for the cool uplands, the country air, the dateless wild olive and the uncatalogued cuckoo."

Lee escaped by walking south along the Chiantigiana, the Chianti Way, shown on maps as the N222 road, which takes you to Siena via several pretty towns in the Chianti Classico wine-growing region. If you are driving, the journey will take little more than an hour, unless you are tempted to stop along the route at the scores of *fattorie* (wine estates) offering free tastings and wine sales direct to the public (*vendita diretta*). This is one way to learn about the region's famous red wines; another is to leave the N222 road at Castellina in Chianti and drive east, stopping for a walk round the pretty town of Radda in Chianti before heading south on the N408 and N484 to Castello di Brolio.

The **Castello di Brolio** ❷ is the birthplace of the modern Chianti industry and offers well-organised guided tours of the vineyards, castle and winery (open daily; entrance fee). It was here, in 1870, that Barone Bettino Ricasoli established the formula for making Chianti wines that has been used ever since, requiring a precise blend of white and red grape juice and the addition of dried grapes to the vat to give the wine its softness and fruit-filled flavour.

LEFT: the pageantry of Siena's Palio.
BELOW: a door knocker, typical of the Tuscan nobility's taste for elaborate decoration.

City of narrow medieval lanes

Knowledgeable about the region's wines, you can tackle the traffic headaches that await in **Siena** ❸. Finding space to park may prove difficult, but the medieval core of the city is largely traffic free, because the alleys that thread between high *palazzi* of rose-pink brick are too narrow for vehicles. All roads in Siena eventually lead to the **Campo** ❹, the huge main central square, which is shaped like an amphitheatre – the Sienese say that it is shaped like the protecting cloak of the Virgin, who, with St Catherine of Siena, is the city's patron saint.

From the comfort of a pavement café on the curved side of the Campo you can note the division of the paved surface into nine segments, commemorating the beneficent rule of the Council of Nine Good Men which governed Siena from the mid-13th century to the early 14th, a period of stability and prosperity when most of the city's main public monuments were built.

Twice a year, on 2 July and 16 August, the Sienese faithfully recreate their medieval heritage in the Palio, a sumptuous pageant-cum-horserace around the Campo. This is no mere tourist event; the residents of the city's *contrade*, or districts, pack the square as their represen-

A statue by the Duomo shows Remus and the she-wolf. Remus's son is said to have founded Siena.

tative horses and riders career around the Campo, and the rider who wins the race and the Palio, a heraldic banner, becomes an instant local hero. At the square's base is the **Palazzo Pubblico**, with its crenellated facade and waving heraldic banners. Erected in the early 14th century, it housed the offices of the city government. At its left corner is the slender tower fondly called the **Mangia**, or Wastrel, after an early bellringer (open daily 10am–1 hr before sunset). Climb more than 500 steps for a panorama of the city.

Although bureaucrats still toil in parts of the Palazzo, as they have for some seven centuries, much of the complex is now devoted to the **Museo Civico ❸** (open in summer Mon–Sat 9.30am–6.30pm; 9.30am–1.30pm in winter; entrance fee) which houses some of the city's greatest treasures. Siena's city council once met in the vast **Sala del Mappamondo**, although the huge globe that then graced the walls has disappeared. What remains are two frescoes attributed to the medieval master Simone Martini: the majestic mounted figure of Guidoriccio da Fogliano and, opposite, the *Maestà*. The *Maestà* is signed in Simone Martini's own hand, but in recent years doubts have been cast on the authenticity of

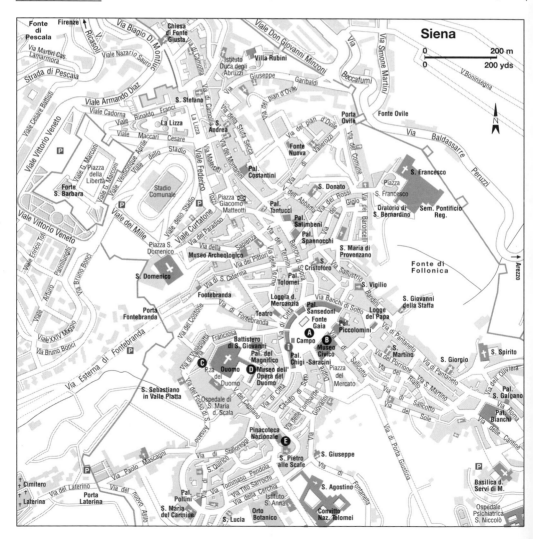

the Guidoriccio. A smaller fresco recently uncovered below the huge panel may be Simone Martini's original, and the Guido Riccio may have been executed long after the artist's death.

Map, pages 264 & 268

In the Sala della Pace is Ambrogio Lorenzetti's *Allegory of Good and Bad Government*. Intended as a constant reminder to the city fathers of their responsibilities, it depicts the entire sweep of medieval society, from the king and his court down to the peasants working the terraced hillsides outside the city walls.

Exiting again to the Campo, turn left and head up the hill via one of the winding streets to **Piazza del Duomo** ⊙. The facade of the vast striped cathedral is a festival of green, pink and white marble, which will help prepare you for the stunning black-and-white geometric patterns of the interior. Take special care to study the 15th and 16th-century marble inlaid paving of the Duomo, which depicts allegories and scenes from the New Testament (unfortunately, many are covered most of the year to protect them from heavy traffic). Off the north aisle is the decorative Libreria Piccolomini, built in 1495 to house the personal papers and books of Pope Pius II. The frescoes by Pinturicchio show scenes from the life of the pope, and in the centre of the room is the famous *Three Graces*, a Roman copy of a sculpture by the Greek artist Praxiteles.

For those with more time, Siena has two other important museums: the **Museo dell'Opera del Duomo** (Cathedral Museum) ⊙ (open daily in summer 9am–7.30pm; 10am–1pm, 2.30–5pm in winter; entrance fee), to the right (south) of the cathedral, and the **Pinacoteca Nazionale** (Picture Gallery) ⊙ (open Tues–Sat 9am–7pm, Sun–Mon 9am–1pm; entrance fee), in the Palazzo Buonsignori on the Via San Pietro, just south of the Campo. The Cathedral Museum's main attraction is the entire room devoted to the works of Duccio, including his moving *Maestà*, the Virgin enthroned.

ABOVE: fresco in Monte Oliveto Maggiore. **BELOW:** Siena's Palazzo Pubblico.

Rounded hills of the Crete

Siena sits at the geographical centre of Tuscany and whichever way you drive you will be spoilt for choice in terms of attractive historic towns and beautiful countryside. Drive southwest along the N438 to **Asciano** ❹ and you will pass through the dramatic Crete region, the Tuscany that appears on countless postcards and posters. Here the bare, rounded clay hills have no trees except for the occasional stately avenue of cypresses, winding across the landscape and marking the way to an isolated farm, a simple Romanesque church or a *borgo*, a small defended village.

Asciano's main street, Corso Giacomo Matteotti, is lined with smart shops and classical *palazzi*, some with pretty balconies. At the top end is the simple Romanesque **Collegiata** and the **Museo di Arte Sacra** (Religious Art Museum) (open by appointment; tel: 0577-718 207) which houses an unusually good collection of Siena School masterpieces. The **Museo Amos Cassioli** (open in summer Tues–Sun 10am–12.30pm, 4.30–6.30pm; 10am–12.30pm in winter; entrance fee) on Via Mameli has a good collection of 19th- and early 20th-century paintings by local artists.

A short drive on is the **Abbazia di Monte Oliveto Maggiore** ❺ (open daily 9.15am–noon, 3.15–5.45pm), a 15th-century Benedictine monastery with an air of

Church in the well-preserved town of Buonconvento.

aloof dignity, set among groves of cypress trees. The Great Cloister is covered in frescoes on the *Life of St Benedict*, begun by Luca Signorelli in 1495 and completed by Sodoma from 1505. The excellent monastery guidebook gives a detailed description. In one scene Sodoma portrays himself with his pet badgers (one wearing a scarlet collar) looking like a pair of well-trained dogs.

Buonconvento ❻ is worth a brief stop, if only to admire the massive medieval city gates of iron-bound wood, before driving through fertile countryside, scattered with vineyards, to the hilltop town of **Montalcino** ❼, a wine-producing town where every other shop seems to sell the famed Brunello wines. It is also a town of timeless character with several old-fashioned wood-panelled bars where vineyard workers shelter from the midday sun. The streets are narrow and steep and from the airy heights of the walls there are entrancing views. The highest point is the **Fortezza** (Fortress), housing a wine centre (open Tues–Sun 9am–1pm, 2–6pm; till 8pm in summer; entrance fee) where various regional vintages can be sampled and purchased.

Romanesque abbey church

BELOW: antique shop in Montalcino.

South again is another sight that features on postcards, but which is far more beautiful in the flesh. The ancient abbey church of **Sant'Antimo** ❽, built of creamy travertine and set against tree-clad hills, has inspired numerous poets and painters. The main part of the church was built in 1118 in a style that owes much to the influence of French Romanesque. The simple interior has capitals carved with biblical scenes, and recorded plainsong echoes around the walls as you explore. The small community of Augustinian monks who tend the church sing the Gregorian chant at Mass every Sunday afternoon throughout the year.

A tortuous mountain route will take you through **Castiglione d'Orcia** and **Rocca d'Orcia**, both with medieval castles built to watch over the valley of the River Orcia, and down to the tiny spa town of **Bagno Vignoni** ❿. This has, at its heart, where the main square ought to be, a large stone-lined pool where sulphurous vapours rise above the hot, bubbling waters which well up from volcanic rocks deep under the earth. Some famous bodies have bathed in this pool in times past, including St Catherine of Siena. Bathing is now forbidden but there is a spa hotel nearby, the Posta-Marcucci (tel: 0577-887112), with modern hydrotherapy facilities and a swimming pool.

Just north of Bagno Vignoni, a minor road takes you east along the wide vale of the Orcia river and then up to **Castellúccio** and **La Foce** ⓫, from where there are spectacular views of a cypress-lined, ancient Etruscan road zig-zagging up the hill. The next town is **Chianciano Terme** ⓬, a post-war spa town noted for water therapy. More interesting is **Chiusi** ⓭, one of the most powerful cities in the ancient Etruscan league. The **Museo Nazionale Etrusco** (open Mon–Sat 9am–2pm, Sun 9am–1pm; entrance fee) is packed with funerary urns excavated from various tombs around the town. Arrangements can be made at the museum to visit one of the tombs in the vicinity, but many, including the famous Tomba della Scimmia (Tomb of the Monkey), are now closed to protect their fragile wall paintings from further deterioration. However, you can now explore "underground Chiusi" in a new exhibition.

The town's Romanesque church is a delight, built from recycled Roman pillars and capitals and with "mosaics" on the nave walls that were painted by Arturo Viligiardi in 1887. The **Museo della Cattedrale** (open daily; entrance fee) displays a fascinating collection of Roman, Lombardic and medieval sculp-

People have been taking the therapeutic waters of Tuscany since Roman times. Lorenzo il Magnifico, ruler of Florence, who suffered from arthritis, was one notable spa enthusiast.

BELOW: the timeless Tuscan landscape.

Some of the best producers of Vino Nobile di Montepulciano are Avignonesi, Le Casalte and Poliziano.

ture and you can arrange to visit an underground gallery running beneath the city, dug by the ancient Etruscans and reused as Christian catacombs in the 3rd to 5th centuries.

Chiusi stands almost on the border with Umbria, but our Tuscany tour continues north, up the fertile Val di Chiana, where cattle are bred to supply the restaurants of Florence with the raw ingredients of *bistecca alla fiorentina* (steak Florentine), then west to **Montepulciano ⓮**. This splendid hilltop town, with its pedestrianised historic centre, deserves long and leisurely exploration, with frequent stops to sample the local Vino Nobile wines, either in the city's rock-cut cellars, or in Caffè Poliziano (Via di Voltaia nel Corso 27), a characteristic Art Deco bar with an art gallery in the basement.

The spacious main square, the **Piazza Grande**, sits at the town's highest point. On one side is the 15th-century **Palazzo Comunale** (Town Hall), a miniature version of the Palazzo Vecchio in Florence. Nearby is the **Duomo**, which contains a masterpiece of the Siena School, the huge *Assumption* triptych (1401) by Taddeo di Bartolo over the high altar.

As the road to Pienza leaves Montepulciano, it is worth diverting right for the church of the **Madonna di San Biagio**, perched on a platform below the walls of the city. This domed church of honey and cream-coloured stone, a Renaissance gem begun in 1518, is the masterpiece of Antonio da Sangallo.

Model Renaissance city, built for a pope

BELOW: view along Pienza's town walls.

Pienza ⓯ is a tiny town that would be famous for nothing but its sweet sheep's milk cheeses, had not the future Pope Pius II been born here in 1405. He decided to rebuild the village of his birth as a model Renaissance city, but was swindled

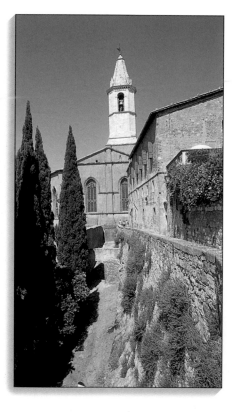

by his architect, Bernardo Rossellino, who embezzled most of the funds. Only the papal palace and the cathedral were completed and both are now suffering from serious subsidence – see them before they collapse.

Despite the great cracks and buckled pillars, the cathedral is uplifting, and flooded with light from the great windows that the pope requested – he wanted a *domus vitrea*, a house of glass, to symbolise the enlightenment of the Humanist age. The **Palazzo Piccolomini** (open Tues–Sun 10am–12.30pm, 3–6pm; entrance fee) alongside is filled with the pope's personal possessions and the loggia at the rear was designed to frame views of Monte Amiata, the distant, cone-shaped peak of an extinct volcano.

The last stop after Pienza is **San Quirico d'Orcia ⓰**, with its splendid Collegiata whose Romanesque west portal is carved with dragons and mermaids.

Back in Siena, the N73 will take you southwestwards on a winding and often empty road through the green and sparsely populated foothills of the Colline Metalliferre, the Metal-bearing Hills, so-called because they have been a rich source of iron, copper, silver and lead ores since ancient Etruscan times.

Some 20 km (12 miles) out of Siena, be sure to stop off at the ruined Cistercian abbey of **San Galgano ⓱**, with its huge and roofless abbey church, where swallows skim in and out of the glassless Gothic windows and sunlight plays on the richly carved capitals of

Map, pages 264–5

the nave. On a hill above the church is the beehive-shaped oratory built in 1182 on the site of San Galgano's hermitage. Look out for the sword in the stone, thrust there by the saint when he renounced his military career to become a hermit. An excellent shop alongside sells local herbs, wines, toiletries and books on the history and sights of the region.

Massa Marittima ⓲ is the ancient mining capital of the region, but there are no ugly industrial scars, just two museums devoted to the history of mining in the region (which flourished in the 13th century) and one of Tuscany's finest Romanesque churches, decorated with humorous sculptures illustrating the adventures of St Cerbone, the town's patron saint. Massa Marittima is the gateway to Tuscany's south, a holiday land with many fine and unspoilt beaches and a Mediterranean climate, notably different from that only a short way north.

From **Piombino** ⓳ ferries take visitors to the island of **Elba**, either on day trips to see the villa where Napoleon spent a short period in exile, or for a relaxing week in one of the island's many luxury hotels. Further south along the busy coastal road, the Via Aurelia, the city of **Grosseto** ⓴ is worth a stop only if you want to visit the excellent archaeology museum (due to re-open after its restoration; tel: 0564-455 132). This has displays and finds that will help you understand the ruins of nearby Etruscan cities such as **Vetulonia** (22 km/13 miles northwest of Grosseto) and **Roselle** (7 km/4 miles north).

Just south of Grosseto is the **Parco Naturale della Maremma** ㉑ (open daily; entrance fee), a protected nature reserve partly ravaged by fires in 1996. The park office in Alberese sells tickets and information on the unspoiled beaches within the park and the rich wildlife. Another wildlife haven is the lagoon north of Orbetello, an important wintering spot for birds. **Orbetello** ㉒ was, in the

ABOVE: the symbol of Massa Marittima's "New Town". **BELOW:** the harbour of Porto Ercole, on Monte Argentario.

16th century, a Spanish garrison town and the baroque architecture reflects this fact. The sea laps right up to the stout city walls and visitors come from afar for the excellent restaurants specialising in fish that are found here and on the island of Monte Argentario.

Inland, tiny villages like **Capalbio** ㉓ specialise in more robust Tuscan dishes, such as wild boar and even baked porcupine (both are hunted locally). For a totally sybaritic experience, you can swim beneath the stars in the hot falls just south of Saturnia before heading into the town for a leisurely meal.

The other villages of this beautiful region, known as the forgotten corner of Tuscany, are situated above dramatic cliffs of soft tufa. These are especially spectacular at **Pitigliano** ㉔, where local people have excavated caves in the rock for storing wine and olive oil, and at **Sovana** ㉕, where the ancient Etruscans excavated tombs in the soft rock below the town. Sovana was the birthplace of Hildebrand, who became Pope Gregory VII in 1073. The tiny one-street village has two outstanding proto-Romanesque churches of the same period.

West of Siena

More spectacular sights await to the west of Siena. Taking the N2, you will first pass **Monteriggioni** ㉖, a hilltop town built in 1213 to guard the northern borders of Sienese territory, encircled by walls and 14 towers.

Next, drive through the lower, modern town of **Colle di Val d'Elsa** ㉗ and, taking the Volterra road, look for the more ancient upper town. Here the main street is lined with 16th-century *palazzi* of unusual refinement and, at one point, the stately procession of buildings is interrupted by a viaduct from which there are splendid views of the surrounding landscape. Your nose will help you find the old-fashioned bakers (Via del Castello 28) in the oldest part of the town that lies beyond, along with several antique shops and museums.

Perhaps the most spectacular sight anywhere in Tuscany is the town of **San Gimignano** ㉘, bristling with medieval towers, scarcely changed in appearance since the Middle Ages and richly rewarding – despite the huge number of visitors it gets. (It is best to stay overnight here, in one of the characteristic hotels, to savour the peaceful beauty of the town in the evening and early morning, after the coach trippers have gone.) The main street is lined with shops, many of them selling good quality crafts as well as locally produced Vernaccia wines and wild-boar ham.

The tall defensive towers lining the two squares at the highest point of the town were built as status symbols rather than for genuinely defensive purposes. They alone make a visit here worthwhile, but the town also possesses such an embarrassment of artistic riches that few visitors get to see everything. The highlights are the *Wedding Scene* frescoes in the **Museo Civico** (open in summer Tues–Sun 9.30am–7.30pm; 9.30am–1pm, 2.30–5pm in winter; entrance fee), showing the newly married couple taking a bath together and climbing into bed, plus the frescoes that cover every inch of wall space in the **Collegio**, the collegiate church, depicting the *Last Judgement* and stories from the Old and New Testaments.

Today there are 15 towers in San Gimignano, but historians say there were once 72 in the small, hilltop town.

BELOW: one of the medieval towers of San Gimignano.

Volterra ㉙ is another rewarding place, sited high on a plateau with distant views to the sea. The entrance to the city is dominated by a Medicean castle, now used as a prison, and if you wander through the park that lies beneath its walls you will come to the **Museo Guarnacci** (open daily in summer 9.30am–7pm, 9.30am–2pm, 3–6.30pm in winter; entrance fee) in Via Don Minzoni. This is packed with ancient Etruscan urns excavated from cemeteries uncovered by landslides in the 19th century. The urns are arranged according to the subjects carved upon them and give an intriguing glimpse into everyday Etruscan life and beliefs. The *Married Couple* urn is a masterpiece of realistic portraiture and even more stunning is the bronze statuette known as *L'Ombra della Sera* (*The Shadow of the Night*), resembling a Giacometti sculpture but cast in the 5th century BC.

The attractive main square of Volterra has some of the oldest civic buildings in Tuscany, dating from the 13th century, and provides a showroom for the local alabaster carving industry; galleries selling alabaster are located all over the town. The cathedral has a wealth of carvings from an earlier age, including a balletic *Deposition*, sculpted in wood in the 13th century.

As one drives west or north from Volterra, the landscape changes rapidly from hilly terrain to flat marshy coastline. You could be forgiven for missing out **Livorno** ㉚, for, although it has an interesting harbour area and a famous Renaissance statue (the *Four Moors* monument), World War II bombing and modern industry have stripped the city of its character.

Pisa ㉛, by contrast, is a must. All the main attractions lie in the northwestern angle of the city walls, around the well-named **Campo dei Miracoli** (the Field of Miracles). The bizarre appearance of the cathedral and baptistry owes much

ABOVE: getting the picture, by Pisa's baptistry. **BELOW:** the Tower, and a statue nearby.

Be sure to see the tomb of Ilaria del Carretto in Lucca's Duomo. The effigy of the young noble-woman was carved by Jacopo della Quercia in 1405.

to the influence of Islamic architecture which Pisan merchants and scholars experienced through their extensive trade contacts with Moorish Spain and North Africa. The marble surfaces of these buildings are covered in arabesques and other ornamentation, as densely patterned as an oriental carpet.

The famous Torre Pendente, the **Leaning Tower**, is still standing but is closed to the public while experiments are conducted to try and resolve the imminent threat of collapse. It is estimated that the tower will fall by the year 2200 if nothing is done to arrest the continuing subsidence, caused by building on too shallow foundations in unstable, silty soil.

Lucca ③, a short way north, is a city of many seductive charms, not least the ramparts encircling the city, which were transformed into a tree-lined promenade in the 19th century. The city has more than its fair share of splendid churches in the Pisan-Romanesque style, with ornately patterned facades of green, grey and white marble. Many are locked, because the interest is on the outside, but there are exceptions: the church of **San Michele**, with its tiers of arcading and hunting scenes, the church of **San Frediano**, with its massive Romanesque font, and the splendid **Duomo** (cathedral). The Duomo contains one of the most famous relics of medieval Europe, the *Volto Santo* (Holy Face), said to have been carved by Nicodemus, who witnessed the Crucifixion – hence it was believed to be a true portrait of Christ (in fact, the highly stylised figure is probably a 13th-century copy of an 11th-century copy of an 8th-century original).

BELOW: decorated columns on the facade of Lucca's Duomo.
BELOW RIGHT: marble quarry in Carrara.

Lucca is the gateway to several regions of Tuscany which all have their own special character. To the west is the Tuscan Riviera, known as the **Versilia**, a string of coastal towns devastated by floods in 1996. The beaches here are regimented (you pay for access but get facilities such as sun loungers, showers,

beach cabins and a bar or restaurant). **Viareggio** ❸ is the most interesting for its Liberty-style (art nouveau) architecture, its plentiful fish restaurants specialising in *cacciucco* (a hearty fish soup) and its atmospheric harbour area.

To the north is the **Garfagnana**, a wild area of high mountains, seemingly covered in snow all year round because the peaks are made of marble. Recently designated as a huge nature reserve, this is a paradise for those who like pony trekking and walking. Information on waymarked trails is available from the region's main town, **Castelnuovo di Garfagnana** ❸. On the fringe of the region is the marble town of **Carrara** ❸ with several quarries offering guided tours and workshops. Just outside Carrara is **Luni** ❸, once a Roman town and now a place of well-preserved ruins.

Nearer to Lucca, there are several ornate villas and gardens open to the public, notably the **Villa Reale** (guided tours Mar–Dec, Tues–Sun from 10am; entrance fee), at **Marlia** ❸, whose *teatro verde* (green theatre), surrounded by clipped yew hedges, is the setting for concerts during Lucca's summer music festival. Another splendid villa, with theatrical gardens spilling down the steep hillside, is the **Villa Garzoni** (villa closed for restoration; garden open daily 8.30am–sunset; entrance fee) at **Collodi** ❸. Collodi was also the pen name of Carlo Lenzini, the author of the *Adventures of Pinocchio* (1881), who spent his childhood here. The Pinocchio theme park in the village is a wonderful distraction for children and is dotted with sculptures based on episodes from the book.

Montecatini Terme ❸ is the most elegant spa town in Tuscany, with ornate buildings surrounded by flowerbeds and manicured lawns. You can buy day tickets which will allow you to sample the waters and admire the marble-lined pools, splashing fountains and art nouveau tile pictures of water nymphs at the **Terme Tettuccio** (open May–Oct, tel: 0572-778501).

Medieval and modern sculpture

Pistoia ❹ and its neighbour, Prato, are both industrial towns specialising in textiles and metal working, but with attractive historic centres awaiting those prepared to drive to them through the dreary suburbs. Pistoia's churches together contain a remarkable number of carved fonts and pulpits dating to the period just before the Renaissance; they include Giovanni Pisano's pulpit of 1301 in **Sant'Andrea church**, which art historians consider to be his masterpiece, more accomplished even than the pulpit he made for Pisa's cathedral in 1302. You can also see the work of one of Italy's best-known modern sculptors, Marino Marini (1901–66), in a new museum, the **Centro Marino Marini** (open Tues–Sat 9am–1pm, 3–7pm, Sun 9am–12.30pm; entrance fee), on Corso Silvano Fredi.

Prato ❹ was the birthplace of Francesco di Marco Datini (1330–1410), better known as The Merchant of Prato, the title and subject of Iris Origo's historical biography. Datini died one of the richest men in Europe and left his money to city charities so, as you might expect, the town has several statues of the great man. Another local merchant married a Palestinian woman in 1180 and discovered that her dowry included the Virgin's girdle. The relic is exhibited four times a year from the external pulpit on the cathedral facade. Inside are fres-

Map, pages 264–5

ABOVE: terracotta by della Robbia in Pistoia's Ospedale del Ceppo. **BELOW:** statue at Collodi.

*The chapterhouse of
Prato's church of
San Francesco
contains splendid
frescoes by Niccolò
Gerini.*

BELOW: starting life
together in Arezzo's
Piazza Grande.

coes by Fra Filippo Lippi, the monk who seduced the nun Lucrezia Buti and
often incorporated her features into his paintings. Here she plays the role of
Salome dancing at Herod's feast and demanding the head of John the Baptist.

City of Leonardo

South of Pistoia is the tiny hilltop village of **Vinci** ㊷, birthplace of Leonardo
da Vinci, where the castle has been turned into an entertaining **museum** (open
daily 9.30am–6pm; entrance fee) dedicated to the great man and his inventions.
The displays consist of wooden models of a bicycle, a submarine, a tank, a heli-
copter, etc., beautifully crafted and based on Leonardo's notebooks.

From Vinci, you can take a winding rural road into Florence, stopping at **Pog-
gio a Caiano** ㊸ (open daily 9am–6.30pm; entrance fee), the villa built for
Lorenzo de' Medici which became the archetype for many others. Skirting Florence, you can speed south to Arezzo on the A1 *autoroute*, or break the journey
by leaving at the Incisa intersection and following signs for **Vallombrosa** ㊹.
The reward is not so much the 18th-century monastery as the splendid beech
wood that surrounds it; the poet John Milton, visiting in 1638, was so impressed
that he wrote a description of Vallombrosa's autumnal leaves in *Paradise Lost*.

More delights await if you go north and take the N70 to **Stia** ㊺. From here,
you can visit two sacred sites set high in spectacular woodland, cut by mountain streams and waterfalls. One is the hermitage at **Camáldoli** ㊻ (open only to
male visitors), 17 km (10 miles) east of Stia; the other is the monastery at **La
Verna** ㊼ further south, best reached by driving east from Bibbiena (open daily).
It was here that the hands and feet of St Francis were miraculously marked with
the stigmata in 1224. The monastery commands panoramic views.

On the way south from here to Arezzo, it is also worth seeking out little **Caprese Michelangelo** . There is little to see, except for a sculpture park in the grounds of the castle where Michelangelo was born, but the views over alpine countryside explain why Michelangelo always attributed his good brains to the mountain air he breathed as a child.

Arezzo contains many sights, including a good **archaeological museum** (open Tues–Sun 9am–1.30pm; entrance fee) full of Arretine tableware, fashionable for a time during the Roman period. For most visitors, though, the highlight will be Piero della Francesca's fresco cycle in the church of **San Francesco**. The frescoes illustrate the *Legend of the True Cross*, a complex story whereby the wood of the Tree of Knowledge, which bore the fruit that Adam and Eve ate, becomes the Cross on which Christ died and then is instrumental in converting Constantine the Great, who made Christianity the religion of the Roman world.

The artist's style, compelling and mysterious, attracts superlatives from art historians and you can easily become hooked on his work, following the Piero della Francesca trail, like the heroine of *A Summer's Lease*, a novel by the English writer John Mortimer. If so, the trail leads from here to **Monterchi** , 25 km (15 miles) west along the N73, where a former schoolhouse displays his striking *Madonna del Parto*, the Pregnant Madonna. From there, you should continue 12 km (7 miles) north to **Sansepolcro** , the town where Buitoni pasta is produced. Here the **Museo Civico** (open daily Oct–May 9.30am–1pm, 3.30–6.30pm; entrance fee) has della Francesca's 1463 masterpiece, the *Resurrection*, hailed by Aldous Huxley as "the best picture in the world". To complete the trail, you should visit **Urbino**, in the Marches, to see *The Flagellation of Christ* and other works in the Ducal Palace (*see page 291*). ❑

Map, pages 264–5

The Casentino region, north of Arezzo, is much loved by walkers. It is also well known for its plentiful wild mushrooms.

BELOW: the terracotta roofscape of Arezzo.

ROLLING HILLS, CYPRESS TREES AND TOWERS

The distinctive Tuscan countryside has, for centuries, been a favourite haunt of travellers looking to escape the madding crowds of the cities

As glorious as its historic cities and artistic treasures may be, Tuscany's timeless landscape has long been a draw to visitors. After a hectic, sticky visit to Florence, Siena, Pisa or any of the other major towns, the relative coolness and freshness of a rural ride out is a welcome treat. Small medieval towns, perched on hills to benefit from cooling breezes, overlook a rolling landscape which embraces both controlled agriculture and nature at its wildest. Terraces of vines and silvery groves of olives vie for attention with Tuscany's own peculiar landmark – tall, slender cypresses, often planted in rows as windbreaks. These elegant trees have studded the skyline here for centuries, prompting the writer D.H. Lawrence to accuse them of hiding the secrets of the Etruscans, the early settlers of these parts. He described them as "… the sinous, flame-tall cypresses/That swayed their length of darkness all around/ Etruscan-dusky, wavering men of old Etruria". These and other images of the Tuscany countryside feature strongly in the background of some of the greatest works of Renaissance art.

▷ HIDDEN GEMS

The domed, 16th-century church of Santa Maria Nuova lies just beyond the ancient Etruscan walls of Cortona. Churches like this would stand out in any other environment, but in Tuscany their simple, elegant forms and the colour of the local stone blend in with the other visual delights of the countryside.

▷ FLORA AND FAUNA

The backdrop to the 12th-century church of Sant'Antimo provides a fine example of Tuscan nature at work. Wild flowers (best seen in late spring) fight for room with ancient olive trees and coarse shrubs and grasses. These provide a habitat for moths, lizards and cicadas, whose song is heard in summer.

△ OLIVE GREEN
The silvery leaves of olive groves bring a distinctive colour to a Tuscan hillside. Some wine estates now produce very high quality (and highly priced) olive oils. Badia a Coltibuono also offers cookery courses in which you can learn how best to appreciate its wines and oils.

▽ CULTIVATION CULTURE
Tuscan farmers use their land for a variety of purposes. Olives, fruit and tobacco are just some of the crops produced alongside cereals like barley and maize. Chianina cattle, native to the region, provide the meat for *bistecca alla fiorentina*, the classic Florentine steak dish.

△ CHIANTI COUNTRY
South of Florence, the hills are dominated by rows of vines growing predominantly Sanglovese grapes, which are pressed to make Chianti wines. Some vineyards are centred around medieval castles; many of these offer tastings and sell wine to visitors.

◁ BURNT SIENNA
The hills around the city of Siena are known for their reddish-brown clay, which is used for brick-making and the construction of most of the city's buildings. The distinctive pigment in the clay has become internationally known as burnt sienna.

TOWERS OF POWER AND WEALTH

In the Middle Ages, towers protected the wealthiest families in times of internal and external strife; today, they mark out some of Tuscany's oldest towns, catching the traveller's eye from afar. No better example exists of this distinctive skyscape than San Gimignano (*above*), which boasts more than a dozen towers – although at one time it had more than 70.

San Gimignano's many towers date from the 12th and 13th century, and are mostly windowless, possibly to afford further protection; families could retreat into the many rooms inside for months at a time. Defence was not the only purpose of these lofty extensions, however: they were also status symbols. Building a tall, imperious tower was a way of flaunting your wealth and social standing.

Another theory about the the towers concerns the textile trade for which San Gimignano was noted. Towers may have been built to house and protect valuable dyed fabrics, as there was little room to spread them out at ground level.

As many of Tuscany's medieval towns were built on hilltops, a climb to the top of a tower is usually rewarded with magnificent views over the town and the beautiful surrounding countryside.

UMBRIA AND THE MARCHES

Castles cling to ravines and woodland cloaks
wild mountains in the green heart of Italy

Map,
pages
264–5

Perugia **52** is the sun around which the other towns of Umbria orbit. Like so many of its neighbours, the city suffered considerable damage during the series of violent earthquakes that hit Umbria during the autumn of 1997. Following the earthquakes, many historic churches and buildings were closed as a precautionary measure. Some have since reopened while others remain resolutely closed. Even so, many towns in Umbria are attractive in their own right – worth visiting even if you cannot get into every church, museum or gallery.

Perugia's **Piazza IV Novembre** is freshened by the 13th-century **Fontana Maggiore**. This splendid fountain is one of the great works of the Pisan sculptors Nicola Pisano and his son, Giovanni. Carved in 1277, it is covered in elegant figures representing sundry subjects: the *Labours of the Months*, Adam and Eve, scenes from Aesop's *Fables*. Such accomplished art, used to decorate a fountain, reveals just how important a reliable water supply was to the survival of any medieval city. Just to the north of the fountain, the steps of the Gothic cathedral are where people and pigeons gather to preen and flirt. Inside, the mystic *Deposition*, painted by Barocci while under the influence of poison fed to him by a rival, inspired the famous painting by Rubens known as the *Antwerp Descent*.

Sweeping down from the piazza is the **Corso Vannucci**, choked with pedestrians day and night. On the right hand is the 13th–15th-century **Palazzo dei Priori** (Town Hall). Up its steps is the **Sala dei Notari**, painted at the end of the 13th century and since restored.

LEFT: Urbino. **BELOW:** St Francis, Umbria's best-loved son.

Work of local artists

In the same building is the **Galleria Nazionale dell' Umbria** (open Mon–Sat 9am–7pm, Sun 9am–1pm; closed 1st Mon of month; entrance fee) containing works by the most important of the many artists who lived in Umbria, including Francesco da Rimini, Fra Angelico, Piero della Francesca and Pinturicchio. Next door to the gallery is the 15th-century **Collegio del Cambio** (open in summer Mon–Sat 9am–12.30pm, 2.30–5.30pm; Tues–Sat 8am–2pm in winter, Sun 9am–12.30pm all year; entrance fee), distinguished by frescoes of Perugino and his school, and by 17th-century inlaid woodwork.

The rest of the Corso Vannucci is best appreciated at night. Relax in one of the cafés on the street and watch the students watching you. Stop at the end of the Corso in the **Giardini Carducci** to enjoy the second best view in Perugia: the hills twinkling under the stars.

South of the town is **San Pietro** with its 16th-century choir stalls, carved with a whole medieval bestiary – ducks, crocodiles and elephants included. Nearer in is the barn-like **San Domenico** with a little-visited tomb that ranks as one of the finest of its age in Italy – that of

Pope Benedict XI, who died in Perugia in 1304 having eaten poisoned figs. The adjacent cloister contains Umbria's **Museo Archeologico** (open Mon–Sat 9am–1.30pm, 2.30–7pm, Sun 9am–1pm; entrance fee), the gathering place for vast quantities of ancient Etruscan pottery and metalwork. West of the city centre is the church of **San Bernardino**, its facade decorated with angels and musicians with diaphanous robes, looking like a stone version of the figures in Mucha's art nouveau posters, except that these date to 1451, not the 1890s.

To the north of the city is another rarity, the 5th-century round church of **Sant' Angelo**, while closer to the city centre is **Sant'Agostino**, with its operatic baroque plasterwork, created by French artists in the early 17th century.

Assisi and the Vale of Spoleto

There is no place quite like **Assisi** ❺. Despite the crowds, despite the damage caused by the 1997 earthquakes, it remains an inspiring and spiritual city. The sight, as you approach Assisi, of the mighty arches supporting the **Basilica di San Francesco** (upper basilica closed for restoration; lower basilica open daily in summer 7am–7pm; 7am–12.30pm, 2–6pm in winter; entrance fee), rising above the perpetual Umbrian haze, and of **Monte Subasio**, the great peak towering behind, is sufficient to make the rest of the world seem blissfully far away.

The streets are almost too postcard perfect: cascades of flowers fall from wall sconces, alleyway gardens hoard every scrap of sunlight, the smell of roses and wood smoke permeates the air. The Basilica di San Francesco is perfectly situated for sunsets. The facade of the basilica, designed by a military architect, is like the saint it commemorates, beautiful in its poverty. The basilica is entered through the lower of its two naves, which are stacked one on top of the other. The walls of

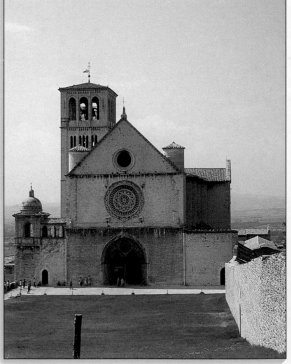

the Basilica Inferiore (Lower Basilica) are a jigsaw puzzle of frescoes by many hands, all of them inspired by the example and life of St Francis. They vary between the sweetly cheerful frescoes of Simone Martini, where even the horses seem to smile, to the sternly didactic vault frescoes depicting the monastic virtues of Chastity, Poverty and Obedience. Equally stern is the crypt where St Francis is buried, but the face of the little monk, with his jutting out ears, painted in the transept by Cimabue and said to be a faithful portrait, tells a different story.

Upstairs in the Upper Basilica, Giotto's famous fresco cycle on the *Life of St Francis* is undergoing restoration following the 1997 earthquake: optimists hope it will be open for the millennium. With this cycle, Giotto singlehandedly revived the art of fresco painting in Italy (he learned by copying artists from Greece) and this is his most accomplished work, admired by all the great artists of the Renaissance for the degree to which it introduced realism into Western art.

Chronologically, a tour of the rest of Assisi begins with the **Roman Forum** (open daily in summer 10am–1pm, 3–7pm; 10am–1pm, 2–5pm in winter; entrance fee) beneath the **Piazza del Comune**. The forum's above-ground vestige is the **Tempio di Minerva** (Minerva's Temple), whose interior has been revamped in an unfortunately gaudy manner. In the northeast sector of town, the **Anfiteatro Romano** (Roman Amphitheatre), where live naval battles were staged, has been topped by homes that follow its original oval structure.

The **Rocca Maggiore** (open daily sunrise–sunset; entrance fee), grim and immobile above the town, destroyed and rebuilt, was part of a string of towers guarding Assisi. The **Duomo** (12th-century, dedicated to San Rufino) is best appreciated for the carving of its Romanesque exterior details; its interior was revamped in 1571.

Map, pages 264–5

BELOW: *Francis Casts off His Clothes,* from Giotto's fresco cycle in San Francesco.

Chiesa Santa Chiara's pink and white exterior is supported by buttresses that are decidedly feminine in their generous curves, their airiness and strength. The chapel houses a 12th-century crucifix supposed to have spoken to St Francis. In an adjoining chapel hang the tunics of Sts Francis and Clare.

To experience something of the solitude and spirituality that matched the lives of both these saints, it is well worth visiting a couple of churches on the outskirts of Assisi. **San Damiano,** nearly 2 km (1 mile) south of the town, is the convent where St Clare spent most of her reclusive life, and it retains the air of a simple religious retreat. More rural still is the favourite hermitage of St Francis, the **Eremo delle Carceri**, a tranquil spot nestling into the tree-covered slope of Monte Subasio, 3 km (2 miles) east of the town.

Assisi sits on the rim of a dried-up lake bed, called the Vale of Spoleto, which was drained of water in the 16th century. Several other towns of great character line the eastern shore, including **Spello ㉞**, which has renowned frescoes by Pinturicchio, one of the main artists of the Umbrian school. **Spoleto ㉟** sits at the southernmost point of the former lake, a city of great cosmopolitan sophistication, renowned for its summer arts jamboree, the Festival dei Due Mondi (of the Two Worlds, meaning Europe and the Americas). The emphasis in this festival is on the avant garde, and the legacy is a number of modern sculptures dotted about the town, plus numerous art galleries selling work of dubious merit.

The town's dominant building, the **Rocca Albornoz**, was built as a papal stronghold, became the home of Lucrezia Borgia, served as a prison where members of the Red Brigade were held and will soon reopen as a cultural complex and art gallery– see it if you can. Alongside is the striking **Ponte delle Torri** spanning the gorge that yawns between the castle and the opposite hill. The

BELOW: Assisi's weeping lion.
BELOW RIGHT: the Eremo delle Carceri on Monte Subasio, outside Assisi.

Bridge of the Towers, as the name translates, was built as an aqueduct in the 13th century and you can walk across the top of the (now dry) water channel.

Spoleto's outstanding treasure is the **Duomo** (12th-century). Its medieval porch is surmounted by a rose window. The cathedral floor has an intricate herringbone and spiral Romanesque design. The chapel to the right was decorated by Pinturicchio. The apse is ablaze with Filippo Lippi's final work, the coronation of an exquisite Madonna surrounded by a rainbow and an arc of angels.

On the north side of the stairs leading to the Piazza del Duomo is the jewel-like 12th-century **Chiesa Sant'Eufemia** whose chaste perfection contrasts with the cathedral's perfect grandeur. Note Sant'Eufemia's massive and ancient stone throne behind the altar.

Visitors to Spoleto with time and a taste for the wild can use the town as a base for exploring the mountainous area to the east of Umbria, where winding narrow roads carry you up to the snowy peaks of the Monti Sibillini range, part of the Apennines.

You can drive, via Triponzo, to **Norcia** ⓾, the birthplace of St Benedict and a major centre of the truffle and salami industries. From here, roads climb ever higher to the spectacular **Piano Grande**, a vast open plain that is covered in wild flowers and rare alpine plants in summer. On the return journey you can take in the pleasing 8th-century monastery at **San Pietro in Valle** ⓾ with its Lombardic sculpture and 12th-century frescoes.

Hill-top Todi

West of Spoleto is the hill-top town of **Todi** ⓾. Here the lovely view from the **Piazza Garibaldi** is enhanced by the fragrance of a garden beneath. Nearby is

Map, pages 264–5

The Edicola, or Tempietto, in Norcia is a curious structure. The 14th-century tower is covered with inscriptions and reliefs of Christian and masonic symbols.

BELOW: the view from Monte Subasio.

the grand **Piazza Vittorio Emanuele** or **Piazza del Popolo**. Facing the **Duomo** is the **Palazzo dei Priori** (13th-century). To the right, up the steps, are the 14th-century **Palazzo del Capitano** and 13th-century **Palazzo del Popolo** (open in summer 10.30am–1pm, 4.30–7pm; 10.30am–1pm, 2–5pm in winter; entrance fee), the former in the Gothic style with a bay of triform windows, the latter in the Lombardic style resting on an impressive network of pillars.

At the head of the square stands the Duomo, begun in the early 12th century. The Gothic campanile, built 100 years later, strays from the fine Romanesque style. The Duomo's rear wall is decorated by a Ferraù da Faenza fresco. To the right is a 16th-century Giannicola di Paolo painting of the Madonna. The interior is softly lit by some of the finest stained glass in the region.

A brisk walk around the hill will bring you to the church of **San Fortunato**. The structure was begun in 1292 and built in stages over a period of 200 years during the architectural revolution. The central portal's sculptures deserve close examination for their tiny, whimsical depictions of humans and beasts. The interior is light and airy; the eggshell whiteness of the stone is enhanced by the deep sable colour of the carved choir and the formidable pillar-mounted lectern. In the crypt, Jacopone, the Franciscan poet who wrote the *Stabat Mater*, is buried.

Through the **Parco della Rocca**, replete with good views, and on down the mountain, the **Tempio di Santa Maria della Consolazione** is perched on a little shelf of green. The 16th-century structure was long thought to be the work of Bramante because of the similarities with St Peter's in Rome, but it is now attributed to one Cola di Capsorala. The altar may seem to some a bit too much, but the space is light and airy, the intricate sunburst of stones on the floor a marvel of geometrics.

BELOW and **BELOW RIGHT:** Santa Maria della Consolazione in Todi.

Vine-growing Orvieto

The hill which supports **Orvieto ⑤** is volcanic in origin, therefore porous, therefore in danger of bringing the city down as it crumbles. The volcanic slopes are covered in the vineyards that produce Orvieto's famously crisp white wines.

After climbing up serpentine curves and through scaffolding-clad streets, you will burst into the unexpected expanse of the **Piazza del Duomo**. With any luck, the late-afternoon sun will be glittering off the mosaics of the 14th-century cathedral's astonishing facade. The cathedral's steps are generally crowded with a mixture of visitors, Orvietans and soldiers garrisoned just down the street.

The cathedral was begun on 15 November 1290 to house relics of the miracles of Bolsena (1263): principally a chalice-cloth onto which blood flowed from the host during a celebration of the Mass. Although the identity of the original architect is a matter of some debate, by its completion the Duomo's construction required the input of legions of architects, sculptors, painters and mosaicists. The facade, designed by Lorenzo Maitani, is bolstered by zebra horizontals of basalt and travertine.

Inside the cathedral, the black and white stripes point up the curvilinear arches. The wall of the apse is decorated with scenes from the *Life of the Virgin*. These were begun by Ugolino di Prete Ilario and completed by Pinturicchio and Antonio Viterbo during the late 14th century. On the left-hand side of the altar is the **Cappella del Corporale**, painted by Ugolino and his assistants and depicting the *Miracle of Bolsena*. To the right of the altar is the **Cappella Nuova** (open daily 10am–1pm, 2.30–6pm; entrance fee) whose decoration was begun by Fra Angelico in 1447 and completed by Luca Signorelli at the turn of the next century. The frescoes (now under restoration) feature lurid scenes of hellfire with a deep contextual nod to Dante.

Via Duomo and **Corso Cavour** are lined with shops selling Orvietan ceramics whose simple, medieval designs are some of the prettiest in the region. Nearby are elegant restaurants, chic clothiers, and more shops selling wood sculptures. To the right, off Corso Cavour is the striking 12th-century **Palazzo del Popolo**.

Straight ahead are the **Palazzo Comunale** and the church of **Sant'Andrea** in the **Piazza della Repubblica**. To the left is the **Old** or **Medieval Quarter**, which is easily the most delightful part of the town, with its antique walls hung with pots of tumbling geraniums, high-walled gardens and the songbirds they attract, and tiny cave-like workrooms of Orvietan artisans.

Lakeside pursuits

The road north from Orvieto will take you to **Città della Pieve ⑥**, birthplace of Perugino, father of the Umbrian School of painting and best-known for his ability to capture the limpid blues and greens of the Umbrian sky. The town has several of his works, including the *Adoration of the Magi*, which features Lake Trasimeno in the background.

Today that lake is Umbria's summer holiday playground, ringed by campsites offering tennis, swimming and trekking on horseback. **Castiglione del Lago ⑥** is the lake's capital, and there are splendid views from the ramparts of the castle which gave the

Map, pages 264–5

TIP

Orvieto has lent its name to a white wine of variable quality. Orvieto Classico, though, refers to a special classification and can be very good. Look for wines by Antinori and Bigi. *Secco* wines are dry; *amabile* are semi-sweet.

BELOW: medieval tower in Orvieto.

town its name. Here, and at the restaurants around the lake, you can sample the locally caught fish, including eel, pike and trout.

North of the lake, the road through Umbertide takes you to the atmospheric town of **Gubbio** ❷, once known as the "city of silence" because of its desolate position in the Umbrian backwoods, but now, thanks to modern roads, a town within easy reach of those who love good food and architecture. Gubbio clings to the side of Monte Ingino, and its major buildings just fit on the narrow terraces that step up the mountainside. At the top of Monte Ingino (it's best to take the funicular railway up, then walk down) rises the **Basilica di Sant'Ubaldo** where lie the remains of the saint in stately, if somewhat grisly, splendour. Legend has it that St Ubaldo intervened in a battle against Perugia, gaining a decisive victory for the badly outnumbered Gubbians. The basilica also displays the three immense *ceri* (candles) with which the sturdy men of Gubbio race up the hill in an orgiastic celebration of the saint's day every 15 May.

Returning to the town, your path should take you to the fine **cathedral** to see the great Gothic ribs of the vault and the 13th-century stained glass. Across a small passage from the cathedral is the **Palazzo Ducale** (open daily 9am–1.30pm; entrance fee), begun in 1476 by Federico da Montefeltro, Duke of Urbino, inspired by the palace in that town. The Ducal Palace's rooms sport frescoes and various interesting architectural features.

The outstanding element of Gubbio's skyline is the belltower of the 14th-century **Palazzo dei Consoli** (open daily; entrance fee), whose Great Hall houses a quixotic collection of medieval paraphernalia, including examples of medieval plumbing. On the first floor are the **Tavole Eugubine**: seven bronze plates upon which a precise hand has translated the ancient Umbrian language into Latin.

BELOW: the Corso dei Ceri festival in Gubbio, which takes place in May.

The Marches

After the stunning hilltowns of Umbria, the neighbouring region of the Marches holds very few sights that can compete, with the singular exception of **Urbino** ⬤ with its stronghold of the wise old warrior Duke Federico da Montefeltro. Here he constructed one of the great treasures of 16th-century architecture. Urbino is an eyrie of a town whose golden buildings are set high amid spectacular mountains. Urbino remains one of the few hill towns left in Italy not ringed by the unsavoury intrusions of modernity. The original old city remains almost completely "unimproved", perched at the top of its two peaks.

The **Piazza del Popolo** is a tourist centre by day. By night, some of the University of Urbino's 16,000 students recline here on the steps or in the cafés, or stand in the street and discuss politics, the latest foreign film, or last night's poetry reading. The facades are old; the faces are generally young. The contrast exemplifies the relaxed symbiosis that exists between Urbino's walls and the lives they enclose.

The duke and his Humanist contemporaries felt man was the centre of the universe – a significant break with Christian philosophy. The courtyard of his **Palazzo Ducale** is paved with a hub, with radiating spokes of marble to symbolise man's central position. The building itself is part palace and part fortress: a graceful, secure nest in the rarefied mountain air for the duke to feather with marvellous works of art. The **Galleria Nazionale delle Marche** (open Tues–Sun 9am–7pm, Mon 9am–2pm; entrance fee), now housed in the palace, has several fine works by Piero della Francesca and by the town's most famous artist, Raphael. Also remarkable is the *trompe l'oeil* inlay work in the duke's study.

Down the street from the ducal palace is **Casa di Raffaello** (open Mon–Sat 9am–1pm, 3–7pm, Sun 10am–1pm; entrance fee) the house where Raphael spent his first 14 years. The middle-class house contrasts with the ducal splendour. Outside in the courtyard is the stone upon which Raphael and his father, Giovanni, also an artist, ground their pigments.

Urbino was not on any major trade routes, and had few natural assets, so Federico brought wealth to the town by offering himself and his army as mercenaries.

Pocket-sized republic

Urbino stands a little inland from the Adriatic, a sunny coastline lined with hectare after hectare of orchards growing peaches and nectarines for export, and of regimented beaches and seaside hotels. You will see something of this if you visit the **Republic of San Marino** ⬤, a self-governing state within Italy that has remained independent for 1,600 years. Stamp collectors will know it as a republic that issues big pictorial postage stamps in a variety of shapes other than square – the philatelic ouput is there to see in specialist museums.

The republic stands on the peak of Monte Titano, with sweeping views out over Rimini to the Adriatic. You can do a complete circuit of the town's historic walls, visiting the several museums that are housed in the bastions, and visit the diminutive building that serves as the parliament of this pocket-sized republic.

Just west of San Marino is Federico's hill-top fortress of **San Leo**, one of the most impressive sights in Italy. In the 18th century, the alchemist Cagliostro was imprisoned here; his specially designed cell can still be seen.❏

BELOW: the citadel of San Marino.

ABRUZZO AND MOLISE

*Two huge national parks – Abruzzo and Gran Sasso
– make this a region where nature rules supreme*

Map,
page 294

he Apennine Mountains, a geologically unruly region long ignored by most travellers, unravel into three strands as they twist down between Rome and the Adriatic. It is characteristic of this area, formerly known by the single name Abruzzo, that it should have been the birthplace of the priest in Hemingway's *A Farewell to Arms* who recommended it for winter sport. That has been Abruzzo's traditional image among foreigners and Italians alike.

The image, like all caricatures, leaves out many of the finer points of this old region, but it persists. Visitors flock to the Gran Sasso, the central mountain chain, to climb, ski, birdwatch and hunt, and to Pescara and other beach towns. Yet the region has an indigenous history that may be the oldest in Italy, and its lovely towns, surrounded by snow-capped mountains even in June, contain first-rate monuments. Molise split off from Abruzzo to form an autonomous region in 1963, and has managed to retain its wild spirit more completely than its populous and faster-developing neighbour.

A dip into history

Human habitation of the region goes back more than 13,000 years to the so-called Fucino (or Marsicano) Man, whose fragmented bones have been discovered in caves in Ortucchio and Maritza. Archaeological evidence of a flourishing indigenous civilisation in the 6th century BC is gathering, hastened by the find of the famous Capestrano Warrior, now at the **Museo Nazionale** (open daily 9am–7pm; entrance fee) in Chieti. Signs of later Roman domination can be seen throughout the region, particularly at the interesting archaeological site of Alba Fucens, near **Avezzano ❶**.

In the Middle Ages and later, the region came under the sway of the various invading kingdoms from the south. The Spanish, for example, were responsible for most of the castles that pepper the region. Earthquakes, particularly the very severe one in 1703, have caused considerable damage, as did the two world wars. Massive migrations of farm workers into the cities after World War II resulted in economic imbalances between the town and the country, but recent efforts to encourage tourism and industry, and the completion of the *autostrade,* have started to reverse the trend of post-war impoverishment.

Shy animals

Italy's voluptuous landscape is at its most magnificent in the **Parco Nazionale d'Abruzzo ❷**, where over 400 sq. km (154 sq. miles) of high-altitude meadows, beech groves and snow-capped peaks are protected from Abruzzian housing developers. It is still possible to see the shy brown Apennine bear, of which there are

LEFT: one step at a time, in Scanno.
BELOW: flower-filled corner.

between 70 and 100. They feed on berries and insects in the remote upper pastures. The Abruzzo chamois, distinguished by the black-and-white pattern on its throat, also thrives here, as do the Apennine lynx and foxes, wolves, otters, song birds, hawks and eagles. About 150 well-marked trails provide access to even the highest sections, most of them within a day's walk of the main road.

Pescasséroli ❸, the administrative headquarters for the park (tel: 0863-91955), was the birthplace of the philosopher Benedetto Croce. Today it is dedicated to physical pursuits such as hiking and skiing, and you can pick up trail maps for the park here. If you are coming at Christmas, Easter or during August, book accommodation in advance – these are the peak seasons. Buses ply daily between Pescasséroli and Avezzano, a more convenient base if time is short.

The road and railway skirt the edge of the **Piana del Fucino**, a lake in Roman times but subsequently drained. In what was once the centre of the lake is the important Telespazio station, with its forest of satellite dishes. In the surrounding fields bright red poppies burst forth in May.

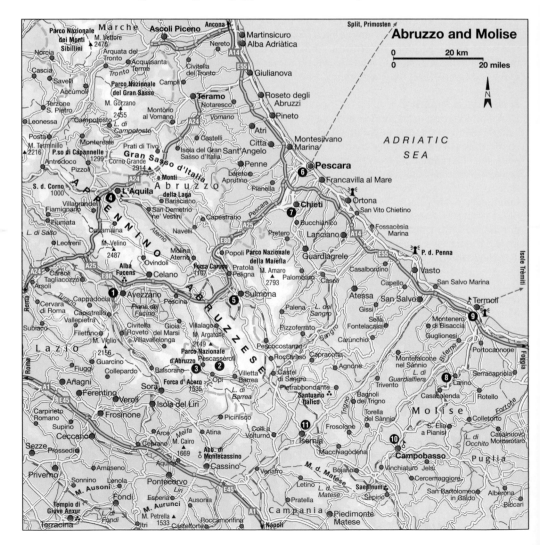

Fountain of 99 spouts

See map opposite

L'Aquila ❹, chief town of Abruzzo, has a turbulent history belied by its fine architecture and the relaxing coolness of its arcaded streets. Founded in 1240 by Frederick II of Hohenstaufen as an outpost against the papacy, the city converted to papal rule shortly after Frederick's death in 1250. Nine years later, Frederick's son, Manfred, reclaimed the city after a siege that destroyed the city walls and led to its abandonment for seven years. Charles I of Anjou began rebuilding it after defeating Manfred at Benevento in 1266.

According to legend, the city of L'Aquila was formed from 99 palaces, 99 churches, 99 fountains and 99 squares, and in commemoration of this numerical coincidence, the city authorities commissioned a fountain of 99 spouts in 1272. The **Fontane delle Novantanove Cannelle** is one of the highlights of the city. The pleasant courtyard of red and white stone and the sound of water issuing from the 99 masks combine to convey a sense of peace.

Pietro da Morrone, a local hermit, was crowned Pope Celestine V at the age of 85. He served only five months in office, claiming that his inexperience with the ways of the world made him unfit to sit on the throne of St Peter.

L'Aquila's best-known monument is the 13th-century church of **Santa Maria di Collemaggio**, outside the city wall on the southeast corner of town. It is impossible to miss its red and white facade, whose three rose windows and corresponding doorways subtly combine the Gothic and the Romanesque. The church was begun in 1277 under the guidance of Pietro da Morrone. His lovely Renaissance tomb can be seen to the right of the apse inside. The interior, relieved of baroque flourishes in 1973, has a fine wooden ceiling.

The newly-cleaned church of **San Bernardino** is arguably the finest Renaissance monument in the Abruzzo. The interior, completely rebuilt after the earthquake of 1703, is dominated by its baroque ceiling and organ, both designed by Ferdinando Mosca of nearby Pescocostanzo. In a chapel on the right, the Renaissance tomb of San Bernardino (1488) has a classical precision carried over in its delicate floral frieze. The tomb and the monument to Maria Pereira (1496) in the apse are the work of Silvestro dell'Aquila, a local artist. The floor repeats the theme of red and white marble.

BELOW: entrance to Santa Maria di Collemaggio.

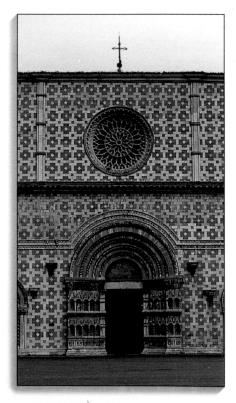

On weekday mornings in the **Piazza del Duomo** there is a vibrant open-air market where local cane, wool, lace and copper are sold. The Duomo, completely destroyed by the 1703 earthquake, was rebuilt in the 1900s.

Defensive "ears"

One of the best museums in Abruzzo is L'Aquila's **Museo Nazionale d'Abruzzo** (open in summer Tues–Sat 9am–7pm, Sun 9am–1pm; Tues–Sun 9am–1pm in winter; entrance fee), located in the castle at the north end of town. The Castello itself, built in 1532 by Piero Luigi Escriba (or Scriba), the architect of Castel Sant'Elmo in Naples, is known for its four protruding "ears" which enabled soldiers to cover every possible angle of approach. The archaeological section on the ground floor has an amusing Medusa's head frieze. On the first floor is a collection of medieval religious art, most of it from local churches, while on the second floor are 16th–18th-century works. The modern art on the third floor includes some interesting paintings by local artists.

Unlike the Parco Nazionale, which is of interest for its wildlife and majestic beech groves, the **Gran Sasso**

talia, just outside L'Aquila, attracts mountaineers. The Gran Sasso itself, at 2,914 metres (9,560 ft), is the highest peak in the Apennines; the many trails, both for hiking and skiing, that radiate from the nearby Campo Imperatore are known throughout Europe. Trail maps are available at the Agenzia di Viaggi-Centro Turistico Gran Sasso in L'Aquila.

Sulmona

One of the most spectacular drives in Abruzzo takes Route 261 from L'Aquila to **Sulmona ❺**, following the valley of the Aterno river past a number of medieval villages, each with its ruined castle and its church. Sulmona, the birthplace of Ovid, is considered by many Abruzzians to be the most beautiful town in the province. The evening *passeggiata* is also worth seeing, when the streets, lined with shops selling *confetti* – sugared almonds that have been made here since the Middle Ages – become packed with people pouring arm-in-arm up the Corso. Others stroll through the Piazza Garibaldi, where shops sell traditional copper pots and pans and where the remains of a medieval aqueduct can be seen.

The **Palazzo della Santissima Annunziata**, once a combination of hospital, church and storehouse of food donated for the poor, stands at the ancient centre of town. The harmony of its facade is often praised. Each of the three portals has a different size and shape, corresponding to the three windows above. The left portal is Gothic, dating from 1415, the middle Renaissance, dating from 1483, and the less interesting right portal from still later. A floral frieze running across the face links the three. On the first floor is a museum of local archaeology and paintings by local artists (open daily 9.30am–1pm). The church, originally more visibly connected to the palazzo, was rebuilt after an earthquake in 1706.

BELOW: L'Aquila's Fountain of 99 Spouts.

Map, page 294

Pescara ❻ is the birthplace of the writer Gabriele d'Annunzio (1863–1938), whose home is off Piazza Unione (closed for restoration). But it is the 16 km (10 miles) of wide, sandy beach rather than d'Annunzio that draws so many visitors to this Adriatic coast.

Half an hour outside Pescara is the ancient hill-top town of **Chieti ❼**, famous today for its archaeological museum, but known since antiquity for its views across mainland Abruzzo and the sea. Remains of three Roman temples can be seen off the main Corso Marrucino, just behind the post office. The recently modernised **Museo Archeologico di Antichità** (closed for restoration), at the far western edge of town in the Villa Comunale, has an extensive coin collection. Particularly interesting is the case containing coins from Alba Fucens: a diagram charts the trenches in which the different coins were found. The museum also contains local anthropological and archaeological finds, including some from the Iron Age, and an interesting collection of Roman statues. The sculpture of the 6th-century BC Capestrano Warrior is the most famous exhibit.

The local delicacy in Chieti is torrone di fichi secci, or nougat with figs.

A festival in Molise

If you happen to take the train from Termoli to Campobasso between 25 and 27 May, stop at the medieval village of **Larino ❽**. The Sagra di San Pardo, Larino's annual festival will be taking place, when ox-carts are paraded through the streets. While there, visit the old cathedral, with its beautiful facade, and climb up the monumental staircase of the Palazzo Reale. Larino is one of the least-known places in Italy, yet one of the most rewarding to visit.

Termoli ❾, on the Adriatic, is a popular beach resort whose old town on the promontory offers fine views in all directions. Well garrisoned behind a small castle built by Frederick II are labyrinthine streets and a fine cathedral. Boats leave from Termoli for the **Isole Trémiti**, a group of offshore islands celebrated for their mysterious grottoes and other marine phenomena.

The town that best illustrates the difference between the old and the new in Molise is **Campobasso ❿**, the region's capital. Presided over by the 15th-century Castello Monforte, from which tumble the steeply stepped streets of the old town, Campobasso's modern quarters spread out to the station below. It is in the new town that two of Campobasso's best-known features can be found: a top-security prison and a training school for the *Carabinieri*, the Italian police. Smartly uniformed young men stroll up the streets in twos and threes or stand talking in the square. Ask them for directions to the old town, in particular to San Giorgio, the 12th-century Romanesque church.

Ninety minutes away by train is **Isernia ⓫**, rich in regional lore and a good starting point for exploring the remote hill towns. In 1979, an ancient settlement was discovered on the outskirts. No human remains were found, but there is evidence that man lived here a million years before the birth of Christ – the oldest traces of humanity discovered in Europe. The discovery of a fireplace indicated that these people used fire. Bones of elephants, rhinoceroses, hippos, bison and bear were also discovered, some now displayed in the excellent **archaeological museum** (open daily; entrance fee). ❑

BELOW: the hilltop village of Villalago, south of Sulmona.

THE SOUTH

*To discover one of Europe's most interesting regions,
venture beyond Naples and Sicily into the* Mezzogiorno

When foreign travellers visit Apulia, Basilicata and Calabria, they are usually greeted by stares. The stares are not hostile. Nor are they necessarily suspicious. They're just surprised. So few foreigners – so few northern Italians, even – visit these remote and sunbaked regions that anybody who does is looked upon as a bit of an oddball.

This was the case when the English writer Norman Douglas visited in 1911; it was the case when the anti-Fascist Carlo Levi was banished here in 1935. So few people have come to this area for pleasure or insight that nobody knows of the pleasures and insights to be found. Those who do come, follow in the footsteps of the Greeks and Romans to Naples, Pompeii, Cumae and Capri. They flock to Sicily and its temples. But Apulia? Basilicata? Calabria? Italy's heel? Her instep? Her toe?

Then there is northern prejudice. Northerners are industrial, pragmatic, fair-skinned. The southerners are agricultural, superstitious, dark. The northerners are rich. The southerners are poor, and emigrate if they get the chance. Nobody moves south to take their place. This is *Il Problema del Mezzogiorno*.

The truth is that southern Italy is one of the most interesting places to visit in Europe. It is a romantic land of castles and churches; vast, wheat-covered plains; and misty mountains where shepherds roam. Apulia is a place for novel architectural forms: the Apulian Romanesque; Leccian baroque; castles by Frederick II – and odd, conical, peasant dwellings known as the *trulli*. In Basilicata are the *sassi*, cave-dwellings carved into the side of a ravine, many adorned with frescoes, and La Trinità, an unfinished 11th-century Benedictine monastery covered with Roman inscriptions. In Calabria visitors rediscover the Greeks – in particular, two made of bronze, recently dredged up by fishermen off Riace. There are Norman castles, Byzantine churches, rich red wines and landscapes which were first described by Homer.

Naples, the Bay of Naples and Sicily are the richest regions historically, and this is reflected in this guide. Apart from the chapter on Naples, which is best explored on foot, the descriptions are geared towards travelling by car. A car is especially important in the *Mezzogiorno*, where sights are too scattered to justify spending long hours waiting for infrequent trains. ❑

PRECEDING PAGES: the typical Basilicata landscape, unchanged for centuries.
LEFT: an ancient fresco of *Spring* in Naples' Archaeological Museum.

NAPLES

Noisy, crowded, but thrilling, Naples has it all – fine buildings, world-class museums and cosmopolitan verve

Map, pages 304–5

Naples (Napoli) has always been the black sheep of Italian cities, the misfit, the outcast, the messy brother that nobody knew quite what to do with. It is burdened by the densest population of any city in Europe, intense poverty, unemployment, bureaucratic inefficiency and organised crime, and has come to be seen as an Italian Calcutta. That Naples is, in fact, one of the most beautiful Italian cities, with a friendly population and a long cultural heritage evidenced in art, churches, castles and pizza, does not deny its less appealing side. In the end, like all black sheep, troubled Naples is the most interesting member of its family.

Orientation

The city has its own special shape, defined partly by landscape, partly by chance and partly by governmental edict. The only way to get a feel for the place is to walk its different quarters. To orientate yourself, find **Piazza Garibaldi ❶**. From here, the long **Corso Umberto I** juts down to the southwest to **Piazza Bovio ❷**, where, changing its name to Via Agostino Depretis, it continues on to **Piazza Municipio ❸**. By day, the corso, one of the main traffic routes in Naples, is jammed with buses, taxis, cars and motorbikes. At night, it is lined with prostitutes. The thoroughfare was forced through the narrow, crowded streets that surround it in 1888 in an effort to improve air circulation following a cholera epidemic. The rather drab **Università ❹** looms halfway down, on the right-hand side.

From Piazza Municipio and the nearby **Piazza Plebiscito ❺** the city fans out to the east, the north and the west. Directly north, up the Via Toledo, also known as the Via Roma, is the red palazzo housing the **Museo Archeologico Nazionale**. East of the museum, in the triangle it forms with the Piazza Plebiscito and the Piazza Garibaldi, lies most of Old Naples, with its medieval streets and its churches. North of the museum, on a hilltop, stands the art gallery of **Capodimonte**. Farther south, on a spur of land out in the bay, rises the egg-shaped **Castel dell'Ovo** and, along the waterfront, the Via Partenope, where the city's most expensive hotels overlook the water. The shoreline then curves away west, passing the **Villa Comunale** with its famous aquarium, to the Marina at **Mergellina**, near Virgil's tomb. From Mergellina views stretch back over the entire city, with Mount Vesuvius looming in the background haze.

The city's roots

The name Naples derives from Neapolis, the New City founded by settlers from Cumae in the 6th century BC. Nearby stood Paleopolis, the Old City, founded in the 9th century BC, also by Greeks from Cumae. The two cities grew side by side like brother and sister until their

LEFT: Via Tribunali, in the historic quarter. **BELOW:** sealing a marriage vow with a toast.

violent overthrow by Samnites in 400 BC. Rome wrested them away after a three-year siege in 326 BC, at which point they began to grow into a single entity called Neapolis. From the beginning, Romans flocked here, drawn by the mild climate, the sparkling bay and the political freedom which retention of the Greek constitution allowed. Virgil wrote the *Aeneid* here; emperors built gardens and bathed.

Eight dynasties

The Dark Ages were indeed dark in Naples – nobody knows quite what happened – and until shortly after the first millennium the city was ruled by dukes loosely allied to Byzantium. Then, in 1139, Roger the Norman took Naples under the wing of his Kingdom of Sicily. The seven dynasties that followed produced most of the architectural landmarks that can be seen today. Their statues, together with one of Roger, peer out from niches in the facade of the Palazzo Reale at the centre of town: Frederick II of Hohenstaufen, who founded the university; Charles I of Anjou, who lived here and left his mark; Alfonso I of Aragon, Charles I of Austria, Charles I of Bourbon, Joachim Murat and Victor Emmanuel II. They line up like wrinkles in the building's broad face, testimonies to the city's past.

Castles and music

When Charles I of Anjou built the **Castel Nuovo ❻** (open Mon–Fri 9am–7pm, Sat 9am–1.30pm; entrance fee) in 1282, he could not have known that seven centuries later it would still serve as the political hub of the city. The Municipal Council of Naples meets in the huge **Sala dei Baroni**, where Charles is said to have performed some of his bloodiest executions. The finest architectural element in this imposing fortress is the Triumphal Arch, built from 1454–67 to commemorate Alfonso I's defeat of the French. It is the only Renaissance arch ever to have been built at the entrance to a castle.

A short walk up the Via San Carlo leads to the **Teatro San Carlo ❼** (tours Sat–Sun 2–4pm; entrance fee), the largest opera house in Italy and one of the finest

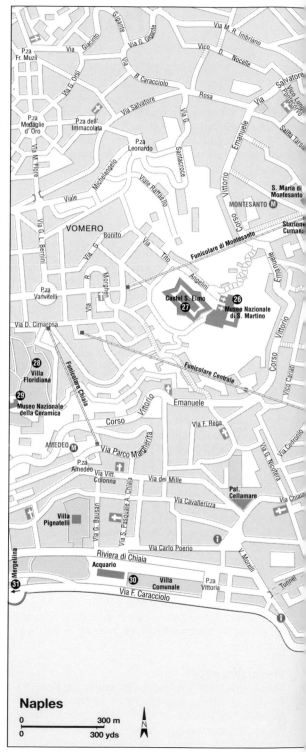

Naples

0 ————————— 300 m
0 ————————— 300 yds

N

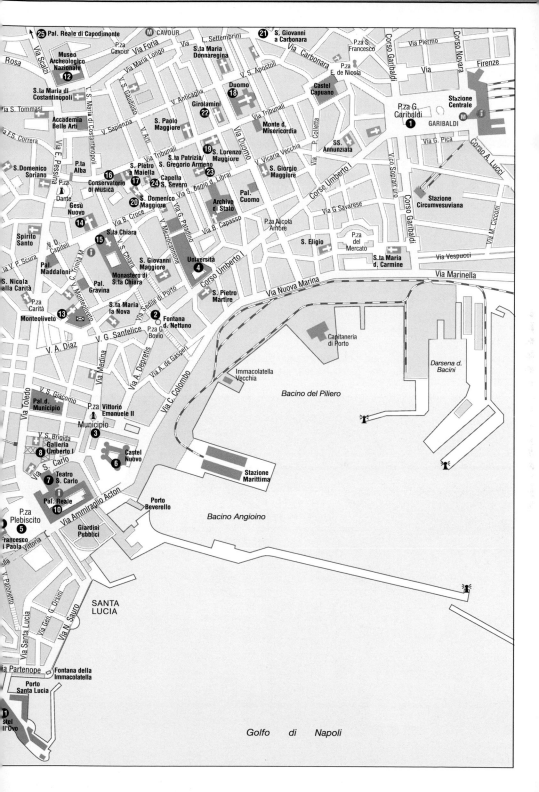

25 Pal. Reale di Capodimonte   Ⓜ CAVOUR

Rosa

Via Scalzi

12 Museo Archeologico Nazionale

S.ta Maria di Costantinopoli

Via S. Tommasi

Via F.S. Correra

Accademia Belle Arti

S. Domenico Soriano

P.ta Alba

P.za Dante

16 Conservatorio di Musica

17 S. Pietro a Maiella

Gesù Nuovo 14

20 S. Domenico Maggiore

Spirito Santo

V. D. Capitelli

15

S.ta Chiara

Pal. Maddaloni

V. a V. P. Scura

S. Nicola alla Carità

P.za Carità

Monteoliveto 13

Via A. Diaz

V. G. Sanfelice

V. S. Giacomo

Pal.d. Municipio

P.za Vittorio Emanuele II

Municipio 3

V. S. Brigida

Galleria Umberto I 8

S. Carlo

Teatro S. Carlo 7

Pal. Reale 10

P.za Plebiscito 5

Francesco i Paola

Vittoria

Giardini Pubblici

Via Ammiraglio Acton

SANTA LUCIA

ia Partenope

Fontana della Immacolatella

Porto Santa Lucia

stel ll'Ovo

P.za Cavour

Via Foria

Via Maria Longo

V. S. Gaudioso

V. S. Maria di Costantinopoli

V. Sapienza

V. Arti

S. Paolo Maggiore

V. Anticaglia

Girolamini 22

Via Tribunali

S.ta Patrizia/ S. Gregorio Armeno

S. Pietro a Maiella

24 Capella S. Severo 23

V. B. Croce

V. G. Paladino

V. B. Capasso

V. S. Sebastiano

Via Settembrini

S.ta Maria Donnaregina

V. S. Apostoli

Duomo 18

Via Tribunali

19 S. Lorenzo Maggiore

Via Duomo

S. Giorgio Maggiore

Pal. Cuomo

Archivio di Stato

S. G. de Librai

P.za Nicola Amore

21 S. Giovanni a Carbonara

Via Carbonara

P.za S. Francesco

P.za E. de Nicola

Castel Capuano

Monte d. Misericordia

Via Vicaria Vecchia

SS. Annunziata

Corso Umberto I

V.co Soprani ur o

S. Eligio

P.za del Mercato

P.za G. Garibaldi 1

GARIBALDI Ⓜ

Stazione Centrale

Corso Garibaldi

Via Piermo

Corso Novara

Via

Firenze

Via G. Pica

Corso A. Lucci

Stazione Circumvesuviana

Corso Garibaldi

Via M. Cicconi

S.ta Maria d. Carmine

Via Vespucci

Via Marinella

Via G Savarese

Via Nuova Marina

Universitá 4

Monastero di S.ta Chiara

Pal. Gravina

S.ta Maria la Nova

2 Fontana d. Nettuno

P.za Bovio

Via Medina

V. A. Depretis

Via A. de Gasperi

Via C. Colombo

S. Pietro Martire

Immacolatella Vecchia

Capitaneria di Porto

Darsena d. Bacini

Bacino del Piliero

Castel Nuovo 6

Stazione Marittima

Porto Beverello

Bacino Angioino

Golfo   di   Napoli

Via Toledo

V. Monteoliveto

C. Trinità M.

V. S. Chiara

S. Giovanni Maggiore

V. Sedile di Porto

Via Santa Lucia

Via Gen. G. Orsini

Via N. Sauro

V. Palonetto

vittoria

ABOVE: street vendor.

in the world. It is all red velvet and gold trim, with six tiers of boxes rising from the stage. Built in 1737, under the direction of Charles III of Bourbon, the theatre retains its perfect acoustics, helped by the insertion, after a fire in 1816, of hundreds of clay pitchers between the walls. The monthly tourist magazine *Qui Napoli*, available at tourist offices, gives listings of concerts, operas and recitals. Even on the sixth tier, you can sit on a red velvet seat in your own private box.

Across the street is the **Galleria Umberto I** ❽, erected in 1887 on a neoclassical design similar to that of its older brother in Milan. Its glass ceiling, 56 metres (184 ft) high, and its mosaic-covered floor were reconstructed after bomb damage in World War II. Pleasant cafés permit a moment's rest.

The wide **Piazza Plebiscito** around the corner is embraced by the twin arcades of the **Chiesa di San Francesco di Paola** ❾ (1817–32), modelled after the Pantheon in Rome. The interior of this imposing church has little to offer tourists other than the pungent shade of its dingy arcades.

Reminder of turbulent times

The sprawling red facade of the **Palazzo Reale** ❿ (open Thurs–Tues 9.30am–10pm, Sun–9am–1pm, entrance fee) looms across the street with its eight statues illustrating the eight Neapolitan dynasties. At the foot of its monumental marble staircase stand the original bronze doors from the Castel Nuovo. The cannonball lodged in the left door is a reminder of an early siege. Upstairs are a throne room and a small but lavish theatre. Further rooms stretch off in a seemingly endless series of period furniture and Dresden china.

Another famous castle, the **Castel dell'Ovo** ⓫ (closed to the public), on the waterfront, is also still in use, this time for scientific conventions. Its oval shape

BELOW: the Castel Nuovo, built in 1282.

(hence the name) was commissioned by the Spanish viceroy Don Pedro de Toledo in 1532, but the original castle was built by William I in 1154, finished by Frederick II and enlarged by the not-to-be-outdone Charles I of Anjou. Pleasant restaurants line the shore, children bellyflop from the causeway, and the speedboats of the Guardia di Finanza (Fraud Squad) lurk just along the quay.

Map, pages 304–5

House of history

The **Museo Archeologico Nazionale di Napoli** ⓬ (open daily 8am–2pm, till 10pm in summer; entrance fee) is one of the great museums of the world, housing the most spectacular finds from Pompeii and Herculaneum and fine examples of Greek sculpture. A trip to the museum will take an entire morning.

The ground floor is devoted to classical sculpture and Egyptian art. In the main entrance hall, a monolithic sarcophagus depicts a famous and important scene: Prometheus creating man out of clay. Another awesome sarcophagus presents a raucous Bacchanalian celebration. Through a doorway to the right, a pair of statues of Harmodius and Aristogeiton, who killed the tyrant Hipparchus, fairly leap out at you as you enter the room. These are actually Roman copies of originals once installed in the Agora in Athens.

In a further room stands a Roman copy of the famous statue of Doryphorus by Polycleitus (440 BC), considered the "canon of perfection" of manly proportions. This statue, found at Pompeii, and others of its period are evidence of the refined tastes of early Greek settlers. The Farnese Collection includes a Hercules and the *Farnese Bull* (the largest piece of antique sculpture ever found) from Rome's Baths of Caracalla.

ABOVE: relief in the Galleria Umberto I.
BELOW: a flying leap off the Castel dell'Ovo.

The rich collection of mosaics on the mezzanine floor at the back of the building come from the floors, walls and courtyards of houses unearthed at Pompeii. The freshness and colour of these works after centuries buried in ash are an amazing tribute to the craftsmanship of their ancient makers. Room LIX contains two of the most famous of the mosaics, both signed by a master of the craft named Dioscorides from the island of Samos. The one labelled 9987 depicts, according to some, two women consulting a sorceress, or, according to others, three women gossiping. This mosaic and 9985, which depicts a dwarf, two women and a man with musical instruments, are thought to represent scenes from a Greek comedy.

The Nile scenes in room LX, from a later period, feature ducks, crocodiles, hippopotami and snakes. These mosaics originally framed the *Battle of Issus*, in Room LXI. In this scene, Alexander the Great is presented in his victorious battle against the Persian emperor Darius in 333 BC. The thicket of spears creates the illusion of an army far larger than that actually shown.

Through the large Salone dell'Atlante at the top of the stairs is a series of rooms containing wall-paintings from various Campanian cities. Especially startling is the 6th-century BC *Sacrifice of Iphigenia*, the Greek equivalent of the biblical sacrifice of Isaac. The deer borne by Artemis in the top of the picture replaced Iphigenia at the last minute, just as Isaac was replaced by a ram. Far happier is *The Rustic Concert*, in which Pan and nymphs tune up for a Roman celebration.

Neapolitan churches

The churches of Naples, like the churches of any Italian city, offer glimpses into Italian life. In Italy, a visit to a church, a quick confession, a curtsy in front of an altar are still a daily ritual for many people. Because of this, most churches are open all day every day (usually no entrance fee), so no opening times are given.

The church of **Monteoliveto** ⑬, about halfway up the Via Roma, contains a wealth of Renaissance monuments hidden away in surprising corners. Far in the back of this aisleless basilica, begun in 1411, stands a bizarre group of terracotta figures by the artist Guido Mazzoni. The eight statues, looking almost alive in the dim light that filters into the chapel, represent the *Pietà*, and are said to be portraits of Mazzoni's 15th-century friends. Further back, down a side passage, is the Old Sacristy, containing frescoes by Vasari and wooden stalls, inlaid with biblical scenes. In the very front of the church, to the left of the entrance, another passage leads to the Piccolomini Chapel where a relief of a Nativity scene by the Florentine Antonio Rossellino (1475) is a delight to behold.

Unlike in Rome, which is heavily baroque, no single architectural style dominates Naples. The Gothic, the Renaissance and the baroque are all represented. The late 16th-century church of **Gesù Nuovo** ⑭, at the top of the street called **Trinità Maggiore**, presents perhaps the most harmonious example of the Neapolitan baroque. The embossed stone facade originally formed the wall of a Renaissance palace. At noon on Saturdays, when weddings take place here, the massive front doors are thrown open to give a splendid view of fully lit baroque at its best. The interior has a unique design, being almost as wide as it is deep. The coloured marble and bright frescoes seem to spiral up into the dome. Directly above the main portal, just inside the church, stretches a wide fresco

ABOVE and **BELOW:**
exhibits in the
Museo
Archeologico.

by Francesco Solimena (1725) depicting Heliodorus driven from the temple. The ubiquitous Solimena dominated Neapolitan painting in the first half of the 18th century.

Map, pages 304–5

Robert the Wise

A more austere, and older, architectural approach is demonstrated by the Gothic church of **Santa Chiara** ⓰, just across the street. Founded between 1310 and 1328 by Robert the Wise for his queen, Sancia, the huge church – the biggest in Naples – became the favourite place of worship of the Neapolitan nobility. Unfortunately, extensive bomb damage during World War II destroyed many of its most important works of art and 18th-century decorations, but worth seeking out in its vast, now relatively empty, interior is the Tomb of Robert the Wise (1343) behind the main altar, by the brothers Giovanni and Pacio Bertini of Florence. Through a courtyard to the left of the church is the entrance to its immense and peaceful cloister (built in the 15th century but much altered in the 18th), where majolica-tiled pathways meander through a wild and beautiful garden of roses and fruit trees.

The steep **Via Santa Maria di Costantinopoli** leads up to the **Conservatorio di Musica** ⓰, founded in 1537, the oldest musical conservatory in Europe. It has an important library and museum (closed for restoration), but it is also enjoyable to wander through its courtyard listening to the music of violins, organs, harps and pianos spilling down from upper storeys. Just down the block, the church of **San Pietro a Maiella** ⓱, built between 1313 and 1316, has one of the most famous ceilings in Italy. The Calabrian Mattia Preti began painting it in 1656, at the age of 43, a few months after leaving his native Taverna for the more rigorous artistic challenges of Naples. Five years later he completed his work, establishing himself as one of the most talented painters of his generation. The panels in the nave tell the story of St Celestine V, while the panels in the transept present the life of St Catherine of Alexandria, the virgin martyr who was beheaded for out-arguing pagan scholars.

ABOVE and **BELOW:** majolica tiles in Santa Chiara.

Reliable miracles

The Naples **Duomo** ⓲ is a magnificent Gothic warehouse of relics from every period of the city's history. Kept in a chapel off the right aisle are the head of St Januarius, the patron saint of the city, and two phials of his blood. The mysterious powers of the crusted blood are the subject of what Mark Twain called "one of the wretchedest of all the religious impostures in Italy – the miraculous liquefaction of the blood". The miracle has been taking place every year on the first Saturday in May, 19 September and 16 December since the saint's body was brought to Naples from Pozzuoli, the place of his martyrdom, by Bishop Severus in the time of Constantine. It is said that if the blood fails to liquefy, a disaster is in store for the city.

Other notable churches, all in the historical centre of the city, include **San Lorenzo Maggiore** ⓳, where archaeological excavations have revealed the old Decumano (main street) running through its cloister, the Gothic **San Domenico Maggiore** ⓴, the 14th-century

San Giovanni a Carbonara ㉑, Girolamini ㉒ and Santa Patrizia ㉓ with its monastery of San Gregorio Armeno. Via San Gregoria Armeno is famous for its workshops producing *presepe* (Christmas cribs), an important Neapolitan tradition.

The **Cappella San Severo** ㉔, a small unconsecrated church near the church of San Domenico Maggiore, should not be missed. It contains the famous *Cristo Velato* (Veiled Christ) by the sculptor Giuseppe Sammartino. The remarkable realism of this statue, carved out of a single piece of marble, combined with the setting of the chapel, conjures up an eerie atmosphere, which is sacred and superstitious at the same time. The chapel was once the workshop of Prince Raimondo, a well-known 18th-century alchemist who was excommunicated by the pope for dubious activities.

Museums in the clouds

Two of the greatest museums in Naples stand high on bluffs overlooking the city. The National Gallery of Naples, formerly in the **Museo Nazionale**, has been relocated to the **Palazzo Reale di Capodimonte** ㉕ (open daily 10am–8pm; entrance fee), the 18th-century palace of King Charles III, set in a shady park directly north of the museum. The gallery contains some of the best paintings in southern Italy. Among the high points are Masolino da Panicale's *Foundation of Santa Maria Maggiore in Rome*, in which Christ and Mary ride a cloud as if it were a magic carpet; Bellini's *Transfiguration*; various works of Titian; two startling allegorical paintings by Pieter Breughel the Elder (*The Blind Leading the Blind* and *The Misanthrope*); and, perhaps the most famous of all, Caravaggio's *Flagellation*.

ABOVE: various liqueurs and digestives on display.
BELOW: view from Castel Sant'Elmo.

A trip up the Montesanto funicular brings the visitor to the top of the Vomero hill, home of the **Museo Nazionale di San Martino** (open Tues–Sun 9am–2pm; entrance fee), located in the Carthusian monastery of the same name. Like so many buildings in Naples, the Certosa di San Martino was built in the 14th century, but had a complete baroque makeover a few hundred years later. Here are 90 rooms of paintings, furniture, ceramics and costumes illustrating the life and history of the city. Some of the top painters of the Neapolitan baroque are represented here, including Salvator Rosa, Francesco Solimena and the prolific Luca Giordano. Belvederes give access to the best views in town – the wide sweep of the Bay of Naples.

Map, pages 304–5

Good views can also be had from the **Castel Sant'Elmo** (open Tues–Sun 9am–2pm; entrance fee) next door, a 14th-century fortress long used as a prison for political troublemakers. The stately gardens of the **Villa Floridiana** (open daily 9am–1 hr before sunset; free), also on the Vomero, are favoured among young mothers as a place to teach infants to walk. The gardens house the **Museo Nazionale della Ceramica** (open daily 9am–1.30pm; entrance fee), which contains one of the most extensive collections of European and Chinese porcelain in Italy.

TIP

Be prepared to walk to see the best of Naples – the traffic can be horrendous.

A secret known to sailors in navies around the world is that the Bay of Naples is one of the most beautiful ports in Europe. To appreciate the splendour of the bay, walk through the **Villa Comunale gardens** to the far-western district of **Mergellina**, from where boats depart to the islands in the bay. The Villa Comunale itself is a mile-long public garden containing, in the centre, a small **aquarium** (open daily; entrance fee) where 200 species of fish, including eels and stingrays, cavort in murky tanks.

BELOW: Neapolitan personality.

Birthplace of the pizza

The **Piazza Sannazzaro**, at the heart of the Mergellina district, repays walkers with some of the best pizza in Naples. Pizza was born in Naples and genuine Neapolitan pizza is unbeatable. Its secret, aside from the fact that it is made with fresh mozzarella – another speciality of the Naples region – lies in the baking. It is baked in an oven shaped like a mound, over a wood fire. Generally the chef, usually an old man, works only in the evening, so it is often difficult to order pizza for lunch. But local specialities invariably available include octopus (*polpo*), mussel soup (*zuppa di cozze*), numerous varieties of fish, various spaghettis made with a fish-sauce, such as the Neapolitan catch-all *spaghetti alla pescatora* (fishwife's spaghetti); and various kinds of *mozzarella e prosciutto* (cheese and ham), swordfish, baked mozzarella, fried mozzarella and *spaghetti alla mozzarella*.

After dinner, you can take a stroll down to the marina, where half a dozen cafés with comfortable swinging chairs and views of Vesuvius siphon off the wealthy yachting crowd.

Naples is a big, brawling city that exists for nobody, ultimately, but itself. It neither actively discourages visitors nor makes any real attempt to draw them in. It just continues on its crowded, noisy, irremediable way, a gypsy caravan of all that is best and worst in Italy. ❑

THE CAMPANIA COAST

*An endless succession of jewel-like coves ripples
down the Naples coast, with Pompeii
and Herculaneum just inland*

Map,
page 314

In Greek times, Naples was a mere stripling overshadowed by its powerful parent **Cumae** (Cuma) ❶, 30 km (19 miles) to the west. Founded by Aeolians from Asia Minor around 750 BC, Cumae had become by the 6th century BC the political, religious and cultural beacon of the coast, controlling the Bay of Naples and its islands.

Here Aeneas came to consult the Sybil before his descent into the underworld. The famous **Antro della Sibilla Cumana** (Cave of the Cumaean Sybil; open daily; entrance fee), recently uncovered by archaeologists, consists of a trapezoidal *dromos* (corridor), 44 metres (144 ft) long, punctuated by six airshafts. At the far end is a rectangular chamber cut with niches where the Sybil apparently sat and uttered her prophecies. The eerie echo of footsteps in the corridor recalls Virgil's description of "a cavern perforated a hundred times, having a hundred mouths with rushing voices carrying the responses of the Sybil." From the cave's mouth it is possible to climb up to the acropolis, whose ruined, lizard-haunted temples offer fine views of the coastline and the sea.

The region between Cumae and Naples, known traditionally as the **Campi Flegrei** (Burning Fields), has been a centre of volcanic activity for the whole of recorded history. Unexpected rumblings and gaseous exhalations from below have linked the area to the mythical Greek underworld, Hades. The **Lago di Averno**, a once gloomy lake in the crater of a now extinct volcano, is the legendary "dark pool" from which Aeneas began his descent into the underworld. No bird was said to be able to fly across this lake and live, due to the poisonous gases. For many years this theory was cruelly tested at the **Grotta del Cane** on the nearby Lago d'Agnano. Dogs were subjected to the carbon dioxide that issued from the floor of the cave until knocked out or killed. "The dog dies in a minute and a half – a chicken instantly," reported Mark Twain. The experiment was repeated nine or ten times a day for the benefit of tourists.

Volcanic crater

Pozzuoli ❷, a wealthy trading centre in Greek and Roman times but later devastated by wars and malaria, is now famous for its **Solfatara**, a volcanic crater releasing jets of sulphurous gases. The Solfatara is thought to have inspired Milton's description of Hell in *Paradise Lost*. Pozzuoli also boasts a magnificent amphitheatre. On the waterfront, enclosed in a small park, lies a rectangular structure formerly known as the **Serapeo** (Temple of Serapis), but now thought to have been a *macellum* (market place). Shellfish encrustation around the bases of its four Corinthian columns has led to speculation that the ground once sank 5 metres (16 ft) below sea level before rising again to its present height.

LEFT: the Amalfi coast.
BELOW: the Arco Felice, an ancient brick archway near Cumae.

Baia ❸ apparently derives its name from Baios, Odysseus's navigator. Here Roman society came to swim. The modern town, with its view across the Gulf of Pozzuoli, contains extensive ruins of Roman palaces enclosed in a picturesque **Parco Archeologico** (open daily; entrance fee) on the hillside. At the lowest level of the park is a rectangular *piscina* from which an arched pathway, hidden in foliage, leads to a domed building believed to have been a bath. Archaeologists have pinpointed this perfect circular structure as the model for the Pantheon in Rome. The hall, partially filled with brackish water, is a natural echo chamber: the slightest scuff of a shoe is broadcast throughout the dome.

Pompeii and Herculaneum

The two Roman cities of **Pompeii ❹** (open daily; special night openings in summer; tel: 081-8545111; entrance fee), and Herculaneum, buried by the eruption of **Mount Vesuvius** in AD 79, have solved what the archaeologist Amedeo Maiuri has called "the essential problem in the history of civilisation: the origin and development of the house". Pompeii, originally settled by indigenous Oscans some time before the 8th century BC and later ruled by Etruscans, Greeks and the warlike Samnites, was a commercial centre at the time of its sudden immersion in pumice stone and ash. It was a city of shops, markets and comfortable townhouses, with paved streets, wide pavements, a stadium, two theatres, temples, baths and brothels. Its rediscovery during land reclamation operations in the 16th century, and subsequent years of excavation (sometimes piratical but increasingly respectful) have revealed an intimate picture of life in a 1st-century Roman city.

The Pompeiian house is thought to have evolved from the relatively simple design of the Etruscan farmhouse. The structure was built around a central court-

PERICOLO
DANGER

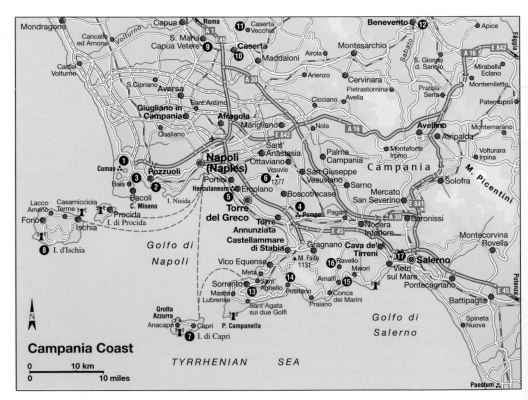

Campania Coast

0   10 km
0   10 miles

N

TYRRHENIAN   SEA

yard (*atrium*) whose roof sloped inwards on all four sides to a rectangular opening in the centre known as the *compluvium*. Through the *compluvium*, rainwater fell into a corresponding rectangular tank called the *impluvium*. Around the *atrium* itself were the various family quarters, including the bedrooms (*cubicula*), the dining rooms (*triclinia*), and directly opposite the narrow entranceway (*vestibule*), the living room (*tablinum*), the most important room in the house.

As the plan developed, a further peristyle courtyard was added, often containing a fountain. Shops were built into the front of the house; sections of the house were blocked off and rented out, with separate entranceways, to strangers (for example, the **Villa di Julia Felix**); another storey was added up top, until the Etruscan prototype had metamorphosed into the comfortable and palatial townhouses typified by the **Casa dei Vettii** and the **Casa del Fauno**.

Wedding whips

A striking feature of the Pompeiian house was the colourful and often highly refined artwork covering its walls. Many of the most beautiful frescoes have been taken to the Museo Nazionale in Naples, but at the **Villa dei Misteri**, just outside the Porto Ercolano, a series of 10 scenes, apparently depicting the initiation of brides into the Dionysiac mysteries, has been left *in situ*.

The meaning of these paintings, which depict, among other things, the whipping of a young bride, is still far from clear, although it is generally agreed that the mantled woman in the final scene is probably a portrait of the mistress of the house, who may have been a Dionysiac priestess.

The most remarkable thing about Pompeii is the mass of detail. Carved into the polygonal paving stones of the streets, for instance, are small phalluses pointing to the centre of the city. These are thought by some to have warded off evil spirits, by others to have pointed to the brothel district. And walls and monuments throughout the city are covered with inscriptions of every kind, from lists of upcoming plays to the scribbled accounts of shopkeepers, from election notices to *billets-doux*. "It is a wonder, O Wall," wrote one cynic on the wall of the basilica, "that thou hast not yet crumbled under the weight of so much written nonsense."

Unlike Pompeii, **Herculaneum ❺** (open daily; tel: 081-7390963; entrance fee), was a bedroom community built for the enjoyment of sea breezes and views across the Bay of Naples. Instead of the compact townhouses of Pompeiian businessmen, there are sprawling villas of wealthy patricians. There is a free, more spontaneous form of architecture, and the houses, freed of the mud in which they were encased for so long, are generally in a better state of preservation than those at Pompeii.

One of the pleasures of Herculaneum (aside from the fact that it is less crowded with tour groups than Pompeii) is the carbonised pieces of wooden furniture, door mouldings and screens still inside the houses. Fine frescoes, such as the *Rape of Europa* in the **Casa Sannitica**, adorn the walls, and carpet-like mosaics cover the floors. Particularly striking are the black-and-white mosaics on the floor of the **Casa dell'Atrio a Mosaico**. The city derives its name from Hercules, and was originally called *Herakleia* by its Greek founders.

ABOVE: faun in the Casa del Fauno.
BELOW: fresco at Villa dei Misteri.

Herculaneum is the best starting point for an afternoon ascent of **Mount Vesuvius ❻**, which looms directly over the modern city of **Ercolano**. No longer is it necessary, as in Dickens's time, to be carried up the mountain on a litter borne by 15 attendants. Buses leave regularly from the Ercolano train station and drop passengers at the roadhead, from which there is a 20-minute climb up a well-beaten track.

Since the volcano's first eruption about 10,000 years ago, periods of violent activity have alternated with periods of calm. Just before the infamous eruption of AD 79, trees and olive groves covered Vesuvius up to its very peak. In this century, a constant plume of smoke billowed from a cone inside the crater until 1944, when, during the volcano's last eruption to date, the cone was destroyed. Now only a few scattered *fumarole* (whisps of smoke) around the brim of the crater indicate that the volcano is still active and could erupt again.

Islands of pleasure

Of the three islands just outside the Gulf of Naples, **Capri ❼**, on the Sorrento side, has traditionally been the most popular. Its mild climate, luxuriant vegetation and seemingly inaccessible coast have drawn visitors for centuries. Emperor Tiberius retired here in AD 27, either to pursue his lifelong love of privacy or to indulge in the secret orgies which the historians Tacitus and Suetonius claim characterised the closing years of his reign. While on Capri, writes Suetonius, the

ABOVE: transport on Ischia.
BELOW: Ischia's Maronti Beach.

emperor "devised little nooks of lechery in the woods and glades … and had boys and girls dressed up as pans and nymphs posted in front of caverns or grottoes; so that the island was now openly and generally called 'Caprineum' because of his goatish antics". The writer Norman Douglas, who also lived on

Capri, attributed such legends to the idle exaggerations of resentful peasants.

The modern traveller, arriving by ferry or hydrofoil from Naples or Sorrento, can reach the remains of **Tiberius's Villa** (open daily; entrance fee) by bus from the town of Capri. The most famous sight on the island, however, is the **Grotta Azzurra** (Blue Grotto), a cave on the water's edge. Its strange light has made it the most visited attraction in Campania after Pompeii.

From **Anacapri**, on the far side of the island, you can take a chair-lift up **Monte Solaro**. Its 360° view encompasses the southern Apeninnes, Naples, Vesuvius, Sorrento and Ischia. In Anacapri itself, the church of **San Michele** is worth a visit for its majolica-tiled pavement depicting the *Story of Eden* by Francesco Solimena.

On Capri, as on the islands of Ischia and Procida, the pleasures of the body take precedence. **Ischia ❽**, the largest island off Naples, is famous for its hot mineral springs. The island is of volcanic origin. Some say the Giant Typhoeus, struck by Zeus's thunderbolt, was buried under Ischia, and is the cause of the occasional groanings and shakings that have marked its long history. Visitors generally stay in a comfortable hotel in the town of **Ischia**. One of the most pleasant, with a luxurious spa, is the modern Jolly Hotel.

The town of **Lacco Ameno**, on the coastal road, is known for its mud baths, which contain the most radioactive waters in Italy. **Sant'Angelo** has some of the best beaches on the island. At **Ischia Ponte**, a causeway crosses to the **Castello Aragonese**, built by Alfonso I of Naples in 1450. The crypt of the ruined cathedral is adorned with frescoes in the style of Giotto. The nearby convent has an interesting cemetery where the dead sisters were placed upright in chairs. **Procida**, the smallest of the islands, has good beaches and a thriving fishing industry. It is quiet and serene and generally free of tourists.

Old Campania

Inland from Naples, at **Santa Maria Capua Vetere** ❾, are the remains of the second largest amphitheatre in Italy. Few tourists are aware of this magnificent crumbling structure, where visitors can actually climb down into the subterranean passages where wild beasts roamed.

The basilica of **Sant'Angelo in Formis**, 6 km (4 miles) north of Capua, is a musty structure containing bright Byzantine frescoes illustrating the *Life of Christ*. **Caserta** ❿, often called the Versailles of Naples for its lavish **Reggia** (Royal Palace) (open Tues–Sun 9am–2pm; gardens till 6pm; entrance fee), is of no great interest, but **Caserta Vecchia** ⓫, on a mountaintop 10 km (6 miles) northeast, is one of the most beautiful towns in Campania. Founded in the 8th century, it still looks much as it did then. Its Romanesque cathedral has a wonderful facade with a cow over the central portal. Inside are a pair of holy water stoups supported by lions and a monolithic, 4th-century baptismal font in which baptism by total immersion was practised. There are some excellent restaurants scattered around the town where you can eat wild boar, the local speciality.

One of the most important cities in Campanian history is **Benevento** ⓬, where the noble king Manfred voluntarily died in battle after the defection of his allies

Map, page 314

Caserta's Palazzo Reale, an enormous building in questionable taste, was designed in 1752 by Luigi Vanvitelli for the Bourbon King Charles III. The state apartments and huge formal gardens can be visited.

BELOW: view of Sant'Angelo on Ischia, and a neighbouring island.

The freshness and quality of local produce in Campania is superb.

in 1266. The city was named Beneventum upon becoming a Roman colony in 268 BC. In the centre of town, on the route of the ancient **Via Appia** from Rome to Brindisi, stands the **Arch of Trajan**. Of the splendid reliefs depicting scenes from Trajan's life, those on the side facing Rome celebrate the emperor's domestic policies while those on the side facing Brindisi record his foreign policies. The **Museo del Sannio** (open Tues–Sun 9am–1pm; entrance fee) is worth visiting not only for its collection of local antiquities but also for the hunting scenes on the column capitals that surround its 12th-century cloister.

Paradise regained

The visitor to **Sorrento** ⓭, whether arriving from the noisy streets of Naples or from the scorched ruins of Pompeii, will find a cool and peaceful town of lemon groves, with a small beach and plentiful cafés. There's not much more to Sorrento, save for a 15th-century **Loggia** with fine column capitals on the Via San Cesareo, and the fact that the poet Tasso was born here in 1544, but that is exactly why the town is such a popular resort among Italians and foreigners alike. It's a good place in which to relax, and an excellent starting point for excursions to Capri and the **Amalfi Coast**.

This dramatic coast stretches from **Positano** to **Salerno** and boasts some of the most spectacular scenery in Italy. The **Amalfi Drive** faithfully follows its length, keeping a respectful distance above the waves but doggedly following each frightening twist of the shoreline. Bright houses cling to the slopes and gardens descend in steps to the sea. Its climate, views and picturesque gorges draw artists and honeymooners.

BELOW: Ravello.

Positano ⓮ consists of a semi-circle of houses set back in a cove, with numerous hotels, good swimming and wonderful views. The road then passes through several tunnels before reaching the **Grotta di Smeraldo**, famous for its greenish light. Through yet more tunnels (watch out for cyclists) lies **Amalfi** ⓯, a major trading centre in Byzantine times and now a major tourist centre. From the main piazza, with its fountain, a flight of steps ascends to the 11th-century bronze door of Amalfi's **Duomo**. In the crypt lies the body of St Andrew the Apostle, delivered from Constantinople in 1208. On either side of the main altar are ambones (pulpits) with fine mosaics.

The loveliest town on the Amalfi coast is **Ravello** ⓰, famous for its architecture, its gardens and admirers. Ravello's **Duomo** is celebrated for its bronze doors by the Apulian Barisano da Trani. Cast in Trani in 1179, the doors were transported to Ravello by ship. Inside, the floor slopes upwards towards God and a fine marble pulpit supported by pillars resting on the backs of six hungry lions. The pulpit was presented to the church in 1272 by Nicola Rufolo and his wife, Sigilgaida, who built the splendid **Villa Rufolo** across the street. The villa's lush gardens and Moorish cloister overlook the sea several miles away. The best view, however, is from the more extensive gardens at the **Villa Cimbrone**, built at the end of the 19th century by a wealthy Englishman, Ernest William Beckett. Beckett's ashes are buried beneath the **Temple of Bacchus**, which he built on the edge of the cliff.

Salerno and Paestum

It was just south of **Salerno ⑰** that the Allies began their assault on Italy on 9 September 1943. The city, strung out along the shore, has a good beach and one of the loveliest cathedrals in southern Italy, which is reached through an atrium incorporating 28 columns from Paestum. Inside, as the removal of 18th-century plaster continues, more medieval frescoes are coming to light. Particularly beautiful is a fresco of the Virgin (behind the fourth pier in the right aisle). As at Ravello, this cathedral contains a pair of exquisite ambones, dating from the 12th century. The great Hildebrand is buried in a tomb in the right apse. The crypt contains the body of St Matthew.

The English writer George Eliot regarded the **Temple of Neptune** at **Paestum** (open daily; entrance fee) as "the finest thing, I verily believe, we have seen in Italy". Her words echo the sentiments of many 19th-century travellers for whom this Greek city, founded in the 6th century BC, was the final stop on the Grand Tour. There are few sights so arresting as Paestum's three well-preserved Doric temples standing empty on the grassy plain that surrounds them. The Temple of Neptune, the most majestic of these, was built in the 5th century BC of a reddish travertine whose warmth, as Eliot wrote, "seems to glow and deepen under one's eyes".

The so-called **basilica,** of a greyer tinge, beside the Temple of Neptune, dates from the 6th century BC. The third temple, the **Temple of Ceres**, is separated from the other two by the **Roman forum** and **baths**, and a **Greek theatre**. Across the street, in the **museum** (open daily; closed 1st and 3rd Mon of month; entrance fee) are famous mural paintings from the **Tomb of the Diver** (480 BC), rare and beautiful examples of Greek painting. ❑

Map, page 314

BELOW: Temple of Neptune at Paestum.

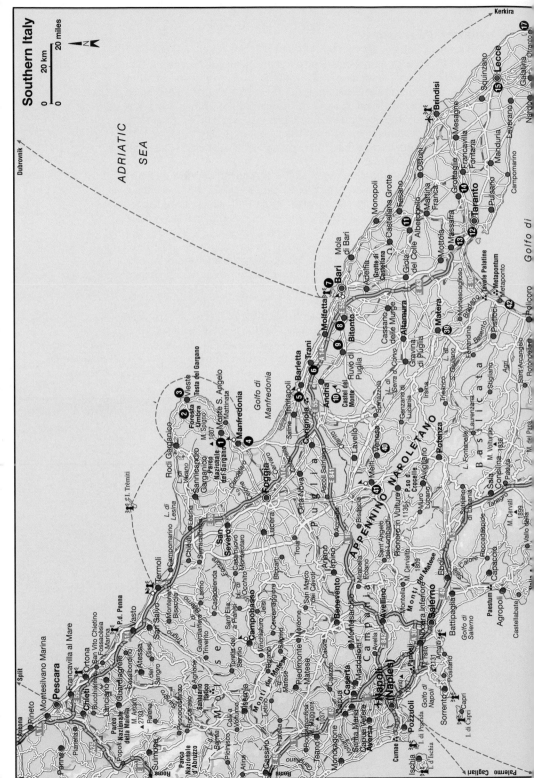

Southern Italy

ADRIATIC
SEA

Golfo di
Taranto

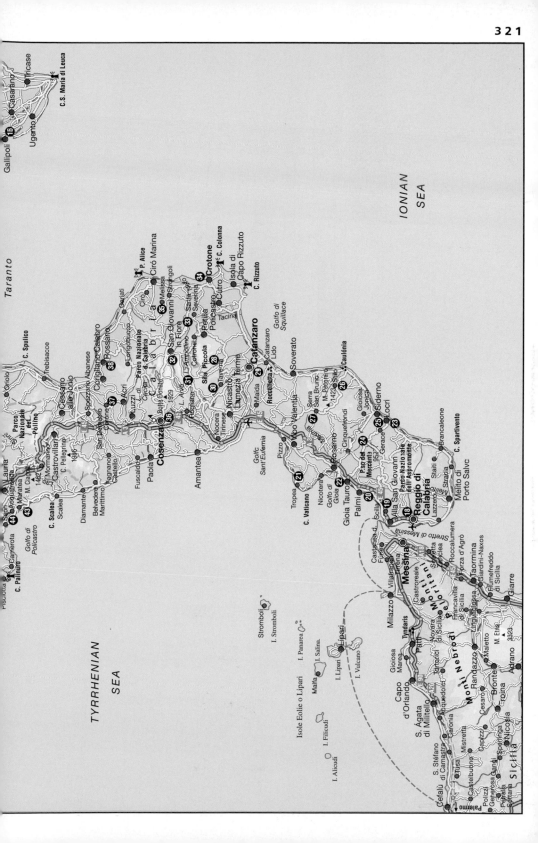

Taranto

IONIAN
SEA

TYRRHENIAN
SEA

Gallipoli
Ugento
C.S. Maria di Leuca
Casarano
Tricase

C. Spulico
Oriolo
Trebisacce
Cerchiara
alle'Jodio
Spezzano Albanese
Corigliano Calabro
Rossano
Longobucco
Cariati
Ciro
Ciró Marina
P. Alice
Crotone
C. Colonna
Isola di
Capo Rizzuto
C. Rizzuto
Cutro
Strongoli
Melissa
Santa
Severina
San Giovanni
in Fiore
Petilia
Policastro
Tacina
Cotrone
Cropani
Catanzaro
Catanzaro
Lido
Golfo di
Squillace
Soverato
Caulónia
Stilo
M. Federico
1142
San Bruno
Serra
San Bruno
Gioiosa
Jonica
Siderno
Locri
Geraci
Brancaleone
Staiti
C. Spartivento
Melito di
Porto Salvo
Motta
Lazzaro
Reggio di
Calabria
Villa San Giovanni
Parco Nazionale
dell'Aspromonte
P. di
Montalto
1955
Scilla
Palmi
Bagnara
Calabra
Gioia Tauro
Rosarno
Cinquefrondi
C. Vaticano
Tropea
Nicotera
Golfo di
Gioia
Vibo Valentia
Pizzo
Golfo
Sant'Eufemia
Amantea
Maida
Lamezia Terme
Roccelletta
Nicastro
Nocera
Tirinese
Rogliano
Sila Piccola
L. Arvo
1929
Botte Donato
Cosenza
San Demetro
Corone
Luzzi
Acri
Cosenza
Parco Nazionale
della Calabria
Parco
Nazionale
del
Pollino
Lauria
Maratea
Acquafredda
M. Ciagola
1462
Mormanno
C. Pellegrino
Castrovillari
Castello
Fagnano
Belvedere
Marittimo
Diamante
Scalea
C. Scalea
Paola
Fuscaldo
C. Palinuro
Capo
Sapri
Golfo di
Policastro
Camerota
Pisciotta
Isole Eolie o Lipari
I. Filicudi
I. Alicudi
Stromboli
I. Stromboli
I. Panarea
I. Salina
Malfa
I. Lipari
Lipari
I. Vulcano
Milazzo
Tindaris
Patti
Gioiosa
Marea
Capo
d'Orlando
S. Ágata
di Mililtello
S. Stéfano
di Camastra
Caronia
Mistretta
Tusa
Cefalù
Castelbuono
Pollina
Gangi
Generosa
Polizzi
Sclafani
Nicosia
Sperlinga
Gagliano
Palermo
Monti Nebrodi
Montalbano
di Sicilia
Novara
di Sicilia
Santa
Lucia del
Mela
Castroreale
Francavilla
di Sicilia
Roccella
Giardini-Naxos
Taormina
Fiumefreddo
di Sicilia
Giarre
Roccalumera
Furnari
Castanea d.
Furie
Villafranca
Tirrena
Messina
Stretto di Messina
M. Etna
3323
M. Soro
Cesarò
Troina
Maletto
Bronte
Randazzo
Linguaglossa
Adrano
Sicilia
Monti Peloritani

C. Spartivento

APULIA

Forming the heel and spur of Italy's boot,
Apulia is a region of glorious churches, castles
and sun-bleached beaches

Map, pages 320–1

ome people visit Apulia (known in Italian as Puglia) for its architecture, some for its landscape, some for its archaeology and some for its food, but all go away haunted by memories of a single man: Frederick II of Hohenstaufen, Holy Roman Emperor, King of Germany and King of Sicily. Known to Dante as "the father of Italian poetry" and to his 13th-century contemporaries as *stupor mundi et immutator mirabilis* – wonder of the world and extraordinary innovator – Frederick built most of the castles that are still the dominant architectural feature of the region.

He also founded many of Apulia's most splendid churches, carrying on the tradition of the Apulian Romanesque begun by his Norman predecessors a century before. An enlightened ruler who waged a bitter and ultimately unsuccessful feud with the popes in Rome, he was also an avid sportsman whose brilliant treatise on falconry still ranks among the most accurate descriptions of the subject. His just laws and tolerance of the Islamic beliefs of the Saracens are legendary. Frederick's death in 1250 and the tragic defeat of his illegitimate son, Manfred, at the Battle of Benevento in 1266 ushered in a period of economic and spiritual decline that is only now being reversed.

Apulian Romanesque

If Frederick II is the dominant figure in Apulia's long and varied history, the Apulian Romanesque is its most important architectural legacy. The style, fusing Byzantine, Saracenic and Italian decorative techniques with the French architectural forms introduced by the Normans, first appeared in the church of San Nicola at Bari in 1087. The plans of most other Apulian churches of the period derived from this elegant cathedral with its short transepts, three semicircular apses corresponding to three naves and three portals, a tall, plain facade, and richly decorated doorways carved with animals, flowers and biblical scenes.

The food of Apulia is fresh and simple, making good use of the abundant tomatoes, wine and olive oil. The most famous pasta here is *orecchiette*, an ear-shaped variety sometimes made with whole-wheat flour.

The visiting Archangel

The landscape of northern Apulia is dominated by vast inland plains planted with wheat. The only real mountains are clustered on the Gargano Promontory, a thickly forested peninsula that juts out into the Adriatic to form the "spur" of the boot of Italy. Here, in the medieval town of **Monte Sant'Angelo ❶**, is the **Santuario di San Michele** (open daily; closed 1–3pm in winter), a cave where the Archangel Michael is said to have revealed himself to local bishops in AD 490, 492 and

LEFT: Ostuni, a white hilltown. **BELOW:** rich-flavoured southern tomatoes.

TIP

From Vieste you can
catch a ferry to the
Tremiti Islands, 40 km
(25 miles) offshore,
which are sparsely
populated but offer
good beaches and
clear water to visitors.

493. The cave is entered through a pair of bronze doors made in Constantinople in 1076 and decorated with the numerous deeds of the Archangel; brass rings
in the doors were supposed to be knocked loudly to wake the Archangel within.
This pleasant town also has a fine municipal museum devoted to the popular
arts of the Gargano. Particularly interesting are the presses once used to make
wine and olive oil, and a stone flour mill originally turned by mules.

Monte Sant'Angelo is a good place to buy components for a lunch in the
Foresta Umbra ❷, a parkland in the centre of the peninsula where 100-year-old
beech trees, oaks and chestnuts shade winding trails and pleasant picnic spots.
From here, you can drive along the coastline to **Vieste ❸**, a bright town on the
tip of the promontory containing a castle built by Frederick II. The road continues west along a serpentine coastline studded with beaches and grottoes, passing en route an odd, phallic rock formation known as *Pizzomunno*. Signs indicate
turnings for the grottoes.

Manfredonia ❹, back on the mainland, is a port and beach resort with a
pretty historic centre including a Castello, begun by Manfred (son of Frederick
II) in 1256 and later enlarged by Manfred's enemy, Charles I of Anjou. Near
Manfredonia are the beautiful medieval churches of **Santa Maria di Siponto**,
with a 5th-century crypt and an altar made from an early Christian sarcophagus, and **San Leonardo**, with a facade guarded by two stone lions. Siponto also
has good, if crowded, sandy beaches.

Coastal route

The coastal route to Bari is lined with seaport towns, all carrying on a brisk trade
in vegetables, fruit and wine. The oldest, most important and, today, least attrac-

BELOW: Trani's
Duomo. **BELOW
RIGHT:** Bari.

tive of these is **Barletta** , where Manfred established his court in 1259. Here, at the intersection of the Corsos Garibaldi and Vittorio Emanuele, stands the intriguing **Colosso**, a 4th-century Byzantine statue thought to represent the Emperor Valentinian I (364–75). Only the head and torso are original; the rest was recast in the 15th century. Behind rises the **Basilica di San Sepolcro**, with a nice Gothic portal and an octagonal cupola reminiscent of Byzantine designs. Barletta's **Duomo** is a confusing edifice built on a Romanesque plan, with five radiating apses in French Gothic style and a Renaissance main portal. By the sea rises Manfred's 13th-century castle, much expanded in later centuries.

A far more picturesque town, 13 km (8 miles) south of Barletta, is **Trani** ⑥, the centre of the local wine trade and fairly prosperous. Its Romanesque cathedral, founded in 1097 but not completed until the middle of the 13th century, is perhaps the most beautiful church in Apulia. Beneath its richly carved rose window is a smaller window flanked by pillars resting on the backs of elephants. The wonderful bronze doors are the work of the local artist Barisano da Trani, who is also responsible for the celebrated doors on the cathedral at Ravello. The interior of the church, bright and austere, has the usual three apses and three naves, with triforium arcades above the side-aisles supported, here, by six pairs of columns on either side. Steps descend to the underground church of **Santa Maria della Scala** and the crypt. Even further down is the underground **Ipogeo di San Leucio**, 1.5 metres (5 ft) below sea level, containing two primitive but delightful frescoes.

Windy Bari

Ancient **Bari** ⑦, founded by the Greeks and developed by the Romans as an important trading centre, was destroyed by William the Bad in 1156 and restored by William the Good in 1169. Today it is the largest and most important commercial centre in Apulia. The city is divided into two distinct parts, the Città Vecchia, with its tight tangle of medieval streets and dazzling white houses, and the Città Nuova, the modern city, with wide boulevards laid out at perfect right angles to each other. The tortuous alleyways of the old city protected the inhabitants from the wind and from invaders.

The church of **San Nicola** was founded in 1087 to contain the relics of St Nicholas, patron saint of Russia, stolen from Myra in Asia Minor by 47 sailors from Bari. Its facade bears many resemblances to the facade of the cathedral at Trani, though it is even plainer. A small round window (oculus) crowns three bifora windows, a monofora window, and a richly carved portal flanked by columns borne by a pair of time-worn bulls.

The interior of the church is best visited in the evening, when sun shoots through the windows of the facade, creating unusual light effects on the three great transverse arches (structural additions of 1451). Among the many noteworthy objects in this church are the beautiful column capitals of the choir screen separating the nave from the apse, and the *ciborium* (freestanding canopy) over the high altar, dating from the early 12th century. Behind the *ciborium* is the church's best-known work of art, an 11th-century episcopal throne

Map, pages 320–1

TIP

When in Bari, be sure to try the local ear-shaped pasta – *orecchiette* – often served with cauliflower.

BELOW: in the old city of Bari.

ABOVE: window of the Castel del Monte.

BELOW: the Duomo (cathedral) in Bitonto.

supported by three grotesque telamones. To the left is a Renaissance altarpiece, *Madonna and Four Saints*, by the Venetian Bartolomeo Vivarini. The crypt contains the precious relics of St Nicholas, said to exude a wonder-working oil and visited by pilgrims for centuries. The Byzantine icon of St Nicholas in the central apse of the crypt was presented to the church by the king of Serbia in 1319.

Bari's **Duomo**, a short walk west of San Nicola, was erected between 1170 and 1178 over the remains of a Byzantine church destroyed by William the Bad during his rampage through the city in 1156. Basilican in plan, the church follows San Nicola in most details of its design, with deep arcades along both flanks and a false wall at the rear that masks the protrusions of the three semi-circular apses. A particularly fine window adorns the rear facade. Nearby, off the Piazza Federico II di Svevia, is the **Castello** (open Tues–Sat 9am–1pm, 3.30–7pm, Sun 9am–1pm; entrance fee), built in Norman times, refurbished by Frederick II, and considerably enlarged by Isabella of Aragon in the 16th century.

Bari's **Pinacoteca Provinciale** (open Mon–Sat 9.30am–1pm, 4–7pm, Sun 9.30am–1pm; entrance fee), containing paintings from the 11th century to the present, is in the Città Nuova, along the Lungomare Nazario Sauro. The best painting is undoubtedly Bartolomeo Vivarini's *Annunciation* in Room II. Further rooms contain Giambellino's startling *San Pietro Martire* and a number of works by Neapolitan baroque painters including Antonio Vaccaro and the prolific Luca Giordano. Francesco Netti, the Italian impressionist, a native son of Bari, is also represented and there is a new collection of contemporary art. Bari's small but worthwhile **Museo Archaeologico** (closed for restoration), in the Piazza Umberto I, has a rich collection of Attic black- and red-figure vases.

Around Bari

An interesting one-day excursion into Apulia's architectural past begins 18 km (11 miles) west of Bari in the olive oil centre of **Bitonto ❽**, whose famous cathedral, built between 1175 and 1200, represents perhaps the most complete expression of the Apulian Romanesque. The beautiful facade has a rose window and an elegantly carved portal, flanked by the usual lions. The pelican above the doorway is a symbol of Christ – in medieval times, the pelican was thought to peck at its own flesh to feed its young. Bitonto has an attractive historic quarter, and is worth an excursion from Bari.

The town of **Ruvo di Puglia ❾**, 18 km (11 miles) farther west, was known as Rubi in Roman times, when it was famous for its ceramics. The 13th-century **Duomo** was widened in the 17th century to provide room for baroque side-chapels and, though restorations have shrunk the interior's width back to its original Romanesque proportions, the wide facade retains its baroque girth, giving the church a somewhat squat appearance. Fortunately, the medieval sculpture on the facade largely remains; the seated figure at the top is thought to represent the ubiquitous Frederick II. Beneath the nearby **Chiesa del Purgatorio** lie some Roman remains. Ruvo's excellent **Museo Jatta** (open Mon–Sat 8.30am–1.30pm, Fri–Sat also 2.30–7.30pm; free) is devoted to Rubian ceramics excavated from nearby necropoli and dating from the 5th to the 3rd century BC.

On a hilltop 30 km (19 miles) west of Ruvo stands the **Castel del Monte** (open daily in summer 9am–7pm; 9am–1pm in winter; entrance fee) ❿, often cited, as is the Colosseum in Rome, as a supreme example of the architectural aims of an age. The eight-sided building has two storeys and eight Gothic towers; curiously enough, the main entrance is adorned with a Roman triumphal arch. Historians differ as to whether Frederick II erected the small fortress as a hunting lodge or as a military outpost, but all agree that he married his daughter, Violanta, to Riccardo, Count of Caserta, here in 1249. In 1266 the implacable Charles I of Anjou imprisoned the hapless sons of Manfred after their father's tragic defeat – and voluntary death – at Benevento. The castle served as a refuge for the noble families of Andria, a nearby town, during the plague of 1665, and was later abandoned, becoming a hideout for brigands and political exiles. Restoration began in 1876. The eerie emptiness of the building is reinforced by its isolation in the middle of wheat-covered plains.

An entirely different kind of architectural unit – the odd, conical, whitewashed peasant dwellings known as *trulli* – can be seen in the town of **Alberobello** ⓫, 50 km (32 miles) southeast of Bari. Nobody knows the exact origins of these houses (the oldest date back to the 12th century), but they did allow for easy home-extension by the addition of another unit, and modern building in the area is often based on the *trulli* shape. Now many of them have been turned into gift shops. South of Alberobello, the pleasant hill-top village of **Locorotondo** is another place to find *trulli*.

The **Grotte di Castellana** (open for guided tours daily; entrance fee), another of the region's great tourist attractions, are also surrounded by gift shops, but the caves themselves (20 km/12 miles back towards Bari from Alberobello) are

Map, pages 320–1

BELOW: *trulli* farm buildings.

*Flamboyant
decoration on the
facade of Sant'Irene,
which also has one
of Lecce's most
spectacular baroque
altars.*

BELOW: Piazza Sant'
Oronzo in Lecce.

really quite interesting, containing pools, grottoes and ceilings that literally drip with stalactites.

Spartan Taranto

Taranto ⑫, the ancient Taras founded by Spartan navigators in 706 BC, was in the 4th century BC the largest city in Magna Graecia, boasting a population of 300,000 and a city wall 15 km (9 miles) in circumference. It was, like many towns on this coast, a centre of Pythagorean philosophy and visited by such luminaries as Plato and Aristoxenes (author of the first treatise on music). Today the city, much damaged in World War II, is the home of one of Europe's most important iron works. The old town is effectively an island separated from the modern and industrial quarters by canals.

Taranto's **Museo Nazionale** (open Tues–Sat 8.30am–1.30pm, 2.30–7.30pm, Sun–Mon 8.30am–1.30pm; entrance fee), in the modern quarter, is the second most important museum in southern Italy, rivalled only by the Museo Archaeologico in Naples for the splendour of its antiquities. The collection includes Greek and Roman sculpture and a series of wonderful Roman floor mosaics, including a fragment depicting a lion and a boar fighting. Rooms on the first floor house one of the most complete collections of ancient ceramics in Italy. Of particular interest are the many proto-Corinthian ointment boxes decorated with geometric and human figures; the Corinthian vases; a rare Laconian cup dating from the 6th century BC, with a design of radiating fishes; and numerous Attic black- and red-figure vases.

In Taranto's old city is the church of **San Domenico Maggiore**, founded by Frederick II in 1223, rebuilt in 1302 by Giovanni Taurisano, and much altered in

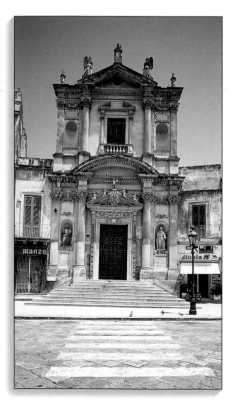

baroque times. Nearby, on the Via Cariati, is a lively fish market. Taranto's **Duomo** contains fine mosaic floors and antique columns from pagan temples.

For those with the time, a fascinating side trip (21 km/13 miles) can be made from Taranto to the nearby town of **Massafra** ⑬, known for its early Christian cave churches hewn into the sides of a deep ravine that snakes through the centre of the town. The Santuario della Madonna della Scala contains a 12th-century *Madonna and Child* fresco. It can be reached via a baroque staircase from the town centre. At the bottom of the ravine is the Farmacia del Mago Gregorio – a maze of caves and tunnels once used by monks as a herb store. Ask in the town about access to these and other cave churches, but avoid coming in the middle of the day when there will be very few people around.

From Massafra by back roads (37 km/23 miles), or from Taranto by *superstrada* (22 km/14 miles), you can reach **Grottaglie** ⑭, a hill-top town where you can watch Apulian potters make the ceramic pitchers, plates, bowl and cups available in gift shops across the region. The decorative spaghetti plates produced in the town are known throughout Italy.

Baroque Lecce

Lecce ⑮ is known for its profusion of baroque houses and churches. The city owes its appearance to the malleable characteristics of the local sandstone, which is easy to carve when it comes out of the ground but hardens with time. The growth of religious orders, particularly the Franciscans, Jesuits and Theatines, in the 17th and 18th centuries led to intensive building which created an architectural uniformity unique in southern Italy. Churches drip with ornate altars and swirling columns. Outside, shadeless streets meander past curving yellow palaces bright with bursts of bougainvillea.

At the centre of town, in the cobblestoned **Piazza Sant'Oronzo**, stands a single Roman column stolen from its twin in Brindisi. The pair originally marked the southern terminus of the Via Appia from Rome. A bronze statue of St Orontius, patron saint of the city, stands on top of the column. The southern half of the square is dominated by excavations of part of a well-preserved Roman amphitheatre, while the strange Renaissance pavilion, which has been glazed, used to be the town hall but now houses the tourist information office.

Lecce's harmonious **Piazza del Duomo**, just off the **Corso Vittorio Emanuele**, is framed by the facades of the **Duomo**, the **Palazzo Vescovile** and the **Seminario**, all built or reworked in the 17th century. The Duomo actually has two facades: the lavish one facing the Corso, with its statue of St Orontius, and the more austere (and older) one facing the Palazzo Vescovile. The altars inside the Duomo, carved with flowers, fruit and human figures, are typical of the ornate local style.

Bright basilica

The most complete expression of Leccian baroque is the **Basilica di Santa Croce**, built in 1549–1679. Its exuberant facade sports a balcony supported by eight grotesque caryatids. The bright interior has an overall restraint that unifies the different designs of its chapels. A chapel in the left transept contains a series of 12 bas-reliefs by the local artist Francesco Antonio Zimbalo showing the life of San Francesco di Paola.

Lecce's modern and informative **Museo Provinciale** (open Mon–Fri and Sun am; free), just outside the old city, is built around a spiral ramp reminiscent of the Guggenheim Museum in New York. In the archaeological section, Attic black- and red-figure vases are nicely arranged around a central core containing bronze tools and suits of armour. The picture gallery, on the third floor, contains paintings by various southern Italian artists, including the great Calabrian Mattia Preti.

The rewards of travelling in Apulia, as in its neighbours Basilicata and Calabria, include the pleasure of ending the day on a beach. Apulia has the longest coastline in Italy, a fact which has made it peculiarly attractive to foreign invaders, from the ancient worshippers of Zeus to the sun-worshipping visitors of today. Lecce is within easy reach of beaches at **Gallipoli** ⑯ on the Ionian Sea, and **Otranto** ⑰ on the Adriatic. Otranto has the added attraction of a Romanesque cathedral with an impressive mosaic floor.

In the peace and the wave-song of the pristine Apulian sands, you could lie dreaming for many months, lost in reveries on the passage of so many heroes through these parts, from wily Odysseus to the broad-minded, gallant, brooding Frederick II. ❏

BELOW: elaborate figures on the facade of the Basilica di Santa Croce.

Map, pages 320–1

CALABRIA AND BASILICATA

Rugged mountains, cave dwellings and ancient Greek cities combine here with a beautiful and unspoiled coastline

Map, pages 320–1

Calabria is closer in spirit than any other region in Italy to the Italy of Byron and Shelley – the land of mouldering ruins that inspired the romantic thoughts of 19th-century travellers. But the region is fast changing. The completion of the *autostrada* from Salerno to Reggio Calabria, governmental support of housing and industry, and vast improvements in the quality of hotels have begun to lure both northern entrepreneurs and foreign tourists to this long isolated part of Italy. No major city is now without its *Zona Industriale*, no village without its roar of motorcycle engines. But the tourist industry is still in its infancy here. Much of Calabria's heritage still lies buried among the roots of the many olive trees.

The landscape of the region is dominated by the backbone of mountains that descends, in a series of fantastic foothills to the sea. Only 9 per cent of the territory consists of flat land. It was from the sea that Calabria's first invaders, the Greeks, came in the 8th century BC, crossing the Straits of Messina from Sicily.

LEFT: doorway of San Giovanni, in Matera. **BELOW:** one of the Greek bronzes found in the sea in 1972, and now in the museum in Reggio di Calabria.

Spectacular treasure trove

Also from the sea have come the **Bronze Warriors**, Calabria's most celebrated reminder of those early settlers. Discovered by fishermen off Riace in 1972, these two colossal Greek statues, thought to have been lost overboard from a ship sailing between Calabria and Greece 2,000 years ago, are the star attractions in the **Museo Nazionale della Magna Graecia** in **Reggio di Calabria** ⓲ (open daily 9am–7pm; closed 1st and 3rd Mon of month; entrance fee).

The coastline just north of Reggio was first described by Homer in Book XII of the *Odyssey*, the earliest navigational guide to the Tyrrhenian sea. Here lurked the infamous monster Scylla, whose "six heads like nightmares of ferocity, with triple serried rows of fangs and deep gullets of black death" did away with six of Odysseus's best men. Today the Rock of Scilla provides the foundation for a youth hostel. Modern **Scilla** ⓳ has an excellent view across the Straits of Messina.

Farther north, **Palmi** ⓴ is worth visiting for its **ethnographic museum** (open Mon–Fri; entrance fee), with an extensive collection of ceramic masks designed to ward off the evil eye. The museum is housed, along with other collections, in a newly built complex just outside the town. **Tropea** ㉑, suspended from a cliff over one of the many fine beaches that line the shore, is perhaps the most picturesque town on the coast. The old town has a beautiful Norman **cathedral** containing, behind the high altar, the *Madonna di Romania*, a portrait said to have been painted by St Luke.

Highway 111 is the loneliest road in Calabria. It twists across the central mountain chain following what is

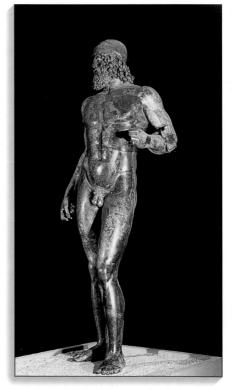

believed to be an ancient trade route connecting **Gioia Tauro ㉒** on the Tyrrhenian with **Locri ㉓** on the Ionian sea. Fierce brigands once ruled the woods through which it passes. From the **Passo del Mercante ㉔**, the road's highest and loneliest point, both seas are visible. From here the road descends to the beautiful town of **Gerace ㉕**, situated on the hump of a nearly inaccessible crag. It is best to visit Gerace in the evening, and on foot, to appreciate the romantic sunset views from the grassy ruins of its castle. It is said that in the 10th century the city's inhabitants survived an Arab siege by subsisting on ricotta cheese made from mothers' milk.

In still earlier times, a miracle-working saint, San Antonio del Castello, conjured up a spring of pure water in a cave in the cliff that surrounds the castle. The imprint of the saint's knees, they say, can be seen in the floor of the cave.

Gerace is a city of many layers, justifying the phrase, "If you know Gerace, you know Calabria". Its cathedral is the largest in Calabria. It was begun in 1045 on top of an older church – now in the crypt. Both cathedral and crypt contain columns from the Greek settlement at Locri. Some parts of this 7th-century BC town, including walls and temples, can still be seen.

The famous **Cattolica** at **Stilo ㉖**, one of the best-preserved Byzantine churches in existence, is a reminder that in medieval times Calabria's rugged interior was a vibrant religious centre. The tiny church, built on a square floor plan with five cylindrical cupolas, clings to the flank of Monte Consolino, just above Stilo, like a miniature castle overlooking its town. Its bright interior is adorned with fragments of frescoes.

Another important religious centre further inland is the Carthusian monastery at **Serra San Bruno ㉗** (monastery open to male visitors only Mon–Sat 11am–noon, 4–5pm; museum daily in summer 9am–1pm, 3–8pm; restricted hours in winter). In this peaceful sanctuary, reconstructed around the ruins of an abbey destroyed by earthquake in 1783, 16 bearded, white-robed monks live according to the vows of silence, solitude and poverty prescribed by Bruno of Cologne in the 11th century. The monks eat no meat, but make an excellent cheese, which is sold in the town.

The four columns supporting the vault of Stilo's Cattolica are from a pre-Christian temple. They are placed upside-down as symbols of the church's victory over paganism.

BELOW: the 10th-century Cattolica at Stilo.

Where shepherds wander

Of Calabria's four great mountain clusters – the Aspromonte, the Sila Piccola, the Sila Grande and the Sila Greca – the **Sila Piccola ㉘**, in the middle, has most to offer. Among its dense pine groves and cool meadows shepherd boys still wander with their flocks. The climate up here is refreshing after the dry heat of the coast. The twisty road up from **Catanzaro ㉙** climbs first to **Taverna ㉚**, a serene town whose name suggests that it was once a way-station. In 1613, the baroque painter Mattia Preti was born here. He left Calabria at the age of 43 to become one of the most influential painters in Naples. The church of **San Domenico**, just off the main square, contains the best of Preti's local work; paintings of his may also be seen in the churches of **Santa Barbara** and **San Martino**.

A few "tourist villages" have been developed in the vast pine-covered area of the inner Sila as skiing or fishing centres but they have not altered its sense of isolation. The roads are empty and winding and barred when the snow gets too deep in winter. Even the **Lago Ampollino** , a man-made lake created earlier this century to encourage tourism and produce electricity, lacks the crowds found at even the most remote Italian vacation spots. Here, nature still rules the day.

San Giovanni in Fiore ㉜, the biggest town in the Sila, is noted for the black and purple costumes of its women. More compelling is the lovely hill-top town of **Santa Severina** ㉝, famed for its medieval scholastic tradition. Attached to the cathedral is an 8th- to 9th-century Byzantine baptistry of circular design, built originally as a *martyrium* (a shrine for the sacred relics of honoured members of the local Christian community) when it stood alone. One of its four "arms", or entrances, was removed in the 16th century to accommodate the abutting cathedral sacristy. At the entrance to the town, the Byzantine church of **San Filomena** has a cylindrical dome of Armenian inspiration, and three tiny apses that seem to anticipate Romanesque designs. The long central Piazza Vittorio Emanuele leads to the 10th-century Castello which is now a school.

A city worth visiting for its memories of former inhabitants is the coastal town of **Crotone** ㉞, corresponding to the ancient Croton, founded by Greeks in 710 BC. Here the mystical mathematician Pythagoras came up with his theorem about right-angled triangles and taught the doctrine of *metempsychosis*, in which the soul is conceived as a free agent which, as John Donne later imagined, can as easily attach itself to an elephant as to a mouse before briefly inhabiting the head of a man. The English novelist George Gissing composed some of the most amusing passages of *By the Ionian Sea* in Crotone before his death here in 1901. The modern town, on its crowded promontory, has little to offer the tourist other than an excellent wine from the nearby village of **Melissa** ㉟, an interesting **archaeological museum** (open Tues–Sun; entrance fee) and indifferent hotels.

Northern Calabria and Basilicata

Steamy **Cosenza** ㊱ is a flat, modern and very large city surrounding an old town on a hill. Its beautiful Gothic cathedral, in the old town, was consecrated in the presence of Frederick II in 1222. In the **Tesoro dell'Archivescovado** behind the cathedral (apply to the marriage office) is a Byzantine reliquary cross that Frederick II donated to the church at the time of its consecration. The partially ruined **Castello** at the top of the old town has excellent views over the town. Its interior is being slowly restored.

When Norman Douglas visited the Albanian village of **San Demetrio Corone** ㊲ in 1911, he was told by the amazed inhabitants that he was the first Englishman ever to have set foot in the town. The modern visitor may feel equally unique as he confronts the curious stares of barbers, policemen, shopkeepers and women in bright Albanian dresses.

The Albanians first fled to Calabria in 1448 to escape persecution by the Arabs. Today they form the largest ethnic minority in the region. They possess their own language, literature and dress, and their own Greek Orthodox bishop. As isolated as San Demetrio is in the backhills of the Sila Greca, it was once one of the most important centres of learning in Calabria, the site of the

Map, pages 320–1

The inimitable Norman Douglas, during his lengthy sojourn in the "flesh-pots of Crotone", speculated that the cows he encountered wandering along the beach might very well be "descendants of the sacred cattle of Hera".

BELOW: mending nets in a fishing village.

The Tavole Palatine at Metaponto was built in the late 6th century BC. A nearby museum displays vases, coins and jewellery found at the site.

BELOW: Matera.

famous Albanian College where the revolutionary poet Girolamo de Rada taught for many years. The little church of Sant' Adriano stands just inside the college. Inside it contains a Norman font and a wonderful mosaic pavement.

On the Ionian coast, overlooking the sea, stands lonely **Rossano 38**, which was the most important city in the South between the 8th and 11th centuries. Today Rossano is home of the famous **Codex Purpureus**, a rare 6th-century Greek manuscript adorned with 16 colourful miniatures drawn from the Gospels and the Old Testament. This extraordinary book can be seen in the **Museo Diocesano** (open daily 9.30am–noon; entrance fee) beside the cathedral. At the top of the grey stone town stands the Byzantine church of **San Marco**, with five domes and a breathtaking view across the valley. Below the old town lies the bustling resort of Rossano Scalo.

Land of poverty and history

Basilicata is the poorest and most underdeveloped region in southern Italy, yet it is a land of considerable historical and sociological interest with a remarkably varied landscape. Its beaches on both the Tyrrhenian and Ionian coasts are among the finest in the South.

Matera 39, the second largest city after Potenza, presents perhaps the most unsettling example of the clash between the ancient and modern in southern Italy. Until quite recently, people in Matera literally lived in caves. Their rock-cut dwellings, called *sassi* by local inhabitants, date back to Byzantine times when they were built as churches. In later years, many of the churches were converted into homes where humans and livestock crowded together in unsanitary dankness, watched over by Byzantine frescoes painted on the rock.

Map, pages 320–1

Recently Matera has developed the *sassi* area as a tourist attraction and you can pick up maps and itineraries from the **tourist office** at Via de Viti de Marco, 9. The church of **Santa Lucia**, in the main part of town, contains the two most famous frescoes in Matera, the *Madonna del Latte* and *San Michele Arcangelo*, both dating from the second half of the 13th century. Nearby, the Apulian Romanesque **Duomo** has a striking rose window.

Venosa ④, in northern Basilicata, was the birthplace of Horace, the 1st-century BC Roman poet and satirist. Here lie the remains of **La Trinità**, a Benedictine abbey begun in the 11th century and never completed. The structure, built of stones from an earlier Roman temple on the site, is a topless treasure trove of inscriptions, portals, sarcophagi and frescoes romantically situated in a grassy park, surrounded by olive trees and close to some Roman remains. **Melfi** ④, just to the west, has a fine Norman castle containing the **Museo Nazionale del Melfese** (open daily; entrance fee) with interesting archaeological finds. It was here that Frederick II promulgated his *Constitutiones Augustales*, the just code of laws for which his regime is still remembered by local inhabitants.

Of the many beautiful coastal towns in Basilicata, **Metaponto** ④, on the Ionian sea, is best known, mainly on account of its **Tavole Palatine**, a Doric temple dating from the 6th century BC, with 15 standing columns. The Greek city of Metapontum was founded in the 7th century BC and is today undergoing archaeological excavation. **Maratea** ④, over on the Tyrrhenian coast, rivals Ravello in Campania for its pleasant streets and its breathtaking views over the sea. Above the abandoned medieval town (Maratea Superiore) rises *The Redeemer*, a monumental statue sculpted in 1963 by Bruno Innocenti. The nearby resort of **Acquafredda** ④ has a charming hotel, the Villa Chieta, just above a beach. ❏

Built into a hillside across the valley from Matera is the church of the Madonna delle Tre Porte, with an exquisite fresco of the Virgin.

BELOW: the Norman castle at Melfi.

SICILY

Map, page 340

The island of Sicily, set in the middle of the Mediterranean and once the centre of the known world, has the finest array of classical and Moorish sites in Italy

Nature and history have made Sicily a land of considerable and striking contrasts. The greatest island in the Mediterranean Sea, Sicily was for centuries the centre of the known world. Its peculiar geographic position – smack in the middle of the Mediterranean – made the island vulnerable to attacks by foreigners, but at the same time a meeting-place of Mediterranean civilisations, a bridge between East and West. Witness the Greek colonisation (8th–3rd century BC), the Arab invasions (9th–10th century) and the Norman domination (11th–12th century). These were Sicily's great epochs, when commercial towns were founded and developed along the coast.

Invaders generally confined themselves to the coast, because of the difficult, mountainous terrain inland. Sicily's volcanic features, represented by Mount Etna and the Aeolian Islands, testify to relatively recent geological origins. The island still suffers violent earthquakes occasionally, and intermittent lava flows have made the plain below immensely fertile.

The reasons for the island's relative state of underdevelopment are rooted in its feudal past. Land in the interior is still organised along semi-feudal lines while industry suffers from mis-management and Mafia involvement.

PRECEDING PAGES: the hill-top town of Calascibetta, in the centre of the island. **LEFT:** Arab-Norman cloisters at Monreale. **BELOW:** under the almond trees, near Etna.

The Ionian coastline

A ferry plies between Villa San Giovanni in Calabria and **Messina ❶** in half an hour. Travellers arriving at Messina are invariably surprised to find themselves in a modern city with low-rise buildings and wide avenues; the surprise turns to astonishment when they see the wonderful scenery which is offered by the **Peloritani Mountains** that cradle the city.

Although founded in the classical age by Greek settlers and developed mostly between the 15th and 17th centuries, Messina has little to show for its ancient origins. On a fateful morning in the year 1908, terrifying earthquake jolts, followed by a violent seaquake, shook the city and razed it to the ground. Despite this disaster, several fine churches survived, including the **Duomo** and the nearby Orion fountain, by a pupil of Michelangelo, Giovanni Montorsoli. At midday, the astronomical clock of the Duomo's campanile puts on a spectacular show with mythological and religious figures and sound effects such as a cock crowing and a lion's roar.

In the shadow of Etna

After 45 km (28 miles), the road from Messina winds up to a town that is the essence of Sicily. "It is the greatest work of art and nature!" exclaimed Goethe in *Italian Journey*. **Taormina ❷** knows no greys. Its beauty is made up of light, colour and sea. Lying on a short terrace of the coast against a mountain, it slopes down a

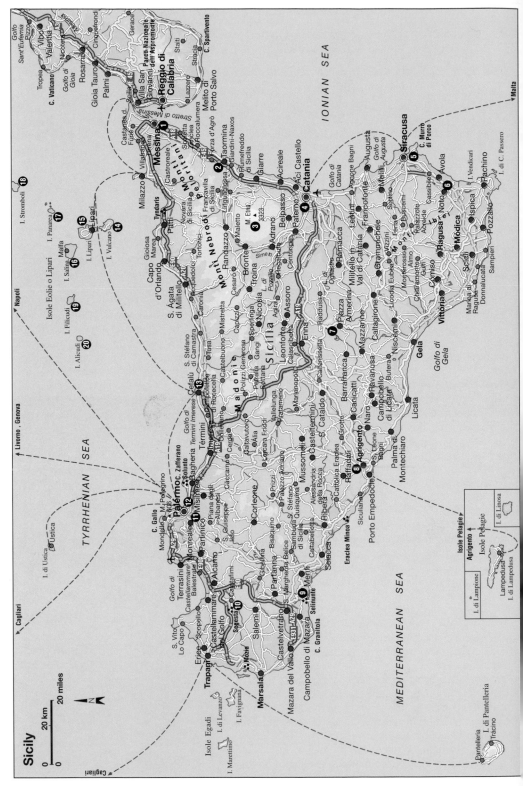

Sicily

cliff "as if", wrote Guy de Maupassant, "it had rolled down there from the peak". Its shoulders are embraced by the enormous, sometimes puffing, Etna.

See map opposite

Climb the hill to the **Greek Theatre** (open daily; entrance fee), Taormina's most famous monument, celebrated by many writers for its magnificent position. Built in the 3rd century BC, but completely remodelled by the Romans, it illustrates the Greeks' knack of choosing settings where nature enhances art. The jagged coastline of Taormina is dramatic: outcrops of rocks are intercut by narrow creeks, ravines and inlets.

In town, **Corso Umberto,** which cuts through the old centre, is the place for shopping and people-watching. The bars here are usually packed with an international crowd, but the atmosphere somehow remains that of a village. You can see this village in its churches or in the grand *palazzi* with their mullioned windows, marble tracery, scrolls and billowing balconies. The village atmosphere, however, does not disguise the fact that Taormina is a resort for the well-heeled – nowhere else could one find such a concentration of Valentino and Armani.

Sicily's smokestack

The landscape south of Taormina is dominated by **Mount Etna** ❸, the majestic volcano (3,323 metres/10,959 ft) with its snow-capped peak. It is one of only a few volcanoes in the world which are active. Its surface is punctuated by about 200 cones, smaller craters, accumulated layers of lava, gashes and valleys. Etna's history is a series of more or less ruinous eruptions, from the one in 396 BC, which halted the Carthaginians, to one in 1981, which destroyed part of the cableway. Even a smaller eruption in 1992 required help from the American marines to staunch the lava flow.

ABOVE: traditional puppets of Crusader knights. **BELOW:** grapevine on Etna.

In the fertile plain stretching from the southern foot of Mount Etna rises the city of **Catania** ❹. It was an important Greek and Roman colony and suffered from the various powers that succeeded in dominating the island. Destroyed twice by violent earthquakes (in 1169 and 1693), the city was covered in 1669 by lava which even advanced into the sea for about 700 metres (2,300 ft).

Catania is the economic centre of the richest area of Sicily: its continuing development is based mainly on citrus fruits, vineyards and market gardening, but commercial and industrial enterprises also flourish and have earned it the title "Milan of the South", a double-edged compliment given recent corruption scandals in both cities. It also has a high crime rate; beware of bag-snatchers in the fish market, and avoid the castle quarter, port and San Cristoforo area at night.

The city feels modern, with an urban plan characterised by wide streets designed in the 18th century baroque style. Catania's main axis is **Via Etnea**, where people gather for the *passeggiata* and window shopping. But Catania's baroque soul is better tasted in the smaller **Via dei Crociferi** in which churches and monastic buildings open like wings of a theatre. The street is covered by a wonderful arch, also baroque, leading to **San Benedetto**, a vast yet unfinished Benedictine monastery.

Another landmark in the history of the baroque style is the church of **San Niccolò**, which is reached by fol-

Sicilian bread comes in a variety of shapes.

BELOW: nuns visiting the archaeological park at Syracuse.

lowing Via Gesuiti. Be sure to go up to the cupola from where there are wide views of Mount Etna and Catania. Any visit would be incomplete without seeing **Castello Ursino** (open Tues–Sat 9am–noon, 3–6pm, Sun 9am–1pm; free), erected by Emperor Frederick II (1239–50) and since restored. Rest in the landscaped gardens of **Villa Bellini**.

Town of tyrants

From the wide plain of Catania head for **Syracuse ❺** (Siracusa) through landscapes of classical beauty, counterpointed by archaeological remains. Built in 734 BC by a group of Corinthian farmers who settled on the small isle of **Ortigia**, Syracuse developed so rapidly that in a short time it was establishing new colonies along the Sicilian coast. In 485 BC, when it had developed into a prosperous town, it was conquered by the tyrant Gelon. Syracuse then enjoyed its greatest political, economic and artistic magnificence, becoming one of the most important centres of the Mediterranean. It defeated the Carthaginians, Etruscans and even Athenians until it ruled over almost the whole of Sicily. After a dalliance with democracy, Syracuse flourished under despotism. Dionysius, the city's most enlightened tyrant, presided over Syracuse's golden age.

Great monuments and public works testify to the epoch's glory and wealth; at **Ortigia**, the ancient, but still lively heart of town, you can admire some exceptional temples: **Tempio di Apollo** (7th–6th century BC), and the grandiose **Tempio di Atena** (5th century BC), which later became the **Duomo**.

Leave Ortigia across the **Ponte Nuovo** and head north to **Neapolis** (open daily until 2 hrs before sunset; entrance fee), the sprawling archaeological park with the **Teatro Greco**, one of the greatest theatres in the Greek world (138

metres/452 ft in diameter; 15,000 seats). Here, during May and June, a series of high-quality classical performances is held; if you buy a ticket, you may end up in the very spot where Plato or Archimedes sat for their night on the town.

Nearby lie the **Latomie**, which are ancient honeycombed quarries. Later, the *latomie* were used as prisons for Athenians sentenced to hard labour. In the **Latomia del Paradiso**, there is a man-made cave known as Dionysius's Ear, which has an amazing echo. A whisper is amplified by the walls, a phenomenon that permitted the tyrant Dionysius to eavesdrop on prisoners. If you relish ancient legends, stop at the **Aretusa Fountain** back in Ortigia. According to local lore, the beautiful nymph jumped into the sea in order to escape from the river god Alfeo and was transformed into this spring.

An interesting destination close to Syracuse is the small town of **Noto ❻**. It stands on a ridge of the **Iblei Mountains**, furrowed by a long and straight road which widens out into wonderful scenes of inclined squares. Here Spanish baroque architecture triumphs in churches, palaces, monasteries and squares, all in a golden-coloured stone. Noto's most interesting monument is the church and monastery of **Santissimo Salvatore**, a riot of pilasters, adorned windows, loggias, terraces and belltowers. The highlight is **Palazzo Villadorata**: a facade incorporating Ionic columns and baroque balconies awash with lions, cherubs, medusae and monsters.

Sicily's harsh and imposing heart

From the coast, an excursion leads through the bare interior, with its reddish sulphur mines, vivid vegetation and little villages clustered on hills. One hilltop town is **Piazza Armerina ❼**, famous for the **Villa Romana** (open daily

Map, page 340

The original town of Noto was destroyed by an earthquake in 1693. A Spanish-Sicilian noble, Giuseppe Lanza, was put in charge of the rebuilding, and he decided to start the town afresh, 16 km (10 miles) further south.

BELOW: mosaics from the Villa Romana in Piazza Armerina.

At the cloisters in Monreale, 109 groups of capitals were ornately decorated by 12th-century craftsmen.

until 1 hr before sunset; entrance fee), an imperial mansion or grand hunting lodge. This is a complex construction, built between the 3rd and 4th centuries when the great noble families of the Roman Empire relaxed in the country. The villa has a series of extraordinary mosaics, the work of African and Sicilian artists, representing hunting scenes, imaginary creatures, and natural landscapes; an entire ancient world – one which, curiously, included bikinis – comes to life before your eyes.

Also of interest is the baroque **Duomo**, crowning a terraced hill. Theatrical staircases also accentuate the spacious belvedere and the Duomo's baroque facade. A Catalan-Gothic campanile with blind arcading remains from the original church and sets the tone for the lavish interior. Decorated like blue and white porcelain, the church boasts a Byzantine icon of a Madonna, a baroque tabernacle and a luminous *provençal* painted Crucifix.

Land of the gods

The neglected landscapes of the mining area lead to the solar beauty of **Agrigento** ❽, described by the Greek poet Pindar as "the most beautiful city of mortals". The symbol of the city is a group of magnificent temples occupying a valley. The origins of Agrigento (Akragas to the Greeks) date from 581 BC. The 5th century marked the apogee of the town, and it was then that the main temples were erected.

The town was later conquered by the Carthaginians and the Romans. Its importance diminished under the successive Byzantine and Arab dominations, but grew again with the arrival of the Normans. The classical city (open daily until 1 hr before sunset; entrance fee) comprises magnificent temples and tombs. The finest are: Tempio di Giove (Olympian Zeus), the largest Doric temple ever known; Tempio di Giunone (Juno/Hera), which commands a view of the valley; and Tempio della Concordia, one of the best preserved temples in the world.

The temples of **Selinunte** ❾ (open daily 9am–1 hr before sunset; entrance fee) can be seen from afar, on a promontory between a river and a plain in the middle of a gulf with no name. The massive but slender columns lift up to the skies from a sea of rocks that crush the dark red earth. Selinunte looks like a puzzle made of stone pieces: divided columns, chipped capitals, and white and grey cubes are all heaped together, as if a giant hand had mixed the pieces to make the reassembling of the original image more difficult. However, the stones speak volumes, revealing libraries, warehouses, courthouses, temples – all testifying to a prosperous ancient town in the middle of fertile lands. Amid the stones grows *selinon*, the wild parsley which gave its name to the powerful Greek colony.

Selinunte was destroyed in its attempt to expand at the expense of Segesta: in 409 BC, 16,000 citizens of Selinunte were slain by their Carthaginian rivals. To complete the plunge into the past, go to the rival **Segesta** ❿ (hours as for Selinunte). In spite of the frequent devastations of wars between the Greeks and the Carthaginians, an imposing Doric **Temple** has survived. It stands on the side of an arid and wind-beaten hill and is propped up by 36 columns. A few hundred feet further up is the **Theatre**, constructed in the 3rd century over the top of Mount Barbaro and from which stretches a splendid view over the **Gulf of Castellammare**.

Map, page 340

The Conca d'Oro

Enclosed by a chain of mountains, the Conca d'Oro, an evergreen valley that widens as it approaches the sea, is still irrigated and cultivated according to old custom. The valley is dominated by **Monreale ⓫**, which was founded in the 11th century around the famous Benedictine abbey bearing the same name.

Next to the monastery is the **cathedral**, a masterpiece of 12th-century Norman architecture. The church owes its fame to the mosaics, made by Byzantine and Venetian artists and craftsmen. The mosaics illustrate biblical scenes, from the Creation to the Apostles, in a golden splendour which fades away into grey, giving a tone of "sad brightness" summed up by the gesture and glance of the huge Pantocrator (Almighty). To pass from the cathedral to the cloister is to move from the East to the West. Here, the beauty lies in the 109 groups of capitals

The puppet theatre in Sicily goes back centuries, re-telling the story of the battles between Charlemagne's knights (the Paladins) and the Saracen invaders.

BELOW: in the gardens of Villa Giulia.

whose sculptures show an unusual freedom in execution, typical of the Romanesque style.

After admiring the view of the Conca d'Oro from the church's terraces (180 steps), proceed to **Palermo** ⑫, chief town and port of Sicily, at the bottom of a wide bay enclosed to the south by Capo Zafferano and to the north by Mount Pellegrino, which Goethe described as "the most beautiful promontory in the world". When you first arrive, it is difficult to understand why Palermo has been celebrated as an extraordinary cultural crossroads; miserable shacks and desolate old buildings greet the eye. But the city has a fascinating history – settled by the Phoenicians in the 8th century BC, it changed hands (like the rest of the island) many times. In the 10th century, under Arab rule, it was the world's second largest city (after Constantinople) and a multi-ethnic metropolis; two centuries later, the Normans had made it one of Europe's most magnificent cities. So be patient and set out to discover the city without preconceived ideas.

The best place to start an itinerary is from the **Palazzo dei Normanni** ⓐ, the splendid Norman palace and seat of the Sicilian parliament. Inside are the **Cappella Palatina** (open Mon–Fri 9am–noon, 3–5pm, Sat 9am–noon, Sun 9–10am, noon–1pm), and the **Sala di Re Ruggero** (open Fri–Sat and Mon 9am–noon, guided tours only; enquire at Cappella Palatina), glittering chambers encrusted with mosaics of Eastern influence. From there, follow the city's oldest thoroughfare, the former **Cassaro** – nowadays **Via Vittorio Emanuele** ⓑ – where it is easy to imagine the picturesque commercial life of Arab and Norman times.

Main crossroads

Via Vittorio Emanuele goes down to the **Quattro Canti** ⓒ, in the centre of the old town, a busy crossroads cut by **Via Maqueda**, the other axis of Palermo. Here the baroque dominates in four monuments decorated with fountains and statues. Another beautiful fountain stands in nearby **Piazza Pretoria** ⓓ. A few more steps lead to the Norman age, when Palermo was defined by the geographer Idrisi as the "town which turns the head of those who look at it". Here are two churches: the **Martorana** ⓔ, decorated with Byzantine mosaics, and **San Cataldo** ⓕ, which preserves three red, Moorish domes. The nuns of the church of Martorana are famous for inventing *pasta reale,* the popular marzipan fruit-shaped sweets.

Between Via Maqueda and the Palazzo dei Normanni extends the **Albergheria Quarter**. In spite of the desolate facades of new buildings, it is still possible to discover old Palermo near an open market in the quarter's centre. Isolated by an oasis of green is the small church of **San Giovanni degli Eremiti** ⓖ, a masterpiece of medieval architecture. Its five Moorish domes recall the 500 mosques that once dotted the town, as described by the traveller Ibn Hawqal in the 10th century. The southeastern quarter of the old town, called the **Kalsa**, is largely reduced to crumbling houses. But a witness to its turbulent history is the massive **Palazzo Chiaramonte** ⓗ (closed to the public), also called the Steri. This Catalan-Gothic fortress was a feudal stronghold before becoming the seat of the Inquisition in 1598. Not far away, the church of **Santa Maria della Catena** ⓘ is

a synthesis of Gothic and Renaissance art. Along Via Alloro is the **Palazzo Abatellis ❶**, built in the 15th century and now housing the **Galleria Regionale della Sicilia** (open daily till 1.30pm; also 3–7.30pm Tues and Thur; entrance fee), which contains an intimate art collection.

Rest in the park of **Villa Giulia ❶**, a typical Italian garden, planted in 1777 with rigorous symmetry. Close by is the **Orto Botanico ❶** (open daily, Sat and Sun am only) which offers exotic plants and rare trees among which Goethe loved to rest. You can then continue along the **Foro Italico**, an esplanade leading to the **Cala ❶**, the old port. Although it no longer functions as a port, the Cala remains a picturesque shelter for gaily-coloured fishing boats. Today's city centre is in **Via Ruggero Settimo** and the first part of **Viale della Libertà ❶**. Here are the best shops, several bookstores and cinemas, but few bars. Palermo's picturesque side is still visible in the food market of the **Vucciria**, a triumph of colour, light and sound, and in the **Zisa** palace (open daily, Sat–Sun am only; entrance fee), built in 1160 by William the Bad, which recalls the time when Palermo was virtually the centre of the known world.

Along the Tyrrhenian coast

Along the intense blue Tyrrhenian Sea the road is bordered by flowers and luxuriant citrus and olive groves. The winding road offers glimpses of **Cefalù ❸**. A panoramic view of the town, possible only from the sea, is extraordinary: a little town clinging to a promontory at the foot of an enormous rock and, to the west, a beautiful sandy beach crowded with bathers and flanked by hotels. Cefalù's fame lies in its medieval charm and great Norman cathedral.

Aeolian Islands

The Sicilian experience should end with a taste of adventure. The best place for this is an archipelago of seven little isles emerging in the **Golfo di Patti** off the north coast of Sicily: the **Aeolian Islands**, a name alluding to Aeolus who, in Greek mythology, is the god of the winds. **Vulcano ❹**, the first stop for the ferry, offers yellow sulphurous baths and volcanic craters. **Lipari ❺**, the largest and most populated island, is the most complex geologically and the richest historically. Its pumice beach has the only white sand in the whole archipelago. **Salina ❻**, the highest and the greenest, is topped by two symmetrical volcanos.

Exclusive **Panarea ❼**, with its little white houses framed by luxuriant vegetation, is a refuge for rich tourists and luxury yachts. **Stromboli ❽**, on the other hand, is the "black giant". Like Etna, it is constantly active and rumblings can be heard 5, 15 and even 25 minutes apart. Stromboli is nothing more than lava, ash and slag. It is the youngest of the seven "sisters", born only 40,000 years ago.

The visitor to **Filicudi ❾** and **Alicudi ❿** has to forget modern comforts, for there is neither electricity nor running water on these islands. Despite such inconvenience, they are a paradise not only for divers and fishermen (the offshore contours are very rocky and irregular so destructive trawling is impossible), but also for people who love peace and solitude. ❏

Maps, pages 340 & 345

BELOW: a freshly caught swordfish in Lipari.

THE LIVING EARTH: ITALY'S VOLCANOES

Bubbling, seething and angry, or silent, solemn
and threatening, Italy's volcanoes dictate the
way of life of those in their shadow

The area from the island of Sicily north to Campania on the Italian mainland is notoriously unstable geologically. Here, the earth's crust continues to suffer earthquakes, changes in land levels and volcanic activity. From Vesuvius brooding over the Bay of Naples to imperious, seething Etna on Sicily, Italian volcanoes have shaped the way of life for local people for centuries. The destruction and devastation that has followed major eruptions has on the one hand caused trepidation and exodus but, on the other, has also offered long-term compensation in the legacy of fertile soil enriched with volcanic extract.

SPREADING THE WORD

The fame of Italy's volcanoes owes much to its classical writers. Virgil and Pliny the Younger both described the might of volcanic activity in the region. Pliny, in particular, left us a detailed account of the eruption of Vesuvius in AD 79 which saw the death of his uncle, Pliny the Elder, and destroyed the towns of Herculaneum and Pompeii. In turn, Vesuvian mud and ash has preserved for us a unique picture of life in Roman times (*see page 314*).

▽ VOLCANIC ISLES

Stromboli, one of the volcanic Aeolian (or Lipari) Islands northeast of Sicily, was believed by the ancient Greeks to be the home of Aeolus, the god of wind. The waters around these islands are enriched with minerals and are known for their curative properties, making them popular with bathers.

△ **THE TOURIST TRAIL**
Volcano tourism really began in the 19th century when Vesuvius, then Etna (*above*) became part of the traveller's itinerary. Sedan chairs or donkey-power were used to convey lazy visitors to the top, and wily, business-minded local guides led the way.

▷ **FIRE PREVENTION**
Vesuvius, although officially "active", has not shown any major activity since 1944. Etna, however, remains a constant threat. In 1992, lava was only prevented from reaching nearby towns when the US Navy dropped concrete blocks in its path.

▷ **MUD, GLORIOUS MUD**
The seas around the Aeolian Islands can be radioactive and in places are warmed by underwater jets of steam. Sulphurous mud pools are sought out for the treatment of rheumatism. The island of Lipari also has the notable hot springs of San Calogero, where the water temperature rises to over 60°C (140°F).

◁ **KEEP YOUR DISTANCE**
Etna is Europe's largest active volcano and is Italy's highest mountain outside of the Alps. Even though it is prone to eruption, and the area around the main crater is now out of bounds, it is still generally safe to climb – providing common sense and local advice are heeded. Wear warm clothing.

△ **ROCKY RAVINE**
Etna's Valle del Bovo (Valley of the Ox) is a bleak, rocky chasm, 5 km (3 miles) wide, on the mountain's eastern face. It was created by a volcanic explosion and pot holes still puff out plumes of smoke. Geologists marvel at the clear stratification of rock forms in the valley walls.

▷ **RIVERS OF FIRE**
Awesome rivers of fire like this lava flow on Etna reveal the raw power of volcanoes and the wonder they have induced over the centuries. In *Le Spéronare*, Alexandre Dumas described Etna's "immense crater, roaring, full of flames and smoke; heaven above one's head, hell beneath one's feet".

THE MIGHT AND POWER OF GODS

The power of Italy's active volcanoes is a phenomenon which defied explanation in ancient times. The Romans attributed the fiery convulsions to Vulcan, the god of fire and metal-working, whom they believed lived deep beneath the island of Vulcano in the Aeolian Islands. In addition, the poet Virgil told of the giant Enceladus who, he declared, was interred below Mount Etna, his groanings and rumblings accounting for the earth-shaking, violent eruptions.

Early Christians, too, saw divine activity in volcanic outbursts. In the year 253, the mere production of the veil covering the tomb of the recently martyred St Agatha was said to have staunched the lava flow from Etna that threatened to envelop Catania and its people. Even in relatively modern times, the citizens of Naples have been quick to turn to their patron saint, Januarius, for help whenever Vesuvius has begun to belch smoke.

However, some observers over the centuries have been more pragmatic about the causes of volcanic activity. One anonymous Roman poet suggested that the phenomenon was wind induced: "It is the winds which arouse all these forces of havoc: the rocks which they have massed thickly together they whirl in eddying storm ..."

SARDINIA

Seven thousand prehistoric stone towers, countless beaches and more sheep than people make Sardinia the perfect place to get away from it all

Sardinia has little in common with the rest of Italy. The Mediterranean's second-largest island offers a very restricted diet of art and architecture; rather, its appeal lies in its beaches and rugged landscape. Much of its 1,600-km (1,000-mile) coastline is given over to duney sands and romantic coves nestling in pine and juniper woods. A large part of its interior, where sheep outnumber humans, is wild and mountainous, and covered in a knotty carpet of herby, shrubby *macchia*. Even the island's cuisine is different from the mainland's. Here, robust, country fare comes in the form of *pecorino* cheese made from ewes' milk, roast lamb and suckling pig, *seadas* or cheese pastries served with honey, and *carta da musica* – crisp, wafer-thin bread said to resemble sheets of music.

Most holidaymakers come for stay-put beach holidays. Many base themselves in the purpose-built, ritzy resorts which has put the island on the tourist map, but there are more down-to-earth alternatives. The large distances involved and the paucity of sights make Sardinia less than ideal for a touring holiday. There are, however, some unique attractions, notably the intriguing remnants of the prehistoric, nuraghic civilisation: an astonishing 7,000 stone towers, or *nuraghi*, which from a distance look like giant dung heaps, litter the countryside.

BELOW: Cala di Volpe, a luxury hotel in the form of a medieval castle.

Lying within Gallura, the sparsely inhabited northeastern region of Sardinia where pinky, granite rocks tower like castles over swathes of *macchia* and juniper, cork and oak woods, is the **Costa Smeralda ❶**, or Emerald Coast. In the early 1960s, the Aga Khan and associates bought up this impossibly picturesque little piece of coastline – a mere 10 km (6 miles) end to end by road   and turned it into a hedonistic bolthole, now the flagship of the island's tourism. Development is rigorously controlled. Virtually every hotel and apartment complex comes in regulation "Mediterranean" style, of pantiled roofs, and pink and russet walls, distressed to give the appearance of age.

Even if you can't afford to partake in the jet-set lifestyle, it makes great spectator sport. Head for **Porto Cervo**, the only resort, where Armani and Versace boutiques compete for attention with extravagant yachts, and **Cala di Volpe**, a make-believe medieval castle, is the most ostentatious of the hotels. Many of the gorgeous coves are inaccessible, but you can wander through groves to those on the Capriccioli peninsula. Impressive **Cala Liscia Ruja**, just south, is the area's biggest beach. The resort of **Baia Sardinia**, just north of the Costa Smeralda proper, is equally contrived, but far less pretentious and more affordable.

Much of the rest of the Galluran coastline is being spoilt by the onset of ranks of apartments and self-catering villages. This is true of scruffy **Palau**, the departure point for ferries to **Isola Maddalena ❷**. The island is part of a NATO military zone but has good beaches, and is connected to **Caprera ❸**, where you can visit the house in which Garibaldi spent his last years. Back on the mainland, **Santa Teresa Gallura ❹** is a study in pink, and there are a couple of great sandy beaches at nearby **Capo Testa**, fringed by rocks the size of houses.

Alghero

Northwestern Sardinia is a more benign, softer region than the northeast, with sandy strands cupped in pine woods. But its big draw is **Alghero ❺**, the only resort on the island which has genuine character and history:in the 14th century, the port was occupied by Catalans, and street names are still written in that language.

Its old centre, half surrounded by medieval walls, could hardly be more entrancing: cobbled lanes are lined with high-sided, shuttered buildings dripping in peeling stucco and washing. The best beach in the vicinity is **Spiaggia di Maria Pia**, and there is a popular boat trip across the bay to the **Grotta di Nettuno ❻**, a cave system at the foot of a towering, tilted cliff with memorable rock formations. Untouristy **Sassari ❼**, a 45-minute drive inland, is Sardinia's second city, which has enjoyably earthy backstreets between the overblown, neo-Gothic **Piazza d'Italia** and the baroque-fronted cathedral; and a large **archaeology museum** (open Tues–Sat and Sun am; entrance fee), which, after Cagliari's, is the best place to immerse yourself in the nuraghic culture.

Sardinia's dramatic interior – with imposing tablelands, pine woods, massive walls and granite amphitheatres – is the historic, cultural and geographic heart of the island. Here, safely sheltered from foreign invaders, a population of shepherds developed a fierce and isolated society.

Map, page 352

TIP

Alghero is arguably the best place on the island for fresh seafood. Stop at the market in Via Sassari for lobster, sea urchins and squid, or try the local restaurants.

BELOW: oleanders and *macchia* in the Monti del Gennargentu, south of Nuoro.

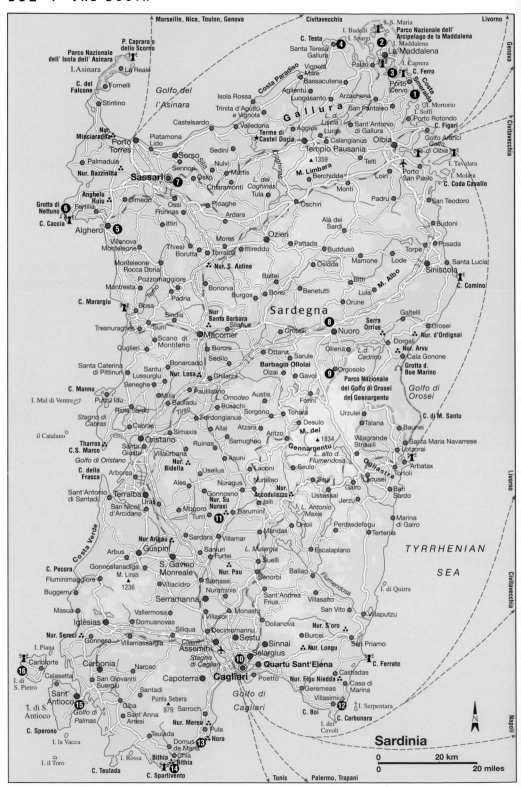

Sardinia

There are no urban centres of interest – **Nuoro** , the area's capital, is only worth visiting for its folklife museum, the **Museo della Vita e delle Tradizioni Popolari Sarde** (open Tues–Sat 9am–7pm; entrance fee). Immediately south is the most accessible part of the region, where vineyards and olive groves are intensively cultivated across the hillsides. Many visitors end up at the **Hotel Su Gologone** near Oliena, which lays on superb Sardinian cooking and guided expeditions into the mountains. Just down the road lies unwelcoming but fascinating **Orgosolo** ❾, the Barbagia's "bandit capital", where politicised, anti-capitalist murals cover virtually every inch of wallspace along its high street. The long lonely drive south on the SS125, which clings unnervingly to mountainsides from Dorgali to Arbatax and beyond, is the island's most exhilarating.

The south

Cagliari ❿, the island's hectic capital, is rewarding if you ignore the traffic-ridden port and climb up into **Castello**, the medieval centre where steep, gloomily atmospheric streets lie within 13th-century walls and towers. The cathedral, a hotchpotch of styles, and a Roman amphitheatre are outshone by the **Museo Archeologico** (open daily 9am–1pm, 3.30–7pm; entrance fee), famous for exquisite spindly bronze statuettes and votive boats from the nuraghic culture.

An hour's drive north, skirting the fertile **Campidano** plain, brings you to the island's most impressive *nuraghe*, **Su Nuraxi** ⓫ (open daily 9am–1 hr before sunset; entrance fee) at Barumini. Dating from the 15th century BC, the colossal fortification is made up of beautifully formed beehive-shaped rooms; the maze of low stone walls at its base was once a dependent village.

The coastal road east from Cagliari leads to enormous tranches of the finest sand in the island's isolated southeastern corner. However, **Villasimius** ⓬ and the **Costa Rei**, the unfancy resorts that have grown up around them, are rather characterless, comprising mainly campsites and self-catering complexes.

The gentle, pine-clad coastline southwest from Cagliari, scattered with holiday homes and a few smart hotels, is more interesting. Punic and Roman **Nora** ⓭ (open daily 9am–sunset; entrance fee) is Sardinia's most extensive classical site, with clearly defined houses and mosaics and a temple and small theatre. Equally rewarding is the waterside location, on a little peninsula next to a long curve of sand. Many of the finds from Nora are housed in the **Museo Archeologico** (open daily 9am–sunset; entrance fee) in nearby **Pula**. A few miles south lies the **Forte Village**, a luxurious, beautifully landscaped and family-orientated complex where the service runs to flower petals being placed in bedroom lavatory bowls. It sits next to a good beach, but the area's best is at **Chia** ⓮, backed by hillock-high dunes. The drive beyond along the **Costa del Sud** passes craggy headlands and azure waters in deep inlets on its way to **Sant'Antioco** ⓯. Linked to the mainland by an ancient causeway, the island's eponymous town has Christian catacombs under its main church.

Ferries run to **San Pietro** ⓰, known for the bloody *mattanza* in early summer, when schools of tuna are slaughtered en masse. ❑

See map opposite

Traditional folk costume can often be seen at festivals.

BELOW: the sandy beach at Nora. **OVERLEAF:** door of San Zeno, Verona.

INSIGHT GUIDES
Travel Tips

Insight Guides portray destinations in depth, providing the complete picture and the top photography

Insight Pocket Guides focus on the best choices for places to see and things to do and include large fold-out maps

Insight Compact Guides' portability makes them the perfect books to carry with you for on-the-spot reference

Three types of guide for all types of travel

INSIGHT GUIDES Different people need different kinds of information. Some want *background information* to help them prepare for the trip. Others seek *personal recommendations* from someone who knows the destination well. And others look for *compactly presented data* for on-the-spot reference. With three carefully designed series, Insight Guides offer readers the perfect choice. Insight Guides will turn your visit into an experience.

The world's largest collection of visual travel guides

Contents

Getting Acquainted

The Place

Area 301,245 sq. km/116,280 sq. miles.
Capital Rome.
Highest Mountain Mont Blanc (4,760 metres/15,616 ft).
Principal rivers Po, Tiber, Arno and Volturno.
Population 57 million.
Language Italian.
Religion Roman Catholic.
Time Zone Central European Time (GMT plus 1 hour).
Currency Lira.
Weights & Measures Metric.
Electricity 220 volts. You will need an adaptor to operate British three-pin appliances and a transformer to use 100–120 volt appliances.
International Dialling Code 0039.

Geography

The Alps form a natural boundary between Italy and neighbouring countries France, Switzerland and Austria. A little further south, running at a right-angle to the Alps and extending right down the country, are the Apennines. Between the two is the fertile Po valley, where most of the country's cereals are grown. Below the Alps are the Italian Lakes – notably Maggiore, Lugano and Como.

The country has four active volcanoes, including Etna, near Catania on the island of Sicily, and Vesuvius, on the Gulf of Naples. Sicily and the other major island, Sardinia, have largely mountainous terrains.

Climate

There are three main kinds of climate affecting Italy:

● In the mountainous areas (Alps and Apennines), the winter is long and cold and the summer is short and cool. Even for summer visits, you are advised to bring sweaters and light boots.
● In the Pianura Padana (region around Milan), the climate is characterised by foggy winters and hot, humid summers.
● In the rest of Italy, the winters are fairly mild and the hot, dry summers are tempered by sea-breezes (more along the Tyrrhenian coastline than along the Adriatic). Summers can be torrid in the south and on the islands.

Population

About 57 million people live in this democratic republic which has a Western-style economy. Parliament and government are based in Rome, the capital and largest city (around 3 million inhabitants). The second largest city is Milan (just over 1.5 million), the third largest is Naples (just over 1 million) and the fourth largest is Turin (about 1 million people).

Government

Italy's president is elected for a term of seven years by Parliament, which is composed of two houses. These are the Senate (with 315 members) and the Chamber of Deputies (comprising 630 members). The president nominates the prime minister and, on the prime minister's recommendations, the Cabinet.

Recently, after a period of constitutional corruption in the early 1990s, Italy reduced its dependence on proportional representation and moved towards a "first-past-the-post" system, more in line with the British or French electoral systems. Under the new system, the country elected its first left-wing government, a loose centre-left coalition, in 1996. The individual regions tend to have strong political affiliations, with the North influenced by Federalist tendencies, the centre historically left-wing, along with certain major cities, and the South in a transitional phase, though traditionally more right-wing.

Economy

Industry (motor and electrical goods manufacturing, chemicals, sulphur, mercury, iron and steel) is concentrated in Northern Italy, while agriculture is concentrated in the South. Carrara marble (from Carrara in northwest Italy) is famous throughout the world. Italy is the world's largest producer of wine and olive oil and Europe's foremost producer of silk.

Milan is the centre of the Italian design industry and rivals Paris as the fashion capital of Europe. Italy's economic strength lies in the creativity and industry of its small and medium-sized companies, especially those in Lombardy, Piedmont, the Veneto and Emilia-Romagna. No solution has yet been found to the struggling economy of the South and its huge levels of unemployment.

Planning the Trip

What to Wear

The Italians are known for their sense of style. However, this does not mean that one has to dress formally. However, when sightseeing, both men and women are advised to cover their shoulders and avoid wearing shorts (or short skirts in the case of women), as some churches bar visitors who are unsuitably dressed.

Unless you are going to visit mountain areas, the moderate climate makes heavy clothing unnecessary in summer. A light jacket will be adequate for summer evenings. In winter (November–March), the climate can be cold and wet throughout Italy.

Visas and Passports

EU citizens do not need a visa or a passport to enter Italy: an identification card valid for foreign travel is sufficient.

Visitors from the following countries need a passport but are exempt from needing a visa providing they do not stay for more than three months: Australia, Austria, Barbados, Canada, Iceland, Jamaica, Japan, Kenya, South Korea, Kuwait, Malaysia, Maldives, Malta, Mexico, Monaco, New Zealand, Niger, Norway, Paraguay, Poland (for a stay up to 30 days), Singapore, Switzerland, Trinidad and Tobago, United States, Uruguay, Venezuela (up to 60 days).

Other nationalities should contact their nearest Italian consulate.

You are supposed to register with the police within three days of arriving in Italy. In fact, this procedure will be taken care of by your hotel, whatever the level of accommodation. If you are not staying in a hotel, contact the local police station.

Money Matters

The monetary unit is the *lira* (plural *lire*). Travellers' cheques are recommended as they can be replaced if stolen or lost. However, commission will be charged for changing them. Most shopkeepers and restaurateurs will not change money, so it is best to change a limited amount at the airport when you arrive, especially if it is the weekend, when banks are closed. Try to avoid changing money in hotels, where the commission tends to be higher than in banks.

Animal Quarantine

Pets must be vaccinated against rabies and you should obtain an officially stamped document stating that your animal is healthy. This should be done no more than one month before you arrive in Italy.

Banks are generally open 8.30am–1.30pm and for one hour in the afternoon (usually between 3 and 4pm). You can also change money at airports and main railway stations.

You will find current exchange rates are published in the press and posted in banks. Rates fluctuate considerably.

Credit Cards and Cash Machines In cities, many restaurants, hotels, shops and stores will take major credit cards (Visa, American Express, Mastercard, Diner's Club and Carte Blanche), but most petrol stations require cash. Don't bank on being able to use credit cards in country areas.

Getting There

By Air
In addition to the national airline, Alitalia, most airlines run direct flights to Italy, including many charter flights offering bargain tickets.

Italy has 29 main airports, but only two of them are for intercontinental flights: Roma Leonar-

Customs Regulations

Used personal effects may be imported and exported without formality.

The import of narcotics, weapons and pirated materials is forbidden. Alcoholic drinks, tobacco and perfume can be imported in limited quantities, depending on your nationality. EU citizens are free to import duty-free up to 800 cigarettes/400 cigarillos/200 cigars or 1 kg tobacco; 10 litres of spirits; 20 litres of fortified wines (sherry, port); 90 litres of wine (no more than 60 litres of which should be sparkling); and 110 litres of beer. Goods on which duty has already been paid in another European country may be freely imported, provided the amount falls within what might be described as "for personal use".

For US citizens, the duty-free allowance is: 200 cigarettes, 50 cigars or 3 lb tobacco; 1 US quart of alcoholic beverages and duty-free gifts worth up to $100.

The following airports have duty-free shops: Genoa, Milan, Pisa, Turin, Venice, Rome Fiumicino, Rome Ciampino, Naples, Rimini and Bologna.

do da Vinci (known as Fiumicino) and Milano Malpensa. Roma Ciampino serves some charter flights.

Leonardo da Vinci Airport (Fiumicino) is 35.5 km (22.5 miles) southwest of downtown Rome. It is the fourth busiest airport in Europe.

There is a direct hourly train service between Fiumicino Airport and Stazione Termini, from which taxis, metro and bus services are available. The journey takes 28 minutes. Another train runs every 20 minutes to alternative train stations Tiburtina and Ostiense,

Public Holidays

- **January** New Year's Day (1)
- **March/April** Good Friday, Easter Monday
- **April** Liberation Day – *Anniversario della Liberazione* (25)
- **May** Labour Day – *Festa del Lavoro* (1)
- **August** Assumption of the Blessed Virgin Mary – *Ferragosto* (15)
- **November** All Saints – *Ognissanti* (1)
- **December** Immaculate Conception of the Blessed Virgin Mary – *Immacolata Concezione* (8), Christmas Day (25), St Stephen's Day (26)

In addition to these national holidays, almost all cities have a holiday to celebrate their own patron saint, for example St John the Baptist, 24 June (Turin, Genoa and Florence); St Ambrose, 7 September (Milan); St Mark, 25 April (Venice); St Petronius, 4 October (Bologna); St Gennaro, 19 September (Naples); St Nicholas, 6 September (Bari); St Rosalia 15 July (Palermo); Saints Peter and Paul, 29 June (Rome).

from which taxis, metro and bus services are also available. The ride takes about 30 minutes.

Taking a yellow or white taxi with a meter (unofficial taxis can charge extortionate fares and may even be dangerous) from the airport can be a good alternative to fussing with public transport. There are surcharges for luggage, at night, and on Sunday, and there is a special airport supplement. Typical fares range from L70,000–90,000. Fares can be negotiated in advance.

Roma Ciampino There is a bus service roughly every 30 minutes from the airport to the Anagnina metro station – the very end of *Linea A*. From there, the journey takes 25 minutes to the centre of town. Taxis are far more convenient and typically cost L60,000–70,000 .

Marco Polo Airport is located at Tessera on the mainland 9 km (5.5 miles) north of Venice. To reach Venice there is a choice of public bus to Piazzale Roma (30 minutes); private land taxi (20–25 minutes); the Coopera-tiva San Marco water launch which crosses the lagoon to Piazza San Marco via the Lido (45 minutes); or a water-taxi, which costs six times as much as the public launch.

Treviso Airport is an alternative for travellers to Venice or the Lakes. Charter flights are available from London Gatwick, and a coach service runs to Venice.

Verona Airport is probably the most convenient for reaching the Lakes or the Veneto region. Charter flights arrive from London, Frankfurt, Paris and some other cities.

Milano Malpensa Airport, Milan's intercontinental airport, is 46 km (28.5 miles) from the centre of Milan. An Air Pullman bus ferries passengers between the airport and the Air Pullman office outside the Central Railway Station. You can buy a ticket

for this shuttle service up to a few minutes before departure from the Air Pullman office.

Milano Linate, Milan's other airport, is about 8 km (5 miles) from the centre. The ATM bus 73 travels regularly (5.30am–midnight) from the front of the airport (Piazzale del Aeroporto) to its terminus on the Piazza S Babila at the corner of Corso Europa.

Peretola, Florence, is 4 km (2 miles) northwest of the city centre. Some international flights land at Peretola, but these tend to be more expensive than flights to Pisa (see below). From the UK, Meridiana flies regularly to Florence.

Galileo Galilei Airport, Pisa, is the more usual airport for inter-national visitors to Florence. Trains to Florence (leaving every hour and taking an hour to reach the city) leave from just outside the airport.

Punta Raisi airport is 32 km (20 miles) west of Palermo. Sicily's other main airport, Fontanarossa, is 7 km (4 miles) southwest of Catania.

Cagliari-Elmas is the main airport on Sardinia, but there are also airports at Olbia and Alghero.

By Car

When calculating the cost of travelling to Italy by car, allow for motorway tolls as well as accommodation en route and petrol. If you want to travel by toll-free roads in Italy, get hold of the Italian State Tourist Office's *Traveller's Handbook*, which lists them.

The usual route from France to Italy is via the Mont Blanc Tunnel (between Chamonix and Courmayeur) or from Switzerland through the Gran San Bernardo Tunnel (between Bourg St Pierre and Aosta). Some of the many alpine passes are seasonal, so it is best to check the viability of your route with the tourist board or a

Car Trains

The following rail services will transport cars to Italy:

• Paris–Milan
• Boulogne–Lille–Milan
• Schaerbbeek (Brussels)–Milan
• Hertogenbosch (The Netherlands)–Domodossola –Genoa–Milan
• Hertogenbosch–Chiasso– Milan
• Düsseldorf–Cologne–Milan– Genoa
• Hamburg–Hanover–Verona
• Munich–Rimini
• Düsseldorf–Cologne– Bolzano
• Vienna–Venice
• Boulogne–Bologna
• Boulogne–Rome
• Boulogne–Alessandria
• Boulogne–Livorno

motoring organisation before setting off.

To take your car into Italy, you will need your current driving licence (with an Italian translation unless it is the standard EU licence), your vehicle registration document (which must be in the driver's name or supported by the owner's written permission for the driver to use the vehicle) and Green Card insurance. You are also required to carry a warning triangle in case of breakdown.

By Coach

The cost of travelling to Italy from Great Britain by scheduled coach is not much cheaper than travelling by air. National Express Eurolines runs coaches from London Victoria, via Paris and Mont Blanc, to Aosta, Turin, Genoa, Milan, Venice, Bologna, Florence and Rome. To book from London, contact: National Express Eurolines, Victoria Coach Station, Buckingham Palace Road, London SW1, tel: 0990-808080.

By Rail

This is not a particularly cheap option unless you are travelling as part of the Inter-Rail scheme (providing a month's unlimited train travel in Europe for anyone under the age of 26 at a very reasonable price). However, it can be an attractive option, especially if you are planning to stop off en route.

When travelling from Great Britain via Paris (the usual route when travelling to Rome, for example), it is necessary to change in Paris (from Gare du Nord to Gare de Lyon).

EC (Eurocity) and TEE (Trans Europe Express) trains are luxury first-class only trains running between the main European cities. A special supplement is charged and seat reservation is obligatory.

Practical Tips

Business Hours

Shops are open for business 9am–12.30pm and 3.30 or 4pm–7.30 or 8pm. In areas serving tourists, hours are generally longer than these. Shops often close on Monday (or Monday morning only). Some close on Saturday. Almost everything closes on Sunday.

Tipping

Unless otherwise indicated on the menu, service is included. Therefore it is not necessary to tip your waiter. A modest amount of change left on the table is sufficient to express apprecia- tion for good service. Although *pane e coperto*, an outdated cover and bread charge, has been officially eliminated in most cities, some restaurants have been slow in phasing it out. Only in the finest hotels, and for lengthy stays, is a tip for the maids/head waiters necessary.

Media

The Italian press is concentrated in Milan and Rome. The biggest papers are *La Repubblica* and *Il Corriere della Sera,* which publish regional editions. Most major cities publish weekly listings magazines which are worth getting, even for visitors with basic Italian. Rome and Florence both produce English versions of such magazines. *Romanc'e* is a weekly guide to everything going on in Rome, and is available from news-stands every Thursday. It has a section in English at the back. The local tourist office will have information on current happenings.

Television stations include RAI (the national network with three channels), the Vatican network, plus seven national and over 450 local commercial stations.

Postal Services

Post office hours are usually 8am–1.30pm, but many towns have a main post office which is open throughout the day.

Stamps may also be purchased from tobacco shops (*tabacchi*).

The post office can provide such services as *raccomandata* (registered) and *espresso* (express).

You can receive mail addressed to *Posta Restante*, held at the *Fermo Posta* window of the main post office in every town, picking it up personally with identification.

Remember that you do not have to line up to post your mail: you can simply post it in the red letter-boxes near the tobacconists or at the station.

Telephone

Public telephones are often found in bars and on main squares. From some bars, but mostly from post offices, you can call *scatti* (ring first, pay later). Most accept phonecards (*carte telefoniche* or *schede telefoniche)* and these are available from tobacconists or post offices for L5,000, L10,000 or L15,000. Alternatively, you can buy a *gettone* token which costs L200 (these are sometimes given as change when buying goods). Few telephones accept coins, but those that do take L100, L200 and L500. Directory enquiries is available by dialling 12, at a charge of roughly L1,000.

The cost of long-distance calls depends on the distance and the time of day. Within Italy, the cheapest time to call is 6.30pm–8am, after 1pm on Saturday or all day Sunday.

If you are telephoning to outside Italy, it costs least 10pm–8am and all day Sunday. Off-peak rates are affected by whether it is the peak or off-peak period in the country you are calling.

Tourist Offices

General tourist information is available at the **Ente Nazionale per il Turismo** (ENIT), Via Marghera 2/6 Rome, tel: 4971222.

In the UK, contact ENIT, 1 Princes Street, London W1R 8AY, tel: 0171-408 1254, fax: 0171-493 6695.

In the US, contact ENIT, Suite 1565, 630 Fifth Avenue, New York, NY 10111, tel: 212-2454822, fax: 212-5869249.

In every major town you will find the **Azienda Provinciale per il Turismo** (APT). For addresses and phone numbers, check the directory or the *Yellow Pages*

Calling Home

To call abroad from Italy, dial 00, followed by:

Australia 61
Canada..............................1
Ireland 353
New Zealand 64
UK....................................44
USA...................................1

Then dial the number, omitting the initial "0" if there is one.

European Directory Enquiries: 176
European operator assistance: 15
Intercontinental operator assistance: 170
Telegrams and cables: 186

Area Codes

For numbers **both** inside and outside your area, dialling must be preceded by "0" and then the area code, which you can obtain free from Information (dial 12). The area codes (including the initial "0") of main cities are:

Rome (06), **Milan** (02), **Bologna** (051), **Genoa** (010), **Florence** (055), **Pisa** (050), **Venice** (041), **Turin** (011), **Naples** (081), **Como** (031), **Palermo** (091).

From outside Italy, **keep** the initial zero, ie (06) for Rome.

under "ENIT". Together with helpful information, main APT offices offer a free city map, a list of hotels, and museum hours and addresses. APT in the main cities are listed on the page opposite.

Almost every town in Italy has a **Touring Club Italiano** (TCI) office, which provides free information about points of interest. Telephone numbers are listed in the local telephone book. The club also produces some of the best maps and food – and wine – guides i

Emergencies

Security and Crime
Terrorism resurfaced in the form of bomb blasts in Milan, Florence and Rome in the early 1990s, but the main problem for tourists is pick-pocketing, bag-snatching and robbery. It is advisable to have insurance coverage against these. If you are the victim of a crime (or suffer a loss) and wish to claim against your insurance, it is essential to make a report at the nearest police station and get documentation to support your claim. When you need a policeman, dial **113** (or 112 for

Provincial Tourist Offices (APT)

Rome
The main headquarters are located in Via Parigi 5, tel: 06-48899253, and there are also offices at Stazione Termini, tel: 06-4871270, and Fiumicino Airport, tel: 06-65956074. These are open 8.15am–7pm.

Milan
APT offices are located at Stazione Centrale, tel: 02-6690432/6690532 – open in summer 9am–12.30pm and 2–6.30pm; in winter until 6pm; closed Sunday. There is also an office at Piazza del Duomo, tel: 02- 809662, fax: 02-72022999. This office serves Milan and the surrounding region and is open Monday–

Saturday 8am–7pm; Sunday 9am –noon and 1.30–6pm.

Florence
The APT office is far from the centre of the city, in Via Manzoni 16, tel: 055-23320. This is open Monday–Friday 8.30am–1.30pm and 4–6.30pm; Saturday 8.30am–1pm. More central and efficient, but open to personal callers only, is the Azienda Autonoma di Turismo, Provincia-Comune di Firenze, Via Cavour 1R, tel: 055-290832/290833; fax: 055-2760383 – open Monday–Saturday 9am–2pm. You can also visit the tourist office south of Piazza della Signoria, at Chiasso Baroncelli

17, tel: 055-2302124; fax: 055-2302033. Alternatively, try the office at the station, tel: 055-212245; fax: 055-2381226.

Venice
The APT office is in San Marco 71F, tel: 041-5226356, under the arcades of the piazza – open Monday–Saturday 9am–12.30pm and 3–7pm. There is also an office in the train station, tel: 041-719078 – open daily 8am–7pm. The APT provincial headquarters is at Castello 4421, tel: 041-5298711; fax: 041-5230399.

the *Carabinieri*, a national police force which is technically a branch of the army).

If driving, lock your car and never leave luggage, cameras or other valuables inside. This applies particularly in major cities and in the South.

Medical Services
In cases of real need, such as medical aid or ambulances, call the Public Emergency Assistance number, **113**. This service operates on a 24-hour basis, and, in the principal cities, response will be in the main foreign languages. Dial 112 for the Carabinieri immediate action service. Certain tourist cities, such as Florence, offer medical interpreting services.

To receive free treatment in cases of illness, accident or even childbirth, EU citizens (and citizens of countries with other ties to Italy, such as Brazil, Monaco, and the former Yugoslavia), must obtain (in their country of residence before arriving in Italy) the E-111 form. This form is to state that the

bearers are registered with their national health service and therefore have the right to the

Personal Security

To safeguard your personal safety, it is wise to observe these few simple rules:

● Don't linger in non-commercial areas after dark. The more people there are around, the less likely it is that you will be targeted.
● Don't carry all your cash with you, even if you think it is safely hidden.
● Use travellers' cheques or Eurocheques rather than large quantities of cash
● Never leave your luggage unattended
● Ask hotel staff to put your valuables in the hotel safe (most hotels provide a storage service)
● Always deposit your room key at the desk before leaving your hotel, however quickly you think you might return

same assistance offered to Italian citizens. (Note: it won't provide repatriation, which you may require in the case of serious illness.) Citizens of non-EU countries must pay for medical assistance and medicine.

Health insurance is recommended for travelling in Italy. Keep receipts for medical expenses if you want to claim.

Most hospitals have a 24-hour emergency department called *Pronto Soccorso* but a stay in an Italian hospital can be a grim experience.

For more minor complaints, seek out a *farmacia*, identified by a sign displaying a red cross within a white circle. Trained pharmacists give advice and suggest over-the-counter drugs, including antibiotics. Normal opening hours are 9am–1pm and 4–7.30 or 8pm, but outside these hours the address of the nearest *farmacia* on duty is posted in the window.

Women Travelling Alone
The difficulties encountered by women travelling in Italy are

often overstated. However, women – especially if young and blonde – usually have to put up with much male attention. Though this is often annoying, it is rarely dangerous, but take particular care in Genoa, Bari, Naples, Palermo and Catania. Ignoring whistles and questions is the best way to get rid of unwanted attention. The less you look like a tourist, the fewer problems you are likely to have.

Embassies

Normal opening times of embassies vary, so telephone to check. If your passport is lost or stolen and you need a new one, you will need a police report, proof of identity and suitable photos, but check requirements first. These are the addresses of the embassies of the main English-speaking countries:

Australia: Via Alessandria 215, Rome, tel: 06-852721.
Canada: Via Zara 30, Rome, tel: 06-44598421/ 44598900.
Ireland: Piazza Campitelli 3, Rome, tel: 06-6979121.
New Zealand: Via Zara 28, Rome, tel: 06-4404035/ 4402928.
United Kingdom: Via XX Settembre 80A, Rome, tel: 06-4825551.
United States: Via Vittorio Veneto 121, Rome, tel: 06-46741.

Getting Around

By Air

The major centres – Rome, Milan, Florence, Venice, Naples – and towns of touristic interest are connected by flights provided mostly by Alitalia. Smaller airlines are ATI, Alisarda (to and from Sardinia) and Aligiulia. Flying in Italy is expensive compared to taking the train, but it can be useful for long distances. Discount flights are often available if you are prepared to arrive and return on certain days, but such fares must be booked in Italy. For detailed information, contact your nearest travel agent or Alitalia office.

Remember that infants under two years accompanied by an adult have a 90 percent discount; children over two years and under 12 have a 50 percent discount, and young travellers of 12–21 years have a 25 percent discount.

By Rail

The cheapest, fastest and most convenient way to travel is by train. Train information is available from the *Uffici Informazioni* at most major stations, listed in the telephone directory under *Ferrovie dello Stato*.

Local trains are called *Regionale, Diretto, Interregionale* and *Espresso*. When travelling considerable distances or along major lines, the faster *InterCity* and *EuroCity* services are the best bet – the

supplemental charge being well worth the time saved and the comfort. The *Pendolino* is the fastest and most comfortable train, and requires a supplemental charge and a reservation. It is a good idea to buy tickets and make reservations for the *IC/EC* and *Pendolino* in advance, and this can be done at any travel agency as well as at the station.

If you are planning to make more than several train journeys, it is worth buying the inexpensive official train timetable book from any station kiosk. If travelling a fair distance, it is worth reserving a seat as trains tend to be crowded.

Trains are generally cheaper and more convenient than buses – at least on main routes such as Milan–Bologna–Florence– Rome. However, in the South, especially in Sicily, buses are faster and more convenient.

Significant fare reductions and special offers are available for groups and young travellers, and it is worth making enquiries about these when you arrive in Italy. Train tickets are valid for two months. Passengers must stamp their tickets in the station before boarding. If for some reason that is not possible, you must find the conductor before he finds you.

By Coach

Each province in Italy has its own inter-city bus company and each company has its own lines. It is worthwhile taking buses, especially when you are going to the mountainous interior, where they are generally faster than the train. In the South, too, buses within the province or region tend to be faster and more reliable than trains. However, even in Central Italy, some routes are better by bus: the journey from Siena to Florence, for example, is faster by bus.

Some of the principal coach companies operating long-distance travel from the main cities are listed below.

Rome
Appian Line, Piazza Esquilino 6/8, tel: 06-487861. Services and one-day tours to Florence, Assisi, Naples, Capri, Sorrento, and Pompeii.

Milan
Autostradale, Piazzale Castello 1. Services throughout Lombardy and the Lakes. The company also runs guided tours, which can be booked through the tourist office.

Trentino-Alto Adige
SAD, Via Conciapelli 60, Bolzano, tel: 0471-450111. Close to the train station. Services throughout the Dolomites area.

Genoa
AMT, Piazza della Vittoria 88, tel: 010-5997414. Services from Genoa to Alassio, Rapallo and Milan.
Pesci, Piazza della Vittoria 941, tel: 010-564936. Services from Genoa to many parts of Italy.

Florence
Lazzi, Via Mercadante 2, tel: 055-215154. Services all over Italy.
Sita, Viale dei Cadorna 105, tel: 055-278611. Services to most of Italy.

Sicily
Etna Trasporti, Via d'Amico 181, Catania, tel: 095-348141. Services to Licata, Gela, Ragusa, Caltagirone and Taormina.
Saistours Travel and Tourist Office, Via Paolo Balsamo, Palermo, tel: 091-6166027.

Services to Catania, Messina, Gela, Enna and Caltagirone.

In Rome

Buses
ATAC bus information and route maps are available from the kiosk in Piazza dei Cinquecento in front of Stazione Termini (8am–8pm, tel: 06-46954444). Buses run 5.30am–midnight. There is also a limited night service (lines indicated by 'N').

Tickets, once validated, are good for 75 minutes on all ATAC (orange) buses and for one journey on the Metro or on some urban railways, including Roma–Lido di Ostia. Bus and Metro tickets must be validated with a time stamp from the machines at the entrance to the Metro and at the rear of buses (use the rear entrance). Each time you board, use the space

Ferries and Hydrofoils

There are a great many ferryboat and hydrofoil speedboat lines that offer connections between the mainland and Italy's many large and small islands. The services run by the State Railways, the Tirrenia, Grandi Traghetti, Trans Tirreno Express and Nav.Ar.Ma. companies provide all the connections with Sicily and Sardinia. Many other lines connect the peninsula with the smaller islands. Here is some basic information regarding some shipping lines:

State Railways:
Civitavecchia–Golfo Aranci (Sardinia): departures many times a day for passengers with cars. The crossing takes nine hours.

Tirrenia Lines:
Civitavecchia–Olbia; Civitavecchia–Cagliari: both direct and via Arbatax. These

connections with Sardinia are daily for passengers and cars, with both day and night runs. Tirrenia Line also runs Genoa–Porto Torres, Genoa–Cagliari, and Naples–Cagliari (all to Sardinia), with an average crossing time of 12–15 hours.

Trans Tirreno Express:
Livorno–Olbia, particularly during the high season.

Grandi Traghetti: This line offers connections from Genoa–Porto Torres (about 11 hours) and Genoa–Palermo (22 hours), both for passengers and cars.

Traghetti Tirrenia: This Genoa-based line operates sailings to Sardinia and Sicily.

Nav.Ar.Ma: This line offers a ferry service from Piombino (Tuscany) to the island of Elba

and to Bastia (Corsica), as well as Genoa–Sardinia.

Toremar-Siremar-Caremar:
Toremar offers connections to the Tuscan islands (Elba, Giglio) while Siremar runs to the Aeolian islands and Caremar has runs from Naples to the Naples Gulf islands (Capri, Ischia).

Alimar-Aliscafi SVAV: This is a hydrofoil speedboat line which connects Naples and Palermo, via Ustica, in only five hours.

Adriatic: This service carries passengers and cars from Venice, Trieste, Ancona, Pescara, Bari and Brindisi both to Adriatic and foreign ports.

To obtain further information about fares and schedules, call in at any of the many travel agencies or the APT offices.

provided on the ticket for multiple validation stamps, making sure that the last (third) space is stamped within 75 minutes of the first. Ticket machines are in every Metro station. A one-day pass (BIG – *biglietto integrato giornaliero*), which expires at midnight on the day purchased, is also available, as well as a weekly pass (CIS – *carta integrata settimanale*) and monthly pass.

Beware of pickpockets on buses.

Metro

Two Metropolitana (under-ground) lines run 5.30am–11.30pm. Linea A runs from Ottaviano, near the Vatican, through the city centre to the eastern edge of the city (Anagnina). Linea B runs from Rebibbia in the northeast to EUR, the modern industrial zone south of the city. The lines intersect at Stazione Termini.

Like bus tickets, metro tickets can be bought from machines at stations, or from tobacconists and some bars. They must be validated in the metro station before starting your journey. They are then valid for two metro or bus trips within 75 minutes of the first validation.

In Milan

The bus and tram service (ATM) is fast and efficient. Tickets must be purchased in advance at tobacconists (*tabacchi*) or news-stands and are good for 70 minutes of travel.

The Metropolitana Milanese (MM) is the best subway in Italy. MM has two lines (1 and 2) which serve almost all the city and the hinterland. Usually tourists get on line 1, which runs south from near Stazione Centrale through Piazza del Duomo and west beyond Piazza Santa Maria delle Grazie.

Tickets are sold at machines in stations and in most *tabacchi*

and news-stands. Tickets allow 75 minutes of travel. A day ticket is valid on all forms of transport. Other good value tickets are the 24-hour ticket, the 2-day ticket, or the book of 10 tickets.

In Florence

ATAF is the city bus company. Tickets are sold at bars, tobacconists and news-stands displaying the ATAF sticker and are dispensed by special machines near bus stops. Each ticket is valid for 60 or 120 minutes of travel, during which you can change from one bus to another as often as you need. You can also get 24-hour tickets and multiple tickets. The ATAF office at Piazza Stazione will give you a free bus map, but the best transportation in Florence remains, simply, your feet.

In Venice

The city is small enough to be covered on foot and a good map is essential for exploring the maze of small streets and squares. Pick one up from the tourist office.

The main form of public transport is the *vaporetto* or water bus. The most scenic line is the No. 1 Accelerato, which takes you slowly down the Grand Canal. Line 82 provides a faster service down the Grand Canal, making only six stops and going west as far as Tronchetto (the car park island) and east to San Zaccaria (and the Lido in summer). The circular line No. 52 provides an enjoyable ride around the periphery of Venice and takes in the island of Murano.

Passengers who have not bought a ticket before boarding will be surcharged; tourists have to pay considerably more than residents, who get reduced rates. Twenty-four-hour or three-day passes are available. Note that children under 1 metre (3

feet) high travel free, but a suitcase costs as much as an adult passenger.

A private and more costly water-taxi service can be hired from most hotels in the city. If arriving at your hotel with luggage, you will need to tip someone to help carry it up to the building.

Water-Taxis & Gondolas

The alternatives to water buses are water-taxis and, of course, gondolas. The former take up to four people and, like regular taxis, display meters. You can find taxi "ranks" at main points in the city; otherwise, call 5220575 or 5222303. To understand the complex system of charges for water transport, pick up a free copy of *A Guest in Venice* from any major hotel.

The flat rate for hiring a gondola is about L80,000 for 50 minutes and L40,000 for each 25 minutes thereafter during the day, and L110,000 at night, though it is advisable to haggle. A singing gondolier costs extra. Gondolas booked as a group convoy may be cheaper – if you can face it! A recommended route is Bridge of Sighs, Santa Maria Formosa and Rialto Bridge, returning via the Grand Canal.

Very much cheaper, for those who want a quick taste, are the *traghetto* gondolas, which simply ferry people across the Grand Canal in six different places where no bridge is convenient.

In Naples

Buses run everywhere and are the only public transportation available along the waterfront. They are generally packed during rush hour. Due to the traffic's intensity, taxis are not much faster than buses and are much more expensive.

The fast, clean and frequent Metropolitana connects Stazione Centrale at one end of the city

Calling a Taxi

You can call for a taxi by dialling one of the following numbers:

Rome: Radio Taxi 3570, 3875, 4994 and 8433.
Milan: 6767, 5353, 8585 and 8388.
Florence: 4390 and 4242.
Main taxi stands are on Piazza della Repubblica and Piazza Beccaria.
Naples: 364444 and 364340.
Venice: see Water-Taxis and Gondolas.

Check the *Tutto Città* (first page) or the *Yellow Pages* for other towns not listed here.

with Mergellina on the other, with only three stops in between. Funicular railways (Funicolare Centrale, Funicolare di Chiaia, Funicolare di Montesanto) run up the steep Vomero hill. The Circumvesuviana commuter line runs from Stazione Centrale around the Bay of Naples, via Ercolano (Herculaneum), Pompeii and Castellammare di Stabia, to Sorrento. There are two lines, so check that you are on the right one.

For complete information, check the monthly tourist publication *Qui Napoli*, available at the tourist office in the train station and at major hotels.

Taxis

Cabs are found at taxi ranks or paged by telephone rather than hailed in the street. When you call, the operator will tell you the call letters of the taxi and approximately how many minutes it will take to arrive.

Fares are clocked up on meters. There is a fixed starting charge and then a charge for every kilometre (and a standing charge for traffic jams). Taxi drivers are obliged to show, if

asked, the current list of additional charges. Extra charges are added for night rides (10pm–7am), luggage, journeys outside town and journeys on Sundays and public holidays. It is a general rule to leave a small tip rounding off the fare to the nearest L1,000 or 2,000.

Private Transport

By Car
In Italy, you must drive on the right. The motorways (*autostrade*) are fast and uncrowded (except in summer), but Italians sometimes drive faster than the speed limit. Nearly all *autostrade* charge tolls and you pay as you exit.

It is compulsory to wear seat-belts at all times and infants up to nine months must occupy a baby seat. Children between nine months and four years must sit on the back seat.

Pay attention to street signs advising no-parking because police are strict on illegal parking and will remove vehicles found in no-parking areas. You'll need plenty of cash to reclaim your car. Try to park in a garage for the night: it will be a little expensive, but much safer.

In the South, especially in Naples and Palermo, where parking is a nightmare, it is best to leave your car with official car parking attendants, who wear white caps. Never leave a car under the guardianship of somebody who is not wearing a white cap; he may only be guarding his right to steal. Never leave valuables in a car.

Hitchhiking is forbidden on the *autostrade* and is not advised for women travelling alone, especially in the South.

When travelling into the mountain areas during the winter months, it is advisable to call 194 for road conditions. When there is ice and snow, chains will be required.

See page 398 for a translation of key road signs and traffic directions.

Car Rentals
Hiring a car is expensive in Italy, as is petrol. Major car rental firms such as Avis, Hertz and Europcar are represented in most cities and at all airports, though local firms often offer better rates. Agencies are listed in the *Yellow Pages* under *Autonoleggio*. Collision damage waiver and recovery in case of breakdown are usually included in the price of hiring a vehicle, but be sure to check exclusions carefully. Additional insurance cover is usually available at fixed rates. Also, make sure that the price you are quoted includes VAT (IVA), which is levied at 19 percent.

The renter must be over 21 and must be in possession of a valid driver's licence (an EU licence, an international driving licence or a national driving licence with Italian translation). A deposit equal to the cost of hiring the vehicle is usually required, or a credit card imprint.

Driving Speeds

The following speed limits apply to cars in Italy:

Urban areas:
50 km/h (30 mph)
Roads outside urban areas:
90 km/h (55 mph)
Dual carriageways outside urban areas: 110 km/h (70 mph)
Motorways (*autostrade*):
130 km/h (80 mph);
for cars less than 1100cc:
110 km/h (70 mph)

Where to Stay

Choosing a Hotel

Italy has a wonderful variety of accommodation in all categories, from grand villas to small family-run hotels, as well as the newly-developing sector of *Agriturismo* – farm holidays. All the major international chains are represented in Italy, with Jolly and Hilton being two of the most common. However, there are also burgeoning groups of highly individualistic hotels that have banded together to present a common front. They tend to be independent hotels that are linked by their atmosphere, style and cost to others in different areas. Be sure to call or write beforehand to verify facilities and make reservations. Smaller hotels are not necessarily cheaper – some of the more exclusive small hotels match the grand hotels in style and expense – but even inexpensive hotels usually offer basic comforts and good service.

Hotel Listings

The following listings offer a selection of hotels at all levels. Your travel agent or the APT offices in Italy can give more complete information on these and other hotels.

ROME

Grand Hotels

The Cardinal
Via Giulia 62
Tel: 06-6542719.
Fax: 06-6786376.

In the medieval part of the city and close to the Vatican. An atmospheric hotel. **LLL**

Cavalieri Hilton
Via Cadlolo 101.
Tel: 06-35091.
Fax: 06-3509 2241.
At the top of the hill of Monte Mario: a resort hotel in Rome, offering a swimming pool, tennis courts and more. **LLLL**

D'Inghilterra
Via Bocca di Leone 14.
Tel: 06-69981.
Fax: 06-69922243.
Very traditional and old-fashioned hotel in a good location in the centre of the main shopping area. Ernest Hemingway, Anatole France and Alec Guinness all stayed here.
LLLL

Excelsior
Via Vittorio Veneto 125.
Tel: 06-47081.
Fax: 06-4826205.
Preferred by Americans, this grand hotel has been a meeting-place for actors, actresses and society people for almost half a century. **LLLL**

Forum
Via Tor de' Conti 25.
Tel: 06-6792446.
Fax: 06-6786479.
Charming hotel in the Roman Forum area, with a view of the ancient city from its roof garden. 82 rooms. **LLLL**

Hassler-Villa Medici
Piazza Trinità dei Monti 6.
Tel: 06-699340.
Fax: 00-6789991.
Ideally located at the top of the Spanish Steps, this hotel is one of the best in Rome. It provides excellent food and service and

Price Categories

Price categories are based on a double room without breakfast:
L = under L150,000
LL = L150,000–250,000
LLL = L250,000–400,000
LLLL = more than L400,000

free bicycles for exploring the city. Particularly beautiful is the roof garden restaurant, with its view of the city (good for Sunday brunch). **LLL–LLLL**

Hotel Select
Via V. Bachelet 6 (off Piazza Independenza).
Tel: 06-4456383.
Fax: 06-4441086.
This comfortable 3-star hotel is part of the *Logis d'Italia* group (see *Hotel Groups* opposite). The hallmarks are value for money and hospitality. The hotel is convenient for Termini station and has a pleasant courtyard for summer drinks. **LLL**

Jolly Hotel Vittorio Veneto
Corso d'Italia 1.
Tel: 06-8495.
Fax: 06-8841104.
High-quality Jolly service, as in the other hotels of the chain. **LLL**

Le Grand Hotel
Via Vittorio Emanuele Orlando 3.
Tel: 06-47091.
Fax: 06-4747307.
Located between the railway station and the Via Veneto area, this formal, dignified hotel belongs to the Ciga chain and, like all the others, is very well run and stylish. **LLL**

Lord Byron
Via Giuseppe de Notaris 5.
Tel: 06-3220404.
Fax: 06-3220405.
Close to Villa Borghese, this first-class small hotel looks like a private club. Only 47 rooms, but also a good restaurant (Le Jardin). **LLL–LLLL**

Nazionale
Piazza di Montecitorio 131.
Tel: 06-695001.
Fax: 06-6786677.
Near the Chamber of Deputies, this is another central hotel famous for former guests, including Simone de Beauvoir and her husband, Jean-Paul Sartre. 78 rooms. **LLLL**

Parco dei Principi
Via G. Mercadante 15.
Tel: 06-854421.
Fax: 06-8845104.

Modern hotel, with a swimming pool, on the edge of Villa Borghese. **LLLL**

Raphael
Largo Febo 2.
Tel: 06-682831.
Fax: 06-6878993.
Close to Piazza Navona and near the Senate and the Chamber of Deputies, this hotel attracts many Italian politicians. Service is good, but not excellent. **LLLL**

Small Hotels

Columbus
Via della Conciliazione 33.
Tel: 06-6865435.
Fax: 06-6864874.
Three-star hotel near St Peter's, with ancient furniture and 107 rooms. **LLL**

Fontana
Piazza di Trevi 96.
Tel: 06-6786133.
Fax: 06-6790024.
In a restored 13th-century monastery next to the Trevi Fountain, with a beautiful rooftop bar. **LLL**

Gregoriana
Via Gregoriana 18.
Tel: 06-6794269.
Fax: 06-6784258.
The attraction here is the Art Deco interior, with room letters by the celebrated 1930s fashion illustrator Erte. The hotel has only 19 rooms and no restaurant. **LL–LLL**

Hotel Doria
Via Merulana 4.
Tel: 06-44465888.

Fax: 06-44465889.
Simple, recently refurbished hotel just five minutes' walk from Stazione Termini. Small and clean, it offers TV and mini-bar in some rooms. A good sightseeing base. **LL**

La Residenza
Via Emilia 22.
Tel: 06-4880789.
Fax: 06-485721.
Situated off the busy Via Veneto, this is a small, quiet hotel with only 27 bedrooms. **LLL**

Margutta
Via Laurina 34.
Tel: 06-3223674.
Fax: 06-3200395.
Near Piazza del Popolo, this hotel has no restaurant, but is still pleasant. **LL**

Hotel Groups

The following is a selection of the most noteworthy hotel groups.

Charming Hotels: This delightful group of luxurious, independent Italian hotels is characterised by its impeccable taste in atmospheric locations, use of authentic antiques and excellent traditional cuisine. There are Charming Hotels in Como, Milan, Florence, Siena and Venice, amongst other places. You can book through head office in Rome: Via Pinciana 25, tel: 06-8411940; fax: 06-85210210, in the UK through Liaisons Abroad, tel: 0171-376 4020; fax: 0171-376 4442, or in the USA through European Connection, Roslyn Heights, New York, tel: 310-541 0028; fax: 310-541 1359; toll free 800 541 5412. Hotel Londra Palace (*see page 370*) is typical of the group.

Sina Hotels: This small hotel group, founded by an Italian aristocrat, runs a collection of stylish and luxurious hotels in six major Italian cities: Milan, Parma, Viareggio, Florence,

Perugia and Rome. The hotels are all different yet have a certain elegance and formality in common. Villa Medici (*see page 372*) is typical of the group. You can book the hotels directly or through Sina Hotels in Rome: Piazza Barberini 23, tel: 06-4870222; fax: 06-4874778.

Turin Hotels: This group began in Turin and manages traditional, classic hotels in the regions of Piedmont and Liguria. The hotels are characterised by high Piedmontese standards of service, classical or neo-classical buildings and excellent cuisine. They are all 4-star and include the Turin Palace Hotel (*see page 368*) and the Excelsior Palace Hotel in Rapallo. Hotels can be booked through Turin Hotels International, Turin, tel: 011-5151911; fax: 011-5617191.

Logis d'Italia: This group operates on the same principles as the better-known French group, Logis de France. The group's 90–100 hotels are found all over Italy and are

listed in the *Logis d'Italia* guide, available from bookshops or the Italian tourist office. The group's principles are founded on value for money, hospitality and size (most are small, and many are family run). Hotels can be booked through a central reservations system in Milan, tel: 02-48519285; fax: 02-48519265, or booked direct. A typical hotel in the group is Hotel Select in Rome (*see page 366*).

Abitare La Storia: This new hotel grouping operates under the banner of 'Living History', or 'Bringing History Alive'. It is an association of independently-run hotels, each of which is housed in an historic palazzo or villa, often with lovely grounds. The keynotes are tradition and atmosphere, which are often matched by a choice of good regional cuisine. This group of keenly-priced 3- and 4-star hotels has a typical representative in Hotel Ripagrande in Ferrara (*see page 372*).

MILAN

Grand Hotels
Duca di Milano
Piazza della Repubblica 13.
Tel: 02-62841.
Fax: 02-6555966.
Impressive hotel with spacious
suites. **LLLL**
Excelsior Gallia
Piazza Duca d'Aosta 9.
Tel: 02-6785.
Fax: 02-66713239.
Luxury-category, historic hotel
located close to Stazione
Centrale, near the air terminal
and business centre. Expensive,
but service is perfection. **LLLL**
Executive Hotel
Via Don Luigi Sturzo 45.
Tel: 02-6294.
Fax: 02-29010238.
First-rate service and a good
restaurant. **LLLL**
Hotel Principe di Savoia
Piazza della Repubblica 17.
Tel: 02-62301.
Fax: 02-6595838.
Located north of the cathedral,
this is a classic luxury hotel,
with superb service. Elegant
reception rooms; 298
bedrooms; swimming pool and
sauna. **LLLL**

Milanese Hotels

During the big seasonal
fashion shows, hotel rates in
Milan double.

Jolly President
Largo Augusto 10.
Tel: 02-77461.
Fax: 02-783449.
Excellent member of the Jolly
chain. **LLL–LLLL**
Jolly Touring
Via Ugo Tarchetti 2.
Tel: 02-6335.
Fax: 02-6592209.
Top class comfort. **LLL–LLLL**
Milano Hilton
Via Galvani 12.
Tel: 02-69831.
Fax: 02-66710810.

Contemporary hotel, decorated
in a provincial/modern style.
Located in the new commercial
centre of the city. **LLLL**
Palace Hotel
Piazza della Repubblica 20.
Tel: 02-63361.
Fax: 02-654485.
Close to the railway station, in
front of the **Principe di Savoia**,
this very comfortable hotel has
been renovated in an ultra-
modern style. Well known
restaurant. **LLL–LLLL**

Small Hotels
Antica Locanda Solferino
Via Castelfidardo 2.
Tel: 02-6570129.
Fax: 02-6571361.
This is a delightful hotel, with
old-fashioned furniture and
atmosphere. From the windows,
you can look out on the Brera
quarter. Romantic restaurant. **LL**
Sant'Ambroeus
Via Papiniano 14.
Tel: 02-48008989.
Fax: 02-48008687.
Friendly, cosy hotel near Solari
Park and the Metro. **L–LL**

LOMBARDY & THE LAKES

Bellagio
Villa Serbelloni
Via Roma 1.
Tel: 031-950216.
Fax: 031-951529.
This fabulous patrician villa has
been converted into one of the
finest hotels in Northern Italy.
The views, grounds, facilities
and service are all impeccable.
LLLL

Bergamo
Excelsior San Marco
Piazza della Repubblica 6.
Tel: 035-366111.
Fax: 035-223201.
Impressive modern hotel with
efficient service and good
facilities. Roof garden. **LL–LLL**

Como
Barchetta Excelsior
Piazza Cavour 1.

Tel: 031-3221.
Fax: 031-302622.
Rather anonymous modern hotel
redeemed by its central location.
Request a room overlooking the
lake. **LLL**

Sirmione
Grand Hotel Terme
Viale Marconi 7.
Tel: 030-916261.
Fax: 030-916568.
Elegant, well-modernised hotel
in attractive grounds. Good
facilities include a pool, sauna
and fitness centre. **LLLL**
Golf & Suisse
Via XXV Aprile.
Tel: 030-9904188.
Fax: 030-916304.
Small, family-run hotel close to
the lake, with a small pool.
Rather anonymous bedrooms
but there's a friendly welcome
and lavish breakfasts. No
restaurant but several nearby. **L**

PIEDMONT

Turin
City
Via F. Juvarra 25.
Tel: 011-540546.
Fax: 011-548188.
Small, comfortable hotel close
to the station of Porta Susa,
with 61 bedrooms. **LL–LLL**
Jolly Hotel Ambasciatori
Corso Vittorio Emanuele 104.
Tel: 011-5752.
Fax: 011-544978.
Favoured by business people.
Good location and service. **LLL**
Jolly Hotel Principe di Piemonte
Via Piero Gobetti 15.
Tel: 011-5629693.
Fax: 011-5620270.
The most central hotel in Turin.
Very comfortable, with excellent
service. **LLLL**
Turin Palace Hotel
Via Sacchi 8.
Tel: 011-5625511.
Fax: 011-5612187.
Flagship of Turin Hotel Group
(see *Hotel Groups* page 367): a
classic and elegant hotel

convenient for Porta Nuova station. **LL–LLL**
Villa Sassi
Strada Traforo del Pino 47.
Tel: 011-8980556.
Fax: 011-8980095.
This hotel is housed in an 18th-century villa, in a great park. There are only 12 bedrooms, but excellent service and comfort. Exclusive. **LLL**

VALLE D'AOSTA

Aosta
Europe
Piazza Narbonne 8.
Tel: 0165-236363.
Fax: 0165-40566.
Set in the historic centre, this is a traditional hotel, noted for its peace and quiet as well as elegance. **LL–LLL**
Hostellerie du Cheval Blanc
Via Clavité 20.
Tel/Fax: 0165-239140.
Functional yet friendly hotel, well set up for winter sports, with a sauna and a heated pool. **LL**

LIGURIA & RIVIERA

Genoa
Bristol Palace
Via XX Settembre 35.
Tel: 010-592541.
Fax: 010-561756.
Despite its modest entrance, this is a well-furnished hotel – particularly the dining-room, which is decorated in the Louis XVI style. Good service. **LLL**
Plaza
Via M. Piaggio 11.
Tel: 010-8393641.
Fax: 010-8391850.
Small villa transformed into lodgings in an ideal location near Piazza Corvetto. **LL–LLL**
Savoia Majestic
Piazza Acquaverde.
Tel: 010-261641.
Fax: 010-261883.
Comfortable, good service, in a central position by Principe station. **LLL**

Price Categories

Price categories are based on a double room without breakfast:
L = under L150,000
LL = L150,000–250,000
LLL = L250,000–400,000
LLLL = more than L400,000

Alassio
Grand Hotel Diana
Via Garibaldi 110.
Tel: 0182-642701.
Fax: 0182-640304.
Open April–October, with good service, a swimming pool and a terrace-garden. Half-board mandatory. **LLLL**

Bordighera
Grand Hotel Cap Ampelio
Via Virgilio 5.
Tel: 0184-264333.
Fax: 0184-2642.
Ideally located on the hill of Bordighera, this refined hotel has a splendid view over the sea and coastline. **LL**
Grand Hotel del Mare
Capo Migliarese.
Tel: 0184-262201.
Fax: 0184-262394.
Hotel overlooking the sea, preferred by adults for its quietness, its comfort and its beautiful rooms. **LLL**

Camogli
Cenobio dei Dogi
Via Cuneo 34.
Tel: 0185-7241.
Fax: 0185-772796.
This hotel, in a wonderful spot overlooking the sea, is surrounded by a splendid park. It is well known for its beautiful rooms, restaurant, salt-water swimming pool and solarium, its private beach and its nightclub during the summer. **LLLL**

Portofino
Splendido
Viale Barratta 16.
Tel: 0185-269551.
Fax: 0185-269614.

One of Italy's finest hotels. This hotel is a peaceful oasis along a street lined with olive trees, affording a splendid view of the Portofino promontory. Every comfort and great cuisine. **LLLL**

Rapallo
Hotel Europa
Via Milite Ignoto 2.
Tel: 0185-669521.
Fax: 0185-669847.
Part of the Turin Hotels group, this Art Nouveau hotel was restored to its former glory in 1996. Fine restaurant, as well as fitness centre. **LLL**

Santa Margherita Ligure
Imperial Palace
Via Pagana 19.
Tel: 0185-288991.
Fax: 0185-284223.
Luxury, big hotel in the classic tradition, surrounded by a tropical garden. Old-fashioned decor with antique furnishings, big rooms and excellent service. **LLL–LLLL**

San Remo
Grand Hotel Londra
Corso Matuzia 2.
Tel: 0184-668000.
Fax: 0184-668073.
Set on the seafront, close to the casino. Old, quiet and pleasant. **LLL**
Royal
Corso Imperatrice 80.
Tel: 0184-5391.
Fax: 0184-661445.
Luxury-category hotel surrounded by terraced gardens filled with flowers and palm trees. This is a classic hotel, with big, comfortable rooms which overlook the sea or the hills. **LLLL**

Sestri Levante
Grand Hotel dei Castelli
Via alla Penisola 26.
Tel: 0185-487220.
Fax: 0185-44767.
Very quiet and pleasant hotel In front of the church of S. Niccolò,

surrounded by a big park and overlooking the sea. An elevator descends to the hotel's private beach. The service is excellent. **LLL**

Ventimiglia
La Riserva
Castel d'Appio 71.
Tel: 0184-229533.
Fax: 0184-229712.
Set 5 km outside the town of Ventimiglia, this is a small place with a wonderful view of the Riviera dei Fiori and the Costa Azzurra. The rooms are comfortable and the service, whilst homely, is also courteous. **LL**

VENICE

Grand Hotels
Cipriani
Isola della Giudecca 10.
Tel: 041-5207744.
Fax: 041-5203930.
A small oasis hidden on the tip of the island of Giudecca, the Cipriani feels far removed from the city centre. Among its comforts are lavish bedrooms furnished with Fortuny fabrics, a swimming pool (one of the only private pools in Venice), gardens and tennis courts, a yacht harbour, piano bar and a launch service which whisks you, in a couple of minutes, to San Marco. **LLLL**

Danieli
Riva degli Schiavoni 4196, Castello.
Tel: 041-5226480.
Fax: 041-5200208.
Part of the Ciga chain of hotels, the Danieli is rich with memories of eminent guests: George Sand, Alfred de Musset, Dickens, Balzac, Wagner, kings, princes, stars. The splendid Gothic foyer, built around a courtyard, is an attraction in itself, and the rooms are very comfortable. The roof garden restaurant has a splendid view over the lagoon. **LLLL**

Europa & Regina Hotel
San Marco Corte Barozzi 2159.
Tel: 041-5200477.
Fax: 041-5231533.
In front of the baroque Church of the Salute, with rooms overlooking the Grand Canal, this old hotel has been tastefully redecorated and the service is first-class. **LLLL**

Excelsior Hotel
Lungomare Marconi 41, Lido di Venezia.
Tel: 041-5260201.
Fax: 041-5267276.
A member of the Ciga chain, this is a huge luxury beach hotel with a facade reminiscent of a Moorish castle. Attractions include numerous sports facilities and a free launch service to Venice. **LLLL**

Venetian Hotels

Hotel rates in Venice are about 30 percent higher than those on the mainland, but the prices are worth it for the atmosphere.

Grand Hotel des Bains
Lungomare Marconi 17.
Tel: 041-5265921.
Fax: 041-5260113.
Ciga-run, this grand old hotel is remembered for its role in Thomas Mann's *Death in Venice*. It is located across the road from its private beach. Facilities similar to those at the Excelsior (*see bottom left*). **LLLL**

Gritti Palace Ciga Hotel
Campo Santa Maria del Giglio 2467, San Marco.
Tel: 041-794611.
Fax: 041-5200942.
The most elegant hotel in Venice, renowned for its formal luxury, charming setting (right on the Grand Canal) and discreet, attentive service. Doge Andrea Gritti lived here and the hotel still has the air of a private palazzo. Hemingway, Winston Churchill, Herbert von Karajan and Greta Garbo all stayed here.

The cuisine, which you enjoy on the canalside terrace, is very refined. **LLLL**

Londra Palace
Riva degli Schiavoni 4171.
Tel: 041-5200533.
Fax: 041-5225032.
This elegant hotel is a flagship of the Charming Hotels group (see *Hotel Groups* page 367). It overlooks the lagoon and has a romantic bar and excellent restaurant. **LLLL**

Small Hotels
Accademia
Fondamenta Bollani 1058, Dorsoduro.
Tel: 041-5210188.
Fax: 041-5239152.
Reservations should be made months in advance for this sought-after pensione. Close to the Accademia gallery, it is a 17th-century villa with delightful gardens front and back. **LL–LLL**

Bucintoro
Riva San Biagio 2135, Castello.
Tel: 041-5223240.
Fax: 041-5222424.
Simply furnished, friendly pensione on the waterfront with splendid views over the Basin of San Marco and the island of San Giorgio Maggiore. **LL**

Flora
Calle De La Pegola 2283/A.
Tel: 041-5205844.
Fax: 041-5228217.
Charming, friendly hotel within five minutes' walk of Piazza San Marco. The garden, with fountains and flower beds, is particularly appealing. Bedrooms vary enormously and can be quite basic. **LLL**

La Fenice et des Artistes
Campo San Fantin, San Marco 1936.
Tel: 041-5232333.
Fax: 041-5203721.
Within a stone's throw of the Fenice Opera House (presently closed), this hotel is usually popular with actors, musicians and artists. **LLL**

Metropole
Riva degli Schiavoni 4149.

Tel: 041-5205044.
Fax: 041-5223679.
In front of St George's Island.
Beautifully furnished with
excellent service. **LLLL**
Monaco & Grand Canal
Calle Vallaresso, San Marco
1325.
Tel: 041-5200211.
Fax: 041-5200501.
First-category hotel located
where the Grand Canal flows into
the Laguna. Very intimate and
comfortable, though the rooms
are perhaps a little small and
sometimes noisy. Good service.
LLLL
San Cassiano
Calle della Rosa 2232,
Santa Croce.
Tel: 041-5241768.
Fax: 041-721033.
One of the few hotels actually on
the Grand Canal, the San
Cassiano is converted from a
14th-century palazzo. About half
the rooms have canalside views
looking across to the Ca' d'Oro.
LLL
Saturnia & International
Calle Larga XXII Marzo 2398.
Tel: 041-5208377.
Fax: 041-5207131.
Very romantic hotel housed in a
16th-century palace close to
bustling Piazza San Marco. Both
intimate and comfortable. **LLLL**

THE VENETO

Verona
Due Torri Baglioni
Piazza S. Anastasia 4.
Tel: 045-595044.
Fax: 045-8004130.
This grand classical *palazzo* has
been well converted into a
luxurious hotel and has an
excellent, if rather formal,
restaurant with a fine wine list.
LLLL
Victoria
Via Adua 8.
Tel: 045-590566.
Fax: 045-590155.
Set in the heart of the old
quarter of Verona, this historic

palazzo has been creatively yet
sensitively converted. The
bedrooms are superbly inviting
while the reception rooms
incorporate Roman and medieval
remains, including some
mosaics. **LLL**

Vicenza
Campo Marzio
Viale Roma 21.
Tel: 0444-545700.
Fax: 0444-320495.
A convenient hotel, though not
particularly individualistic. It is
near the park and within easy
reach of the railway station. **LLL**

TRENTINO-ALTO ADIGE

Cognola
Villa Madruzzo
Località Ponte Alto 26 (3 km
from Trento).
Tel: 0461-986220.
Fax: 0461-986361.
A grand hill-top villa set in
charming grounds. An elegant
interior is matched by pleasing
service and good traditional
cuisine, with mushroom dishes
a local speciality. **LL**

Trento
Buonconsiglio
Via Romagnosi 18.
Tel: 0461-272888.
Fax: 0461-272889.
A stylish, modern hotel suitable
for business and leisure
travellers. Well-equipped and
close to the historic centre. **LL**
Hotel America
Via Torre Verde 52.
Tel: 0461-983010.
Fax: 0461-230603.

Long-established hotel set in the
historic heart of Trento. Good
service. **LL**

FRIULI-VENEZIA GIULIA

Trieste
Duchi d'Aosta
Piazza Unità d'Italia 2.
Tel: 040-7600011.
Fax: 040-3660921.
This hotel is small but very
charming, with big, well-
furnished rooms, and efficient
service, in a convenient, central
position. Be sure to try the
excellent restaurant (Harry's
Grill). **LLL**
Jolly
Corso Cavour 7.
Tel: 040-7600055.
Fax: 040-362699.
Jolly-style hotel with the usual
great service and comfort. **LLL**
Savoia Excelsior Palace
Riva del Mandracchio 4.
Tel: 040-77941.
Fax: 040-638260.
Every comfort. **LLL**

EMILIA-ROMAGNA

Bologna
Grand Hotel Elite
Via Aurelio Saffi 36.
Tel: 051-6491432
Fax: 051-649242.
Very modern and comfortable,
with one of the best restaurants
in Bologna. **LLL**
Jolly
Piazza XX Settembre 2.
Tel: 051-248921.
Fax: 051-249764.
Close to the station and the
Alitalia terminal. Large and
comfortable. **LLL–LLLL**
Royal Carlton
Via Montebello 8.
Tel: 051-249361.
Fax: 051-249724.
This large hotel is extremely
comfortable and close to the
centre of Bologna. Excellent
service, but perhaps a little
anonymous. **LLLL**

Ferrara
Duchessa Isabella
Via Palestro 70.
Tel: 0532-202121.
Fax: 0532-202638.
This frescoed 16th-century
palazzo features inlaid ceilings
and a lovely garden. **LLLL**
Hotel Ripagrande
Via Ripagrande 21.
Tel: 0532-765250.
Fax: 0532-764377.
Renaissance palace forming part
of Abitare La Storia (Living
History), a group of historic
independent hotels (see *Hotel
Groups* on page 367). Fine
cuisine and a central location. **LLL**

Parma
Grand Hotel Baglioni
Via Piacenza 14.
Tel: 0521-292929.
Fax: 0521-292828.
Sophisticated modern hotel
within walking distance of the
historic centre. Spacious
bedrooms and a good
restaurant. **LLL**
Villa Ducale
Via del Popolo 35.
Tel: 0521-272727.
Fax: 0521-780756.
Charming villa set in appealing
grounds; welcoming. **LLL**

Ravenna
Bisanzio
Via Salara 30.
Tel: 0544-217111.
Fax: 0544-32539.
Modern, comfortable hotel, with
good service, close to the most
important monuments. **LL**
Jolly
Piazza Mameli 1.
Tel: 0544-35762.
Fax: 0544-216055.
Hotel with excellent standards
and a restaurant. **LL**

FLORENCE

Grand Hotels
Excelsior
Piazza Ognissanti 3.
Tel: 055-264201.

Fax: 055-210278.
In the luxury category,
overlooking the Arno, which you
can admire from the terrace
restaurant. Service tends to be
under par but the location is
ideal. **LLLL**
Hotel de la Ville
Piazza Antinori 1.
Tel: 055-2381805.
Fax: 055-2381809.
Quiet and elegant, located in the
centre of Florence, next to Via
de' Tornabuoni. Good service
and comfort. **LLLL**
Savoy
Piazza della Repubblica 7.
Tel: 055-283313.
Fax: 055-284840.
In the heart of Florence, this
hotel is classic in style and
service. Many rooms are
decorated in Venetian style. **LLL**
Villa Cora
Viale Machiavelli 18.
Tel: 055-2298541.
Fax: 055-229086.
Luxury category. Located on the
hills of Florence but still
convenient for the city centre.
Built by the Baron Oppenheim in
a neoclassical style, this hotel
hosted Eugenia di Montijo, the
widow of Napoleon III, and the
rich Baroness Von Meck,
patroness of Tchaikovsky and
Debussy. It offers a quiet
atmosphere, a huge park and a
pool. **LLLL**
Villa Medici
Via il Prato 42.
Tel: 055-2381331.
Fax: 055-2381336.
With its huge bedrooms, roof
garden restaurant and swimming
pool, this 18th-century villa hotel
offers everything you could
desire, including a good location
near the railway station. **LLLL**

Small Hotels
Beacci Tornabuoni
Via de' Tornabuoni 3.
Tel: 055-212645.
Fax: 055-283594.
This small and attractive
pensione occupies the top floors
of a Renaissance *palazzo* on the

most elegant street in Florence.
LLL
Hotel Regency
Piazza d'Azeglio 3.
Tel: 055-245247.
Fax: 055-2346735
This is the right place for people
who like quiet and comfort. The
hotel offers a charming garden,
beautiful furniture, a gourmet
restaurant and a central
position. **LLLL**
Lungarno
Borgo San Jacopo 14.
Tel: 055-27261.
Fax: 055-268437.
This stylish hotel overlooks the
Arno between Ponte Vecchio and

Price Categories

Price categories are based
on a double room without
breakfast:
L = under L150,000
LL = L150,000–250,000
LLL = L250,000–400,000
LLLL = more than L400,000

Ponte Santa Trinità. **LLLL**
Pensione Annalena
Via Romana 34.
Tel: 055-222402.
Fax: 055-222403.
Located across the Ponte
Vecchio, just beyond the Pitti
Palace, this little place offers a
lovely Florentine experience at
reasonable prices. **LLL**
Pensione Bencistà
Fiesole.
Tel/Fax: 055-59163.
Situated outside the city,
between Fiesole and San
Domenico, this hotel in a 15th-
century villa is small and simple,
with no phones in the rooms.
Rates are moderate. Closed:
November to mid-March. **LL**
Villa Le Rondini
Via Bolognese Vecchia 224,
Trespiano (7 km from Florence).
Tel: 055-400081.
Fax: 055-268212.
Villa in lovely grounds, with a
swimming pool in olive groves.
LLL

TUSCANY

Arezzo
Castello di Gargonza
Monte San Savino 52048.
Tel: 0575-847021.
Fax: 0575-847054.
Meticulously restored country hamlet in the Tuscan hills between Arezzo and Siena. Visitors stay in modernised 13th-century cottages. Excellent restaurant. **LL**

Lucca
Hotel Villa Rinascimento
Santa Maria del Guidice.
Tel: 0583-378292.
Fax: 0583-370238.
This beautifully restored Renaissance villa lies on the road to Pisa and is 9 km from Lucca. The interior is simple yet lovely; the grounds include a pool and olive groves. **LL**

San Gimignano
Villa San Paolo
Strada per Certaldo.
Tel: 0577-955100.
Fax: 0577-955126.
This delightful classical villa lies 4 km from San Gimignano. The grounds include a pool and tennis courts. **LLL**

Siena
Certosa di Maggiano
Via Certosa 82.
Tel: 0577-288180.
Fax: 0577-288189.
This unique 14th-century Carthusian monastery is the oldest in Tuscany. Now a 5-star hotel, it is adorned with antiques and offers a prestigious restaurant, library and lovely cloisters. **LLLL**
Garden
Via Custoza 2.
Tel: 0577-47056.
Fax: 0577-46050.
This 16th-century patrician villa is now a comfortable hotel with formal Italian gardens and a swimming pool. Very welcoming.
LL

UMBRIA & THE MARCHES

Perugia
La Rosetta
Piazza Italia 19.
Tel/fax: 075-5720841.
Good hotel with a new and an old part. Eat in the courtyard under pergolas and palms in the summer. Fine service. **LL**
Le Tre Vaselle
Torgiano Perugia.
Tel: 075-9880447.
Fax: 075-9880214.
A few kilometres from Perugia, this is a wonderful small hotel in a 17th-century villa owned by Giorgio Lungarotti, one of the most famous wine collectors in Italy. Pleasant atmosphere and great cooking. **LLL**

Assisi
Subasio
Via Frate Elia 2.
Tel: 075-812206.
Fax: 075-816691.
The columns of this hotel link to the church of San Francesco, and the terraces command a wonderful view of the town and countryside. Many famous people have stayed here, including the king and queen of Belgium, and actors Charlie Chaplin, James Stewart and Marlene Dietrich. Good rooms and service. **LL**
Umbra
Vicolo degli Archi 6.
Tel: 075-812240.
Fax: 075-813653.
Close to the Piazza del Comune, this is the most central hotel in Assisi. Though small, rooms are comfortable and the restaurant is very good. **LL**

Urbino
Bonconte
Via delle Mura 28.
Tel: 0722-2463.
Fax: 0722-4782.
Charming villa-hotel in the walled town. The interior is comfortable and elegant. **LL–LLL**

ABRUZZO & MOLISE

L'Aquila
Duca degli Abruzzi
Viale Giovanni XXIII 10.
Tel: 0862-28341.
Fax: 0862-61588
A second category hotel that is very well run. From the restaurant there is a wide view of the L'Aquila area. **L**
Campobasso
Skanderbeg
Via Novelli 3B.
Tel: 0874-413341.
Fax: 0874-416340.
The best hotel in town, comfortable. **L**

Pescara
Esplanade
Piazza 1 Maggio 46.
Tel: 085-529241.
Old-style hotel with a modernised interior, right across from the beach. Excellent views.
LL

NAPLES
Best Western Paradiso
Via Catullo 11.
Tel: 081-7614161.
Fax: 081-7613449.
Hotel located in a quiet, residential area on the hill of Posillipo, enjoying views of the sea and the port. **LLL**
Britannique
Corso Vittorio Emanuele 133.
Tel: 081-7614145.
Fax: 081-660457.
Hotel attached to Parker's (see below), in the first category with good service. **LL**
Excelsior
Via Partenope 48.
Tel: 081-7640111.
Fax: 081-7649743.
A Ciga hotel just across the street from the Castel dell'Ovo, with a wonderful view of the Gulf of Naples. **LLLL**
Jolly
Via Medina 70.
Tel: 081-416000.
Fax: 081-5518010.

This modern high-rise hotel has a roof-garden restaurant affording magnificent views of the city. **LLL**

Parker's
Corso Vittorio Emanuele 135.
Tel: 081-7612474.
Fax: 081-663527.
This first-category hotel is located in a 19th-century palace. The decor is casual; the service is good. **LLL**

Royal
Via Partenope 38.
Tel: 081-7644800.
Fax: 081-7645707.
Elegant hotel on the seafront. Good service; large conference hall. Popular with business travellers. **LLL**

Vesuvio
Via Partenope 45.
Tel: 081-7640044.
Fax: 081-7644483.
Another top hotel just down the street from the Excelsior. **LLLL**

CAMPANIA COAST

Capri
La Palma
Corso Vittorio Emanuele 39.
Tel: 081-8370133.
Fax: 081-8376966.
Located in the shopping area. Sauna available. **LLLL**

Punta Tragara
Via Tragara, 57.
Tel: 081-8370844.
Fax: 081-8377790.
Comfortable and quiet with a beautiful view of the Faraglioni. Min. 3 night stay July/August. **LLLL**

Ischia
Il Moresco
Via Emanuele Gianturco, 16.
Tel: 081-981355.
Fax: 081-992338.
Sited on the beach with good service and comfortable rooms. **LL–LLL**

Punta Molino
Ischia Porto, Via C. Colombo 23.
Tel: 081-991544
Fax: 081-991562.

Located near a pine wood. Good service. **LLL**

Regina Isabella
Piazza Santa Restituta 1, Lacco Ameno Ischia.
Tel: 081-994322.
Fax: 081-900190.
Located in a small port. Thermal bath available. Min. 3 night stay July/August. **LLLL**

Sorrento
Ambasciatori
Via Califano 18.
Tel: 081-8782025.
Fax: 081-8071021.
Quiet, with a swimming pool and large garden. **LLLL**

Excelsior Vittoria
Piazza Tasso 34.
Tel: 081-8071044.
Fax: 081-8771206.
This is a very old, elegant hotel, affording views across the port of Sorrento. **LLLL**

Price Categories

Price categories are based on a double room without breakfast:
L = under L150,000
LL = L150,000–250,000
LLL = L250,000–400,000
LLLL = more than L400,000

APULIA

Bari
Jolly
Via Giulio Pietroni 15.
Tel: 080-5564366.
Fax: 080-5565219.
New, comfortable and quiet hotel typical of the Jolly style. **LLL**

Palace Hotel
Via Lombardi 13.
Tel: 080-5216551.
Fax: 080-5211499.
Modern, big, comfortable hotel. **LL–LLL**

Lecce
President
Via Salandra 6.
Tel: 0832-311881.

Fax: 0832-372283.
This is a top-class hotel offering good service. **LL**

BASILICATA & CALABRIA

Cosenza
San Michele
Località Bosco 8/9, Cetraro.
Tel: 0982-91012.
Fax: 0982-91430.
This hotel enjoys a magnificent setting, above a sheer drop to the sea. Located in a wonderful park, it offers plenty of comforts, including tennis courts, a swimming pool and a lift to the beach. **LLL**

Reggio Calabria
Excelsior
Via Vittorio Veneto 66.
Tel: 0965-812211.
Fax: 0965-893084.
First-category hotel offering very comfortable rooms and good service. **LL**

SICILY

Palermo
Jolly
Foro Italico 22.
Tel: 091-6165090.
Fax: 091-6161441.
Big, modern hotel near the seafront, offering all the top-class comforts and service typical of hotels in the Jolly chain. **LLL**

Villa Igea
Salita Belmonte 43.
Tel: 091-543744.
Fax: 091-547654.
Near the Lido di Mondello, under the Monte Pellegrino, this villa was built by the architect Basile for Don Ignazio Florio, a famous Sicilian shipowner. The outside looks like a Norman palace, but the interior is richly decorated with stucco floral decorations in the Liberty style. Outside there are terraces and a park with a swimming pool which overlooks the sea. **LLL**

Agrigento
Jolly dei Templi
Parco Angeli Villaggio Mosé.
Tel: 0922-606144.
Fax: 0922-606685.
This is a modern hotel and, though the surroundings are a little bit noisy, the rooms are comfortable and the service is good. **LL**

Messina
Jolly Hotel dello Stretto
Via Garibaldi 126.
Tel: 090-363860.
Fax: 090-5902526.
First-category hotel situated near Messina's harbour, offering every comfort at moderate prices. **LL**

Siracusa
Jolly
Corso Gelone 45.
Tel: 0931-461111.
Fax: 0931-461126.
Close to the archaeological sites, comfortable and elegant. **LLL**
Villa Politi
Via Maria Politi Laudien 2.
Tel: 0931-412121.
Fax: 0931-36061.
This hotel has an atmosphere similar to that of the hotel in Giuseppe di Lampedusa's *The Leopard*. Quiet rooms and good service. **LLL**

Taormina
San Domenico
Piazza San Domenico 5.
Tel: 0942-23701.
Fax: 0942-625506.
This hotel is famous for its location, its park and its rooms, which have extraordinary views of the temples and sea. **LLLL**

Where to Eat

What to Eat

The gentle lifestyle of Italy is partly a product of its civilised eating habits: eating and drinking in tranquillity at least twice a day are the norm here.

Italian breakfast (*colazione*) is usually light and consists of *cappuccino* (espresso and steamed milk) and a *brioche* (pastry), or simply *caffè* (black and strong espresso).

Except in the industrialised cities, *pranzo* (lunch) is the big meal of the day. It consists of *antipasto* (hors d'oeuvre), a *primo* (pasta, rice or soup) and a *secondo* (meat or fish with a vegetable – *contorno* – or salad). To follow comes cheese and/or fruit. Italians usually drink coffee (*espresso*) after lunch and/or a liqueur, such as *grappa, amaro* or *sambuca*.

Traditionally, dinner is similar to lunch, but lighter. However, in the cities people are tending to eat less at lunchtime and making dinner the major meal of the day.

Every region in Italy has its own typical dishes: Piedmont specialises in pheasant, hare, truffles and *zabaglione* (a hot dessert made with whipped egg yolks, sugar and Marsala wine); Lombardy is known for *risotto alla Milanese* (saffron and onions), minestrone, veal and *panettone* (a sweet, Christmas bread with sultanas and candied fruits); Trentino-Alto Adige is the place for dumplings and thick, hearty soups to keep out the cold; Umbria is best for roast pork and black

truffles; Tuscany is good for wild boar, chestnuts, steak and game; Naples is the home of Mozzarella cheese and pizza and is good for seafood; and Sicily is the place for delectable sweets.

Italy still claims the best ice cream in the world, as well as the Sicilian speciality *granita* (crushed ice with fruit juice or coffee).

The further south you travel, the spicier and heavier is the food and the stronger the wine.

Where to Eat

Italy has thousands of restaurants, *trattorie* and *osterie*. If you do not want to have a complete meal, you can always have a snack at the bar or at *tavole calde* and *rosticcerie* (grills).

If you go to a restaurant, don't order just a salad: the waiters may well look down on your eating habits and treat you with disdain. If you think a complete meal is too big, forego the *antipasto*, but take a *primo* and a *secondo* at least.

The restaurants listed below have been recommended by Italian food writers and/or the authors of this guide. It is difficult to generalise about prices since much depends on the choice of dishes and menu selection. Even noted chefs may offer a less expensive, but restricted, menu in conjunction with the main menu.

Price Guide

The price of a three-course meal for one (not including wine):
L = L50,000 or less per head
LL = L50,000–70,000 per head
LLL = L70,000–100,000 per head
LLLL = L100,000 or more per head

ROME

Al Ceppo
Via Panama 2.
Tel: 06-8419696.
Typical restaurant with cuisine from Le Marche. Closed: Monday and August. **LLL**

Cannavota
Piazza S. Giovanni in Laterano 20. Tel: 06-77205007.
Crowded with tourists and locals alike – very informal. Roman cuisine. Closed: Wednesday and part of August. **L**

Checchino dal 1887
Via Monte Testaccio 30.
Tel: 06-5746318.
Authentic old-time family atmosphere, plus typical Roman cuisine. Closed: Sunday evening, Monday, Christmas and 15 July–15 August. Reserve. **LL**

Chianti
Via Ancona 17.
Tel: 06-44250242.
Rustic *trattoria* with a tavern. Great Tuscan and Roman cuisine. Closed: Sunday and August. **LLL**

Ciceruacchio
Via del Porto 1.
Tel: 06-5806046.
Very touristy place in Trastevere, on the lines of an old-fashioned tavern. Roman cuisine; list of local wines. Open only for dinner. Closed: Monday, and part of August. **LL**

Colline Emiliane
Via degli Avignonesi 22.
Tel: 06-4817538.
Classic ambience; rich Emilian cuisine. Closed: Friday and August. Reserve. **LL**

El Toulà
Via della Lupa 29/B.
Tel: 06-6873750.
Very elegant decor. The cuisine is refined and regional, especially from the Veneto. Impressive wine list. Closed: Saturday lunch, Sunday and part of August. Reserve. **LLLL**

Elettra
Via Principe Amedeo 72.
Tel: 06-4745397.
Crowded with regular diners, this has a pleasant, homely atmosphere and traditional but varied cuisine. Closed: Saturday and part of August. **L**

Girarrosto Toscano
Via Campania 29.
Tel: 06-4823835.
Modern tavern with traditional Tuscan cuisine. Closed Wednesday. **LLL**

Il Falchetto
Via dei Montecatini 12.
Tel: 06-6791160.
Small, family-run restaurant, just off the lively Via del Corso, positioned in a narrow, quiet road which makes eating outside a pleasure. Closed: Friday and part of August. **LL**

Il Tinello
Via di Porta Pinciana 16B.
Tel: 06-486847.
Hidden off the Dolce Vita beaten track, this offers traditional cuisine and service and serves great pizza at lunchtime. Closed: Sunday and part of August. **LL–LLL**

La Vigna dei Cardinali
Piazzale Ponte Milvio 34.
Tel: 06-3333500.
A nice restaurant with a beautiful summer garden. Traditional cuisine, with variations. Closed: Monday evening. **L**

L'Eau Vive
Via Monterone 85.
Tel: 06-68801095.
French cuisine. in a 15th-century palace managed by nuns. Closed: Sunday and August. **LL**

Le Jardin dell'Hotel Byron
Via Giuseppe de Notaris 5.
Tel: 06-3220404.
Ask for the restaurant, which is exquisite, elegant and set in a lovely garden. Closed: Sunday and part of August. **LLLL**

Passetto
Via Zanardelli 14.
Tel: 06-68806569.
Fish dishes and cuisine from Abruzzo. Traditional atmosphere. **LLL**

Pierdonati
Via della Conciliazione 39.
Tel: 06-68803557.
Tavern in front of St Peter's.
Traditional Roman cuisine, plus local wines. Closed: Thursday and part of August. **L**

Piperno
Via Monte de' Cenci 9.
Tel: 06-6542772.
This traditional Roman *trattoria* offers romantic outside dining during the summer on a little piazza in old Rome. It features Roman cuisine such as *ravioli ricotta e spinaci,* and *saltimbocca.* Closed: Sunday evening, Monday and part of August. **LLLL**

Ranieri
Via Mario de' Fiori 26.
Tel: 06-6791592.
Founded in 1849, this restaurant is ideal for *tête-à-tête* dinners. *Fin de siècle* furniture; historic motif. Closed: Sunday. **LLL**

Romolo
Via di Porta Settimiana 8.
Tel: 06-5818284.
The Trastevere ambience here is enhanced by the opening of a courtyard in summer. There is good Roman cuisine as well. Closed: Monday and part of August. Reserve. **LLL**

Taverna Giulia
Vicolo dell'Oro 23.
Tel: 06-6869768.
Classic restaurant which serves food outside during the summer. Great national and Genoese cuisine. Try *trenette al pesto* and *stinco al forno* (roast shank of veal or pork). Closed: Sunday and part of August. **LL**

Tavernetta Sistina
Via Sistina 147.
Tel: 06-4741939.
Centrally located in the chic Via Sistina, close to the Spanish Steps. Here you will find good, Roman cuisine and a wide variety of fish dishes combined with a fun, comfortable atmosphere. **LL**

ROME'S ENVIRONS

Civitavecchia
L'Angoletto
Via P. Guglielmotti 2.
Tel: 0766-32825.

Good, traditional seafood, soups and home-made pasta. Closed: Monday, parts of January and July. **LL**

Nemi
La Taverna
Via Nemorese 13.
Tel: 06-9368135.
Nice and simple with a great fireplace. Traditional cooking. Closed: Wednesday and January. Reserve. **LL**

Ostia
Allo Sbarco di Enea
Via dei Romagnoli 657.
Tel: 06-5650034.
Crowded with tourists. Closed: Monday, 15 days in January. **LLL**

Palestrina
Stella
Piazza della Liberazione 3.
Tel: 06-9538172.
Modern ambience; regional cuisine. **LL**

Subiaco
Belvedere
Via dei Monasteri 33.
Tel: 0774-85531.
Wonderful restaurant in a small hotel, specialising in cuisine from Lazio. Closed: Monday. **LL**

Tarquinia
Le Due Orfanelle
Vicolo Breve.
Tel: 0766-856307.
Simple trattoria. Try the galletto al mattone (chicken cooked on a hot brick) and maialino (baby pig). Closed: Tuesday. **L**

Tivoli
Cinque Statue
Largo S. Angelo 1.
Tel: 0774-335366.
Great ambience, plain cuisine from Lazio, and, in summer, tables outside. Closed: Friday and Sunday evening, last 2 weeks in August. **LL**

MILAN
Al Mercante
Piazza di Mercanti 17.

Tel: 02-8052198.
Friendly restaurant overlooking the piazza. In summer you can eat outdoors under a very old loggia. Closed: Sunday and August. Reserve. **LL**
Boeucc
Piazza Belgioioso 2.
Tel: 02-76020224.
A temple of Milanese gastronomy. Closed all day Saturday and Sunday lunch. **LLL–LLLL**

Brasera Meneghina
Via Imperia 7.
Tel: 02-89503255.
Genuine osteria of old Milan, dating back to the 17th century. It features a fireplace and a small porch painted with frescoes, and offers outdoor dining in summer. Closed: Friday, Saturday lunch and Sunday. **LL**
Casa Fontana
Piazza Carbonari 5
Tel: 02-6704710.
About 25 different types of risotto to taste. Closed: Monday and Saturday lunchtime. **LL**
Dolce Vita
Via Bergamini 11.
Tel: 02-58303843.
Romantic and sophisticated spot with candles and coffered ceilings. Lombard specialities, nouvelle cuisine and gourmet menus (less pricey at lunchtime). Closed: Sunday. **LL–LLL**
Gran San Bernardo
Via Borghese 14.
Tel: 02-3319000.
Large, friendly restaurant

serving some of the best regional cooking. Try casseoeula (a stew of pork, sausages and carrots served with cornbread) and polenta. Closed: Sunday and August. Reserve. **LLL**
Bistro Duomo
Piazza del Duomo.
Tel: 02-877120.
The temple of Italian cuisine, the best in Italy. Modern ambience. For the élite. Closed: All day Sunday and Monday Lunch; 3 weeks in August. Reserve. **LLL**
La Bella Pisana
Via Sottocorno 17.
Tel: 02-76021803.
Pleasant ambience, with a garden for summer. Padana plain cooking and fresh fish. Closed: Tuesday and August. Reserve. **LL**
La Scaletta
Piazza Stazione di Porta Genova 3.
Tel: 02-58100290.
Modern ambience, with a library and international level cuisine. Very fashionable. Closed: All day Sunday, Monday lunch, Easter and Christmas. Reserve. **LLLL**.
Savini
Galleria Vittorio Emanuele 11.
Tel: 02-72003433.
Exquisite decor, ultra-professional service and typical classic Italian cuisine. Close to Duomo. Closed: Sunday and August. Reserve. **LLLL**
Taverna Gran Sasso
Via Principessa Clotilde 10.
Tel: 02-6597578.
Kitsch restaurant, serving typical Abruzzese cooking; live music. Closed: Sunday and August. Reserve. **LLL**

LOMBARDY & THE LAKES

Bergamo
Agnello d'Oro
Via Gombito 22.
Tel: 035-249883.
Good regional food in an old hotel in the upper part of town. Closed: Sunday evening, Monday and January. Reserve. **LL**

Lio Pellegrini
Via San Tomaso 47.
Tel: 035-247813.
Atmospheric former sacristy,
serving Tuscan specialities.
Closed: Monday and Tuesday
lunch. **LL**

Taverna del Colleoni
Piazza Vecchia 7
Tel: 035-232596.
Lombard specialities. Closed:
Monday. **LLL**

Trattoria del Teatro
Piazza Mascheroni 3.
Tel: 035-238862.
Nineteenth-century furniture,
plus simple, but delicious food.
Closed: Monday. **L**

Cremona
Ceresole
Via Ceresole 4.
Tel: 0372-30990.
Classic national cuisine. Closed:
Sunday evening, Monday and
August. Reserve.**LLLL**

Mantova (Mantua)
Cigno
Piazza Carlo d'Arco 1.
Tel: 0376-327101.
In a wonderful piazza, in an
ancient building. The service is
as excellent as the regional
cooking. Closed: Monday and
Tuesday. Reserve. **LL–LLL**

Pavia
Ferrari da Tino
Via dei Mille 111.
Tel: 0382-539025.
Old-fashioned, homely *trattoria*.
Closed: Sunday evening,
Monday and 15 July–
15 August. **L**

PIEDMONT

Turin
Del Cambio
Piazza Carignano 2.
Tel: 011-546690.
Opened in 1757, one of the
most beautiful restaurants in
Italy. Nineteenth-century
furniture and atmosphere.
International and national

cuisine. Closed: Sunday and
August. Reserve. **LLLL**

La Capannina
Via Donati 1.
Tel: 011-545405.
The ambience is rustic, though
this restaurant is set in a fine
palazzo. The food is strictly
cooked in the Langarola style
(the Langhe are a part of
Piemonte). The *fritto misto* is
superb. Closed: Sunday and
August. Reserve. **LL**

Price Guide

The price of a three-course
meal for one (not including
wine):
L = L50,000 or less per head
LL = L50,000–70,000 per
head
LLL = L70,000–100,000 per
head
LLLL = L100,000 or more
per head

Ostu Bacu
Corso Vercelli 226.
Tel: 011-2464579.
Modern ambience. Come here to
taste plain, old-fashioned
Piemontese cooking. Closed:
Sunday and August. Reserve. **LL**

Spada Reale
Via Principe Amedeo 53.
Tel: 011-8171363.
Modern-style, Tuscan and
Piemontese cuisine. Closed:
Saturday lunch and all day
Sunday. Reserve. **LL**

Tre Galline
Via Bellezia 37.
Tel: 011-546833.
Typical old-fashioned *piola* (a
meeting-place to drink wine and
eat snacks), serving regional
cooking. Closed: Monday and
August. Reserve. **LL**

Villa Sassi
Strada Traforo del Pino 47.
Tel: 011-8980556.
In a cardinal's villa, this is a
restaurant for VIPs, with an
attached hotel (only 17 rooms).
Exclusive, with superb cuisine.
Closed: Sunday. Reserve. **LLLL**

VALLE D'AOSTA

Aosta
Le Foyer
Corso Ivrea 146.
Tel: 0165-32136.
Set just outside Aosta, this
restaurant offers excellent fish
and Italian cheeses. Closed:
Monday evening and all day
Tuesday. **LL**

Vecchia Aosta
Piazza Porte Pretoriane 4.
Tel: 0165-361186.
Set within part of the old city
gateway, this restaurant serves
French and regional specialities,
ravioli, various stuffed pastas
and tournedos with juniper
berries. Closed: Wednesday
(October-May). Open all Summer.
LL

Breuil-Cervinia
Les Neiges d'Antan
Località Cret Perrères, Statale
406.
Tel: 0166-948775.
Situated on a mountain 4 km
from Breuil-Cervinia, this quiet
house serves typical Valdostana
cuisine. Try the *fonduta*. Closed:
May-June, September-November,
all day Sunday and Monday
lunch. Reserve. **LL**

Gignod
Locanda La Clusaz
Località La Clusaz, Statale Gran
San Bernardo.
Tel: 0165-56075.
Set north of Aosta, this
charming inn has a number of
rooms as well as a frescoed,
medieval interior. Restaurant
specialities include grain soups,
polenta and dishes made with
chestnuts or bacon. Closed:
Tuesdays in low season, Dinner
only Monday-Friday. **L–LL**

LIGURIA & RIVIERA

Genoa
Antica Osteria del Bai
Via Quarto 12, Genova-Quarto.

Tel: 010-387478.
Historic restaurant where Garibaldi once ate, inside a fortress overlooking the sea. Typical Genoese cuisine. Closed: Monday and 20 July–12 August. **LLLL**

Gran Gotto
Viale Brigata Bisagno 69.
Tel: 010-564344.
Near Stazione Brignole. Classic and elegant, with a rustic atmosphere and regional cooking. Try the *trenette al pesto*. Closed: Saturday lunch and all day Sunday. Reserve. **LLLL**

La Pergola
Via Casaregis 52R.
Tel: 010-588543.
Comfortable atmosphere, regional cooking. Closed: Sunday evening, all day Monday. **LLL**

Panson
Piazza delle Erbe 5.
Tel: 010-2468903.
This charming Genovese restaurant is situated in a safe but slightly dilapidated square close to Via XX Settembre. All Genovese dishes are on offer, including *pansoti al sugo di noci* (pasta with walnuts), and the famous *pesto alla genovese* (pasta with basil sauce). Closed: Sunday evening and August. **LL**

Piro
Salita Bertora 5/R, zona Struppa.
Tel: 010-802304.
Elevated restaurant offering views of Genoa. This is a typical simple *trattoria*, with pretty good Genoese cooking. Closed: Sunday evening, all day Monday and 15 August–15 September. **L**

Zeffirino
Via XX Settembre 20.
Tel: 010-591990.
In the centre of the city, with modern furniture and mixed cuisine. Reserve. **LL**

Lerici
Conchiglia
Via Mazzini 2.
Tel: 0187-967334.
Along the seafront, with

especially fresh fish. Closed: Wednesday and 20 December–10 January and 2 weeks in November. **LLL**

Portofino
Il Pitosforo
Molo Umberto I 9.
Tel: 0185-269020.
Meeting place for yachtspeople with a modern atmosphere. Ligurian specialities as well as international cooking. Closed: Sunday and 1 January–28 February. Reserve. **LLLL**

Stella
Molo Umberto I 3.
Tel: 0185-269007.
Marine atmosphere; regional cooking. Closed: Wednesday and 6 January–3 March. Reserve. **LLL**

San Remo
Del Porto da Nicò
Piazza Brescia 9.
Tel: 0184-501988.
The classic *trattoria* of the port, with good seafood. Closed: Wednesday and 1 November–20 December. Reserve. **LL**

Giannino
Corso Trento e Trieste 23.
Tel: 0184-504014.
Very comfortable establishment offering high-class cooking. Closed: All day Sunday, Monday lunch. Reserve. **LLL–LLLL**

Vernazza
Gambero Rosso
Piazza Marconi 7.
Tel: 0187-812265.
Close to the port: a small *osteria* noted for its seafood. Closed: Monday and mid-December to February. **LL–LLL**

VENICE

Castello
Al Covo
Campiello della Pescaria 3968.
Tel: 041-5223812.
Enthusiastically-run restaurant serving fish fresh from the lagoon, wild duck (seasonal) and

wonderful home-made desserts. Great wine list. Lunch is less expensive than dinner. Closed: Wednesday and Thursday. **LLL–LLLL**

Dorsoduro
La Furatola
Calle Lunga San Barnaba 2879.
Tel: 041-5208594.
Unpretentious restaurant where local gourmets go for fish and seafood. Closed: Thursday and sometimes Monday, January and August. **LLL**

Riviera
Zattere 1473.
Tel: 041-5227621.
Good home-made pasta and fish. Weather permitting, tables are set outside, overlooking the island of Giudecca. Closed: Sunday and Monday. **LL**

Taverna San Trovaso
Fondamenta Priuli 1016.
Tel: 041-5203703.
Cheap, cheerful taverna serving standard Italian food. Closed: Monday. **L**

San Marco
Al Graspo de Ua
Calle de Bombaseri,
San Marco 5095 .
Tel: 041-5200150.
Close to the Rialto Bridge. This restaurant, under its wooden roof, is centuries-old, and is a delight for those seeking local colour. National cuisine. Closed: Monday and Tuesday in July and August. **LLL**

Alle Colonnete
San Marco 987.
Tel: 041-5237082.
Typical Venetian cuisine. Closed: Thursday and Friday lunch. **LLL**

Vecia Carbonera
San Marco 4648.
Tel: 041-5225479.
Rebuilt, but maintaining its 19th-century ambience, with good Italian cooking. Closed: Tuesday, Wednesday, January and 15 July–16 August. **LLL**

Antico Martini
Campo San Fantin 1983.
Tel: 041-5224121.

Close to the site of the former Fenice opera house. Elegant and intimate, serving Venetian and international cuisine. Closed: Tuesday and Wednesday lunch. Reserve. **LLLL**

Da Arturo
Calle degli Assassini 3656.
Tel: 041-5286974.
Very small, and unusual for Venice as it does not serve fish. Excellent meat, pasta and salads. Open late. Closed: Sunday, three weeks in August. **LL**

Harry's Bar
Calle Vallaresso 1323.
Tel: 041-5285777.
This bar/restaurant was a favourite haunt of Hemingway; it is now mainly patronised by very wealthy Venetians, expatriates and American tourists. Good home-made pastas at exorbitant prices. **LLLL**

San Polo
Da Fiore
Calle del Scaleter 2202, San Polo.
Tel: 041-721308.
Small restaurant near Campo San Polo. Well worth seeking out for its good food, wine and elegant ambience, which also attracts Venetian celebrities. Closed: Sunday and Monday. **LLLL**

Do Leoni
Londra Palace, Riva degli Schiavoni 4171.
Tel: 041-5200533.
Venetian delicacies in an elegant ambience overlooking the island of San Giorgio. **LLL**

Poste Vecie Antica Trattoria
Mercato del Pesce di Rialto 1608.
Tel: 041-721822.
Inviting rustic *trattoria* specialising in fish from the nearby market and also home-made *ravioli*. Closed: Tuesday and 20 November–20 December. Reserve. **LLL**

Trattoria alla Madonna
Calle della Madonna 594.
Tel: 041-5223824.

This is a popular fish and seafood restaurant near the Rialto. It offers good value for Venice, and hence is always crowded – the service can be brusque. Closed: Wednesday. Reserve during the week. **LL–LLL**

Santa Croce
Antica Bessetta
Salizzada de Calzusto 1395.
Tel: 041-721687.
Near San Giacomo dell'Orio, off the beaten track. Authentic family-run *trattoria* serving regional cuisine. Good value. Closed: Tuesday, Wednesday lunch, Christmas and 15 July–16 August. **LL**

VENETO

Padova (Padua)
Dotto
Via Squarcione 23.
Tel: 049-8751490.
Classic furniture, typical cuisine. Try *pasta e fagioli* (pasta and beans) and *baccalà* (stockfish). Closed: Sunday evening, Monday and August. Reserve. **LL**

Verona
12 Apostoli
Vicolo Corticella San Marco 3.
Tel: 045-596999.
One of the best restaurants in Italy, this is located in an ancient building decorated with frescoes by Casarini. Closed: Sunday evening, Monday, Christmas and mid-June to mid-July. Reserve. **LLL**

Marconi
Via Fogge 4.
Tel: 045-591910.
Elegant place serving regional classic cuisine, especially fish. Closed: Sunday, Tuesday afternoon and August. **LL**

Vicenza
Cinzia e Valerio
Piazzetta Porta Padova 65/67.
Tel: 0444-505213.
Set on the ancient city walls, an elegant restaurant with fish

specialities. Closed: Sunday evening, all day Monday, August and first week of September. **LL–LLL**

TRENTINO-ALTO ADIGE

Bolzano
Da Abramo
Piazza Gries 16.
Tel: 0471-280141.
Set in the old town hall, and with a garden, serving good regional fish dishes. Closed: Sunday. **LL**

Trento
Chiesa
Via Marchetti 9.
Parco San Marco.
Tel: 0461-238766.
On the first floor of a 17th-century palace with a cloister. Very refined. Closed: Sunday. **LL**

FRIULI-VENEZIA GIULIA

Trieste
Al Bragozza
Riva N. Sauro 22.
Tel: 040-303001.
Traditional seafood restaurant. Closed: Sunday and Monday, 3 weeks in June and July. **LL**

Antica Trattoria Suban
Via Comici 2.
Tel: 040-54368.
Friendly and simple, with a summer bower. Good regional cuisine. Closed: Monday lunch and all day Tuesday. Reserve. **LL–LLL**

San Marco Caffè Storico
Via Battisti 18.
Tel: 040-371373.
The grandest *belle époque* café in the city. **LL**

Udine
Alla Vedova
Via Tavagnacco 9.
Tel: 0432-470291.
Very old Friulian restaurant, with outdoor tables in summer. Good traditional cooking. Closed: Sunday evening, Monday and August. Reserve. **L**

EMILIA-ROMAGNA

Bologna
Antica Osteria Romagnola
Via Rialto 13.
Tel: 051-263699.
Hearty cuisine in a lively
atmosphere, with live music in
the evenings. Courtyard open in
the summer. Closed: Monday.
L–LL
Cantina Bentivoglio
Via Mascarella 46.
Tel: 051-265416.
Set in the cellars of a palazzo,
this boisterous restaurant
attracts a young crowd. Emilian
specialities; live music. Closed:
Monday. **L**
Da Bertino e Figlio
Via delle Lame 55.
Tel: 051-522230.
Funny Emilian *trattoria*, with
good cooking, especially the
gnocchi. Closed: Monday
evening and 1–15 August. **L**

Ferrara
Romantica
Via Ripagrande 34.
Tel: 0532-765975.
Classic Italian cuisine with
Ferrarese dishes, too. Set in the
historic quarter. Closed:
Wednesday and second week of
July. **L**

Modena
Da Enzo
Via Coltellini 17.
Tel: 059-225177.
Dating back to 1912, this place
has been tastefully renovated.
Typical Modenese cooking.
Closed: Monday and August. **L**
Fini
Piazza San Francesco.
Tel: 059-223314.
Classic, elegant, but homely,
with traditional regional cuisine.
Try *bolliti* (boiled meat). Closed:
Monday, Tuesday and August.
Reserve. **LLLL**

Parma
La Filoma
Via XX Marzo 15.

Tel: 0521-206181.
Refined, with 17th-century
furniture, offering traditional
cooking and service. Closed:
Tuesday and August. **LL**

Ravenna
Al Gallo
Via Maggiore 87.
Tel: 0544-213775.
Wonderful pergola in summer.
Good (not exceptional) local
food. Closed: Monday evening,
Tuesday and February. **LL**

Price Guide

The price of a three-course
meal for one (not including
wine):
L = L50,000 or less per head
LL = L50,000–70,000 per
head
LLL = L70,000–100,000 per
head
LLLL = L100,000 or more
per head

San Marino
Righi-La Taverna
Piazza Libertà.
Tel: 0549-991196.
Rustic, but good, food. Closed:
Monday in winter, and January. **LL**

FLORENCE

Cantinone del Gallo Nero
Via S. Spirito 6R.
Tel: 055-218898.
Always crowded, this very
informal restaurant is located in
a 15th-century wine cellar. The
speciality is its Chianti wine
collection and the Tuscan
peasant dishes, such as
crostini, ribollita and *pinzimonio*.
Closed: Monday and August. **LL**
Dino
Via Ghibellina 51R.
Tel: 055-241452.
This former wine store has an
atmosphere typical of the region
– and good cooking to match.
Closed: Sunday evening and
Monday. **LL**

Enoteca Pinchiorri
Via Ghibellina 87.
Tel: 055-242777.
In the 15th-century Ciofi Palace,
with a delightful courtyard for
dining in the open air. Superb
nouvelle cuisine, with an
impressive wine collection
(almost 60,000 bottles). Closed:
Sunday and August. Reserve.
LLLL
La Loggia
Piazzale Michelangelo.
Tel: 055-2342832.
The beautiful view of Florence
will bewitch you. This restaurant
serves international and Italian
delicacies. Good service.
Closed: Monday. **LL–LLL**
Omero
Via Pian de' Giullari 11R.
Tel: 055-220053.
A rustic *trattoria* with outside
tables in summer. Splendid view.
Closed: Tuesday and August.
Reserve. **LL**
Otello
Via degli Orti Oricellari 36R.
Tel: 055-216517.
Typical Florentine restaurant.
Reserve. **LL**

TUSCANY

Arezzo
Cecco
Corso Italia 125.
Tel: 0575-20986.
Bar and *tavola calda*, but good
cooking with no pretensions.
Closed: Monday. Cecco is also a
small, inexpensive hotel. **L**

Cortona
La Loggetta
Piazza Peschiera 3.
Tel: 0575-630575.
Mellow atmosphere, with good
regional cooking in a 16th-
century palazzo. Closed: Monday
and January. Reserve. **LL**

Lucca
Da Giulio
Via delle Conce 45.
Tel: 0583-55948.
Just plain good food with

minestrone and beans on the menu. Closed: Sunday, Monday and August. **L**

Pisa
Sergio American Bar
Lungarno Pacinotti 1.
Tel: 050-580580.
Elegant decor in a medieval setting with excellent regional cuisine. Closed: Sunday and August. **L**

San Gimignano
La Cisterna
Piazza della Cisterna 23.
Tel: 0577-940328.
Restaurant in a 15th-century monastery, with a wonderful view over the village. Popular among tourists. Closed: Tuesday. Reserve. **LL**

Siena
Grotta Santa Caterina
Via della Galluzza, 28.
Tel: 0577-282208.
Characteristic tavern. Closed: Sunday evening and Monday. **L**
Guido
Vicolo Pier Pettinaio 7.
Tel: 0577-280042.
Fourteenth-century building, with a big kitchen, good service and traditional regional cooking. Home-produced oil and wine. **L**
Tullio ai Tre Cristi
Vicolo Provenzano 1/7.
Tel: 0577-280608.
Trattoria attached to a shrine representing the Crucifixion. Managed for 40 years by the same family. Try the *pici*, a kind of hand-made spaghetti. Closed: Tuesday. **L**

UMBRIA & THE MARCHES

Perugia
Falchetto
Via Bartolo 20.
Tel: 075-5731775.
Authentic local food using the best ingredients, no pretences. Closed: Monday. **L**

Ancona
Passetto

Piazza IV Novembre 1.
Tel: 071-33214.
Elegant and exquisite, serving traditional seafood cuisine. Sea views from the terrace.Closed: Wednesday. Closed: Sunday evening and all day Monday. Reserve. **LLL**

Assisi
San Francesco
Via S. Francesco 52.
Tel: 075-812329.
Umbrian dishes served in front of a fine fireplace. Views over the basilica. Closed: Wednesday and 2 weeks in July. **LL**

Foligno
Da Remo
Viale Battisti 49.
Tel: 0742-340679.
The decor and the menu are simple, but the family that runs this restaurant has a long tradition of fine cooking. Eat outdoors in summer. Closed: Sunday evening and Monday. **L**

Price Guide

The price of a three-course meal for one (not including wine):
L = L50,000 or less per head
LL = L50,000–70,000 per head
LLL = L70,000–100,000 per head
LLLL = L100,000 or more per head

Orvieto
I Sette Consoli
Piazza San Angelo 1.
Tel: 0763-343911.
Refined, excellent interpretations of local cuisine, especially good value. Closed: Wednesday. **L**
La Grotta
Via Lucca Signorelli 5.
Tel: 0763-341348.
Just off the Piazza Del Duomo, a restaurant particularly recommended for its roast meats. **L**

Spoleto
Il Tartufo
Piazza Garibaldi 24.
Tel: 0743-40236.
Quiet and dignified with well-prepared traditional cuisine. The dining room preserves a 4th-century Roman floor. Closed: Wednesday and 15 July–8 August. Closed: Sunday evening and all day Monday, January and 2 weeks in July. Reserve. **LL–LLL**

Todi
Umbria
Via S. Bonaventura 13.
Tel: 075-8942390.
In a 14th-century building, with a delightful terrace overlooking the hills for relaxed dining in summer. Good local food. Closed: Tuesday and Christmas–9 January. **LL**

ABRUZZO & MOLISE

Campobasso
Il Potestà
Vico Persichillo 1,.
Tel: 0874-311101.
An excellent list of local wines accompanies the menu of traditional food with a modern slant. Closed: Monday and Tuesday evening. **LL**

Chieti
Venturini
Via de Lollis 10.
Tel: 0871-330663.
Restaurant with a traditional atmosphere and a terrace. Special roast game and fish dishes. Closed: Tuesday and some of July. Reserve. **LL**

L'Aquila
Tre Marie, Via Tre Marie 3.
Tel: 0862-410109.
Old-fashioned restaurant with a 17th-century fireplace and a homely atmosphere. Traditional local cuisine – sample the *ciufolotti*. Closed: Sunday evening and Monday all day. Reserve. **LL**

Teramo
Duomo
Via Stazio 11.
Tel: 0861-241774.
Modern restaurant serving a good choice of old-fashioned local cooking. Closed: Monday and part of August. Reserve. **LL**

NAPLES
Ciro a Santa Brigida
Via S. Brigida 71.
Tel: 081-5524072.
Classic well-known restaurant, with good (not great) Neapolitan cooking. Closed: Sunday and August. Reserve. **L**
Da Ettore
Via Santa Lucia 56.
Tel: 081-7640498.
Good food served in a simple *trattoria*. Closed: Sunday and August. **L**
Dante e Beatrice
Piazza Dante 44.
Tel: 081-5499438.
Genuine Naples *trattoria*, crowded with Neapolitans enjoying the good local cooking. Bear in mind that no credit cards are accepted. Closed: Monday and 20–30 August. **L**
Giuseppone al Mare
Via Ferdinando Russo 13.
Tel: 081-5756002.
At Posillipo, right on the seafront. Great seafood. Closed: Sunday evening and all day Monday. **LLL**
La Bersagliera
Borgo Marinaro, Via Santa Lucia 10/11.
Tel: 081-7646016.
Old restaurant located in a small port with a view of Castel dell'Ovo. Closed: Tuesday. **LLL**
La Cantinella
Via Cuma 42.
Tel: 081-7648684.
Very elegant and expensive restaurant, with a telephone on every table. Closed: Sunday and part of August. **LLLL**
La Fazenda
Via Marechiaro 58/A.
Tel: 081-5757420.

Restaurant overlooking the Gulf of Naples and Capri, serving fine Mediterranean food. In summer, the terrace-garden is open. Closed: Monday and 15 August–1 September. Reserve. **LL–LLL**
La Sacrestia
Via Orazio 116.
Tel: 081-664186.
At Mergellina, with a wonderful view back over the Gulf of Naples, in a building reminiscent of an old monastery. In summer you can enjoy typical Neapolitan food in the garden. Closed: Sunday evening, Monday Lunch and August. Reserve. **LLL**
Sbrescia
Rampe San Antonio a Posillipo 109. Tel: 081-669140.
Restaurant offering fresh seafood and a beautiful view of the Gulf. Closed: Monday and part of August. Reserve. **LLL**
Zi Teresa
Borgo Marinari 1.
Tel: 081-7642565.
Very old, atmospheric restaurant. Seafood specialities. Closed: Monday and part of August. **LL**

CAMPANIA COAST

Amalfi
Da Gemma
Salita Fra' Gerardo Sasso 10.
Tel: 089-871345.
Good, traditional cooking, especially seafood. Tables on the street in summer. Closed: Wednesday and January. Reserve. **LL**

Benevento
Pina e Gino
Via G. Cassella 48.
Tel: 0824-24947.
Friendly *trattoria* with a wide variety of pasta dishes and good pizzas. Closed: Sunday and August. **L**

Capri
Ai Faraglioni da Giuliano
Via Camerelle 75.
Tel: 081-8370320.

Elegant dining rooms overlook the *faraglioni* and the countryside. Reliable traditional cuisine. Closed: Monday except summer, and mid-November–mid-March. Reserve. **LLL**
La Capannina
Via delle Botteghe 12.
Tel: 081-8370732.
Fashionable restaurant serving classic, traditional seafood. Closed: Mid-January to mid-February. Reserve. **LLL**
La Fontelina
Località Faraglioni.
Tel: 081-8370845.
A quiet, intimate corner ideal for lovers of vegetables. Lunch only. Closed October–April. **LL**
La Pigna
Via Roma 30.
Tel: 081-8370280.
The ideal place for a romantic dinner: elegant, international and local. The dining-room has a porch and a citrus orchard around. Patio and fountain. Neapolitan cuisine with personality and flair. Closed Monday. **LL**
Le Grottelle
Via Arco Naturale 5.
Tel: 081-8375719.
Cheerful atmosphere and unique view of the Arco Naturale. Home-reared chicken and rabbit and barbecued fresh fish. Closed: Thursday except summer and late December–Easter. **LL**

Ischia
Da Peppina di Renato
Località Forio, Via Bocca 42.
Tel: 081-998312.
Furnished with old barrels, this *trattoria* offers solid local cuisine, like *pasta mischiata* (pasta with beans, lentils or chickpeas) and *coniglio all'ischitana* (rabbit). Home-made *crostate* (tarts) and cakes. Closed: Monday, except summer. **LL**
Gennaro
Via del Porto 66.
Tel: 081-992917.
Restaurant overlooking the port, serving traditional fish dishes. Closed: November – March. **L**

Paestum
Nettuno
Via Principi di Piemonte 2.
Tel: 0828-811028.
Good view of the temples, and good Italian cooking. Closed: evenings and Monday in September–March. Reserve. **LL**

Positano
La Buca di Bacco
Via Rampa Teglia 8.
Tel: 089-875699.
Simple and genuine atmosphere and cuisine. Closed: November–March. **L**
'O Capurale
Via Regina Giovanna 12.
Tel: 089-811188.
Genuine atmosphere and simple seafood and pasta, pastries and home-made *limoncello* (lemon-scented liqueur). Closed: Late October to Easter. **L**

Salerno
Al Cenacolo
Piazza Alfano I 4/6.
Tel: 089-238818.
Good fish and pasta dishes, followed by delicious desserts. Closed: Sunday evening, Monday and part of August. **L**

Sorrento
Antico Frantoio
Località Casarlano, Via Cala 5.
Tel: 081-8785845.
Trattoria among olive groves, with a view of the Gulf. Home-made bread and beer, and plenty of pasta. Closed: Tuesday in winter. **L**
La Favorita
Corso Italia 71.
Tel: 081-8781321.
Time-honoured restaurant, filled with strange old furniture; beautiful garden. Mainly seafood is served. Closed: Wednesday October–April. **L**

APULIA

Bari
Ai due Ghiottoni
Via Putignani 11.
Tel: 080-5232240.

Smart restaurant with excellent food and superb wine list. Closed: Sunday. **LL**
La Credenza
Via Verrone 15/Arco Sant'Onofrio, Borgo Antico.
Tel: 080-5244747.
Well-restored restaurant in the heart of old Bari. Traditional dishes like *orecchiette* with cauliflower *(orecchiette e cime de cole)* and pecorino cheese and garlic rolls *(brasciole)*. Closed: Wednesday and August. **L**
Murat
Via Lombardi 13.
Tel: 080-5216560.
The elegant, panoramic restaurant of the renowned hotel of the same name offers an interesting choice of regional dishes including a good selection of cheeses. Less exciting desserts. Set menus are moderately priced. Closed: Sunday and August. **LL**

Barletta
Il Brigantino
Viale Regina Elena 30.
Tel: 0883-533345.
Large, elegant restaurant with a terrace overlooking the sea, traditional cuisine and efficient service. **LL**

Brindisi
La Lanterna
Via Tarantini 14.
Tel: 0831-564026.
Between the Colonno and the cathedral. Local specialities in new recipes. Closed: Sunday and August. **LL**

Foggia
Cicolella
Viale XXIV Maggio 60.
Tel: 0881-688890.
Elegant, with a summer terrace, this restaurant is attached to a hotel dating back half a century. Mostly regional cuisine, with ear-shaped pasta *(orecchiette)* and fish-soup among the best dishes. Closed: Saturday, Sunday, part of August and Christmas. Reserve. **L**

Lecce
Plaza
Via 140° Reg. Fanteria 10.
Tel: 0832-305093.
Good Pugliese cooking, including *orecchiette*. Closed: Sunday and August. **LL**

Manfredonia
Coppola Rossa
Via dei Celestini 13.
Tel: 0884-582522.
Friendly *trattoria* offering good local fish dishes, plus home-made desserts. Closed: Sunday evening, Monday, some of January and some of June. **L**

Taranto
Al Gambero
Vicolo del Ponte 4.
Tel: 099-4711190.
Big and well-lit, overlooking the Mar Piccolo, with the best crawfish in Apulia. Closed: Monday and November. **LL**

Trani
La Darsena
Via Statuti Marittimi 98.
Tel: 0883-487333.
Traditional restaurant, specialising in seafood. Closed: Monday. Reserve. **LL**
Ostello di Federico
Castel del Monte.
Tel: 0883-569877.
Close to Frederick II's famous castle, with a beautiful terrace-garden. Regional cooking with variations. Closed: Monday, January and November. Reserve. **L**

BASILICATA & CALABRIA

Cosenza
La Calavrisela
Via G. de Rada 11A.
Tel: 0984-28012.
Comfortable. Calabrian cuisine, heavy and spicy. Closed: Monday. **L**

Matera
Da Mario
Via XX Settembre 14.

Tel: 0835-336491.
Inside a natural cave *(lamione)* in the centre of Old Matera in the Sassi region; the rustic furniture makes the place look like the inside of a big barrel. The cuisine is typical of Basilicata; try *orecchiette* (the ear-shaped pasta) with *rape* (turnip-tops). Closed: Sunday. **L**

Reggio Calabria
Bonaccorso
Via Bixio 5.
Tel: 0965-896048.
Elegant and intimate restaurant with an old-fashioned atmosphere. The owner is the chef, and also happens to be an artist. Traditional cuisine, with variations. Closed: Sunday and August. Reserve. **L**

SICILY

Palermo
La Scuderia
Viale del Fante 9.
Tel: 091-520323.
In the green "Favorita" park, with a summer garden in the Moorish manner. National and Sicilian cuisine. Closed: Sunday evening and last two weeks in August. **LL**

Catania
La Siciliana
Viale M. Polo 52/A.
Tel: 095-376400.
Elegant and classic restaurant, with a long family tradition of cooks (good Sicilian fare). Summer garden. Closed: Sunday evening and Monday. **LLL**

Monreale
La Botte
Contrada Lenzitti 20.
Tel: 091-414051.
Restaurant with farmhouse-style furniture, and classic cooking. Closed: Monday and parts of July and August. **L**

Noto
Il Barocco
Via Cavour.

Tel: 0931-835999.
Located in the centre of baroque Noto, at the corner with the Duomo, this traditional restaurant is in the apartments of an old palace, and serves inventive cuisine. **L**

Price Guide

The price of a three-course meal for one (not including wine):
L = L50,000 or less per head
LL = L50,000–70,000 per head
LLL = L70,000–100,000 per head
LLLL = L100,000 or more per head

Ragusa
Antica Macina
Località Ragusa Ibla, Via Giusti 123. Tel: 0932-248096.
Traditional cooking with variations. Try the fish soup, served in a terracotta bowl covered with a layer of pizza dough and baked in a wood-fired oven. Closed: Monday and September. **LL**
Villa Fortugno
Road to Marina di Ragusa, exit after 4 km (2.5 miles).
Tel: 0932-667134.
Old country farm with a summer garden and good regional cooking. Closed: Monday and August. **LL**

Selinunte
Lido Azzurro
Località Marinella, Via Marco Polo 51. Tel: 0924-46211.
Beautiful view of the Acropolis and simple seafood cooking. Astonishing variety of starters in the best Sicilian tradition. Closed: Monday except summer. **L**

Siracusa
Arlecchino
Via dei Tolomei 5.
Tel: 0931-66386.
Modern restaurant with first-rate service and regional cuisine: try

pasta con le sarde. Closed: Monday and part of August. Reserve. **LL**

Taormina
Gigi Mangia
Via Principe di Belmonte 104D.
Tel: 091-587651.
Interesting seasonal cooking for all tastes. A well-stocked cellar makes this small restaurant the meeting point for local wine lovers. Closed: Sunday. **L**
Luraleo
Via Bagnoli Croce 27.
Tel: 0942-24279.
Friendly, rustic restaurant, serving Sicilian cooking, especially fish, lobsters and mussels. There is also a barbecue. Open daily, May-October. **LL**

SARDINIA

Cagliari
Dal Corsaro
Via Regina Margherita 28.
Tel: 070-664318.
During the summer, it is better to go to the restaurant of the same name located at Marina Piccola-Poetto, tel: 370295. Both places serve great Sardinian cuisine, but the restaurant offers a more elegant and romantic atmosphere. Closed: Sunday and August. **LLL**

Palau
Da Franco
Via Capo d'Orso 1.
Tel: 0789-709310.
The right place for a business meeting, with refined service and a terrace overlooking the little port. Seafood dominates the menu. Closed: Monday. **LL**

Porto Cervo
Gianni Pedrinelli
Golfo Pevero.
Tel: 0789-92214.
Rustic farmhouse with a huge fireplace where meat is roasted on spits; typical Sardinian cooking. Closed: Open daily. **LL**

Culture

Attractions

Italy has such a long recorded history that the biggest problem facing the traveller is how to choose from among the nation's endless cultural attractions. All main centres, most provincial cities and many quite small towns have museums. Theatres, galleries, and concert halls also offer something for every interest.

Concerts

Classical music lovers will find themselves at home in Italy. Noteworthy concerts occur all year almost all over the country.

The opera season in Rome is December–June at the **Teatro dell'Opera**, Piazza Gigli, tel: 06-48160255. October–May, the **Auditorium of the National Academy of Santa Cecilia** on Via della Conciliazione, tel: 06-68801044, and the **Sala dei Concerti** on Via dei Greci. Concerts are also held in various churches around town, as well as some smaller auditoriums. Check with the tourist office.

In Florence, the most important musical event is the International Music Festival, **Maggio Musicale Fiorentino** in May and June at the Teatro Comunale, the principal opera house and concert hall. Open air concerts are held in the Boboli Gardens and in the cloisters of the Badia Fiesolana on July and August evenings. Another important summer festival is **Estate Fiesolana**, which lasts from June till August. This event

fills the ancient Roman theatre in Fiesole and several churches in Florence with opera, concerts, theatre, ballet and movies.

The very famous **La Scala** in Milan, tel: 021-8053418, is a must for every opera fan. The opening evening (usually 7 December) is the city's main cultural event. Ballets and concerts are also held here.

During the summer, parks are crowded with people enjoying a variety of outdoor cultural events sponsored by the city.

In Turin, classical music is at its peak from late August until the end of September, when **Settembre Musica**, an international music festival, featuring the best national and international performers, takes over the town.

Venice's famous **La Fenice** opera house is closed at present, following a devastating fire in 1996. It is due to open in the millennium. Until then, concerts are performed at the Pala Fenice, a tented structure on the island of Tronchetto.

Naples boasts the largest opera house in Italy, **San Carlo**, tel: 081-7972111. The hall's perfect acoustics draw performers and audiences throughout the year. Bari's **Teatro Petruzzelli** is another fine music hall in the South.

Theatres

If you would like to see an Italian play, ask the city's APT (Azienda Provinciale del Turismo) or check local newspapers for information on performances. Ticket prices vary depending on the show and venue. The principal theatres are: in Rome, **Teatro Sistina**, Via Sistina 129, tel: 06-4826841 (mainly a music hall), **Teatro Valle**, Via Teatro Valle 23, tel: 06-68803794, and **Argentina Teatro di Roma**, Largo Argentina 52, tel: 06-68804001.

In Milan, you can go to the **Piccolo Teatro**, Via Rovello 2,

and its offshoot, the **Teatro Studio**, Via Rivoli 6, as well as the new **Nuovo Piccolo Teatro** next door (booking number for all three theatres: 02-77333222).

If in Florence, you can take in an Italian production at the **Teatro Comunale**, Corso Italia 12, tel: 055-2779236, **Teatro della Pergola**, Via della Pergola 12/32, tel: 055-2479652, **Teatro Verdi**, Via Ghibellina 101, tel: 055-213220, or at **Teatro Niccolini**, Via Ricasoli 3, tel: 055-213282.

In Naples there are two theatres worth visiting: the **Mercadante Piazza Municipio**, tel: 081-5524214, a small but beautiful theatre rebuilt in the 1940s, and the **Bellini**, Via Conte di Ruvo, tel: 081-5491266.

Nightlife

Late Spots

Nightlife in Italy follows the American and English fashions. There are a great many nightclubs, pubs and discos where young people gather to listen to music, dance and talk. Many of these places go in and out of popularity (or in and out of business) in the space of a few months, so check details in local newspapers or listings magazines.

In recent years, Milan and Florence have been tops for hip nightlife: Milan for its rock and discos, Florence for its clubs, while Naples has elegant and stylish nightclubs for the smart set.

In Rome, jazz is very fashionable; blues music is popular in Naples. Venice is less of a city for nightlife and many people prefer sitting in cafés and walking through the beautiful, labyrinthine streets.

Below is a list of only the more up-to-date clubs:

Rome
Alibi
Via di Monte Testaccio 39.
Gay disco on Tuesday nights only. On other nights it is open to all and there is a theme for dancing. New music.
Black Out
Via Saturnia 18.
Fashionable only on Fridays, when you can meet post-modern and graffiti artists.
El Trauco
Via Fonte dell'Olio 5.
Classic place for Brazilian music.

Il Bagaglino al Salone Margherita
Via due Macelli 75.
Cabaret in Italian.
La Macumba
Via degli Olimpionici 19.
Refuge for African, Caribbean and Latin music lovers. The rhythms are wild, with the music of Fela Kuti, Dibango and Prince.
Mississippi Jazz Club
Borgo Angelico 16.
Tel: 06-6540348.
Intimate club with the best Roman big or little jazz bands. Its most famous performers include Maurizio Gianmarco & C., Enrico Pierannunzi and Bruno Biriaco.
Smania
Via S Onofrio.
Here you will find Brazilian music, but not just samba. More fashionable is the swing of the Yemaia and of the Serpiente Latina every night.
Yellow Flag
Via della Purificazione 41.
Tel: 06-465951.
White new wave, including English psychedelic music.

Milan
Nightlife, of the hot, youthful variety, is centred on the Navigli district, the canal quarter. It is enough to turn up at night and see what is on offer, from restaurants with live music to outré clubs.
Acqua Sporca
Performances of 1940s-style big bands, every night. In the Navigli area.
Beau Geste
Piazza Velasca 4.
Tel: 02-8900692.
Part-club, part-disco, with music for most tastes.
Café Teatro Nobel
Via Asciano Sforza 81.
Tel: 02-89511746.
Shows, jazz and cabaret.
Capolinea
Via Lodovico Il Moro 119.
Tel: 02-89122024.
All big-name be-bop bands meet here. It is possible to eat while

listening to the music.
El Brellin
Via Alzaia.
Tel: 02-58101351.
Sophisticated piano bar and restaurant in the Navigli area. Closed Sunday.
Le Scimmie
Via Asciano Sforza 49.
Tel: 02-189402874
Traditional good jazz in the Navigli area. Closed Tuesday.

Florence
Caffè Strozzi
Piazza Strozzi.
Refined meeting-place popular for drinks.
Caffè Tornabuoni
Lungarno Corsini 12–4/R.
Elegant piano bar on the banks of the Arno.
Caffè Voltaire
Via della Scala 9.
Open every night. A meeting-place with recorded music.
Dolce Vita
Piazza del Carmine.
Tel: 055-284595.
Trendy and glamorous spot, especially in summer. The place for cocktails, live music and just hanging out.
Du Monde
Via di San Niccolò 103R.
Piano bar frequented by the beautiful people and poseurs. Open 10pm–5am.
Rivoire
Piazza della Signoria. Still the bar to be seen at.
Space Electronic
Via Palazzuolo 37.
Tel: 055-293082.
One of the most popular discos for youngsters.
Taragua
Via dell'Erta Canina 12.
Tel: 055-2346543.
'Tropical' bar, nightclub and Latin American disco. Closed Monday.

Naples
City Hall
Corso Vittorio Emanuele.
Good jazz, fusion-style; here you can rub elbows with all the great Neapolitan musicians, including

Bennato, De Piscopo and Esposito.
Kiss-Kiss
Via Sgambati 47.
Tel: 081-5466566.
Large disco with restaurant and cabaret attached.
La Mela
Via dei Mille 50, and **Chez Moi**, Via del Parco Margherita 20.
Two of the most elegant nightclubs in Naples.
Virgilio Sports Club
Via Tito Lucresio Caro 6.
Tel: 081-5755261.
Smart piano bar with a sea view from the terrace.

Turin
The Big Club
Corso Brescia 28.
New wave disco, rock and jazz concerts.

However, in Turin, the best nightlife from a visitor's point of view lies in the seductive 19th-century cafés. The most famous are **Barattie Milano** in Piazza Castello, and **Caffè Torino** in Piazza San Carlo (well-known for its cocktails).

Festivals

Special Events

The year is packed with special events, some linked to festivals of the Catholic church, others to the changing seasons. Every little village in Italy has its own wonderful festivals, so take every opportunity to attend. Many are associated with the harvest (especially wine) or to local products (*polenta*, *prosciutto*). The remainder tend to be historical re-enactments linked to jousting or to costumed cavalcades.

Here are some of the highlights in the Italian festival calendar:

Biennale. This is a major exhibition of international modern art, held in Venice every June–October in even-numbered years.

Carnevale. This period of festivities preceding Lent (February and March) is celebrated in unrivalled style in Venice.

The **Festa del Redentore** is also staged in Venice, on the night of the 3rd Saturday of July. A bridge of boats is built across the Giudecca Canal to the Redentore – the church which was built in gratitude for deliverance from plague in 1567. People row out to picnic on the water to watch the wonderful firework displays launched from Giudecca island.

The **International Film Festival**, once again in Venice, is held at the Lido, at the end of August each year.

The **Festa di Noiantri** is celebrated during the latter half of July. This street festival, involving music, fireworks and food, is centred in Trastevere, one of the oldest quarters of Rome.

The **Festival dei Due Mondi di Spoleto**, held late June–early July, at Spoleto, in Umbria, offers opera, theatre, concerts, ballet and exhibitions. The future of the festival is currently under threat, but it may yet be saved.

The **Scoppio del Carro,** or Explosion of the Carriage, takes place in Florence every Easter Sunday. A mechanical dove swoops through the cathedral and ignites a golden carriage filled with fireworks. The event symbolises the Resurrection.

Gioco del Calcio (also known as *Calcio in costume*) is another Florentine event, held on 19, 24 and 28 June. This is a type of football played by men wearing 16th-century costumes.

The famous **Palio** horse race is held on 2 July and 16 August in Siena's Piazza del Campo. The bareback riders, who take part in a two-hour procession before the race, wear 15th-century costumes.

Also in Tuscany, the city of Arezzo hosts the **Giostra del Saracino** on the last Sunday in August and the first Sunday in September. This medieval jousting match echoes the events of the Crusades.

Outdoor Activities

National Parks

Italy has some stunningly beautiful national parks, including:

Parco Nazionale del Gran Paradiso

Home of the last steinbocks and chamois in Italy, this Alpine park is the oldest in the country and covers 72,000 hectares (178,000 acres). Spreading over parts of Valle d'Aosta and Piedmont, it has plenty of refuges and trekking facilities, and is a magnet for nature lovers. Tel: 0124-901070.

Parco Nazionale dello Stelvio

This is the biggest park in Italy (135,000 hectares/333,600 acres). It lies close to Switzerland and is rich in forests and animals. The mountains are wonderful and there are plenty of hotels. Tel: 0342-910100.

Parco Nazionale dell'Abruzzo

Here the last brown bear in Italy lives in remote splendour in one of the highest sections of the Apennines. Tel: 0863-91955.

The Alps

If you would like to go hiking in the mountains, pick up a map of the network of walking paths, with more than 80 overnight areas with shelters. Paths are marked with numerous red signs and distinctive small flags. Every stage calls for 5–7 hours of hiking time at an average of about 1,000 metres (3,300 ft) in altitude.

At the overnight rest areas there are shelters with double-decker bunks, essential services and a kitchen. The shelters are generally situated in inhabited localities, where it is possible to buy food, phone home, rest for a day, visit historical-ethnographic museums, chat with the inhabitants and also, last but not least, eat a good meal at an inn.

An itinerary can last a month, a week or a day. From the Maritime Alps in the west to Lake Maggiore, on a route stretching for 650km (400 miles) that spans five provinces, the hiker crosses many splendid parks, such as the Gran Paradiso, the Orsiera-Rocciavrè, the Alta Val Pesio and the Argentera.

All areas are open to the public July–September.

Sport

Spectator Sports

Soccer

The national sport in Italy is soccer. Almost every city and village has its own team. The most important national championship is the "Serie A" (First Division). The winner of this competition is eligible to play in a kind of European championship, the "Champions' League", against the top teams of other European nations.

The "Serie A" championship is played September–May, and each of the 16 teams has to play the other teams twice.

The most successful Italian soccer team is Juventus FC from Turin, followed by Internazionale ("Inter") from Milan. But many other cities are blessed with successful sides, including Verona, Parma, Florence and Rome (which, like Milan, has two teams – in this case Lazio and Roma).

If you would like to see a game, check the newspaper to find out which team is playing, and where. Remember that it is very difficult to get tickets if the match is an important one. Ticket prices vary according to the importance of the team, the game, and the location of the seat you want. Unlike in some other European countries, matches tend to be safe, family affairs.

Motor Racing

The second passion of the Italians is represented by cars and speed. Formula One races attract people interested in the sophisticated technology and the coupling of man and car. This sport attracts mostly a TV audience, because it is expensive to go around the world to see the races. In Italy citizens support the red cars built by Ferrari. There is always a large crowd at the circuits in Imola (where the San Marino Grand Prix is held) and Monza (Italian Grand Prix). Although the car industry is centred on Turin, motor racing is based in the regions of Lombardy and Emilia-Romagna.

Other Sports

Almost every other sport is enjoyed in Italy, including basketball, golf, water polo, horse racing, rugby union, rowing and sailing. In addition, the Alps, Dolomites and the Apennines provide plenty of skiing opportunities.

May is an important month for sport in Italy. The *Giro d'Italia* cycle race, a major event on the cycling circuit, is staged, the Italian Open tennis tournament is held at the Foro Italico in Rome, and equestrian sports followers enjoy their major competition of the year, which takes place in Rome's Villa Borghese gardens.

If you are interested in buying tickets for any match or event, buy the pink *Gazzetta dello Sport* newspaper, where everything under the sun about sports is listed.

Shopping

Shopping Areas

Rome

The best shopping district is around the bottom of the Spanish Steps, with the elegant **Via Condotti** lined with the most exclusive shops (Gucci, Ferragamo and Bulgari).

Other fashionable streets run parallel to Via Condotti, such as **Via Borgognona** (shops of Fendi, Gianfranco Ferrè and Gucci); **Via delle Carrozze** or **Via Frattina** (for ceramics, lingerie and costume jewellery); **Via Vittoria** (where the boutique of Laura Biagiotti can be found) and **Via della Croce**. Most of these streets are closed to traffic. For antiques, go window shopping along **Via del Babuino** (do not miss the Giorgio Armani boutique there) or along **Via Margutta** or **Via Giulia**.

Another fine shopping section is along the Via del Corso between Piazza del Popolo and Largo Chigi, where **Via del Tritone** begins.

Less expensive and more popular shopping streets are **Via Nazionale**, near the railway station, where Fiorucci (sportswear and shoes) has his main outlet, and **Via Cola di Rienzo**.

"The other face of fashion" is represented by the open markets, such as the one in **Via Sannio** which sells new and second-hand clothes and, of course, the famous one at **Porta Portese**, open only on Sunday, where you can find almost everything. "Armani-style" second-hand clothes can be found in **Via delle Carrozze**.

Milan

More than Rome, Milan is the centre for international fashion and the manufactured products of Italy. For those with expensive tastes, the most chic and elegant streets for shopping are: **Via Montenapoleone**, **Via Spiga** and **Via S Andrea**, all near the Duomo and La Scala. These streets feature such fine stores as Krizia, Giò Moretti, Trussardi, Kenzo, Sanlorenzo, Giorgio Armani and Ferragamo, as well as Versace, Gucci, Ermenegildo Zegna, Comme des Garçons, Valentino, Dolce e Gabbana, Hermès, Chanel, Moschino, Prada, Ferre and Fendi.

Florence

The whole centre of Florence could be considered a huge shop, always crowded with tourists and well-dressed local people. Handicrafts are disappearing, leaving the place to smart and strange fashion shops. The most fashionable streets remain **Via dei Calzaiuoli**, **Via Roma** (absolutely "in" is Luisa), **Via de' Tornabuoni** (Gucci and Céline, as well as the famous Ferragamo fashion house – visit its new shoe museum in Palazzo Spini-Feroni), **Via della Vigna Nuova** and **Via degli Strozzi** (Neuber, Principe, Diavolo Rosa).

Ponte Vecchio is famous almost all over the world for gold

Clothing Size Chart

Women's dresses:

Italian	UK	US
38	8	6
40	10	8
42	12	10
44	14	12

Men's shirts:

Italian	UK	US
36	14	14
38	15	15
41	16	16
43	17	17

Shoe Size Chart

Women's shoes:

Italian	UK	US
37	4	6
38	5	7½
39	6	8½
40	7	9

Men's shoes:

Italian	UK	US
40	6½	7½
41	7	8
42	8	8½
43	9	9½

and silver jewellery and some antique shops.The area near the church of **Santa Croce** is full of top-quality leather goods, while for other handicrafts you can check out the city's two open markets, sprawling **San Lorenzo** and covered **Mercato Nuovo**, near Piazza della Signoria.

Venice
The most exclusive shopping area in Venice is the **Via XXII Marzo** and the streets around **St Mark's Square**. The best local shopping areas are the Rialto Bridge and San Polo. A market is held on the **Lido** on Tuesday morning. Bargains to shop for include shoes, clothes, gifts and fur coats.
  Murano glass, hand-blown in Venice, is distinctly gaudy but a popular buy. Also look out for colourful carnival masks, to wear or to hang up.

Naples
The best shopping area is concentrated around the **Piazza Amedeo** to **Piazza Trieste e Trento**. The **Via dei Mille** and **Via Filangieri** have many famous name designer shops. Mariella, one of Italy's most famous and expensive men's wear outlets, is located nearby, in **Via Riviera di Chiaia**. A less expensive street is the **Via Roma**, near the San Carlo Opera House.

Language

Language Tips

The language spoken is Italian, supplemented by regional dialects. In large cities and tourist centres you will find many people who speak English, French or German. In fact, due to the massive emigration over the last 100 years, you may encounter fluent speakers of foreign languages. Do not be surprised if you are addressed in a New York, Melbourne, Brussels or Bavarian accent: the speaker may have spent time working abroad.
  It is well worth buying a good phrase book or dictionary, but the following will help you get started. Since this glossary is aimed at non-linguists, we have opted for the simplest options rather than the most elegant Italian.

Basic Communication

Yes *Sì*
No *No*
Thank you *Grazie*
Many thanks *Mille grazie/tante grazie/molte grazie*
You're welcome *Prego*
Alright/Okay/That's fine *Va bene*
Please *Per favore* or *per cortesia.*
Excuse me (to get attention) *Scusi* (singular), *Scusate* (plural)
Excuse me (to get through a crowd) *Permesso*
Excuse me (to attract attention, e.g. of a waiter) *Senta!*
Excuse me (sorry) *Mi scusi* (singular), *Scusatemi* (plural)

Wait a minute! (informal) *Aspetta!* (formal) *Aspetti!*
Could you help me? (formal) *Potrebbe aiutarmi?*
Certainly *Ma certo*
Can I help you? (formal) *Posso aiutarLa?*
Can you show me...? (formal) *Può indicarmi...?*
Can you help me? (formal) *Può aiutarmi, per cortesia?*
I need ... *Ho bisogno di ...*
I'm lost *Mi sono perso*
I'm sorry *Mi dispiace*
I don't know *Non lo so*
I don't understand *Non capisco*
Do you speak English/French/German? *Parla inglese/francese/tedesco?*
Could you speak more slowly, please? *Può parlare piú lentamente, per favore?*
Could you repeat that please? (formal) *Può ripetere, per piacere?*
slowly/quietly *piano*
here/there *qui/là*
What? *Cosa?*
When/why/where? *Quando/perchè/dove?*
Where is the lavatory? *Dov'è il bagno?*

Greetings

Hello (Good day) *Buon giorno*
Good afternoon/evening *Buona sera*
Good night *Buona notte*
Goodbye *Arrivederci*
Hello/Hi/Goodbye (familiar) *Ciao*
Mr/Mrs/Miss *Signor/Signora/Signorina*
Pleased to meet you (formal) *Piacere di conoscerLa*
I am English/American *Sono inglese/americano*
Irish/Scottish/Welsh *irlandese/scozzese/gallese*
Canadian/Australian *canadese/australiano*
Do you speak English? (formal) *Parla inglese?*
I'm here on holiday *Sono qui in vacanza*
Is it your first trip to Milan/Rome? (formal) *É il Suo primo*

viaggio a Milano/Roma?
Do you like it here? (formal) *Si trova bene qui?*
How are you (formal/informal)? *Come sta/come stai?*
Fine thanks *Bene, grazie*
See you later *A più tardi*
See you soon *A presto*
Take care (formal) *Tia bene,* (informal) *Tammi bene*

New acquaintances are likely to ask you:
Do you like Italy/Florence/ Rome/Venice/my city? (formal) *E piace Italia/Firenze/Roma/ Venezia/la mia città?*
I like it a lot (is the correct answer) *Mi piace moltissimo.*
It's wonderful (an alternative answer) *È meravigliosa/ favolosa.*
(Both responses can be applied to food, beaches, the view, etc.)

Telephone calls

the area code *il prefisso telefonico*
I'd like to make a reverse charges call *Vorrei fare una telefonata a carico del destinatario*
May I use your telephone, please? *Posso usare il telefono?*
Hello (on the telephone) *Pronto*
My name's *Mi chiamo/Sono*

Could I speak to...? *Posso parlare con...?*
Sorry, he/she isn't in *Mi dispiace, è fuori*
Can he call you back? *Può richiamarLa?*
I'll try again later *Riproverò più tardi*
Can I leave a message? *Posso lasciare un messaggio?*
Please tell him I called *Gli dica, per favore, che ho telefonato*
Hold on *Un attimo, per favore*
A local call *una telefonata locale*
Can you speak up please? (formal) *Può parlare più forte, per favore?*

In the Hotel

Do you have any vacant rooms? *Avete camere libere?*
I have a reservation *Ho fatto una prenotazione*
I'd like... *Vorrei...*
a single/double room (with a double bed) *una camera singola/doppia (con letto matrimoniale)*
a room with twin beds *una camera a due letti*
a room with a bath/shower *una camera con bagno/doccia*
for one night *per una notte*
for two nights *per due notti*
We have one with a double bed *Ne abbiamo una matrimoniale.*

Could you show me another room please? *Potrebbe mostrarmi un'altra camera?*
How much is it? *Quanto costa?*
on the first floor *al primo piano*
Is breakfast included? *É compresa la prima colazione?*
Is everything included? *É tutto compreso?*
half/full board *mezza pensione/pensione completa*
It's expensive *É caro*
Do you have a room with a balcony/view of the sea? *C'è una camera con balcone/con vista sul mare?*
a room overlooking the park/the street/the back *una camera con vista sul parco/che dà sulla strada/sul retro*
Is it a quiet room? *É una stanza tranquilla?*
The room is too hot/cold/ noisy/small *La camera è troppo calda/fredda/rumorosa/piccola*
Can I see the room? *Posso vedere la camera?*
What time does the hotel close? *A che ora chiude l'albergo?*
I'll take it *La prendo*
big/small *grande/piccola*
What time is breakfast? *A che ora è la prima colazione?*
Please give me a call at... *Mi può chiamare alle...*
Come in! *Avanti!*

Pronunciation and Grammar Tips

Italian speakers claim that pronunciation is straight-forward: you pronounce it as it is written. This is approximately true but there are a couple of important rules for English speakers to bear in mind: *c* before *e* or *i* is pronounced "ch", e.g. *ciao, mi dispiace, la coincidenza. Ch* before *i* or *e* is pronounced as "k", e.g. *la chiesa.* Likewise, *sci* or *sce* are pronounced as in "sheep" or "shed" respectively. *Gn* in Italian is rather like the sound in "onion", while *gl* is softened

to resemble the sound in "bullion".

Nouns are either masculine (*il*, plural *i*) or feminine (*la*, plural *le*). Plurals of nouns are most often formed by changing an *o* to an *i* and an *a* to an *e*, e.g. *il panino, i panini; la chiesa, le chiese.*

Words are stressed on the penultimate syllable unless an accent indicates otherwise.

Like many languages, Italian has formal and informal words for "You". In the singular, *Tu* is informal while *Lei* is more

polite. Confusingly, in some parts of Italy or in some circumstances, you will also hear *Voi* used as a singular polite form. (In general, *Voi* is reserved for "You" plural, however.) For visitors, it is simplest and most respectful to use the formal form unless invited to do otherwise.

There is, of course, rather more to the language than that, but you can get a surprisingly long way towards making friends with a mastery of a few basic phrases.

Can I have the bill, please? *Posso avere il conto, per favore.*
Can you call me a taxi please? *Può chiamarmi un taxì, per favore?*
dining room *la sala da pranzo*
key *la chiave*
lift *l'ascensore*
towel *l'asciugamano*
toilet paper *la carta igienica*
pull/push *tirare/spingere*

Eating Out

Bar snacks and drinks
I'd like... *Vorrei...*
coffee *un caffè* (*espresso*: small, strong and black)
un cappuccino (with hot, frothy milk)
un caffelatte (like *café au lait* in France)
un caffè lungo (weak)
un corretto (laced with alcohol – usually brandy or grappa. You should specify)
tea *un tè*
lemon tea *un tè al limone*
herbal tea *una tisana*
hot chocolate *una cioccolata calda*
orange/lemon juice (bottled) *un succo d'arancia/di limone*
fresh orange/lemon juice *una spremuta di arancia/di limone*
orangeade *un'aranciata*
water (mineral) *acqua (minerale)*
fizzy/still mineral water *acqua*

Bar Notices

Prezzo al tavolo/in terrazza **Price at a table/terrace** (often double what you pay standing at the bar)
Si paga alla cassa **Pay at the cash desk**
Si prende lo scontrino alla cassa **Pay at the cash desk**, then take the receipt (*lo scontrino*) to the bar to be served; this is common procedure
Signori/Uomini **Gentlemen** (lavatories)
Signore/Donne **Ladies** (lavatories)

minerale gasata/naturale
a glass of mineral water *un bicchiere di minerale*
with/without ice *con/senza ghiaccio*
red/white wine *vino rosso/bianco*
beer (draught) *una birra (alla spina)*
a gin and tonic *un gin tonic*
a bitter (Vermouth, etc.) *un amaro*
milk *latte*
a (half) litre *un (mezzo) litro*
bottle *una bottiglia*
ice cream *un gelato*
cone *un cono*
pastry *una pasta*
sandwich *un tramezzino*
roll *un panino*
Anything else? *Desidera qualcos'altro?*
Cheers *Salute*
Let me pay *Offro io*
That's very kind of you *Grazie, molto gentile*

In a restaurant
I'd like to book a table *Vorrei riservare un tavolo*
Have you got a table for... *Avete un tavolo per ...*
I have a reservation *Ho fatto una prenotazione*
lunch/supper *il pranzo/la cena*
We do not want a full meal *Non desideriamo un pasto completo*
Could we have another table? *Potremmo spostarci?*
I'm a vegetarian *Sono vegetariano/a*
Is there a vegetarian dish? *C'è un piatto vegetariano?*
May we have the menu? *Ci dà il menu, per favore?*
wine list *la lista dei vini*
What would you like? *Che cosa prende?*
What would you recommend? *Che cosa ci raccomanda?*
home-made *fatto in casa*
What would you like as a main course/dessert? *Che cosa prende di secondo/di dolce?*
What would you like to drink? *Che cosa desidera da bere?*
a carafe of red/white wine *una caraffa di vino rosso/bianco*

fixed price menu *il menu a prezzo fisso*
the dish of the day *il piatto del giorno*
VAT (sales tax) *IVA*
cover charge *il coperto/pane e coperto*
That's enough; no more, thanks *Basta (così)*
The bill, please *Il conto per favore*
Is service included? *Il servizio è incluso?*
Where is the lavatory? *Dovè il bagno?*
Keep the change *Va bene così*
I've enjoyed the meal *Mi è piaciuto molto*

Menu Decoder

Antipasti (hors d'oeuvres)
antipasto misto **mixed hors d'oeuvres** (including cold cuts, possibly cheeses and roast vegetables– ask, however)
buffet freddo **cold buffet** (often excellent)
caponata **mixed aubergine, olives and tomatoes**
insalata caprese **tomato and mozzarella salad**
insalata di mare **seafood salad**
insalata mista/verde **mixed/green salad**
melanzane alla parmigiana **fried or baked aubergine** (with parmesan cheese and tomato)
mortadella/salame **salami**
pancetta **bacon**
peperonata **vegetable stew** (made with peppers, onions, tomatoes and sometimes aubergines)

Primi (first courses)
Typical first courses include soup, *risotto*, *gnocchi* or numerous varieties of pasta in a wide range of sauces. *Risotto* and *gnocchi* are more common in the North than in Central Italy.
il brodetto **fish soup**
il brodo **consommé**
i crespolini **savoury pancakes**
gli gnocchi **potato dumplings**
la minestra **soup**

il minestrone **thick vegetable soup**
pasta e fagioli **pasta and bean soup**
il prosciutto (cotto/crudo) **ham** (cooked/cured)
i supplì **rice croquettes**
i tartufi **truffles**
la zuppa **soup**

Pasta Dishes

Common Pasta Shapes
cannelloni (large stuffed tubes of pasta); *farfalle* (bow- or butterfly-shaped pasta); *tagliatelle* (flat noodles, similar to *fettuccine*); *tortellini* and *ravioli* (different types of stuffed pasta packets); *penne* (quill-shaped tubes, smaller than *rigatoni*).

Typical Pasta Sauces
pomodoro (tomato); *pesto* (with basil and pine nuts); *matriciana* (bacon and tomato); *arrabbiata* (spicy tomato); *panna* (cream); *ragù* (meat sauce); *aglio e olio* (garlic and olive oil); *burro e salvia* (butter and sage).

Secondi (main courses)
Typical main courses are fish-, seafood- or meat-based, with accompaniments *(contorni)* that vary greatly from region to region.

La carne (meat)
allo spiedo **on the spit**
arrosto **roast meat**
i ferri **grilled**
al forno **baked**
al girarrosto **spit-roasted**
alla griglia **grilled**
involtini **skewered veal, ham, etc.**
stagionato **hung, well-aged**
stufato **braised, stewed**
ben cotto **well-done** (steak, etc.)
al puntino **medium** (steak, etc.)
al sangue **rare** (steak, etc.)

l'agnello **lamb**
a bresaola **dried salted beef**
la bistecca **steak**

il capriolo/cervo **venison**
il carpaccio **lean beef fillet**
il cinghiale **wild boar**
il coniglio **rabbit**
il controfiletto **sirloin steak**
le cotolette **cutlets**
il maiale **pork**
il fagiano **pheasant**
il fegato **liver**
il filetto **fillet**
la lepre **hare**
il maiale **pork**
il manzo **beef**
l'ossobuco **shin of veal**
la porchetta **roast suckling pig**
il pollo **chicken**
le polpette **meatballs**
il polpettone **meat loaf**
la salsiccia **sausage**
saltimbocca (alla romana) **veal escalopes with ham**
le scaloppine **escalopes**
lo stufato **stew**
il sugo **sauce**
il tacchino **turkey**
la trippa **tripe**
il vitello **veal**

Frutti di mare (seafood)
Beware the word "*surgelati*", meaning frozen rather than fresh.

affumicato **smoked**
alle brace **charcoal grilled/ barbecued**
alla griglia **grilled**
fritto **fried**
ripieno **stuffed**
al vapore **steamed**

le acciughe **anchovies**
l'anguilla **eel**
l'aragosta **lobster**
il baccalà **dried salted cod**
i bianchetti **whitebait**
il branzino **sea bass**
i calamari **squid**
i calamaretti **baby squid**
la carpa **carp**
i crostacei **shellfish**
le cozze **mussels**
il fritto misto **mixed fried fish**
i gamberi **prawns**
i gamberetti **shrimps**
il granchio **crab**
il merluzzo **cod**
le moleche **soft-shelled crabs**

le ostriche **oysters**
il pesce **fish**
il pesce spada **swordfish**
il polipo **octopus**
il risotto di mare **seafood risotto**
le sarde **sardines**
la sogliola **sole**
le seppie **cuttlefish**
la triglia **red mullet**
la trota **trout**
il tonno **tuna**
le vongole **clams**

I legumi/la verdura (vegetables)
a scelta **of your choice**
i contorni **accompaniments**
ripieno **stuffed**

gli asparagi **asparagus**
la bietola **similar to spinach**
il carciofo **artichoke**
le carote **carrots**
i carciofini **artichoke hearts**
il cavolo **cabbage**
la cicoria **chicory**
la cipolla **onion**
i funghi **mushrooms**
i fagioli **beans**
i fagiolini **French (green) beans**
le fave **broad beans**
il finocchio **fennel**
l'indivia **endive/chicory**
l'insalata mista **mixed salad**
l'insalata verde **green salad**
la melanzana **aubergine**
le patate **potatoes**
le patatine fritte **chips/French fries**
i peperoni **peppers**
i piselli **peas**
i pomodori **tomatoes**
le primizie **spring vegetables**
il radicchio **red, slightly bitter lettuce**
la rughetta **rocket**
i ravanelli **radishes**
gli spinaci **spinach**
la verdura **green vegetables**
la zucca **pumpkin/squash**
gli zucchini **courgettes**

I dolci (desserts)
al carrello **(desserts) from the trolley**
un semifreddo **semi-frozen dessert (many types)**
la bavarese **mousse**

la cassata **Sicilian ice cream with candied peel**
le frittelle **fritters**
un gelato (di lampone/limone) **(raspberry/lemon) ice cream**
una granìta **water ice**
una macedonia di frutta **fruit salad**
il tartufo (nero) **(chocolate) ice cream dessert**
il tiramisù **cold, creamy cheese and coffee dessert**
la torta **cake/tart**
lo zabaglione **sweet dessert made with eggs and Marsala wine**
lo zuccotto **ice cream liqueur**
la zuppa inglese **trifle**

La frutta (fruit)
le albicocche **apricots**
le arance **oranges**
le banane **bananas**
il cocomero **watermelon**
le ciliegie **cherries**
i fichi **figs**
le fragole **strawberries**
i frutti di bosco **fruits of the forest**
i lamponi **raspberries**
la mela **apple**
il melone **melon**
la pesca **peach**
la pera **pear**
il pompelmo **grapefruit**
l'uva **grapes**

Basic foods
l'aceto **vinegar**
l'aglio **garlic**
il burro **butter**
il formaggio **cheese**
la focaccia **oven-baked snack**
la frittata **omelette**
il grana **hard grating cheese, similar to parmesan**
i grissini **bread sticks**
l'olio **oil**
la marmellata **jam**
il pane **bread**
il pane integrale **wholemeal bread**
il parmigiano **parmesan cheese**
il pepe **pepper**
il riso **rice**
il sale **salt**
la senape **mustard**
le uova **eggs**

lo yogurt **yoghurt**
lo zucchero **sugar**

Sightseeing

Si può visitare? **Can one visit?**
il custode **custodian**
il sacrestano **sacristan**
Suonare il campanello **ring the bell**
aperto/a **open**
chiuso/a **closed**
chiuso per la festa **closed for the festival**
chiuso per ferie **closed for the holidays**
chiuso per restauro **closed for restoration**
Is it possible to see the church? *É possibile visitare la chiesa?*
Entrata/uscita **Entrance/exit**
Where can I find the custodian/sacristan/key? *Dove posso trovare il custode/il sacrestano/la chiave?*

We have come a long way just to see ... *Siamo venuti da lontano proprio per visitare ...*
It is really a pity it is closed *É veramente peccato che sia chiuso*

(The last two should be tried in desperation – pleas for sympathy can sometimes open a few doors.)

At the Shops

What time do you open/close? *A che ora apre/chiude?*
Closed for the holidays (typical sign) *Chiuso per ferie*
Pull/push (sign on doors) *Tirare/spingere*
Entrance/exit *Entrata/uscita*
Can I help you? (formal) *Posso aiutarLa?*
What would you like? *Che cosa desidera?*
I'm just looking *Sto soltanto guardando*
How much does it cost? *Quant'è, per favore?*
How much is this? *Quanto viene?*
Do you take credit cards?

Accettate carte di credito?
I'd like... *Vorrei...*
this one/that one *questo/quello*
I'd like that one, please *Vorrei quello lì, per cortesia*
Have you got ...? *Avete ...?*
We haven't got (any) ... *Non (ne) abbiamo...*
Can I try it on? *Posso provare?*
the size (for clothes) *la taglia*
What size do you take? *Qual'é a sua taglia?*
the size (for shoes) *il numero*
Is there/do you have ...? *C'è ...?*
Yes, of course *Sì, certo*
No, we don't (there isn't) *No, non c'è*
That's too expensive *É troppo caro*
Please write it down for me *Me lo scriva, per favore*
cheap *economico*
Don't you have anything cheaper? *Ha niente che costa di meno?*
It's too small/big *É troppo piccolo/grande*
brown/blue/black *marrone/blu/nero*
green/red/white/yellow *verde/rosso/bianco/giallo*
pink/grey/gold/silver *rosa/grigio/oro/argento*
No thank you, I don't like it *Grazie, ma non è di mio gusto*
I (don't) like it *(Non) mi piace*
I'll take it/I'll leave it *Lo prendo/Lo lascio*
It's a rip-off (impolite) *Una ruberìa*
This is faulty. Can I have a replacement/refund? *C'è un difetto. Me lo potrebbe cambiare/rimborsare?*
Anything else? *Altro?*
The cash desk is over there *Si accomodi alla cassa*
Give me some of those *Mi dia alcuni di quelli lì*
a (half) kilo *un (mezzo) chilo*
100 grams *un etto*
200 grams *due etti*
more/less *più/meno*
with/without *con/senza*
a little *un pochino*
That's enough/No more *Basta così*

Types of shops

antique dealer *l'antiquario*
bakery/cake shop *la panetteria/pasticceria*
bank *la banca*
bookshop *la libreria*
boutique/clothes shop *il negozio di moda*
bureau de change *il cambio*
butcher's *la macelleria*
chemist's *la farmacia*
delicatessen *la salumeria*
department store *il grande magazzino*
dry cleaner's *la tintoria*
fishmonger's *la pescheria*
food shop *l'alimentari*
florist *il fioraio*
grocer's *l'alimentari*
greengrocer's *il fruttivendolo*
hairdresser's (women) *il parrucchiere*
ice cream parlour *la gelateria*
jeweller's *il gioielliere*
leather shop *la pelletteria*
market *il mercato*
news-stand *l'edicola*
post office *l'ufficio postale*
shoe shop *il negozio di scarpe*
stationer's *la cartoleria*
supermarket *il supermercato*
tobacconist *il tabaccaio* (also usually sells travel tickets, stamps, phone cards)
travel agency *l'agenzia di viaggi* (also usually books train tickets for domestic and international journeys).

Travelling

Transport

airport *l'aeroporto*
arrivals/departures *arrivi/partenze*
boat *la barca*
bus *l'autobus/il pullman*
bus station *l'autostazione*
car *la macchina*
connection *la coincidenza*
ferry *il traghetto*
ferry terminal *la stazione marittima*
first/second class *la prima/seconda classe*
flight *il volo*
left luggage office *il deposito bagagli*
motorway *l'autostrada*
no smoking *vietato fumare*
platform *il binario*
porter *il facchino*
railway station *la stazione (ferroviaria)*
return ticket *un biglietto di andata e ritorno*
single ticket *un biglietto di andata sola*
sleeping car *la carrozza letti/il vagone letto*
smokers/non-smokers *fumatori/non-fumatori*
stop *la fermata*
taxi *il taxì*
ticket office *la biglietteria*
train *il treno*
WC *la toilette*

Days and Dates

morning/afternoon/evening *la mattina, il pomeriggio, la sera*
yesterday/today/tomorrow *ieri/oggi/domani*
the day after tomorrow *dopodomani*
now/early/late *adesso/presto/ritardo*
a minute *un minuto*
an hour *un'ora*
half an hour *un mezz'ora*
a day *un giorno*
a week *una settimana*
Monday *lunedì*
Tuesday *martedì*
Wednesday *mercoledì*
Thursday *giovedì*
Friday *venerdì*
Saturday *sabato*
Sunday *domenica*
first *il primo/la prima*
second *il secondo/la seconda*
third *il terzo/la terza*

At the airport

Where's the office of British Airways/ Alitalia? *Dov'è l'ufficio della British Airways/dell'Alitalia?*
I'd like to book a flight to Venice *Vorrei prenotare un volo per Venezia*
When is the next flight to ...? *Quando parte il prossimo aereo per...?*
Are there any seats available? *Ci sono ancora posti liberi?*
Have you got any hand luggage? *Ha bagagli a mano?*
I'll take this hand luggage with me *Questo lo tengo come bagaglio a mano*
My suitcase has got lost *La mia valigia è andata persa*
My suitcase has been damaged *La mia valigia è rovinata*
The flight has been delayed *Il volo è rimandato*
The flight has been cancelled *Il volo è stato cancellato*
I can put you on the waiting list *Posso metterLa sulla lista d'attesa*

Tourist Signs

Most regions in Italy have handy signs indicating the key tourist sights in any given area:

Abbazia (Badia) **Abbey**
Basilica **Church**
Belvedere **Viewpoint**
Biblioteca **Library**
Castello **Castle**
Centro storico **Old town/ historic centre**
Chiesa **Church**
Duomo/Cattedrale **Cathedral**
Fiume **River**
Giardino **Garden**

Lago **Lake**
Mercato **Market**
Monastero **Monastery**
Monumenti **Monuments**
Museo **Museum**
Parco **Park**
Pinacoteca **Art gallery**
Ponte **Bridge**
Ruderi **Ruins**
Scavi **Excavations/ archaeological site**
Spiaggia **Beach**
Tempio **Temple**
Torre **Tower**
Ufficio turistico **Tourist office**

At the station

Can you help me please? *Mi può aiutare, per favore?*
Where can I buy tickets? *Dove posso fare i biglietti?*
at the ticket office/at the counter *alla biglietteria/allo sportello*
What time does the train leave? *A che ora parte il treno?*
What time does the train arrive? *A che ora arriva il treno?*
Can I book a seat? *Posso prenotare un posto?*
Are there any seats available? *Ci sono ancora posti liberi?*
Is this seat free/taken? *É libero/occupato questo posto?*
I'm afraid this is my seat *É il mio posto, mi dispiace*
You'll have to pay a supplement *Deve pagare un supplemento*
Do I have to change? *Devo cambiare?*
Where does it stop? *Dove si ferma?*
You need to change in Rome *Bisogna cambiare a Roma*
Which platform does the train leave from? *Da quale binario parte il treno?*
The train leaves from platform one *Il treno parte dal binario uno*
When is the next train/bus/ ferry for Naples? *Quando parte il prossimo treno/pullman/ traghetto per Napoli?*
What time does the bus leave for Siena? *Quando parte l'autobus per Siena?*
How long will it take to get

Conversion Charts

Metric–Imperial:
1 centimetre = 0.4 inch
1 metre = 3 ft 3 ins
1 kilometre = 0.62 mile
1 gram = 0.04 ounce
1 kilogram = 2.2 pounds
1 litre = 1.76 UK pints

Imperial–Metric:
1 inch = 2.54 centimetres
1 foot = 30 centimetres
1 ounce = 28 grams
1 pound = 0.45 kilogram
1 pint = 0.57 litre
1 UK gallon = 4.55 litres
1 US gallon = 3.78 litres

there? *Quanto tempo ci vuole per arrivare?*
Will we arrive on time? *Arriveremo puntuali?*
Next stop please *La prossima fermata per favore*
Is this the right stop? *É la fermata giusta?*
The train is late *Il treno è in ritardo*
Can you tell me where to get off? *Mi può dire dove devo scendere?*

Directions

right/left *a destra/a sinistra*
first left/second right *la prima a sinistra/la seconda a destra*
Turn to the right/left *Gira a destra/sinistra*
Go straight on *Va sempre diritto*
Go straight on until the traffic

lights *Va sempre diritto fino al semaforo*
Is it far away/nearby? *É lontano/vicino?*
It's five minutes' walk *Cinque minuti a piedi*
It's 10 minutes by car *Dieci minuti con la macchina*
You can't miss it *Non può non vederlo*
opposite/next to *di fronte/ accanto a*
up/down *su/giù*
traffic lights *il semaforo*
junction *l'incrocio, il bivio*
building *il palazzo*
Where is …? *Dov'è …?*
Where are …? *Dove sono …?*
Where is the nearest bank/ petrol station/bus stop/ hotel/garage? *Dov'è la banca/il benzinaio/la fermata di autobus/l'albergo/l'officina più vicino/a?*
How do I get there? *Come si può andare?* (or: *Come faccio per arrivare a …?*)
How long does it take to get to …? *Quanto tempo ci vuole per andare a …?*
Can you show me where I am on the map? *Può indicarmi sulla cartina dove mi trovo?*
You're on the wrong road *Lei è sulla strada sbagliata*

On the road

Where can I rent a car? *Dove posso noleggiare una macchina?*
Is comprehensive insurance included? *É completamente assicurata?*

Numbers

1 *Uno*	**13** *Tredici*	**70** *Settanta*
2 *Due*	**14** *Quattordici*	**80** *Ottanta*
3 *Tre*	**15** *Quindici*	**90** *Novanta*
4 *Quattro*	**16** *Sedici*	**100** *Cento*
5 *Cinque*	**17** *Diciassette*	**200** *Duecento*
6 *Sei*	**18** *Diciotto*	**500** *Cinquecento*
7 *Sette*	**19** *Diciannove*	**1,000** *Mille*
8 *Otto*	**20** *Venti*	**2,000** *Duemila*
9 *Nove*	**30** *Trenta*	**5,000** *Cinquemila*
10 *Dieci*	**40** *Quaranta*	**50,000** *Cinquantamila*
11 *Undici*	**50** *Cinquanta*	**1 Million** *Un milione*
12 *Dodici*	**60** *Sessanta*	

Emergencies

Help! *Aiuto!*
Stop! *Fermate!*
I've had an accident *Ho avuto un incidente*
Watch out! *Attenzione!*
Call a doctor *Per favore, chiami un medico*
Call an ambulance *Chiami un'ambulanza*
Call the police *Chiami la Polizia/i Carabinieri*
Call the fire brigade *Chiami i pompieri*
Where is the telephone? *Dov'è il telefono?*
Where is the nearest hospital? *Dov'è l'ospedale più vicino?*
I would like to report a theft *Voglio denunciare un furto*

Is it insured for another driver? *É assicurata per un altro guidatore?*
By what time must I return it? *A che ora devo consegnarla?*
underground car park *il garage sotterraneo*
driving licence *la patente (di guida)*
petrol *la benzina*
petrol station/garage *la stazione di servizio*

oil *l'olio*
Fill it up please *Faccia il pieno, per favore*
lead free/unleaded/diesel *senza piombo/benzina verde/diesel*
My car won't start *La mia macchina non s'accende*
My car has broken down *La mia macchina è guasta*
How long will it take to repair? *Quanto tempo ci vorrà per la riparazione?*
The engine is overheating *Il motore si surriscalda*
There's something wrong (with/in the) ... *C'è un difetto (nel/nella/nei/nelle)* ...
... **accelerator** *l'acceleratore*
... **brakes** *i freni*
... **engine** *il motore*
... **exhaust** *lo scarico/scappamento*
... **fanbelt** *la cinghia del ventilatore*
... **gearbox** *la scatola del cambio*
... **headlights** *le luci*
... **radiator** *il radiatore*
... **spark plugs** *le candele*
... **tyre(s)** *la gomma (le gomme)*
... **windscreen** *il parabrezza*

Health

Is there a chemist's nearby? *C'è una farmacia qui vicino?*

Which chemist is open at night? *Quale farmacia fa il turno di notte?*
I don't feel well *Non mi sento bene*
I feel ill *Sto male/Mi sento male*
Where does it hurt? *Dove Le fa male?*
It hurts here *Ho dolore qui*
I suffer from ... *Soffro di ...*
I have a headache *Ho mal di testa*
I have a sore throat *Ho mal di gola*
I have a stomach ache *Ho mal di pancia*
Have you got something for air sickness? *Ha/Avete qualcosa contro il mal d'aria?*
Have you got something for sea sickness? *Ha/Avete qualcosa contro il mal di mare?*
antiseptic cream *la crema antisettica*
sunburn *scottatura da sole*
sunburn cream *la crema antisolare*
sticking plaster *il cerotto*
tissues *i fazzoletti di carta*
toothpaste *il dentifricio*
upset stomach pills *le pillole per mal di stomaco*
insect repellent *l'insettifugo*
mosquitoes *le zanzare*
wasps *le vespe*

Road Signs

Accendere le luci in galleria **Lights on in tunnel**
Alt **Stop**
Autostrada **Motorway**
Attenzione **Caution**
Avanti **Go/walk**
Caduta massi **Danger of falling rocks**
Casello **Toll gate**
Dare la precedenza **Give way**
Deviazione **Diversion**
Divieto di campeggio **No camping allowed**
Divieto di sosta/Sosta vietata **No parking**
Divieto di passaggio/Senso vietato **No entry**
Dogana **Customs**

Entrata **Entrance**
Galleria **Tunnel**
Guasto **Out of order** (e.g. phone box)
Incrocio **Crossroads**
Limite di velocità **Speed limit**
Non toccare **Don't touch**
Passaggio a livello **Railway crossing**
Parcheggio **Parking**
Pedaggio **Toll road**
Pericolo **Danger**
Pronto Soccorso **First aid**
Rallentare **Slow down**
Rimozione forzata **Parked cars will be towed away**
Semaforo **Traffic lights**
Senso unico **One way street**

Sentiero **Footpath**
Solo uscita **No entry**
Strada interrotta **Road blocked**
Strada chiusa **Road closed**
Strada senza uscita/Vicolo cieco **Dead end**
Tangenziale **Ring road/bypass**
Traffico di transito **Through traffic**
Uscita **Exit**
Uscita (autocarri) **Exit for lorries**
Vietato il sorpasso **No overtaking**
Vietato il transito **No thoroughfare**

Further Reading

General

Across the River and into the Trees, by Ernest Hemingway.
A Room with a View, by E.M. Forster.
Andreas, by Hugo von Hoffmannsthal. 1930.
The Architecture of the Italian Renaissance, by Peter Murray.
The Aspern Papers, by Henry James.
Autobiography, by Benvenuto Cellini.
Christ Stopped at Eboli, by Carlo Levi.
Le Città Invisibili, Italo Calvino. Translated as *Invisible Cities*.
The Civilization of the Renaissance in Italy. Jacob Burckhardt.
D.H. Lawrence and Italy, by D.H. Lawrence.
The Doge, by A. Palazzeschi.
Etruscan Places, by D.H. Lawrence.
Florence, a Traveller's Companion, by Harold Acton and Edward Chaney.
The Gallery, by John Horne Burns.
Graziella, by Alphonse de Lamartine (AC Mclurg, Chicago).
Il Fuoco, by Gabriele d'Annuncio. Translated as *The Flame of Life*.
Italian Hours, by Henry James.
Italian Journey, by Johann Wolfgang Goethe.
The Italian Painters of the Renaissance, by Bernard Berenson.
The Italians, by Luigi Barzini.
The Italian World, by John Julius Norwich.
The Last Medici, by Harold Acton.
Lives of the Artists, Vol. 1 & 2, by Giorgio Vasari.
Love and War in the Apennines, by Eric Newby.
The Love of Italy, by Jonathan Keates.
The Mafia, by Clare Sterling.
The Mediterranean Passion, by John Pemble.
The Merchant of Prato, by Iris Origo.
Memoirs, by Giacomo Casanova. Translated into many languages.
Naples '44, by Norman Lewis.
Pictures from Italy, by Charles Dickens.
Renaissance Venice, edited by J.R. Hale.
The Rise and Fall of the House of Medici, by Christopher Hibbert.
Rome, Naples and Florence, by Stendhal (published 1817).
Siren Island, Summer Islands, South Wind and *Old Calabria*, by Norman Douglas.
The Stones of Florence and Venice Observed, by Mary McCarthy.
The Stones of Venice (1851–3), by John Ruskin.
The Story of San Michele, by Axel Munthe.
Those Who Walk Away, by Patricia Highsmith.
Thus Spake Bellavista, by Luciano de Crescenzo.
Der Tod in Venedig, by Thomas Mann. Translated as *Death in Venice*.
A Tramp Abroad, by Mark Twain.
A Venetian Bestiary, by Jan Morris.
Venetian Life, by William Dean Howells. 1866.
Venetian Red, by P.M. Passinetti.
Venice, by Jan Morris.
Venice: A Thousand Years of Culture and Civilisation, by Peter Lauritzen.
Venice and its Lagoon, Giulio Lorenzetti.
Venice for Pleasure, by J.G. Links.
Venice: The Greatness and the Fall, Mark by Twain. 1981.
Venice: The Rise to Empire, by John Julius Norwich.
The Wings of the Dove, by Henry James.

Other Insight Guides

Other *Insight Guides* to Italian destinations are: Rome, Venice, Florence, Umbria, Tuscany, The Bay of Naples, Sicily, Sardinia and South Tyrol; *Insight Pocket Guides* Venice, Rome, Florence, Milan, Sicily, Sardinia and Tuscany, which come complete with a pull-out map; and *Insight Compact Guides* to Florence, Milan, Rome, Tuscany, Venice, the Italian Riviera and the Italian Lakes.
Thoroughly updated and expanded, the best-selling *Insight Guide: Rome* lifts the lid on Italy's capital.
Insight Pocket Guide: Florence provides tailor-made tours of Italy's art capital. Perfect for a short break. Includes a pull-out map.
Insight Compact Guide Venice is excellent for on-the-spot information.

ART & PHOTO CREDITS

INSIGHT GUIDE
ITALY

Maps **ERA Maptec Ltd**
Cartographic Editor **Zoë Goodwin**
Production **Mohammed Dar**
Design Consultant **Klaus Geisler**
Picture Research **Hilary Genin, Monica Allende**

Index

Note: page numbers in italics refer to illustrations

The Insight Approach

guide to bali

The book you are holding is part of the world's largest range of guidebooks. Its purpose is to help you have the most valuable travel experience possible, and we try to achieve this by providing not only information about countries, regions and cities but also genuine insight into their history, culture, institutions and people.

Since the first Insight Guide – to Bali – was published in 1970, the series has been dedicated to the proposition that, with insight into a country's people and culture, visitors can both enhance their own experience and be accepted more easily by their hosts. Now, in a world where ethnic hostilities and nationalist conflicts are all too common, such attempts to increase understanding between peoples are more important than ever.

Insight Guides:
Essentials for understanding
Because a nation's past holds the key to its present, each Insight Guide kicks off with lively history chapters. These are followed by magazine-style essays on culture and daily life. This essential background information gives readers the necessary context for using the main Places section, with its comprehensive run-down on things worth seeing and doing.

Finally, a listings section contains all the information you'll need on travel, hotels, restaurants and opening times.

As far as possible, we rely on local writers and specialists to ensure that information is authoritative. The pictures, for which Insight Guides have become so celebrated, are just as important. Our photojournalistic approach aims not only to illustrate a destination but also to communicate visually and directly to readers life as it is lived by the locals. The series has grown to almost 200 titles.

Compact Guides:
The "great little guides"
As invaluable as such background information is, it isn't always fun to carry an Insight Guide through a crowded souk or up a church tower. Could we, readers asked, distil the key reference material into a slim volume for on-the-spot use?

Our response was to design Compact Guides as an entirely new series, with original text carefully cross-referenced to detailed maps and more than 200 photographs. In essence, they're miniature encyclopedias, concise and comprehensive, displaying reliable and up-to-date information in an accessible way. There are almost 100 titles.

Pocket Guides:
A local host in book form
However wide-ranging the information in a book, human beings still value the personal touch. Our editors are often asked the same questions. Where do *you* go to eat? What do *you* think is the best beach? What would *you* recommend if I have only three days? We invited our local correspondents to act as "substitute hosts" by revealing their preferred walks and trips, listing the restaurants they go to and structuring a visit into a series of timed itineraries.

The result: our Pocket Guides, complete with full-size fold-out maps. These 100-plus titles help readers plan a trip precisely, particularly if their time is short.

Exploring with Insight:
A valuable travel experience
In conjunction with co-publishers all over the world, we print in up to 10 languages, from German to Chinese, from Danish to Russian. But our aim remains simple: to enhance your travel experience by combining our expertise in guidebook publishing with the on-the-spot knowledge of our correspondents.